LUKE AND SCRIPTURE

LUKE AND SCRIPTURE

The Function of Sacred Tradition in Luke-Acts

CRAIG A. EVANS
JAMES A. SANDERS

FORTRESS PRESS   MINNEAPOLIS

BS
2589
.E935
1993

LUKE AND SCRIPTURE
The Function of Sacred Tradition in Luke-Acts

Scripture quotations, unless otherwise noted, are from the New Revised Standard Version of the Bible, copyright © 1989 by the Division of Christian Education of the National Council of the Churches of Christ in the United States of America.

Chapter 6 was first published as "Sins, Debts, and Jubilee Release" by James A. Sanders in *Text as Pretext: Essays in Honour of Robert Davidson* (Sheffield: Journal for the Study of the Old Testament, 1992). Reprinted by permission of Sheffield Academic Press, Ltd.

Interior design by Publishers' WorkGroup

Library of Congress Cataloging-in-Publication Data

Evans, Craig A.
    Luke and scripture : the function of sacred tradition in Luke-Acts
/ Craig A. Evans and James A. Sanders.
        p.   cm.
    Includes bibliographical references and indexes.
    ISBN 0–8006–2676–1 (alk. paper):
    1. Bible.   N.T.   Luke—Relation to the Old Testament.   2. Bible.
N.T.   Acts—Relation to the Old Testament.   3. Rabbinical
literature—Relation to the New Testament.   I. Sanders, James A.,
1927-   .   II. Title.
BS2589.E935   1993
226.4'06—dc20   93-5172
                                                               CIP

The paper used in this publication meets the minimum requirements of American National Standard for Information Sciences—Permanence of Paper for Printed Library Materials, ANSI Z329.48–1984. ∞™

Manufactured in the U.S.A.   1-2676
97   96   95   94   93   1   2   3   4   5   6   7   8   9   10

CONTENTS

PREFACE

Luke and Scripture: The Function of Sacred Tradition in Luke-Acts is a collection of exploratory studies that seek to probe the third evangelist's understanding of Scripture, its nature, and its continuing function. These studies represent work in progress. Both of us plan to produce monographs following up certain aspects of the problems touched upon here. Criticisms and suggestions are therefore welcome.

We wish to express our thanks and appreciation to Gerald Bilkes, Melody Knowles, and Jason Van Vliet, recent graduates of Trinity Western University, who assisted in typing several chapters of the manuscript, and to Ginny Evans who assisted in preparing the indexes.

Craig A. Evans
James A. Sanders

ABBREVIATIONS

AB	Anchor Bible
AGJU	Arbeiten zur Geschichte des antiken Judentums und des Urchristentums
AGSJU	Arbeiten zur Geschichte des Spätjudentums und Urchristentums
AnBib	Analecta biblica
ANQ	*Andover Newton Quarterly*
AOS	American Oriental Series
APOT	R. H. Charles (ed.), *Apocrypha and Pseudepigrapha of the Old Testament*
ATD	Das Alte Testament Deutsch
BA	*Biblical Archaeologist*
BBB	Bonner biblische Beiträge
BDB	F. Brown, S. R. Driver, and C. A. Briggs, *Hebrew and English Lexicon of the Old Testament*
BHS	*Biblia hebraica stuttgartensia*
BHT	Beiträge zur historischen Theologie
Bib	*Biblica*
BibB	Biblische Beiträge
BKAT	Biblischer Kommentar: Altes Testament
BR	*Biblical Research*
BSO(A)S	*Bulletin of the School of Oriental (and African) Studies*
BZ	*Biblische Zeitschrift*
BZAW	Beihefte zur *ZAW*
BZNW	Beihefte zur *ZNW*

CBQ	*Catholic Biblical Quarterly*
CBQMS	Catholic Biblical Quarterly—Monograph Series
DBSup	*Dictionnaire de la Bible, Supplément*
DJD	Discoveries in the Judaean Desert
Ebib	Etudes bibliques
EKKNT	Evangelisch-katholischer Kommentar zum Neuen Testament
EncJud	*Encyclopaedia judaica* (1971)
ETL	*Ephemerides theologieae lovanienses*
ExpTim	*Expository Times*
HKAT	Handkommentar zum Alten Testament
HNTC	Harper's NT Commentaries
HTR	*Harvard Theological Review*
IB	*Interpreter's Bible*
IBC	Interpretation: A Bible Commentary for Teaching and Preaching
ICC	International Critical Commentary
IDBSup	Supplementary volume to *Interpreter's Dictionary of the Bible*
IEJ	*Israel Exploration Journal*
Int	*Interpretation*
ISBE	G. W. Bromiley (ed.), *International Standard Bible Encyclopedia*, rev.
JBL	*Journal of Biblical Literature*
JEH	*Journal of Ecclesiastical History*
JJS	*Journal of Jewish Studies*
JR	*Journal of Religion*
JRS	*Journal of Roman Studies*
JSJ	*Journal of the Study of Judaism in the Persian, Hellenistic and Roman Period*
JSNT	*Journal for the Study of the New Testament*
JSNTSup	Journal for the Study of the New Testament—Supplement Series
JSOT	*Journal for the Study of the Old Testament*
JSOTSup	Journal for the Study of the Old Testament—Supplement Series
JSPSup	Journal for the Study of the Pseudepigrapha—Supplement Series
JSS	*Journal of Semitic Studies*
JTS	*Journal of Theological Studies*
KAT	Kommentar zum Alten Testament
LCL	Loeb Classical Library

MNTC	Moffatt NT Commentary
NCB	New Century Bible
NIBC	New International Biblical Commentary
NICNT	New International Commentary on the New Testament
NIGTC	The New International Greek Testament Commentary
NovT	*Novum Testamentum*
NovTSup	Novum Testamentum, Supplements
NTS	*New Testament Studies*
OTL	Old Testament Library
OTS	*Oudtestamentische Studiën*
PTMS	Pittsburgh (Princeton) Theological Monograph Series
RevExp	*Review and Expositor*
RevQ	*Revue de Qumran*
RHPR	*Revue d'histoire de philosophie religieuses*
RSR	*Recherches de science religieuse*
SANT	Studien zum Alten und Neuen Testament
SBLDS	SBL Dissertation Series
SBLMS	SBL Monograph Series
SBLSP	*SBL Seminar Papers*
SBT	Studies in Biblical Theology
SE	*Studia Evangelica I, II, III* (= TU 73 [1959], 87 [1964], 88 [1964], etc.)
SJLA	Studies in Judaism in Late Antiquity
SNT	Studien zum Neuen Testament
SNTSMS	Society for New Testament Studies Monograph Series
SSEJC	Studies in Scripture in Early Judaism and Christianity
Str-B	[H. Strack and] P. Billerbeck, *Kommentar zum Neuen Testament*
SWJT	*Southwestern Journal of Theology*
TDNT	G. Kittel & G. Friedrich (eds.), *Theological Dictionary of the New Testament*
THKNT	Theologischer Handkommentar zum Neuen Testament
ThViat	*Theologia viatorum*
TLZ	*Theologische Literaturzeitung*
TS	*Theological Studies*
TSJTSA	Theological Studies of the Jewish Theological Seminary of America
TU	Texte und Untersuchungen
USQR	*Union Seminary Quarterly Review*
VT	*Vetus Testamentum*

WMANT	Wissenschaftliche Monographien zum Alten und Neuen Testament
WTJ	*Westminster Theological Journal*
WUNT	Wissenschaftliche Untersuchungen zum Neuen Testament
ZAW	*Zeitschrift für die alttestamentliche Wissenschaft*
ZNW	*Zeitschrift für die neutestamentliche Wissenschaft*
ZTK	*Zeitschrift für Theologie und Kirche*

LUKE AND SCRIPTURE

1

GOSPELS AND MIDRASH: AN INTRODUCTION TO LUKE AND SCRIPTURE

CRAIG A. EVANS

JAMES A. SANDERS

THE QUESTION OF GENRE
C. A. Evans

In the wake of discovering the relevance of rabbinic materials for New Testament study, scholars have increasingly looked to Jewish parallels to resolve the question of the genre of the Gospels. Some have suggested that the Gospels are Targums, midrashim, or even lectionaries modeled after Jewish counterparts. However, none of these proposals has forged a scholarly consensus, and for good reason. The Gospels are not Targums because they do not follow the Tanak or Hebrew Scriptures verse by verse. Even the relationship of Matthew and Luke to Mark cannot be described as that of Targum, though in places the relationship is somewhat "targumic."[1] The main reason that this description does not apply is that Matthew and Luke did not simply intend to write paraphrased versions of Mark. They were not as interested in elucidating for their communities the meaning of Mark as in presenting their own respective views. The

---

1. The Targum arose out of the synagogal practice of accompanying the reading of the Hebrew text with an Aramaic paraphrase for the benefit of Aramaic-speaking Jews. B. D. Chilton ("Targumic Transmission and Dominical Tradition," in R. T. France and D. Wenham, eds., *Studies of History and Tradition in the Four Gospels* [Gospel Perspectives 1; Sheffield: JSOT, 1980] 36; repr. in Chilton, *Targumic Approaches to the Gospels* [Studies in Judaism; Lanham and New York: University Press of America, 1986] 125) rightly cautions against calling the Gospels "Targums." He suggests that the retelling activity of the evangelists (and tradents before them) be considered "cognate" (rather than "identical") to the retelling process of the Targums.

Gospels also are not midrashim,[2] although they exhibit midrashic features and may contain isolated midrashim on specific passages from the Tanak.[3] (To this concern the second part of this chapter addresses itself.) Most problematic is the claim that the Gospels are Jewish-Christian lectionaries.[4] Such a thesis is sheer speculation, since there are no models from a period early enough for meaningful comparison.[5]

The Gospels are attempts to tell the story of Jesus. We do not have access to Mark's sources but we do have access to those of Matthew and Luke (viz., Mark and Q). Comparative analysis reveals that these later Gospels are "retellings" of the Jesus story. These retellings have much in common with the general category of "rewritten Bible," to which scholars have assigned much of the Pseudepigrapha. It is also significant that this category bears affinities to the Targums and the midrashim. In this view, the reason that the Bible was rewritten is primarily exegetical. This is perhaps why James H. Charlesworth has recently described much of the Pseudepigrapha as "exegesis."[6]

---

2. Midrashim are scriptural commentaries (exegetical and homiletical) on either the legal (halakic) or nonlegal (haggadic) materials of the Hebrew Bible. For works that attempt to advance the view that the Gospels are midrashim, see M. D. Goulder, *Midrash and Lection in Matthew* (London: SPCK, 1974); J. Drury, "Midrash and Gospel," *Theology* 77 (1974) 291–96; idem, *Tradition and Design in Luke's Gospel* (London: Darton, Longman & Todd, 1976) 44–45. According to Drury ("Midrash," 294), "midrash [is] the method by which, in historical fact rather than scholarly conjecture, Jews of various colours from the most chauvinistic Pharisee to the most liberal Hellenist did their history writing." As examples of what he regards as "midrash," he cites Josephus, Philo, *Jubilees*, and the *Genesis Apocryphon*. Drury's understanding of midrash is too broad and inclusive to be functional. For recent works that argue that Mark is a great midrash on the Old Testament and the Christian dominical tradition, see J. D. M. Derrett, *The Making of Mark: The Scriptural Bases of the Earliest Gospel* (2 vols.; Shipston-on-Stour: Drinkwater, 1985) 1.38; D. Miller, *The Gospel of Mark as Midrash on Earlier Jewish and New Testament Literature* (Lewiston and Queenston: Mellen, 1990).

3. In this chapter "Tanak" refers to the Old (or First) Testament, in whatever languages, oral or written, it may have been available.

4. For works that argue that the Gospels are lectionaries, see A. Guilding, *The Fourth Gospel and Jewish Worship* (Oxford: Oxford University Press, 1960); Goulder, *Midrash and Lection*; idem, *The Evangelists' Calendar: A Lectionary Explanation of the Development of Scripture* (London: SPCK, 1978). It should be noted, however, that Goulder (*Midrash and Lection*, 172) thinks that a "Gospel is not a literary genre at all" but a "liturgical genre." He links Matthew's five major discourses to major Jewish feasts and holidays: (1) the Sermon on the Mount (chaps. 5–7): Pentecost; (2) the sending of the Twelve (chap. 10): Rosh Hashanah and Yom Kippur; (3) the parables of the Kingdom (chap. 13): Sukka; (4) rules for church order (chap. 18): Hanukkah; and (5) the eschatological discourse (chaps. 24–25): Pesahim.

5. For competent critiques of the lectionary hypotheses, see L. Morris, "The Gospels and the Jewish Lectionaries," in R.T. France and D. Wenham, eds., *Studies in Midrash and Historiography* (Gospel Perspectives 3; Sheffield: JSOT, 1983) 129–56; C. Perrot, *La lecture de la Bible dans la Synagogue* (Hildensheim: Gerstenberg, 1973) 287. The evidence of *b. Meg.* 31b, possibly reflecting second-century tradition, suggests that there was no uniform Jewish lectionary prior to that time.

6. See J. H. Charlesworth, "The Pseudepigrapha as Exegesis," in C. A. Evans and W. F. Stinespring, eds., *Early Jewish and Christian Exegesis: Studies in Memory of William Hugh Brownlee* (Atlanta: Scholars, 1987) 139–52.

Whereas it may not be inaccurate to describe the category of "rewritten Bible" as a broad class that includes Targums, midrashim, and other forms of exegesis, it is probably more accurate to think of the rewritten Bible as the earliest form of reapplication of Scripture. This rewriting activity begins within the Bible itself. It has been described as "haggadah within Scripture"[7] and recently as "inner-biblical exegesis."[8] The Pseudepigrapha are attempts at rewriting the Bible outside of the Bible itself but still via the biblical story ("parabiblical rewriting"); here the exegesis is to some extent camouflaged within the biblical story itself.

As the biblical text increasingly stabilized and as consciousness of canon was heightened, the Targums displaced pseudepigraphal writings. Although the Targums also retell the story, the biblical text exercises much greater control, and the text must be interpreted. Much may be imported into the text, and the obvious meaning of the text may be circumvented or even turned on its head, but in the end the exegesis is always in interaction with the text. The rabbinic midrashim are still more closely tied to the text. In these writings the basic text is cited verse by verse, line by line. The text is not rewritten (re-vocalized perhaps); it is simply repeated and (re-)explained for the new situation. The midrashim are on the way to the modern commentary.

Where do the Gospels fit against this background? Matthew and Luke, the only two Gospels whose sources we possess, seem to represent an early stage of rewritten Bible. But they are not retellings of Tanak; they are retellings of the Jesus story. Like the Jewish retellings of Tanak, however, they do import materials from the rest of Scripture, and here Tanak appears. The presence of Tanak is neither incidental nor insignificant, for it not only contributes various details but often provides the cloth out of which an entire pericope is woven. At times the evangelists' usage of Tanak exhibits midrashic and even targumic traits, but to conclude that the Gospels are themselves midrashim can lead to gross misunderstanding. It is far better to say that the Gospels are midrashic, better still to say that they contain midrash and are in places midrashically driven.

The evangelist Luke edited the materials and adopted the language and themes of Scripture much in the same way as did *Jubilees*, Pseudo-Philo's *Biblical Antiquities*, Qumran's *Genesis Apocryphon*, and Josephus's *Jewish Antiquities*. As in these writings, Luke added genealogical materials,

---

7. S. Sandmel, "The Haggada within Scripture," *JBL* 80 (1961) 105–22.

8. M. Fishbane, *Biblical Interpretation in Ancient Israel* (New York: Oxford University Press, 1985); idem, "Revelation and Tradition: Aspects of Inner Biblical Exegesis," *JBL* 99 (1980) 343–61; idem, *The Garments of Torah: Essays in Biblical Hermeneutics* (Indiana Studies in Biblical Literature; Bloomington: Indiana University Press, 1989).

qualified and summarized the contents of his sources, expanded, abbreviated, and omitted altogether. He did not do these things to produce a commentary on Mark or on any other Gospel source. Nor did Luke attempt to produce a commentary on portions of the Greek Old Testament. Luke rewrote the story of Jesus much as Josephus rewrote Israel's sacred history.[9]

Luke's rewriting of this story was greatly influenced by the language and themes of Scripture and the way Scripture was interpreted in Jewish and Christian circles of his time. The purpose of the present collection of studies is to probe the ways in which the Lukan evangelist retold the story of Jesus and the early church in the light of Scripture and its interpretation. We are not so much interested in Luke's various methods or genres as in his sense of continuity and context, in his understanding of the relationship between the story of Jesus and the church and the story of Israel. Simply put, how does the story of Jesus and the Christian community, which arose from his band of followers, fit within theological history? The Lukan evangelist grappled with this question, the principal question behind the function of Scripture in his two-volume work.

It might be added that the New Testament apocryphal Gospels represent the stage of rewritten Bible which recognizes the stabilized, authoritative status of the canonical Gospels (much as the Pseudepigrapha recognize Tanak's canonicity). Consequently, their authors could not simply rewrite Mark as Matthew and Luke did, but they could retell the Jesus story, incorporating legends and New Testament components. When the New Testament canonical question became increasingly clarified, these apocryphal writings, as their Jewish counterparts before them, also faded from the scene. In their place emerged commentary on a stabilized text and a recognized canon.

THE QUESTION OF METHOD
J. A. Sanders

According to James M. Robinson, the exegete's first obligation is to try to recover points originally scored. But points originally scored cannot be recovered until the words preserved in the text before us are understood in terms as near as possible to those of the original contexts: "full context" should mean this to any professional interpreter. Literary criticism, from form criticism through redaction criticism, rightly insists on context in the

---

9. For a fuller statement of my view on this matter, see C. A. Evans, "Luke and the Rewritten Bible: Aspects of Lucan Hagiography," in J. H. Charlesworth and C. A. Evans, eds., *The Pseudepigrapha and Biblical Interpretation* (JSPSup; Sheffield: JSOT, forthcoming).

sense of perceiving a text in the light of its primary and then full literary units. But this is only a part of the meaning of full context. To deal with such units apart from the context in which they were spoken in antiquity is to deal with truncated, isolated units, disconnected from the focus of their meaning.

One of the valuable emphases in the relatively new field of comparative midrash is that of seeing the contemporization of an ancient tradition in light of the need of the community that recalled, and reflected upon, the tradition.[10] Comparative midrash, rhetorical criticism, and audience criticism are emerging as keys to much of what is going on in biblical work today.[11]

The exegete of any ancient literature must view the text itself as only one of two foci necessary to understand what it says. The second focus is the actual situation into which the textual material was first interjected. This focus is often difficult to reconstruct, but the effort must be made. Here one must seek the complement to what the speaker in the preserved text presupposed. The better the rhetoric or the more "occasional" the writing, the more apt are the presuppositions made by the rhetor. Rhetorical criticism, of all literature of any period, clearly shows that speakers

---

10. Cf. R. Bloch, "Midrash," *DBSup* 5 (1957) cols. 1263–81; D. Boyarin, *Intertextuality and the Reading of Midrash* (Bloomington: Indiana University Press, 1990) 11–19. My colleague R. E Brown has recently expressed ("Gospel Infancy Narrative Research from 1976 to 1986: Part I (Matthew)," *CBQ* 48 [1986] 477) uncertainty about what is meant by midrash in the Second Testament. In part it means there is much less prooftexting in turning to Scripture but much more searching of Scripture to try to understand what God was doing in Christ and in the early Church, than critical scholarship generally allows.

11. J. Muilenburg made a significant start in the area of rhetorical criticism of the Old Testament in his "Form Criticism and Beyond" in *JBL* 88 (1969) 1–18. In the field of early Judaism rhetorical criticism is as important as midrash criticism: cf. H. A. Fischel, "Story and History: Observations on Greco-Roman Rhetoric and Pharisaism," in D. Sinor, ed., *American Oriental Society, Middle West Branch, Semi-Centennial Volume* (Asian Studies Research Institute, Oriental Series 3; Bloomington: Indiana University Press, 1969) 58–88; repr. in Fischel, *Essays in Greco-Roman and Related Talmudic Literature* (New York: Ktav, 1977) 443–72 (and watch for anything Fischel might yet do in this area). The area of comparative midrash has been critically reviewed by a former student, M. P. Miller, "Targum, Midrash and the Use of the Old Testament in the New Testament," *JSJ* 2 (1971) 29–82; cf. the bibliographies in J. Neusner, ed., *The Study of Judaism: Bibliographic Essays* (New York: Anti-Defamation League of B'nai B'rith, 1972) 7–80. In the New Testament, *in sensu stricto*, see J. A. Baird, *Audience Criticism and the Historical Jesus* (Philadelphia: Westminster, 1969); P. S. Minear, "Audience Criticism and Markan Ecclesiology," in H. Baltensweiler and B. Reicke, eds., *Neues Testament und Geschichte: Historisches Geschehen und Deutung im Neuen Testament* (O. Cullmann Festschrift; Zurich: Theologischer Verlag, 1972) 79–90. E. Haenchen ("Das Gleichnis vom grossen Mahl," in *Die Bibel und Wir* [Tübingen: Mohr (Siebeck), 1968] 135–55) engages in audience criticism in comparing Luke 14 to Matthew 22 and *Gospel of Thomas* §64 and is quite right as far as he goes. See, more recently, M. C. Callaway, *Sing, O Barren One: A Study in Comparative Midrash* (SBLDS 91; Atlanta: Scholars, 1986); C. A. Evans, *To See and Not Perceive: Isaiah 6.9–10 in Early Jewish and Christian Interpretation* (JSOTSup 64; Sheffield: JSOT, 1989); R. B. Hays, *Echoes of Scripture in the Letters of Paul* (New Haven and London: Yale University Press, 1989).

make the best and most striking points, not when they belabor the obvious, but when they presuppose in the audience, for example, the concerns and the knowledge of recent events that affect their lives.

Such an observation can be depressing for the exegete of ancient literature. Clearly we shall never recover anywhere near the amount of material necessary for reconstructing the situational focus of a biblical text. But we are all the more obligated to try to do so. The language-event school is clearly open to the criticism that their excitement in other areas has led them very nearly to ignore historical context.[12] The point originally scored, or the concept (*Begriff*) the original speaker or writer intended to convey, depends directly on the extent to which the second focus is available to modern scholars.

Simply locating the place and date of original writing scarcely reconstructs the situational focus. Answers to "introductory" questions are hardly sufficient. One must attempt to recover, as nearly as possible, the mentality, the concerns, the hopes and fears of those to whom the textual material was first addressed. In work on any given text, one may have to test several different "original" contexts. Redaction criticism, once very much in vogue, can be effective only as one seeks to know the concerns and desires of the redactor's congregation. In order to see fully the ideas of the biblical redactor, one needs to know the concerns and needs of the congregation, and the need or concern that was being addressed. In order to probe behind one moment in history to an earlier one, form criticism becomes quite important. But once an early unit has been defined one still must be careful about the stage of development with which one is dealing. Probing too far back may simply leave one with a Hellenistic or Near Eastern proverb (or other small unit); and proverbs are notoriously flexible, always needing full historical context to know how the users were bending their meanings, according to the points they wanted to score with their hearers. Sometimes knowledge of how a proverb or legend was understood outside the Bible is a deterrent in reconstructing what it meant when spoken in the first "biblical orbit" situation before it ended up in our canon. To import meanings from one context to another without regard to the second full context can be disastrous. The exegete must be aware of all the possible questions pertinent to fully contextual exegesis.[13]

How was a text understood by an audience? Was the biblical speaker or writer comforting the congregation or audience or perhaps challenging

---

12. See especially R. W. Funk, *Language, Hermeneutic and Word of God* (New York: Harper & Row, 1966) 124–99.

13. Genesis 22 may serve as an illustration. At the earliest stage of the history of a story of child sacrifice in which (1) the priest who must sacrifice is the boy's father and (2) the boy is

them? How did he wish to move his constituency? If she was "only instruct-ing" them, what was her goal in forming/informing their thinking? The basic hermeneutics of the speaker or writer become extremely important at this stage of work. This is the crucial locus of current work in compara-tive midrash. When one has recovered what First Testament authoritative tradition lies at the base of an early Jewish (including Second Testament) text, one may move to another level and compare the various ways that the same First Testament tradition was being contemporized in that period of Judaism in order to see what the emphases were and how they were used elsewhere. Then one can look for clues in the text to see if the hermeneutics can be determined. In the case of the Second Testament, of course, the matter is complicated by the ever present possibility that the redactor, on the one hand, and Jesus, on the other, might have used the same tradition in opposite ways, that is, with different hermeneutics and convictions.[14] When one thinks that, by the methods of comparative midrash, the use of a First Testament tradition by Jesus has possibly been recovered, one must always suppose that, had the evangelist received the tradition from Jesus, he might have understood and used it in a very different way from Jesus. By reporting what Jesus said exactly as he said it, the redactor or evangelist might have produced in the audience the oppo-site effect from that of Jesus, precisely because the audiences were asking

---

his only son, one has reached a pre-Israelitic, probably Canaanitic provenance. The story's meaning here might have been very different from its meaning when Israel adapted it for its own uses. The archaeological and philological schools of interpreters (such as E. A. Speiser and Nelson Glueck) suggest that the story was understood in Israel as an argument against human sacrifice; probably this is so, but the story had other uses as well. G. von Rad, in his *Genesis* (OTL; Philadelphia: Westminster, 1961), 232–40, was also right when he saw what the story meant in terms of redaction criticism and its place in the Abraham cycle: it addressed the question of whether or not God will inevitably keep a promise. (See also his *Das Opfer des Abraham* [Munich: Kaiser, 1971].) At the canonical-critical level the story surely had great significance in the exilic and post-exilic periods (after so many disasters and dashed hopes) because it said to those generations (who have preserved it for us in canonical process) that the God who had given Isaac in Sarah's barren womb gave Isaac a second time from the altar. Judaism's very existence often reached the stage of contingency represented by the knife over the child's body—and yet there was hope. Comparative midrash begins here and studies the understandings of the same story in early Judaism and New Testament times. See S. Spiegel, *The Last Trial* (Philadelphia: Jewish Publication Society, 1967) 33; cf. D. M. Bossman, " 'In Isaac': A Midrashic Approach to a Study of Paul's 'en Christo' " (unpublished doctoral dissertation, Saint Louis University, 1973). Because the "second focus" always changes, so does the message. This is the base of *all* exegesis, from earliest form criticism and tradition criticism through canonical criticism and midrash criticism, in the history of Jewish and Christian interpretation; the New Testament is located at one stage in that long history. The expression "contextual exegesis" is not limited to its literary-critical aspect, the question of smaller and larger units; "contextual" includes the second focus, the situation to which the text spoke *at any period*.

14. See J. A. Sanders, "Adaptable for Life: The Nature and Function of Canon," in F. M. Cross, ed., *Magnalia Dei: The Mighty Acts of God: Essays on the Bible and Archaeology in Memory of G. E. Wright* (New York: Doubleday, 1976) 31–60; repr. in J. A. Sanders, *From Sacred Story to Sacred Text: Canon as Paradigm* (Philadelphia: Fortress, 1987) 11–39.

different questions. The more one works on the Gospels, the more one suspects that where Jesus might have been issuing a prophetic challenge in *his* day, his words, in a later context, could be taken in an opposite way. For instance, a prophetic critique of Jesus aimed at the coreligionists of his day, when repeated verbatim to an early Christian congregation in 70 C.E., was probably received by them not as a prophetic critique of themselves but statically as a condemnation of the Jews.

These observations again emphasize the need, in exegesis, to understand full context to mean the two foci, text and audience. Material statically transmitted from Jesus' situation to Matthew's can score a point diametrically opposite to that of the earlier situation. In the case of Jesus traditions, if we understand Jesus to be employing prophetic-critique hermeneutics in his situation—that is, to be conveying a challenge from the First Testament to his own Jewish in-group—then the message of Jesus is subverted unless Matthew converts what Jesus did so that it also conveys a challenge to *his own* Christian in-group. One of the reasons that the Gospels appear to be anti-Jewish is that Jesus' own hermeneutics, as the Gospels largely want to insist, were often prophetic. Any prophetic-critique hermeneutic in the Bible (First Testament or Second) statically conveyed to a non-Jewish audience runs the risk of being anti-Jewish if not anti-Semitic. This observation may be used as a rule of exegesis. If Second Testament scholarship maintains that at the redaction-critical level much in the Gospels is anti-Jewish (in the struggle of nascent Christianity to affirm its identity as the New Israel), then conversely that same material in Jesus' situation in Palestine in the first century might have been prophetic in hermeneutics. If, to put it another way, the evangelists after 70 C.E., for their own reasons and needs, intended to put the Jews down, and Jesus had actually conducted a prophetic ministry in his life, then such Jesus traditions, accurately (i.e., statically) received, provided the very anti-Jewish material the early church needed without further ado. It was only necessary to record his ipsissima verba, his very words. The fact that contemporization by static analogy completely subverted the point that Jesus had originally scored would perhaps have hardly occurred to the evangelists. The evangelists were not consciously subverting Jesus' intent; on the contrary, they probably thought they were being faithful to him—faithful in the sense that some modern historians think they have been faithful when they fail to breathe the ambiguity of reality into their work by not seeking out the two foci (textual and contextual) necessary for understanding any text.[15]

---

15. This is an important point overlooked by otherwise responsible historians. R. A. Lively, formerly of Princeton University, now of SUNY Buffalo, calls the exercise New History;

In attempting to reconstruct the Second Testament point originally scored, the first-century foil in the second focus must be sought.[16] We must assume that *both* Jesus *and* the evangelists had reasons for what they said. Methodologically, we cannot assume that they were trying to phrase an eternal verity received by revelation. We must conclude they had something to say (1) that would have been understood by contemporaries and (2) that would have been to some extent different from what contemporaries already were thinking. By informing their audiences, Jesus and the evangelists attempted to form their thinking—they were being relevant to their situation. By this method we set aside the quest for what was "unique" or "original" as genuinely dominical and instead look for an aspect of "overagainstness" in what Jesus is reported to have taught,[17] particularly if, in testing out the method, we assume (until proved otherwise) that the hermeneutic employed was that of prophetic critique.[18]

Integral to the comparative midrash method of work on early Jewish literature is the assumption that what is in the text is there because it met a need of the community to whom it was addressed. But we should keep in mind that the community might have needed a challenge to their thinking about themselves and their life-style. In the case of the First Testament prophets, this point is utterly clear.[19] The Second Testament may also exhibit Jesus' use of such a prophetic-critique hermeneutic, and current efforts to develop sound method in comparative midrash must not exclude this possibility. On the contrary, we need to test the possibility of prophetic-critique hermeneutic before moving to other possibilities.

---

actually it is good history. Lively's ideas are incorporated in my "The New History: Joseph Our Brother" (1968; available from the Baptist Ministers and Missionaries Benefit Board, 475 Riverside Drive, New York, N.Y. 10027). The need for historical context more or less varies with the form and content of the literary unit. At one end of the spectrum is the political diatribe and the occasional homily, and at the other, works such as Euclid's geometry or Einstein's theories of relativity. The supporting arguments in the latter are nevertheless best understood (and in some cases only become clear) when read in the context of where science was at the time and what questions were put when the arguments were composed.

16. Cf. J. A. Sanders, "Dissenting Deities and Philippians 2:1–11," *JBL* 88 (1969) 279–90.

17. The three criteria, often associated with the name of N. Perrin (*Rediscovering the Teaching of Jesus* [New York: Harper & Row, 1967]), by which one tests whether a New Testament tradition derived from the so-called pre-resurrection mission, i.e., from Jesus, are inadequate. The linguistic criterion is not valid; distinctiveness can unfortunately cut two ways, and coherence, in the sense meant, is hardly a first-century category.

18. This means that the authoritative tradition, from the First Testament, was contemporized as a challenge to in-group thinking. One must however remember that by tradition we mean not only a First Testament passage, but also images, patterns, etc. Cf. R. Le Déaut, "Apropos a Definition of Midrash," *Int* 25 (1971) 259–82 (with an introduction by J. A. Sanders).

19. Cf. J. A. Sanders, *Torah and Canon* (Philadelphia: Fortress, 1972) 54–96; idem, "Adaptable for Life," 23–30; and idem, "Jeremiah and the Future of Theological Scholarship," *ANQ* 22 (1972) 133–45.

It is helpful to define comparative midrash and describe how it relates to and complements other critical methods. Comparative midrash differs in two particulars from the method called "history of interpretation." First, whereas the latter emphasizes how a First Testament passage was interpreted in its several uses in post-biblical literature, comparative midrash emphasizes the role an ancient authoritative tradition, whether or not actually quoted or cited as Scripture, played in the life and history of Judaism and Christianity. What function did a particular tradition have in the life of the community where and when it was called upon by that community? What need did the tradition meet? Second, comparative midrash pays close attention to the way the tradition is contemporized by the community to meet its need. This involves hermeneutics in *sensu lato*, that is, the manner in which the tradition is woven by the exegete with other materials to draw benefit from the citation, reference, or allusion.

All translations, and not only the Targums, are more or less relevant to the community for which the translation is made.[20] Early manuscripts of biblical books, such as those from Qumran, exhibit variations that cannot be overlooked. The most fruitful field for study is the so-called sectarian literature, whether this be Qumranian, Christian, proto-rabbinic, or that of some other Jewish denomination from which we might have inherited literature without knowing much about it (such as certain apocrypha). By comparing the available instances of contemporization of authoritative traditions in the Second Temple Period and by considering one in the light of another, the whole tradition, as well as particular instances otherwise unavailable, may be illuminated.

Comparative midrash properly begins by recognizing the peculiar role of Scripture in the life and history of Judaism. Although much benefit derives from comparison with rhetorical-critical work on non-Jewish literature of the same time period in the eastern Mediterranean area, the peculiar role of Torah in the life of Judaism must first be recognized. Experts in Greek and Hellenistic studies recognize that a considerable difference exists between the role or function of a Torah tradition in Judaism and the role of classical mythology in the Hellenistic world.[21]

In both cultures, and indeed all cultures down to the present, traditions are called on for the authority they may offer to the writer who cites them. And many of the rhetorical or midrashic methods of the two worlds were

---

20. "Every translation was an adaptation of the original to the needs of its new readers." So E. Bickerman, *Studies in Jewish and Christian History* (3 vols.; AGJU 9; Leiden: Brill, 1976) 1.196.

21. See Fischel, "Story and History," 59–88; idem, "Rabbinical Knowledge of Greek and Latin Languages," *EncJud* 7 (1972) cols. 884–87; and idem, *Rabbinic Literature and Greco-Roman Philosophy* (Leiden: Brill, 1973). See also Bickerman, *Studies*, 1.199, "The LXX Torah was unique because the Torah was unique."

similar so that it is proper to speak of the eastern Mediterranean as one area in this regard. Morton Smith has shown that "Hellenization" meant not only Greek influence in the Semitic world but also Semitic influence in the Greek and Hellenistic worlds.[22] Nonetheless, for all the work being done in the broader area of comparative midrash,[23] no phenomenon outside Judaism is quite comparable to Torah. Integral to the very essence and character of Judaism is the historic memory of the role the Torah traditions played in the death and resurrection experience of the sixth and fifth centuries B.C.E.[24] In crucial ways, that experience of the death of old Israel and the resurrection/birth of Judaism helped to shape the old pre-exilic traditions into the Torah and Prophets and Psalms as we know them, or, at least, into the form they now have (although much was added during and after the exile without altering the basic shape). Jewish people, wherever they have been, have always known that Torah has life-giving power. It and it alone was thought to provide the power to survive the Babylonian exile, and then the Persian dispersion and Hellenistic temptation; Torah told the Jewish people who they were in the face of despair and of the temptation to assimilate. And Torah was not just the Pentateuch but the Prophets and the Psalms and eventually the Writings, and beyond that the oral Torah as well as the written, the Talmud as well as the Bible. Torah in this sense came to mean Judaism itself. To understand Judaism, indeed, to understand midrash, one must begin with this wellspring of life, Torah.

Study of the function of a biblical tradition properly begins with the Bible itself. Biblical scholarship has over the past two centuries developed a number of tools to understand a biblical passage in its biblical setting. Literary criticism helps to locate the source of the material under study and to determine whether it is an original unit or was composed by some later editor from more than one source. Form criticism, a branch of liter-

---

22. See the chapter on "Hellenization" in M. Smith, *Palestinian Parties and Politics That Shaped the Old Testament* (London and New York: Columbia University Press, 1971) 57–81. See also S. Lieberman, *Hellenism in Jewish Palestine* (TSJTSA 18; New York: Jewish Theological Seminary of America, 1962); and E. Bickerman, *The Jews in the Greek Age* (Cambridge: Harvard University Press, 1988).

23. See the seminal article by Bloch, "Midrash"; cf. also Le Déaut, "Apropos a Definition of Midrash"; the pertinent bibliography by M. P. Miller, "Targum, Midrash and the Use of the Old Testament in the New Testament," 36–78; and the essays by R. Bavier, "Judaism in New Testament Times," and J. T. Townsend, "Rabbinic Sources," in Neusner, *The Study of Judaism*, 7–80.

24. Sanders, *Torah and Canon*, and idem, "Adaptable for Life." The metaphors of rebirth and death/resurrection were used by Jeremiah and Ezekiel. The process of selecting material and shaping canon must be traced primarily in the experiences of the believing communities and not in councils and lists that derived their authority from accurate reflection and expression of communal belief.

ary criticism, attempts to define the basic literary units under consideration, both the smaller component units biblical authors might have used and the larger units they might have penned or uttered. Form criticism often probes behind a principal biblical author to the way the quoted or adapted material was understood in cultic or cultural settings before the author used it. Historical criticism has both a large meaning and a more refined one: it may mean the whole enterprise of biblical scholarship in the sense of the quest for the meaning of the Bible in its own historical settings or, as over against enthusiastic form criticism, the need to reconstruct as completely as possible the historical settings in which the biblical literary units under study scored their basic, primary points.

Tradition criticism studies a tradition, which can be located in more than one biblical passage, by carefully noting through synoptic study of the several loci where it appears, the ways the tradition was used, its functions, and the roles it played for the biblical authors (Jahwist, redactor, prophet, psalmist) who used it. Tradition criticism is the intra-biblical counterpart of comparative midrash, which carries the same kind of study into a later period. Finally, redaction criticism is a tool of study whereby the last editors of the larger literary units of the Bible are assumed to possess their own intelligence and motives. Redaction criticism, as over against the assumptions of old literary criticism that thought of them as faithful collectors, grants to these later contributors their own theological and political ideas displayed in the way they arranged and edited the smaller literary units that they received and collected.

Canonical criticism, the latest and most engaging of the subdisciplines of biblical study, goes beyond redaction criticism, beyond the conscious efforts of individuals (or discrete schools), to those all-crucial moments in the canonical process after geniuses had molded the largest literary units, to the filtering process of the faithful, who either continued to read what the geniuses handed on or, finding such works irrelevant to their needs, set them aside in *genizot* or in drawers throughout the eastern Mediterranean basin to discolor and decay from disuse. Here distinctions were made as to what was Torah and what was Prophets, here the real criteria for canonization lay—in a massive but intensive canonical process where neither benevolence nor malice aforethought of any genius or any council played a hand. Does a work give life to the people? Later councils could but ratify such a plebiscite; they could not foist onto the people what the people in their collective innocence, wisdom, and honesty had set aside. Canonical criticism studies such times and moments in the history of the biblical process to try to understand what needs were being met by the works we call canonical. The Jews were principally a diaspora people in these times; the largest communities lived in Babylonia and Egypt until well into the Middle Ages.[25] Either an old tradition met the people where they were, at some point earlier or later, or we do not have it today.[26]

Midrash criticism picks up that observation and, using all available instances, attempts to understand the various ways in which a given passage or tradition met the people where they were, precisely the ways in which it was adaptable. If a tradition was canonical in any sense, it was adaptable: that is its nature. Hence no biblical passage has only the meaning that modern biblical scholarship assigns to it.[27] To recover the original meaning of a biblical passage is important but is only the beginning of serious study of the passage. The passage may well be in the Bible because of a meaning derived from it by a later generation in the canonical process beyond the last editors! Comparative midrash raises the legitimate question as to what is meant by "original meaning." Do philologists not tend to assign to words meanings that antedate the period of the original biblical author, thus bypassing the original meaning in the opposite direction?[28] Nonetheless, a valid history of a given biblical passage begins, properly, with the meanings we perceive in the situations the biblical author intended.

The essays assembled in the present volume are sensitive to these issues with respect to the Lukan evangelist. How has he understood Jesus, the origin of the early Christian community, and his own experience in terms of Israel's sacred tradition and institutions? In what sense is faith in Jesus commensurate with Israel's heritage? In what ways, if any, is the Gospel clarified by this sacred tradition and rich heritage? Does the Christian community represent a continuation of the story of God's people? It is with these questions that the following studies grapple.

---

25. See the comprehensive work by J. Neusner, *A History of the Jews in Babylonia* (4 vols.; Studia Post-Biblica; Leiden: Brill, 1965–69).

26. See J. A. Sanders, *Canon and Community* (Guides to Biblical Scholarship; Philadelphia: Fortress, 1985).

27. Note the different "original meanings" assigned to crucial biblical passages within the short history of modern biblical scholarship. Even the original meaning varies with the Zeitgeist of our own times.

28. This is evident in the work of M. Dahood: see especially his *Psalms* (3 vols.; AB 16, 17, 17a; Garden City: Doubleday, 1966–70).

— 2 —

ISAIAH IN LUKE

JAMES A. SANDERS

Isaiah is cited or alluded to in the Second Testament more than any other First Testament book.[1] Five hundred ninety references, explicit or otherwise, from sixty-three chapters of Isaiah are found in twenty-three New Testament books (239 from Isaiah 1–39; 240 from chaps. 40–55; 111 from chaps. 56–66).[2]

Isaiah was apparently the single most helpful book of the Old Testament in assisting the early church to understand the sufferings and crucifixion of the Christ; it aided the understanding of nearly every phase of Jesus' life, ministry, death, and resurrection. Isaiah also helped the early churches to understand who they were and what their role was as witnesses

---

This chapter is a revision of my study, "Isaiah in Luke," *Int* 36 (1982) 144–55; repr. in J. L. Mays and P. J. Achtemeier, eds., *Interpreting the Prophets* (Philadelphia: Fortress, 1987) 75–85.

---

1. Y. H. Songer, "Isaiah and the New Testament," *RevExp* 65 (1968) 459–70; J. Flamming, "The New Testament Use of Isaiah," *SWJT* 11 (1968) 89–103. Using the Scripture index in the 26th edition of the Nestle-Aland *NT Graece* one sees that Isaiah appears most often in Revelation with some 155 occurrences, whether citations or allusions. Next is Matthew with 87 occurrences, then Luke with 78, Romans with 46, Acts with 39, John with 37, Mark with 28, and Hebrews with 23. Such statistics have limited value, and the student should be cautious about drawing too many conclusions from them. The compilation of a significant and useful Scripture index for the NT has yet to be done. See H. M. Shires, *Finding the Old Testament in the New* (Philadelphia: Westminster, 1974); and my review of it in *USQR* 30 (1975) 241–46. At the Ancient Biblical Manuscript Center in Claremont we plan to compile a Scripture index of all our films of manuscripts. It will be a massive undertaking, but with computer technology and a clear method of work we hope eventually to provide this service to scholarship.

2. M. Kispert, Ph.D. candidate in biblical studies in the Claremont Graduate School, did some of the basic research for this article, esp. working through the Nestle-Aland *NT Graece* Scripture index, 26th edition.

to the Christ event and as those who prepared for the eschaton's fulfillment by proclaiming what God had done in and through Christ. Christology and ecclesiology were formulated in the early churches with the help of Isaiah.

Although there have been quite a few studies of the First Testament, and more specifically of Isaiah, in the Second Testament,[3] the work has hardly begun. The First Testament in general and Isaiah in particular are sometimes used in the Second as proof texts; but it is becoming clear that early Christians searched Scripture midrashically to understand why Christ suffered the fate of a criminal (or, depending on how we should understand the meaning of *lestes* [cf. its use in Josephus], perhaps even the fate of a defeated insurrectionist), why he was so ignominiously treated, why he was crucified. They found help in the Prophets, especially in Isaiah, to understand how God could turn tragedy into triumph.

Isaiah was particularly helpful in understanding why Christ's own people and contemporaries rejected him. The hard words of Isa 6:9-10 were illuminating: sometimes God hardened the heart of a foreign authority like Pharaoh or sent someone like Isaiah whose proclamation had the purpose, or at least the result, of making his own people's eyes blind, ears deaf, and heart dull.[4] Passages such as Isaiah 42, 49, and 53 and Psalms 22 and 118 illuminated for early Christians the heartbreaking tragedy of the crucifixion in such a way that they could perceive its transformation from ignominy and shame to the symbol of salvation for the world. Just as the old Israel and Judah had died in the Assyrian and Babylonian assaults but were resurrected (Ezekiel 37) as the new Israel, Judaism in the exile, so God was effecting through the crucified and resurrected Christ a new Israel, the church. Such citing of Scripture is not prooftexting but midrash (Scripture searching) at its best.

Early Christian readings of Scripture shaped the thinking of the church about what God had done in Christ and was doing with people—it shaped their writing when they wanted to share that thinking in Gospels, letters, or other literary forms. As the work progresses on the First Testament's use by Second Testament writers, a theocentric hermeneutic continues to emerge. People wanted to know what God was doing and saying to them in their time.

---

3. See the excellent, although now somewhat dated, critical bibliography in M. P. Miller, "Targum, Midrash and the Use of the Old Testament in the New Testament," *JSJ* 2 (1971) 29–82, esp. 43–78. This can now be supplemented by the bibliography in P. E. Dinter, *The Remnant of Israel and the Stone of Stumbling in Zion According to Paul (Romans 9–11)* (unpublished doctoral dissertation; Union Theological Seminary, 1980).

4. See, e.g., C. A. Evans, *To See and Not Perceive: Isaiah 6.9-10 in Early Jewish and Christian Interpretation* (JSOTSup 64; Sheffield: JSOT, 1989).

Luke's knowledge of Scripture was rather remarkable. His Bible was a Greek text of the First Testament as it then was. Abundant evidence in Luke and Acts shows that Luke knew First Testament Scripture, especially certain portions,[5] very well indeed. The Semitisms in Luke's work can be accounted for otherwise, for semitization was widespread in the Hellenistic language and literature of his time. He thought and wrote in the Koine Greek of his world. In no case of Luke's reading and understanding of Scripture need one go to a Pharisaic-rabbinic type of Jewish interpretation for an Old Testament passage to see how Luke moved through the ancient text to the modern message. One must often rummage around in the Targums, midrashim, and Jewish commentaries to learn how a passage of Scripture functioned for Matthew. He was sometimes dependent on a particular interpretation or understanding of a passage of Scripture: indeed, he would have had that interpretation in mind even as he read or cited a text.[6]

By contrast, Luke's knowledge of Scripture apparently came from assiduous reading. Luke had his canon within the canon just as everyone and, indeed, every denomination does. But whether before conversion Luke had been a Gentile or a Reform Jew, he knew certain parts of Scripture in such depth that unless the modern interpreter also knows the Septuagint or Greek Old Testament (LXX) very well indeed he or she will miss major points Luke wanted to score. Those portions were centrally the Torah and the Deuteronomic history, that is, Genesis to 4 Kingdoms (2 Kings).[7] Those

---

5. T. Holtz (*Untersuchungen über die alttestamentlichen Zitate bei Lukas* [Berlin: Akademie, 1968] 37–43 and 166–73) claims that Luke knew best the minor Prophets, Isaiah, and the Psalter, based on passages where he is closest to a recognizable Septuagint text. Holtz also states that Luke did not know the Pentateuch at all, but his conclusions are simply wrong. For more recent studies see G. D. Kilpatrick, "Some Quotations in Acts," in J. Kremer, ed., *Les Actes des Apôtres* (Gembloux: Duculot, 1979) 81–87; E. Richard, "The Old Testament in Acts," *CBQ* 42 (1980) 330–41; J. Jervell, "The Center of Scripture in Luke," in Jervell, *The Unknown Paul: Essays on Luke-Acts and Early Christian History* (Minneapolis: Augsburg, 1984) 122–37; H. Ringgren, "Luke's Use of the Old Testament," *HTR* 79 (1986) 227–35; and D. L. Bock, *Proclamation from Prophecy and Pattern: Lucan Old Testament Christology* (JSNTSup 12; Sheffield: JSOT, 1987).

6. One must apply some sociology of ancient knowledge when interpreting an ancient text, especially when trying to understand how an ancient author used a text or tradition older than that author. In order fully to understand Matthew's parable of the Great Banquet in 22:1-14, one must know *Tg.* Zeph 1:1–16, as J. D. M. Derrett has shown in *Law in the New Testament* (London: Darton, Longman & Todd, 1970) 126–55. But this is unnecessary for understanding Luke's form of the parable in 14:15-24, as I tried to show in "Luke's Great Banquet Parable," in J. L. Crenshaw and J. T. Willis, eds., *Essays in Old Testament Ethics* (New York: Ktav, 1974) 245–71; see Chap. 8 below.

7. For the central or special section of Luke's Gospel, 9:51—18:14, see C. F. Evans, "The Central Section of St. Luke's Gospel," in D. E. Nineham, ed., *Studies in the Gospels* (Oxford: Blackwell, 1955) 37–53, and my study, "Luke's Great Banquet Parable." For other studies following Evans's lead see J. Drury, *Tradition and Design in Luke's Gospel: A Study in Early*

sections of Scripture not only helped shape Luke's understanding of what God was doing in Christ (the Gospel) and in the early church (Acts), it also helped shape Luke's two-volume report of that activity.

Luke's reputation as the Second Testament historian is well deserved if one understands by that term what Luke's Scripture already contained as history. Although he had some acquaintance with Herodotus and perhaps other historians known in the Hellenistic world, Luke's intense acquaintance with the history of God's work in ancient Israel as presented in the (LXX) Deuteronomic history shaped the way he wrote his own. Luke's reputation, since 1954, of being a good theologian is in no way tarnished by re-appreciation of his work as *the* Second Testament historian of the work of God in Christ in the Gospel, and the work of God in the early church in Acts. Like his Old Testament predecessors, he was a good theological historian.[8]

A few observations must suffice. Luke's two annunciations in chapter 1 follow in detail the great annunciations in Genesis 15–18, 1 Samuel 1, and Judges 13, especially the annunciation to Hannah.[9] Mary's Magnificat is but a bare reworking of the song of Hannah (1 Samuel 2). The new kingdom announced by God in the first century, to be fully understood, must be seen in the light of the kingdom introduced by God through Samuel, culminating in David. In many ways, Luke presents Christ as the new David, even reporting that Christ asked Saul of Tarsus, on the journey to Damascus (Acts 9:4), a question very similar to the one the young David had asked King Saul at Ziph (LXX 1 Sam 26:18). King Saul had not joined the new kingdom under David but had fallen on a sword and died ignominiously (1 Sam 31:4). Saul of Tarsus, by contrast, not only joined the new kingdom under the new David but became its greatest herald.

And how does Luke conclude his second volume? "And he [Paul] lived there [Rome] two whole years at his own expense, and welcomed all who came to him, preaching the kingdom of God and teaching about the Lord Jesus Christ quite openly and unhindered" (Acts 28:30-31). Compare that to what we find at the end of 2 Kings: "So Jehoiachin put off his prison garments. And every day of his life he dined regularly at the king's table; and for his allowance, a regular allowance was given him by the king,

---

Christian Historiography (London: Darton, Longman & Todd, 1976) 138–64; R. W. Wall, "'The Finger of God': Deuteronomy 9.10 and Luke 11.20," *NTS* 33 (1987) 144–50; idem, "Martha and Mary (Luke 10.38-42) in the Context of a Christian Deuteronomy," *JSNT* 35 (1989) 19–35; and D. P. Moessner, *Lord of the Banquet* (Minneapolis: Fortress, 1989).

8. With this concern in mind, I much appreciate the balance in I. H. Marshall, *Luke: Historian and Theologian* (Grand Rapids: Eerdmans, 1978).

9. See the brilliant work on the annunciation in R. E. Brown, *The Birth of the Messiah* (Garden City: Doubleday, 1977) 256–329.

every day a portion, as long as he lived" (25:29-30). The point is not that King Jehoiachin was a type for the Apostle Paul but rather that Luke leaves the theological history of what God is doing in God's time as open-ended as the Deuteronomic historian had. Jehoiachin was freed from prison in Babylon at the beginning of the Dispersion of Jews throughout the world; Paul, although awaiting trial, was free to witness in Rome at the beginning of the dispersion of the church throughout the world. Each was in the capital of the dominant power of the time, and each was on the threshold of something new in the work of God. This was undoubtedly Luke's theocentric way of suggesting why the parousia had not taken place on the fall of Jerusalem in 70 C.E. He searched the Scriptures to find an understanding of what God was doing. Without question the eschaton was still expected; but, equally important, it is not for us to know the times and seasons of God (Luke 12:35-56). The God who made the first annunciations to Abraham and Sarah, and especially to Hannah, has announced a new kingdom to come in a spectacular way, and it will come in God's good time. God is continually active.

Luke is the most explicit of the evangelists in insisting that to understand what God was doing in Christ one had to know Scripture. Nowhere is his conviction clearer than in the parable of Lazarus and the Rich Man in 16:19-31. When the rich man finally understands why he is in Hades and asks Father Abraham to send Lazarus back from paradise, where he had gone at death, to explain to the rich man's five brothers how matters lay in ultimate truth, Abraham patiently explains that if they would not read Scripture, Moses and the Prophets, using the right hermeneutics, then they would not be convinced by someone rising from the dead (16:27-31)—and Lazarus would be resurrected if he were sent back to explain. This passage, set near the climax of Luke's central section, when matched with the same kind of emphasis in the last chapter of the Gospel (24:13-49) after another had been resurrected, conveys Luke's deep-seated conviction that a correct reading of Scripture, Moses and the Prophets, gives one the ability to see what is going on in the real world.

In both his volumes, Luke is interested in eyewitnesses, those who can see what God is doing amid current events. Luke makes it clear that it was not just the appearance of the resurrected Christ, on the road to Emmaus and in Jerusalem, that convinced the disciples of what had been going on and what was happening to them; because the resurrected Lord gave them exegesis classes, their eyes were opened, and the disciples finally became witnesses (24:48). They, who had been dull and uncomprehending throughout the Gospel, became wide-eyed apostles upon being instructed by the risen Christ through the Scriptures as to what was really happening (24:25, 27, 32, 44, 45); they were then ready for Pentecost, as Luke makes clear at the beginning of Acts. Luke further underscores his point with a solecism in 24:32 which uses the Greek word *dianoigo*. That verb was used in Greek for the opening of eyes. As in Semitic languages, another word was used for opening a scroll, but Luke used *dianoigo* to refer to Christ's opening the Scriptures to Cleopas and his companion on the road to Emmaus: their eyes were opened.

Luke's Scriptures functioned for him in various ways, not only when he cited a passage or alluded to a First Testament event or figure, but also when he did not do so. That is, his remarkable knowledge of the Greek Testament helped to shape his history of God's work in the first century. When Luke wrote in his prologue of those who from the beginning had been eyewitnesses and servants of the word (1:2), he meant from the beginning of God's work as Creator, Judge, and Redeemer, as revealed in Scripture. Luke constantly wove phrases and images from the Septuagint into his writing. A beautiful example is Gabriel's word of assurance (and also chiding) to Mary that with God nothing is impossible (1:37). Those are exactly the words spoken by the heavenly visitors in LXX Gen 18:14. In Genesis they are in interrogative form while in Luke they are in declarative. Thus Luke not only generally knew the annunciations in the First Testament; he explicitly knew the ones in Genesis.[10] It is as though Gabriel answered his Genesis colleagues back across the centuries, "No, nothing is impossible with God." Again, Luke's basic hermeneutic was theocentric.

One might ask how Luke came to know Scripture so well, or, supposing him to have been a Reform Jew who already knew Scripture in Greek, how his congregation knew it well enough to appreciate the subtle ways in which he used it. The answer is that new converts are usually enthusiasts. Upon conversion, first-century Christians apparently became quickly and intimately acquainted with their only Scripture, the First Testament, in Hebrew or in Greek. The few literate members would read aloud for all, and intense discussion would follow in Koine paraphrases of the Septuagint Greek.[11] Reports from contemporary China describe churches packed with young people seeking copies of the Bible which they then read together avidly. One can imagine the great demand for copies of Greek First Testament scrolls in the Hellenistic churches springing up around the Mediterranean. What an insistent teaching elder Luke must have been in the instructional life of his own congregation.

Part of his program of instruction clearly included reading Isaiah. Only

---

10. Pace Holtz, *Über die alttestamentlichen Zitate bei Lukas*.
11. See my "Communities and Canon" in the Oxford study Bible of the *Revised English Bible* (Oxford: Oxford University Press, 1992), 91–100.

three times does Luke actually cite Isaiah or use a formula introduction for a clear citation. But if the Scripture index of Nestle-Aland reflects the actual situation even relatively speaking, Luke falls behind only Revelation and the Gospel of Matthew in the use of Isaiah in the Second Testament. The three quotations of Isaiah with formulae are in Luke 3:4-6 (Isa 40:3-5); 4:18-19 (Isa 61:1-2 and 58:6); 22:37 (Isa 53:12). Explicit Isaianic phrases also appear at Luke 2:30-32 (Isa 52:10; 42:6; 49:6); 7:22 (Isa 26:19; 29:18; 35:5-6; 61:1); 8:10 (Isa 6:9-10); 19:46 (Isa 56:7); and 20:9 (Isa 5:1-2). Isaiah 49:6, which is explicitly cited in Acts 13:47 and is reflected in Luke 1:79 and 24:47 as well as in Acts 1:8 and 26:20, apparently influenced the shape of Luke's entire work.

To probe seriously and deeply into Isaiah's role in such passages in Luke, one needs to work on them in terms of text criticism, comparative midrash, and canonical criticism in relation to form criticism and redaction criticism. Two passages that have been so treated are the reflection of Isaiah's Song of the Vineyard (5:1-7) in the Luke 20 parable of the Wicked Husbandman[12] and the citation of Isa 61:1-2 (with a phrase from 58:6) in the Luke 4 account of Jesus' sermon at Nazareth.[13] The following remarks are based on these studies, especially for Luke 4. Many other passages in Luke must be studied but the work accomplished during the past twenty years indicates that what we have learned about the function of Isaiah 61 in Luke can be generalized to the rest of the Gospel.

It has been shown that Isaiah 58 and 61, or part of them, constituted the *haftarah* lesson attached to the Torah portion on the death of Israel as lectionary readings already in the first century,[14] but this hardly matters in terms of how Isaiah functions for Luke in Jesus' sermon. Unlike Luke, Mark (6:1-6) and Matthew (13:53-58) focus on Jesus' works rather than on his preaching in their report of this event. Furthermore, the other two synoptists place it in the middle of Jesus' Galilean ministry, whereas Luke puts it at the beginning and provides a citation from Isaiah and a sermon based on it. Luke in effect highlights the event as a harbinger of the crucifixion, for he clearly states that Jesus' own home congregation, his relatives, and friends, reject him because of his interpretation of the Isaiah

---

12. This has been done by M. P. Miller, *Scripture and Parable: A Study of the Function of the Biblical Features in the Parable of the Wicked Husbandmen and Their Place in the History of the Tradition* (unpublished doctoral dissertation; Columbia University, 1973).

13. See J. A. Sanders, "From Isaiah 61 to Luke 4," in J. Neusner, ed., *Christianity, Judaism and Other Greco-Roman Cults. Part One: The New Testament* (M. Smith Festschrift; Leiden: Brill, 1975) 75–106; cf. Chap. 4 below.

14. See R. B. Sloan, Jr., *The Favourable Year of the Lord: A Study of Jubilary Theology in the Gospel of Luke* (Austin: Schola Press, 1977).

passage. This is the opposite of Mark and Matthew's report that it is Jesus who rejects the people for their unbelief. Thus Luke stresses that what offended Jesus' contemporaries most was his hermeneutics, his interpretation of one of their favorite passages of Scripture.

Jesus read the passage from the Isaiah scroll and sat down. The congregation waited to hear how he would comment on the passage or what homily he would give. He electrified them by saying that on this day the Scripture was fulfilled in their ears. One must understand how much that particular passage meant to Jews in the first century under Roman oppression and rule. Isaiah had spoken of a herald anointed by the spirit of God to preach good news to the poor, to heal the brokenhearted, to proclaim release to captives and recovery of sight to the blind, and to proclaim the acceptable year of the Lord. In Luke, Jesus' reading of the passage stopped here. Jesus omitted the phrase about healing the brokenhearted and inserted one from LXX Isa 58:6 about sending the oppressed away in release, literally, or setting at liberty those who were oppressed. The phrase in Luke 4:18 repeats verbatim LXX Isa 58:6.

Why would Luke, or Jesus, mix Scripture like that, and how could he get away with it? In the first century, it was not uncommon to pull two or more passages out of their original literary contexts and read them together. This was most often done by word tallying; that is, both passages would have had in them at least one word that was the same. Here it was the Greek word *aphesis*, meaning release or forgiveness: to preach *aphesis* to captives (Isa 61:1) and to send the oppressed in *aphesis* (Isa 58:6).

To get the full impact of this word tallying one must realize that *aphesis* is the Greek translation of Hebrew *shemittah* in Deuteronomy 15 and Hebrew *deror* in Leviticus 25—the two passages in the Old Testament which provide legislation concerning the Jubilee Year. Luke's Jesus conjoined the two passages from Isaiah fully in the spirit and even the letter of Isaiah 61, which was itself composed out of Jubilee traditions.[15] The central concept of Jubilee was periodic release or liberty: letting the land periodically lie fallow, releasing debts, freeing slaves, and repatriating property. The Lord's Prayer is basically a Jubilee prayer.[16]

The matter of greatest interest to the congregation in Nazareth who heard Jesus read the Isaiah passage was release from the burden of Roman oppression, although they would have been interested in any release the

---

15. As shown by W. Zimmerli, "Das 'Gnadenjahr des Herrn,'" in A. Kuschke and E. Kutsch, eds., *Archäologie und Altes Testament* (K. Galling Festschrift; Tübingen: Mohr [Siebeck], 1970) 321–32.

16. See S. Ringe, *A Gospel of Liberation: An Explanation of Jubilee Motifs in the Gospel of Luke* (unpublished doctoral dissertation; Union Theological Seminary, 1980); cf. idem, *Jesus, Liberation, and the Biblical Jubilee* (Overtures to Biblical Theology 19; Philadelphia: Fortress, 1985).

Jubilee afforded. Release of slaves presented problems (Jeremiah 34), but release of debts had proved the most problematic aspect of the old legislation as was already recognized in Deut 15:7-11. As time passed, the problem was met in early Judaism in two ways: in Pharisaic circles by a juridical ploy called *prosboul* whereby waivers could be obtained when the Jubilee Year was approaching so that the economy would not collapse; in eschatological denominations in Judaism by a growing belief that the real Jubilee would arrive in the eschaton and be introduced by Messiah. God's kingdom would come and God's will be done on earth as it was in heaven precisely at the introduction on earth of the great Jubilee, when the divine economy, or superstantial (not daily) bread of the Lord's Prayer, would be manifest on earth. The congregation in Nazareth might well have thought at first that Jesus was the herald of Isaiah 61 sent to proclaim the great Jubilee release from slavery to Roman oppression.

In order fully to grasp Luke's point in placing this episode at the very beginning of Jesus' ministry and in providing us with one of the most precious passages in the Second Testament for discerning the hermeneutics applied to interpretation of Scripture, it is well in reading Luke 4 to resist the temptation to which we usually succumb of identifying with Jesus when we read a Gospel passage. We should instead identify with the congregation made up of Jesus' family and friends. We now know Isaiah 61 was one of the favorite passages in Judaism at the time of Jesus.[17] If the faithful in the Nazareth synagogue understood the passage in the way others understood it at the time, they would have interpreted it, as Jesus read it, as beneficial to themselves. They would have identified, in their turn, with the poor (for they were poor), the captives (for they felt themselves to be captive to the Romans), the blind (for they felt like dungeon inmates who were blind), and the oppressed (for they surely were oppressed). They had every right to feel that the blessings of Jubilee would devolve on them when the eschaton arrived and when Messiah, or Elijah, the herald of the eschaton, came.

Thus when Jesus said that the passage was fufilled that very day, he seemed to bolster their hope and they spoke well of him. This was not because he spoke graciously, as some translations lead us to think, but because (1) he had read one of their favorite passages about the grace of God and (2) he had apparently said it would be fulfilled immediately. They were hearing it by the hermeneutic of the grace of God; they under-

---

17. See my "From Isaiah 61 to Luke 4," 89–92. See also D. Tiede's study, *Prophecy and History in Luke-Acts* (Philadelphia: Fortress, 1980), including his critique of my own work on pp. 47–49.

stood it in terms of God as Redeemer of Israel. God's purpose in sending the herald would have been to save the people who were enduring a plight comparable to that of the slaves in Egypt when God sent Moses to release them from Pharaoh's bondage. The congregation would have rightly understood the passage in such a manner.

But then Jesus continued, "Truly, I say to you, no prophet is acceptable in his own country" (Luke 4:24). Why? Because he was Joseph's son? On the contrary, all the great prophets of Scripture had been homegrown. Amos had gone from Judah to Israel to preach, but all had the same covenant identity; prophets were commonly known in the communities where they preached. It was the message those prophets bore to their people that made them unpopular and unacceptable. It was the hermeneutics they applied to the most precious traditions, turning them into the authority whereby the prophets exposed the secrets of their people's hearts and thereby exposed corruption of consciousness. Luke's Jesus makes this point very clear in the blessings and woes of Luke 6:20-26.

Luke has Jesus stop his reading of the Isaiah passage after the first phrase of Isa 61:2, ". . . to proclaim the acceptable year of the Lord." The passage then speaks of a day of vengeance when God will bring joy and gladness to a Zion that mourned. Why would Jesus stop short of reading the rest of the passage which gave such explicit comfort? First, he stopped reading just before Isaiah spoke of vengeance, supposedly against Israel's enemies, and comfort, supposedly for Israel. But second, he made a telling rhetorical or midrashic point by ending his reading on the Greek word *dektos*—"acceptable," in this case a year acceptable to God. A Jewish interpretation understood this as a year acceptable to Israel! That indeed would be based on a hermeneutic of grace emphasizing God as Israel's own redeemer God only.

But Luke hereby signals for us his understanding of Jesus' hermeneutic in interpreting the Isaiah passage. No prophet is *dektos* to his own people when he applies their precious, authoritative traditions in such a way as to challenge the thinking of the people and their corruption of consciousness. Here is a word tally in the Lukan passage: the Jubilee will come at a time *acceptable to God*; and the prophet who wrests a prophetic challenge to his own people out of their identifying traditions, precisely by the hermeneutic of the freedom of God as Creator of all peoples, is himself *not acceptable to them*. Isaiah had said to his hearers that they were right to think that God was a holy warrior who had aided David in his battles against the Philistines (Isa 28:21; 2 Sam 5:17-25; 1 Chr 14:10-17), but they were wrong to think that God was shackled to them. On the contrary, Isaiah went on, God as holy warrior and Creator of all peoples would, this time, be at the head of the Assyrian troops fighting Judah. God was not only Israel's redeemer but also Creator and Judge of *all* peoples. Jesus went on to say something similar to Isaiah.

Do we really want Elijah to come? Why do we not look back at what he did when he was here? When he himself needed sustenance and had a blessing to bestow he was sent not to a widow in Israel but to a foreigner: a Phoenician widow (1 Kings/3 Kingdoms 17–18). And when Elisha had a blessing to bestow it was bestowed not on an Israelite leper but on a leper from Syria, Israel's worst enemy (2 Kings/4 Kingdoms 5). The freedom of the God of grace is perhaps the most difficult concept for any generation of believers to grasp.[18] Jesus interpreted Scripture (Isaiah 61) by Scripture (3 Kingdoms 17 and 4 Kingdoms 5) using the hermeneutic of the freedom of the God of grace—free even at the eschaton, in the great Jubilee, to bestow the blessings of Isaiah 61 on other than those who felt sure they were elect.

Little wonder the congregation wanted to lynch him. They put him out of the city and attempted to stone him as punishment for blasphemy (to throw an offender down a cliff is preparatory to stoning). If in reading Luke 4 one identifies with the congregation, one can move with them from the feeling of hope and elation, after Jesus had read the Isaianic passage, to the feeling of intense anger which they understandably would feel at hearing the favorite passage (something like John 3:16 for Christians) interpreted in such a way as to indicate that at the eschaton, when the curtain of ultimate truth was lifted, God might freely bestow favors and blessings on folk outside the in-group of true believers.

The real prophetic offense in Jesus' sermon was theological: it was serious and ultimate. Jesus told the congregation that God was not Jewish. This was comparable to a preacher saying that God is not Christian. Of course God is not Muslim, Buddhist, Communist, or any other faith. But when a people or a church or a denomination so emphasizes God's work as Redeemer that they feel they have God boxed up and domesticated, then a prophet must appear to expose their corruption of consciousness. Whenever we feel we have a corner on truth or a commanding grip on reality, then, if we are fortunate, a prophet will appear to shock us into realizing that God is God. It is not that God is not our Redeemer. Thank God, God is! But God is also the Creator of all peoples. God is both committed in promises and free to surprise and even re-create us. God is free to bestow grace anywhere. Grace is a form of divine injustice—undeserved when God first bestowed it on Israel, and undeserved when God bestows it on Phoenician widows and Syrian lepers. The passage stresses

---

18. See J. A. Sanders, *God Has a Story Too* (Philadelphia: Fortress, 1979) 14–26.

what is acceptable to God, not what is acceptable to the faithful: it disengages any thought that God's agenda must follow Israel's. It also stresses release or forgiveness and God's freedom to dispense this to any creature.

In the context from which Luke's Jesus drew the phrase ". . . set at liberty those who are oppressed" (Isa 58:6), the prophet challenged the people for believing God owed them something because they were faithful. "Why have we fasted but you have not seen it? Why have we humbled ourselves but you take no knowledge of it?" The faithful seem always tempted to feel that God should honor their efforts on God's behalf.

By dynamic analogy Jesus and Luke bring Isaiah to us as a challenge whenever we as Christians feel we have God boxed into *our* ideas of the incarnation. The temptation for Christians to feel they have God tamed in the incarnation is perhaps even greater than for Jews to feel they had God on a leash as children of Abraham (Luke 3:8). If we follow Luke and do a theocentric reading of Isaiah canonically and as a whole without worrying whether it is 1, 2, or 3 Isaiah, we must realize that Luke's Jesus brings Isaiah forward to the first-century, and to the twentieth-century, believer in a canonically true manner.

— 3 —

JESUS AND THE SPIRIT:
ON THE ORIGIN AND MINISTRY
OF THE SECOND SON OF GOD

CRAIG A. EVANS

THE HOLY SPIRIT IN LUKE-ACTS:
GENERAL OBSERVATIONS

The prominence of the Holy Spirit in Luke-Acts is well known.[1] Its principal purpose seems to be to show that the gospel is truly of divine origin, meets with divine approval, and is advanced by divine agency. Several passages in Acts make this quite clear. Through the Holy Spirit the risen Christ commands his Apostles (Acts 1:2). They are to wait in Jerusalem until they receive the Holy Spirit (Acts 1:5, 8). When the Holy Spirit comes upon the Apostles (Acts 2:1-4), Peter preaches his Pentecost sermon (Acts 2:14-41) in which Joel 2:28-32 is cited, a text that had promised the pouring out of God's Spirit (Acts 2:17; Joel 2:28). Those who repent and believe in the risen Jesus will receive the promised Holy Spirit (Acts 2:38). Peter, filled with the Holy Spirit, replies to the ruling priests who had ordered the Apostles to cease their witness and preaching (Acts 4:8). Filled with the Holy Spirit, the entire company of believers speak "the word of God with boldness" (Acts 4:31). Indeed, the Holy Spirit is himself a witness to the Gospel (Acts 5:32). Full of the Holy Spirit, Stephen sees "Jesus standing at God's right hand" (Acts 7:56).

Manifestations of the Holy Spirit make it clear that the Samaritans are genuine Christians (Acts 8:15-17). The Spirit leads Philip to the Ethiopian official (Acts 8:29, 39). The converted Saul/Paul is filled with the Holy Spirit (Acts 9:17). The Spirit informs Peter of Cornelius's quest for the

---

1. For a recent treatment of the Holy Spirit in the Lukan writings, see R. Stronstad, *The Charismatic Theology of St. Luke* (Peabody: Hendrickson, 1984), as well as Chap. 13 below.

Gospel (Acts 10:19), and the subsequent descent of the Holy Spirit upon Cornelius and his household (Acts 10:44) persuades Peter and the Jerusalem council that salvation is indeed possible for Gentiles (Acts 10:47-48; 11:17-18). Full of the Holy Spirit, Barnabas seeks out Paul (Acts 11:24-26). The Holy Spirit directs the church to commission Paul and Barnabas (Acts 13:1-4). Filled with the Holy Spirit, Paul is able to defeat the magician Bar-Jesus (Acts 13:6-12). The converts of Antioch of Pisidia are filled with the Holy Spirit (Acts 13:52). The evidence of the Holy Spirit is appealed to at the second Jerusalem council. "God knows the heart and bore witness to them, giving them the Holy Spirit just as he did to us" (Acts 15:8). The Spirit directs Paul in his missionary journeys (Acts 16:6-7; 19:21). When baptized in the name of Jesus, twelve disciples of John the Baptist receive the Holy Spirit (Acts 19:1-7). Through the testimony of the Holy Spirit Paul knows that he will be persecuted (Acts 20:23). By the Holy Spirit the Ephesian elders are made overseers of the church (Acts 20:28). Through the Holy Spirit the prophet Agabus foretells Paul's imprisonment (Acts 21:10-11). Finally, Paul recognizes that the Holy Spirit had spoken through the prophet the words of Isa 6:9-10 to a stubborn and unbelieving generation (Acts 28:25-28).

Numerous passages in the Lukan Gospel speak of the Holy Spirit. Several of these appear in the infancy narratives and seem to function in essentially the same manner as in Acts. The angel tells Zechariah that his son will be filled with the Holy Spirit even from his mother's womb (Luke 1:15). Later, Elizabeth will be filled with the Spirit, and at the sound of Mary's voice the babe in her womb will leap for joy (Luke 1:41-44). The angel tells Mary that her pregnancy will be the result of the Holy Spirit (1:35). After John's birth, Zechariah is filled with the Holy Spirit and utters the Benedictus (Luke 1:67). Simeon, who had been told by the Holy Spirit that he would not die before seeing the Lord's Christ, is led by the Spirit into the temple where he sees Jesus and utters the Nunc Dimittis (Luke 2:25-27).

JESUS AND THE HOLY SPIRIT

The Lukan evangelist also speaks of the Holy Spirit in close association with Jesus' ministry, and in these passages we can make comparison. The Holy Spirit is mentioned not only in Luke's Gospel but also in passages common to Mark and/or Matthew. (There is of course no opportunity for comparison in Acts because there is no other parallel account, and little in Luke's distinctive infancy narratives as the Matthean version covers very different ground.) It will be useful to survey all of the passages that speak of Jesus and the Holy Spirit.

Luke 1:35. When Mary is told that she will conceive and give birth to a son, she asks how this could be possible since she has no husband. The angel answers her, "The Holy Spirit will come upon you, and the power of the Most High will overshadow you; therefore the child to be born will be called holy, the Son of God." The idea that Jesus' conception is of the Holy Spirit is not, of course, unique to Luke. According to Matthew, "before they came together she was found to be with child of the Holy Spirit" (Matt 1:18b). The point is underscored when the angel assures the troubled Joseph that "that which is conceived in her is of the Holy Spirit" (Matt 1:20b). The unique feature in Luke is the second part of the angel's answer, "Therefore the child to be born will be called holy, the Son of God." Being called "holy" probably anticipates the allusion to Exod 13:12 in Luke 2:23 ("Every male that opens the womb shall be called holy to the Lord"), the heavenly voice at the baptism (Luke 3:22) and the mount of transfiguration (Luke 9:35), and possibly the later exclamations of demons (Luke 4:34: "the Holy One of God") and apostolic preaching (Acts 3:14, "You denied the Holy and Righteous One"; 4:27, 30, "your Holy Servant Jesus"), which in turn are based on Scripture (Ps 16:10, "You will not allow your Holy One to see corruption"; cf. Acts 2:27; 13:35). But being called "Son of God" *because* (*dio*) of the conception through the Holy Spirit is an important component in Luke's christology. To this we shall return later.

Luke 2:40. In a summary that resembles the summary of John's growth (Luke 1:80), the Lukan evangelist states that "the child (Jesus) grew and became strong [in Spirit], filled with wisdom; and the favor of God was upon him." Whether this passage makes a helpful contribution to the study at hand is uncertain for two reasons. First, although the majority of witnesses include the variant (θ and the Byzantine family), the earliest manuscripts omit it (cf. B ℵ D). Second, even if we think that *pneumati* ("in spirit") belongs in the text, it may refer to the Holy Spirit or simply to the spiritual aspect of a human's growth (as the case may very well be in Luke 1:80).

Luke 3:22. According to Mark's version of the baptism of Jesus, "immediately he saw the heavens opened and the Spirit descending upon him like a dove" (Mark 1:10). To this Luke makes two important additions (as noted in italics), "The heaven was opened, and the *Holy* Spirit descended upon him *in bodily form,* as a dove." Luke has added *to hagion* to "the Spirit," something that he will do elsewhere,[2] and he has added the adverb

---

2. Luke possibly emphasized the fact that it was the *Holy* Spirit operating within Jesus in order to fend off the accusation that Jesus was empowered by an unclean spirit (cf. Luke 11:14-23).

sōmatikōs. This adverb probably is meant to underscore the reality of the Spirit's descent as a dove upon Jesus, which was not simply visionary or symbolic but real and enabling. And from it Jesus derived a power that he would shortly employ. Moreover, the descent of the Spirit upon (*epi*) Jesus anticipates the citation of Isa 61:1-2 ("The Spirit of the Lord is upon [*epi*] me").

Luke 4:1-2a. According to Mark, "the Spirit immediately drove [Jesus] out into the wilderness." In anticipation of the pending temptations Luke once again enriches his Markan source, "And Jesus, full of the Holy Spirit, returned from the Jordan, and was led by the Spirit for forty days in the wilderness." Not only has Luke added the phrase, "Full of the Holy Spirit," he has replaced the unceremonious "drive out" (*ekballein*), a verb that customarily describes the casting out of demons (e.g., Luke 9:40, 49; 11:14, 15, 18, 19, 20; 13:32), with "lead" (*agein*). Matthew (4:1) makes a similar modification (*anagein*).

Luke 4:14. Following the temptations Mark states that "Jesus went into Galilee" (Mark 1:14). In keeping with his emphasis on the Holy Spirit and in anticipation of the Nazareth sermon, Luke rewrites, "Jesus returned in the power of the Spirit into Galilee" (Luke 4:14; Matt 4:12, "He withdrew into Galilee").

Luke 4:18. Luke 4:16-30 is probably based on Mark 6:1-6a, although the Lukan evangelist might have made use of a parallel source.[3] Nothing in the Markan version approximates the citation from Isaiah 61. According to Luke, Jesus began his sermon by quoting and commenting upon Isa 61:1-2. "The Spirit of the Lord is upon me, because he has anointed [*echrisen*] me to preach good news to the poor; he has sent me to proclaim release to the captives and sight to the blind, to set at liberty the oppressed, to proclaim the acceptable year of the Lord" (Luke 4:18-19). The Lukan Jesus then claims, "Today this Scripture has been fulfilled in your hearing" (Luke 4:21). Luke's "today" does not mean that very sabbath day, but in the time of Jesus' ministry.[4] Jesus' earthly existence was generated by the Spirit (Luke 1:35), and his ministry was christened by the Spirit at the baptism (Luke 3:22). The notices found in Luke 4:1 and 14 are

---

3. I. H. Marshall (*Commentary on Luke* [NIGTC; Grand Rapids: Eerdmans, 1978] 180) considers the Markan version an abbreviation of the episode, with Luke retaining a fuller account (of what Jesus actually said). J. A. Fitzmyer (*The Gospel according to Luke I–IX* [AB 28; Garden City: Doubleday, 1981] 527) thinks that the Lukan account is a conflation of Mark 6:1-6a and primitive, possibly Aramaic, material (as seen in vv. 25-27).

4. Marshall, *Luke*, 185; Fitzmyer, *Luke I–IX*, 533–34.

reminders of Jesus' filling with the Spirit. Taken together they provide the warrant for Jesus to quote Isaiah 61 and claim its fulfillment in his ministry.

Luke 10:21. The dominical saying contained in Luke 10:21-22 is undoubtedly from Q (cf. Matt 11:25-27), but evidently the evangelists independently composed their respective introductions to the saying. Whereas Matthew reads, "At that time Jesus declared," Luke reads, "In that same hour he rejoiced in the Holy[5] Spirit and said." Once again Luke mentions the Spirit, reminding his readers of what enables Jesus' words and deeds. The evangelist's contextualization of this tradition is also deserving of comment. In the preceding pericope (Luke 10:17-20) the seventy return rejoicing because of their power over demons and spirits, and Jesus says that he saw Satan fall from heaven. (The Matthean context is quite different.) One of the principal points that Luke sees in Jesus' possession of the Spirit is that he is able to defeat Satan. This was, of course, clearly illustrated in the temptation narrative and will be illustrated later in Acts in the ministries of Peter (Acts 8:18-24) and Paul (Acts 13:4-12; 16:16-18; 19:13-20). The significance of this theme for the temptation narrative will be developed below.

Luke 11:13. Jesus urges his disciples to have faith in God, for " . . . how much more will the heavenly Father give the Holy Spirit to those who ask him" (cf. Matt 7:11, which reads "good things" instead of the "Holy Spirit"). Here we have another tradition derived from Q, although commentators disagree about which evangelist followed the source and which modified it. Robert H. Gundry thinks that Luke's "Holy Spirit" is original, with Matthew's "good things" as redaction.[6] I suspect that it is the other way around, given Luke's keen interest in the Spirit,[7] but the point is not that important. What is important is to observe once again Luke's contextualization. Immediately following the statement that God will give the Holy Spirit to those who ask, Jesus casts out a demon and then is accused of performing exorcisms through the power of Satan (Luke 11:14-26).

---

5. Many manuscripts omit "Holy," but the adjective is nevertheless well attested, being read by P[75] ℵ B C D 33 and others, with some confusion over whether or not "Jesus" should be read. See Marshall, *Luke,* 433.

6. R. H. Gundry, *Matthew: A Commentary on His Literary and Theological Art* (Grand Rapids: Eerdmans, 1982) 124–25.

7. J. M. Creed (*The Gospel according to St. Luke* [London: Macmillan, 1930] 158), E. E. Ellis (*The Gospel of Luke* [NCB; Grand Rapids: Eerdmans, 1974] 166), E. Schweizer (*The Good News according to Luke* [Atlanta: John Knox, 1984] 192), J. A. Fitzmyer (*The Gospel according to Luke X–XXIV* [AB 28A; Garden City: Doubleday, 1985] 913–16), and C. F. Evans (*Saint Luke* [TPI New Testament Commentaries; London: SCM; Philadelphia: Trinity, 1990] 487) agree. Marshall (*Luke,* 470) is uncertain.

(Again, Matthew's context is quite different, for the parallel saying falls in the Sermon on the Mount and has nothing to do with exorcism.) As seen in some of the preceding examples, Luke casts the role of the Spirit as enabling Jesus to oppose and defeat Satan.

Luke 24:49. The resurrected Jesus "sends" his disciples the promise of his Father and then commands his disciples to remain in Jerusalem until they "are clothed with power [*dynamis*] from on high." The promise referred to here is doubtless the promise of the Holy Spirit (cf. Acts 1:4-5; 2:33), although curiously this is not made explicit.[8] The context and phrases, "Upon you [*eph' hymas*]" and "From on high [*eks hypsous*]," are probably echoes of LXX Isa 32:15, "Until the Spirit comes upon us from on high [*epelthē eph' hymas pneuma aph' hypsēlou*]." The language of Acts 1:8 adds conviction to this suspicion. "You shall receive power [*dynamis*], when the Holy Spirit has come [*epelthontos*] upon you [*eph' hymas*]."[9] The context of this verse from Isaiah is quite significant. Isaiah had warned the comfortable and complacent that desolation and destruction would be Judah's lot (32:9-14), "until the Spirit comes." Then there would be justice, righteousness, and security (32:16-20).

CHRISTIANS AND THE HOLY SPIRIT

The Holy Spirit's ministry continues in Acts, where the Spirit that empowered Jesus now empowers his disciples. Not every reference to the Spirit concerns us, only those that deal with conversion and renewal.

Acts 1:8. Before ascending, the risen Jesus tells his apostles, "You shall receive power when the Holy Spirit has come upon you; and you shall be my witnesses" (Acts 1:8). The Holy Spirit will enable the apostles to preach the gospel and to bear witness to the resurrection, just as the Holy Spirit filled and enabled the characters of the infancy narrative to speak of the things that God was about to accomplish in John and Jesus.

Acts 2:1-4. Jesus' promise is fulfilled on the day of Pentecost: "Suddenly a sound came from heaven like the rush of a mighty wind [*pnoē*], and it filled all the house . . . and there appeared tongues as of fire, distributed

---

8. See Schweizer, *Luke*, 378; Marshall, *Luke*, 907; Fitzmyer, *Luke X–XXIV*, 1585.
9. The LXX translates "come upon," but the Hebrew is actually "pour out" (*'arah*). The Spirit is "poured out" in Joel 2:28 (LXX/MT 3:1), but a different Hebrew word is used there (*shaphak*). The LXX translates literally (*ekchein*), which the Lukan Peter quotes (Acts 2:17) and alludes to (Acts 2:33).

and resting on each one of them. And they were all filled with the Holy Spirit [*pneuma hagion*] and began to speak in other tongues, as the Spirit gave them utterance."

Acts 2:32-33, 38. " 'This Jesus God raised up. . . . Being therefore exalted at the right hand of God, and having received from the Father the promise of the Holy Spirit, he has poured out this which you see and hear. . . . Repent . . . and you shall receive the gift of the Holy Spirit.' " This Pentecost "promise" seems to be the fulfillment of what Jesus taught earlier in Luke 11:13 and 24:49,[10] but with a different nuance: Jesus received from the Father the promised Holy Spirit, which he then poured out on the day of Pentecost, fulfilling the prophecy of Joel 2:28-32 (LXX/MT=3:1-5).[11] The Father gives the Spirit to Jesus, Jesus, in an intercessory or intermediary role, gives the Spirit to his followers.[12] The Spirit will work for Jesus' followers much as it worked for Jesus: both are able to defeat Satan.

Acts 5:27-32. When brought before the Sanhedrin and reminded that they had been told to cease speaking of Jesus, "Peter and the Apostles answered, '. . . God . . . raised Jesus . . . [and] exalted him at his right hand as Leader and Savior, to give repentance to Israel and forgiveness of sins. And we are witnesses to these things, and so is the Holy Spirit whom God has given to those who obey him.' " Here again is the combination of repentance and the giving of the Holy Spirit. (This is probably related to the "times of refreshing" which Israel may expect if it repents [Acts 3:19].) By obeying God (i.e., believing in his Son, Jesus) one receives the gift of the Spirit.

Acts 8:14-17. "Now when the apostles at Jerusalem heard that Samaria had received the word of God, they sent to them Peter and John, who came down and prayed for them that they might receive the Holy Spirit; for it had not yet fallen on any of them, but they had only been baptized in the name of the Lord Jesus. Then they laid their hands on them and they received the Holy Spirit." Why did the Samaritans not receive the Spirit until the visit of the Apostles? (There is no hint of this need in the earlier episodes.) As the Jerusalem council in chapter 11 makes clear, the pur-

---

10. E. Haenchen, *The Acts of the Apostles* (Oxford: Blackwell; Philadelphia: Westminster, 1971) 183; R. Pesch, *Die Apostelgeschichte* (EKKNT 5; 2 vols.; Zurich: Benziger; Neukirchen-Vluyn: Neukirchener Verlag, 1986) 1.124.

11. The pouring out of the Spirit described by Joel was possibly thought to be the fulfillment of Moses' desire that God place the Spirit upon all of the people (Num 11:29; cf. *Midr.* Ps 14.6 [on 14:7]). This is discussed at greater length below in Chap. 13.

12. Which was something that Moses wished to do but could not.

pose was to offer public proof of the reality of the Samaritan repentance and faith. The reception of the Holy Spirit and the attendant phenomena constitute this proof.[13] This point receives further clarification in the next pericope.

Acts 10:1-48. After his vision and the invitation to visit, Peter proclaimed the Christian gospel to Cornelius. "You know the word which he sent to Israel . . . how God anointed [*echrisen*] Jesus of Nazareth with the Holy Spirit and with power; how he went about doing good and healing all that were oppressed by the devil, for God was with him" (Acts 10:36-38). Clearly the Lukan evangelist intends his readers to recall Jesus' Nazareth sermon where Isa 61:1-2 was cited, "The Spirit of the Lord is upon me, because he has anointed [*echrisen*] me to preach good news." According to Luke, to be Christ is not simply to be anointed (i.e., in a symbolic sense), but to be anointed with the Holy Spirit. Again, Luke tells us that by being empowered with the Holy Spirit, Jesus was able to heal those oppressed by the devil (Satan). But Jesus is also the giver of the Holy Spirit itself (Luke 24:49). As had the Samaritans in the preceding passage, so Cornelius and his household receive the Holy Spirit: "While Peter was still saying this, the Holy Spirit fell on all who heard the word. And all the believers from among the circumcised who came with Peter were amazed, because the gift of the Holy Spirit had been poured out [*ekchein*] even on the Gentiles. . . . Then Peter declared, 'Can any one forbid water for baptizing these people who have received the Holy Spirit just as we have?' " (vv. 44-45, 47). Significantly, Luke uses the word "pour out," which was used in the quotation of the passage from Joel (cf. Acts 2:17). Just as God poured out the Spirit on the Apostles, on Jews, and on Samaritans, so now God has poured it out on Gentiles, and on a Roman centurion and his family at that.

But on what grounds that Jews viewed as legitimate could the Holy Spirit be given to Gentiles? The problem centers on purity. The Holy Spirit is "clean" in the strictest sense, hence the convention of calling the Spirit "Holy." One aspect of the "cleanness" of the Holy Spirit is illustrated in its power to cast out the "unclean" spirits and demons (cf. Luke 4:33, 36; 6:18; 8:29; 9:42; 11:24; Acts 5:15; 8:7). The holiness code required Israelites to be holy, as God is holy, and to be separate from the unclean Gentiles (cf. Lev 19:2; 20:26). Thus the idea of the Holy Spirit indwelling Gentiles would be shocking to Jews and possibly even contrary to the

---

13. I. H. Marshall, *Acts* (Tyndale New Testament Commentaries; Grand Rapids: Eerdmans, 1980) 157; Pesch, *Die Apostelgeschichte,* 1.276; H. Conzelmann, *Acts of the Apostles* (Hermeneia; Philadelphia: Fortress, 1987) 65; C. S. C. Williams, *The Acts of the Apostles* (HNTC; New York: Harper & Row, 1964) 157.

teaching of Scripture. Acts 10 addresses this problem. When Peter was directed in his vision to kill and eat animals that fell outside of kashrut, he protested, "No, Lord; for I have never eaten anything that is common [*koinos*] or unclean [*akathartos*]" (Acts 10:14). In saying this he was only declaring his obedience to what God had commanded his ancestors (cf. Lev 20:25-26). But he is rebuked, "What God has cleansed, you must not call common" (Acts 10:15).[14] This did not happen only once, but three times! (10:16). The heavenly voice would have probably been understood as a *bath qol*, a heavenly confirmation of a point of interpretation (usually in reference to legal matters). That the scene occurred three times was meant to underscore the certainty of Heaven's decision. God can and has made Gentiles clean; with God nothing is impossible (cf. Gen 18:14; Luke 1:37). Gentiles, like Jews, may receive the Holy Spirit if they repent and believe in God's Son, Jesus. Peter's understanding of the heavenly voice received confirmation when the Holy Spirit fell upon Cornelius and his household.

This idea is not, however, unanticipated. It has its roots in the ministry of Jesus (Luke 4:25-27) and is illustrated by the fact that in some of Jesus' parables (most found only in Luke) persons who enter the kingdom of God or paradise or who fulfill the ethical requirements of the covenant are poor, sick, or socially outcast (cf. Luke 14:15-24; 16:19-31; 18:9-14), including Samaritans (cf. Luke 10:30-37; 17:11-19). Although these people are ritually "unclean" and hence should be numbered among the non-elect, they enter the kingdom because they obey Jesus and answer the kingdom's summons. And the evidence of their successful entry is the reception of the Holy Spirit,[15] for the Spirit could not indwell them if they were unclean in God's sight (cf. 2 Cor 6:14—7:1).

Acts 11:1-18. When the "circumcision party" (Acts 11:2) asked Peter why he had eaten with uncircumcised men, the apostle relates his experience of chapter 10. He describes his heavenly vision (Acts 11:9; cf. 10:15) and the falling of the Holy Spirit upon the Gentiles (11:15-16; cf. 10:44-47). With this statement the circumcision party is "silenced. And they glorified God, saying, 'Then to the Gentiles also God has granted repentance unto

---

14. Pesch (*Die Apostelgeschichte*, 1.339) cites *b. Sanh.* 59b, "Nothing unclean comes down from Heaven"; and (339, n. 40) *Midr.* Ps 146.4 (on 146:7, "The Lord will loose the bounds"), "All animals which in this world are declared unclean God will in the future declare clean." It is conceivable, if this approximates first-century thinking, that early Christians understood the "cleanness" of Gentiles as a sign of the eschatological age.

15. Marshall (*Acts*, 194) rightly comments, "The reception of the gift on this occasion stressed the reality of the conversion of the Gentiles over against all possible doubt." Cf. Conzelmann, *Acts*, 84, "Heaven itself points the way to the admission of the 'Gentiles.'"

life' " (11:18). Concern, however, over the admittance of Gentiles into the infant church only subsides; it does not disappear.

Acts 15:1-35. On the heels of Paul's first missionary journey (Acts 13–14) the Gentile problem comes to a head. A party from Judea, probably representing the same constituency identified in Acts 11:1 (some of whom were Pharisees, according to 15:5), insists that the Gentiles be "circumcised according to the custom of Moses" (15:1). Peter answers them by declaring, "God who knows the heart bore witness to them, giving them the Holy Spirit just as he did to us; and he made no distinction between us and them, but cleansed their hearts by faith" (15:8-9). This statement succinctly summarizes the Lukan thrust. By giving the Spirit to Gentiles as well as Israelites, God bears witness to the reality of their inclusion among the people of God. This is possible because God has cleansed (*katharizein*) their hearts, and with the heart cleansed, the Holy Spirit may enter. God therefore no longer distinguishes (*diakrinein*) between Jews and Gentiles. Such a notion flies in the face of Jewish belief. "[God] makes a distinction between the holy and the profane, between light and darkness, between Israel and the other nations" (*b. Hullin* 26b). But in Christ there is no longer a distinction between Jews and Gentiles (cf. Gal 3:28). Peter's argument, combined with James's citation and interpretation of LXX Amos 9:11-12, which speaks of Gentiles seeking and being accepted by God (Acts 15:16-18), convinces the council that circumcision is not necessary for salvation (15:22-27). The instructions of the council's letter (15:28-29), based on the advice of James (15:19-21), are not requirements for salvation but guidelines designed to avoid causing offense to Jewish Christians.[16]

Thus an important element for understanding the pouring out of the Holy Spirit on Samaritans and Gentiles in Acts 8–15 is the concept of "cleanness." Religiously observant Jews were concerned with ritual purity (cf. Luke 7:36-39; 11:37-41; 15:2), and Samaritans and Gentiles were regarded as unclean (cf. Matt 10:5; John 4:7-10; 8:48; Gal 2:15; 2 Macc 6:1-2).[17] The indwelling of the Holy Spirit is proof that the individual has

---

16. Marshall, *Acts*, 255; Pesch, *Die Apostelgeschichte*, 2.81; Conzelmann, *Acts*, 118; Williams, *Acts*, 266–67. The instructions of the council's letter may reflect the "Noachic" code (Gen 9:4), which some rabbis felt was binding on the Gentiles; cf. G. F. Moore, *Judaism in the First Centuries of the Christian Era: The Age of the Tannaim* (3 vols.; Cambridge: Harvard University Press, 1927–30) 1.274–75, 339.

17. "Whenever anyone was accused by the people of Jerusalem of eating unclean food [*koinophagia*] or violating the sabbath or committing any other such sin, he would flee to the Shechemites [Samaritans]" (Josephus, *Ant.* 11.7.7 §347). The Samaritan claim of pure lineage was never accepted by Jewish religious authorities (*m. Qidd.* 4:3; *Gen. Rab.* 94.7 [on 46:8-13]). Samaritans were accused of idolatry (*Gen. Rab.* 81.3 [on 35:4]; *y. Abod. Zar.* 2:1; 5:4),

been "cleansed" through repentance and faith in Jesus. The Cornelius episode offers clear proof of this view, and the Jerusalem councils of chapters 11 and 15 clarify the theological rationale.

THE HOLY SPIRIT AND THE
SONS OF GOD

Because Luke's genealogy of Jesus ends with "son of Adam, son of God"[18] (Luke 3:38) and is immediately followed by the temptation narrative (4:1-13) in which Satan tempts Jesus, "If you are the Son of God," commentators have in the past frequently suggested that the evangelist has in mind an Adam/Jesus typology, though none have worked out a detailed analysis.[19]

Joachim Jeremias, however, offered an analysis in an article on Adam,[20] in which he argued that Mark's version of the temptation (Mark 1:13) reflects an Adam typology. Just as Adam, the first man, had dominion over beasts (Gen 1:26-30; 2:19-20; *Apoc. Moses* 16), so Jesus, the new man, was with beasts, a foreshadowing of the restoration of peace between humankind and the animal kingdom (Isa 11:6-8; 65:25). Just as Adam enjoyed the food of angels (cf. *Life of Adam and Eve* 4:2; *b. Sanh.* 59b), so Jesus, after his lengthy fast, was ministered to by angels. Just as Adam was tempted by Satan (Gen 3:1-7), so Jesus was tempted by Satan. Just as Adam was driven from paradise into the wilderness (Gen 3:22-24), so Jesus defeated Satan in the wilderness and made entry into paradise a possibility. Luke was probably aware of this typology, as his sequence of genealogy followed by temptation suggests. The evangelist moreover might have known of the Pauline Adam/Christ typologies (Rom 5:12-21; 1 Cor 15:45-49).

Jeremias's analysis may be correct, but as stated it is vulnerable at many points. Marshall Johnson has raised three objections.[21] (1) The Pauline Adam/Christ typology comes to explicit expression nowhere in Luke-Acts.

---

were regarded as fools (Sir 50:25-26; *T. Levi* 7:2), and were killed, it was believed, with divine approval (*Jub.* 30:5-6, 23). The evangelist Luke was certainly aware of these attitudes, and his selection of material that put Gentiles and Samaritans in a favorable light was doubtlessly a deliberate challenge to such prejudice; cf. M. S. Enslin, "Luke and the Samaritans," *HTR* 36 (1943) 278–97.

18. Fitzmyer, *Luke I–IX*, 491. "It is almost certain that it is Luke himself who has added the last item, 'son of God.'"

19. E.g., W. Manson, *The Gospel of Luke* (MNTC; London: Hodder & Stoughton, 1930) 35; A. Schlatter, *Das Evangelium des Lukas* (2d ed.; Stuttgart: Calwer, 1960) 218–19.

20. J. Jeremias, "*Adam,*" *TDNT* 1 (1964) 141–43.

21. M. D. Johnson, *The Purpose of the Biblical Genealogies with Special Reference to the Setting of the Genealogies of Jesus* (2d ed.; SNTSMS 8; Cambridge: Cambridge University Press, 1988) 233–35. Fitzmyer, *Luke I–IX*, 498: "Johnson . . . has effectively disposed of most of Jeremias' arguments."

Johnson asks, "Can we imagine, therefore, that we are to see in the genealogy a veiled allusion to such a distinctive idea, which Luke elsewhere
ignores?" (2) The midrashic traditions that Jeremias thinks clarify the
Markan temptation account have no relevance for the *Lukan* account,
which omits reference to the wild beasts and the ministering angels. (3)
The genealogy does not end with Adam but with God. If a comparison is
intended, says Johnson, it is Jesus as Son of God, not son of Adam.
Johnson's criticisms are well taken and his suggestion that the Lukan focus
is on Jesus as the Son of God is right on target.[22] Nevertheless, this does
not necessarily preclude a typology with Adam as apparently he supposes.

The question of an Adam/Jesus typology in Luke has recently been
reopened by Jerome Neyrey.[23] His analysis is free from the many weaknesses of Jeremias's and effectively addresses the concerns raised by
Johnson. Neyrey argues that the Adam typology is found both at the
beginning of Jesus' career (genealogy and temptation) and at its end
(garden and cross). The genealogy, concluding with Jesus' ancestry, "son
of Adam, son of God," links the baptism, where God calls Jesus "my beloved
Son" (3:22), with the temptation, where Satan calls Jesus' sonship into
question, "If you are the Son of God" (4:3, 9). Concurring with William
Kurz,[24] Neyrey thinks that the genealogy has been extended to Adam (1)
to place Jesus in the context of world history (Luke 1:5; 2:1-2; 3:1-2; Acts
26:26), (2) to place Jesus within the biblical framework that begins with
creation (Luke 3:38; Acts 17:24) and ends with judgment (Acts 10:42;
17:31), and (3) to underscore the conviction that with the coming of
Jesus, the old age, which had begun with Adam, had now ended and a
new age had begun. Jesus "is the pivotal figure who marks the turn of the
two ages."[25]

Neyrey thinks that the three temptations in the Lukan account mirror
the temptations that Satan had put before Adam: (1) the temptation to
eat (Gen 3:6; Luke 4:3), (2) the temptation to obtain dominion (Gen 3:5;
1:26-30; Luke 4:5-6), and (3) the temptation to defy death (Gen 3:3, 7;
2:17; Luke 4:9-11).[26] Frustrated, Satan departs "until an opportune time

---

22. See Johnson, *The Purpose of the Biblical Genealogies*, 239.
23. J. Neyrey, *The Passion according to Luke: A Redaction Study of Luke's Soteriology* (New York:
Paulist, 1985) 165–84. Ellis (*Luke*, 93) thinks a comparison is intended. Schweizer (*Luke*, 80–
81) thinks that Luke views Jesus as the "new Adam," as do R. E. Brown (*The Birth of the
Messiah: A Commentary on the Infancy Narratives in Matthew and Luke* [Garden City: Doubleday,
1977] 91, 419), and Marshall (*Luke*, 161), though with some hesitation.
24. W. S. Kurz, "Luke 3:23-38 and Greco-Roman and Biblical Genealogies," in C. H.
Talbert, ed., *Luke-Acts: New Perspectives from the Society of Biblical Literature* (New York: Crossroad, 1984) 169–87, esp. 172, 177–79.
25. Neyrey, *The Passion according to Luke*, 167–68.
26. Neyrey, *The Passion according to Luke*, 173–77.

[*kairos*]" (Luke 4:13). This opportune time comes during the passion, when Satan enters Judas (Luke 22:3-6, "He was seeking an opportunity [*eukairia*] to betray him"), attempts to "sift [Peter] like wheat" (22:31), and, as "the power of darkness," is present when Jesus is arrested (22:53). During this time of Satan's activity Jesus, although sorely tested, resolves to do the will of his Father (22:39-46). Thus Jesus remains the faithful and righteous Son of God.[27]

Finally, Neyrey finds parallels in the crucifixion itself. Three times Jesus is taunted ("Let him save himself if he is the Christ of God," etc., 23:35, 37, 39), just as earlier Satan three times had called his relationship with God into question ("If you are the Son of God"). Because he has defeated Satan, Jesus, although dying on the cross, conquers death itself and reopens paradise, which the first Adam had lost,[28] to humanity. Thus Jesus tells the repentant criminal, "Today you will be with me in Paradise [*paradeisos*]" (23:43).[29]

Without accepting every part of his analysis (such as the proposed parallels between Jesus' three temptations and Adam's temptation), the balance of this chapter will presuppose Neyrey's Adam/Jesus typology. Yet the typology is not complete, for there are several loose ends. It is not clear why Luke thinks of Adam as the "son of God" in the first place. Nor is it clear why Jesus himself is regarded as God's Son. And finally, how Jesus was able to withstand the temptations and defeat Satan also remains obscure. When these questions are answered, we shall see that they are closely related.

The essential ingredient missing from Neyrey's analysis is Luke's pneumatology. To recap the passages surveyed above: Jesus came into existence by the Spirit (Luke 1:35), matured in the Spirit (2:40), received the Spirit in substance at his baptism (3:22), was filled with the Spirit before being tempted (4:1-2), began his public ministry in the power of the Spirit (4:14), proclaimed that he had been anointed by the Spirit (4:18), rejoiced in the Spirit at Satan's fall from heaven (10:21), and promised his disciples the Spirit (11:13; 24:49).

On what grounds could Jesus be called the "Son of God"? Luke 1:35

---

27. Neyrey, *The Passion according to Luke*, 177–79.

28. Neyrey (*The Passion according to Luke*, 182) notes that sinners could not enter paradise. "Paradise whose fruit endures incorruptible . . . shall be manifest, but we cannot enter it because we have passed our lives in unseemly manners" (4 Ezra 7:123; cf. 1 Cor 6:9-10). One pre-Christian text anticipates one who will come and reopen the gates of paradise, "And he shall open the gates of Paradise and shall remove the threatening sword against Adam and shall give to the saints to eat from the Tree of Life and the spirit of holiness shall be upon them" (*T. Levi* 18:10-11; cf. Luke 10:19).

29. Neyrey, *The Passion according to Luke*, 179–82. The Greek word *paradeisos* is used in the LXX translation of "garden" (cf. Gen 2:8).

provides the answer. "The Holy Spirit will come upon you, and the power of the Most High will overshadow you; therefore the child to be born will be called holy, the Son of God." Because Jesus was generated by the Holy Spirit he can be rightly called "holy" and "Son of God."[30] This holiness goes hand in hand with his righteousness (Luke 23:47; Acts 3:14), an element to which Neyrey and others have properly drawn our attention.[31] The Holy Jesus (cf. Acts 4:27, 30) becomes the arch rival of the unholy Satan and the legions of unclean spirits. Jesus' continued obedience to the will of his Father, in the power of the Holy Spirit, preserves his righteous character and safeguards his claim to divine sonship. Explicit heavenly affirmation of this sonship is seen in three passages: in the annunciation (1:35), at his baptism (3:22), and at the transfiguration (9:35). The first, and crucial, passage occurs only in Luke, and the second and third passages, taken from his Markan source, have been edited by the evangelist. The baptism immediately follows the righteous Jesus praying, after which he receives the Holy Spirit "in substance," and the Father declares, "You are my beloved Son." Jesus is now prepared to begin his public ministry as God's Son. His ministry begins with temptation (4:1-13) and with his declaration in his hometown that he has been anointed with the Spirit (4:16-19). Immediately before the transfiguration Jesus again prays (9:28), and then the Father speaks, "This is my Son, my Chosen One." Jesus, tested, tried, and proven, is now declared God's "Chosen One." He is ready to journey to Jerusalem, where his "exodus" (9:31) and his "assumption" (9:51) will be accomplished, where salvation will be realized, where paradise will be regained.

If it was by virtue of his Spirit-generation that Jesus was regarded as the "Son of God," then Luke likewise must have regarded Adam as "son of God" by virtue of his generation by the Spirit (or breath) of God. In fact, this is clearly stated in Scripture. "Then the Lord God formed Adam of the dust from the ground, and breathed [*emphusein*] into his nostrils the breath [LXX: *pnoē*][32] of life; and Adam became a living being" (Gen 2:7).

---

30. A. R. C. Leaney ("The Virgin Birth in Lucan Theology and in the Classical Creeds," in R. Bauckham and B. Drewen, eds., *Scripture, Tradition, and Reason: A Study in the Criteria for Christian Doctrine* [R. P. C. Hanson Festschrift; Edinburgh: T. & T. Clark, 1988] 65–100) has correctly sensed the point of the Lukan evangelist when he states, "Luke's emphasis falls on the miraculous divinely-wrought conception by the Holy Spirit of the Messiah" (92). Leaney (94–95) also cites a few words of the ancient Roman baptismal creed on which the Apostles' Creed is based, "Christ Jesus his only Son, our Lord . . . who was born from the Holy Spirit and the Virgin Mary," words that "clearly recall Luke 1:35."

31. Neyrey, *The Passion according to Luke*, 181–82; cf. Fitzmyer, *Luke I–IX*, 218.

32. Note that *pnoē* usually means "breath," whereas *pneuma* can mean either "breath" or "spirit." See LXX Prov 1:23 which uses *pnoe* to translate the MT's *ruach*. But in *1 Clem.* 21:9 *pneuma* substitutes for *pnoē* (cf. *1 Clem.* 57:3).

Just as God's breath/Spirit generated Adam, so it generated Jesus.[33] If by virtue of this generation Jesus may be called "Son of God," then by the same token Adam may be called "son of God." It is hard to understand on what other basis Luke would have so regarded Adam. Philo apparently followed the same line of reasoning; Adam received "his soul not from any other thing created but through the breath of God [*empneusantos theou*] imparting of his own power [*dynamis*] such measure as mortal nature could receive" (*On the Virtues* 37 §203).[34] Because of this unique creation Philo is able to assert that Adam's "Father was no mortal but the eternal God, whose image [*eikon*] he was" (*On the Virtues* 37 §204).[35] In a highly allegorical discussion of the ideal man, in part based on Adam, and the real meaning of the garden of Eden (Gen 2:8) Philo says, "For that man is the eldest son, whom the Father of all raised up, and elsewhere calls him his first-born, and indeed the son thus begotten followed the ways of his Father" (*On the Confusion of the Languages* 14 §63).[36] In another passage he says: "But if there be any as yet unfit to be called 'son of God,' let him press to take his place under God's First-born, the Word, who holds elder-ship among the angels, their ruler as it were. And many names are his, for he is called, 'the Beginning,' 'Name of God,' 'Word,' and the 'Man after His Image [*kat' eikona*]' [Gen 1:27]" (*On the Confusion of the Languages* 28 §146).[37] In other words, Adam, the man created after God's image, is "son of God" and model for all others who aspire to qualify as "sons of God" (cf. *On the Confusion of the Languages* 28 §147, "For if we have not yet become fit to be thought sons of God . . ."). It is clear therefore that Luke's notion of the divine sonship of Adam was neither unique nor unintelligible to first-century readers of Scripture.

Luke's pneumatology not only provides the basis for understanding why he calls both Adam and Jesus sons of God; it also clarifies why Jesus was successful in facing Satanic temptation and Adam was not. Jesus' success was due to his continual reliance upon the power of the Holy Spirit. The special enabling at his baptism and his continued obedience ("led by the Spirit") in the temptation experience gave him the power necessary to thwart Satan. Adam, however, enjoyed no such empowering, but if he is a

---

33. Cf. John 20:22, "He breathed [*emphusein*] into (them) and said, 'Receive the Holy Spirit.' "

34. Translation based on F. H. Colson, *Philo* (LCL 7; Cambridge: Harvard University Press, 1939) 289.

35. Colson, *Philo* (LCL 7) 289. Neyrey (*The Passion according to Luke*, 168) cites these texts to demonstrate that Adam was "son of God" because of his righteousness. True, but it is significant that Philo links Adam's creation by the breath of God to God as Adam's Father.

36. Translation based on F. H. Colson and G. H. Whitaker, *Philo* (LCL 4; Cambridge: Harvard University Press, 1935) 45.

37. Translation based on Colson and Whitaker, *Philo* (LCL 4) 89, 91.

failure, why compare Jesus to him? Philo's interpretation once again may be of some help. He distinguishes the Adams of the two creation accounts (*On the Confusion of the Languages* 14 §62–63; *Questions and Answers on Genesis* 1.4 [on Gen 2:7]). The Adam of the first creation account was "created in the image of God [*kat' eikona theou*]" (Gen 1:26-27). This Adam did not fall, but remained perfect; he is the "heavenly man." But the Adam of the second creation account was "formed of the dust of the earth" (Gen 2:7); because he was sensual, his need for physical gratification clouded his reason and he fell when tempted. "Yet though he should have kept that image [*eikōn*] undefiled . . . when the opposites were set before him to choose or avoid, good and evil, honorable and base, true and false, he was quick to choose the false, the base, and the evil . . . with the natural consequence that he exchanged mortality for immortality, forfeited his blessedness and happiness, and found an easy passage to a life of toil and misery" (*On the Virtues* 37 §205).[38]

Philo's distinction between the Adams of the two creation accounts might very well have been known to Paul. In his Adam/Jesus typology in 1 Corinthians 15 the apostle quotes from Gen 2:7: "The first man, Adam became a living soul [alluding to Gen 2:7]. The last Adam [i.e., Jesus] became a life-giving spirit" (1 Cor 15:45). Two verses later he adds, "The first man [i.e., Adam] is from the earth, earthy [again alluding to Gen 2:7]; the second man [i.e., Jesus] is from heaven" (1 Cor 15:47). When he subsequently applies the typology to Christian eschatology, he draws an even closer parallel. "Just as we have borne the image [*eikōn*] of the earthy, we shall also bear the image [*eikōn*] of the heavenly" (1 Cor 15:49). Paul's typology may assume a distinction between the two Adams which approximates Philo's exegesis. The first Adam (formed of the dust of the earth) sinned, but Jesus, the second Adam (modeled after the one created in the image of God, the one who is from heaven), was obedient and becomes himself a model for those who wish to aspire to heavenly virtue, or, as Philo puts it, to aspire to becoming a "son of God."

Philo's contribution is valuable because he shows us how Adam can serve both as a poor model, who falls into sin when tempted, and as an ideal model, who is obedient to heavenly laws because he has been created in God's image. This dichotomized interpretation of Adam facilitates the Pauline and Lukan Adam/Jesus typologies. On the one hand, Adam is a sinner who brings death to humanity; this is the aspect with which Jesus stands in contrast. On the other hand, Adam is generated by the breath/Spirit of God, is created in God's image, and may be regarded as "son of God"; these are aspects that Jesus parallels.

---

38. Translation based on Colson, *Philo* (LCL 7) 289.

The parallel between Pauline and Philonic exegesis is intriguing, but we cannot be sure how much of either the Lukan evangelist knew; obviously he did not follow Philo's exegesis exactly. Adam as "son of God" because God breathed into him alludes to the Adam of Gen 2:7, which according to Philo's exegesis in *On the Confusion of the Languages* is the sensual and fallible Adam. This would hardly suit Luke's christology, but even Philo is not consistent. In his discussion in *On the Virtues,* the Adam of Genesis 2 is the noble Adam who has God as his father because he had been created directly by the breath of God. The Lukan evangelist has not followed the Pauline typology exactly either. Whereas Paul compares the first and second Adams, Luke compares the first and second sons of God. Paul seems to show that the second Adam's obedience has reversed the mortal effects of the first Adam's disobedience, but Luke seems to show that the second Son of God has regained the paradise that the first son of God lost. What the Pauline and Philonic exegeses do, however, is provide us with an idea of the range and variety of first-century biblical interpretation both within and outside Christian circles.

ADAM, THE HOLY SPIRIT, AND THE GENTILES

As we have seen above, the Holy Spirit plays an important role in Acts in verifying the authenticity of Gentile conversion. Does this Lukan emphasis bear any relation to the role of the Holy Spirit in Jesus? And further, does it bear any relation to the Adam/Jesus "sons of God" typology? Both of these questions may be answered in the affirmative.

First, the giving of the Holy Spirit to Gentiles (as well as to Jews and Samaritans) fulfills Jesus' promise in Luke 24:49. Having been generated by the Spirit, having been filled with the Spirit, and having never lost the Spirit through disobedience,[39] Jesus is able, in cooperation with his Father, to impart the Spirit as a gift to all who obey the Gospel (Luke 11:13; Acts 2:38; 5:32). Through the power of the Spirit Christians can defeat Satan and his unclean spirits just as Jesus did. Luke 10:17-20, a passage unique to Luke, is instructive:

---

39. In all probability Luke would have viewed the loss of the Spirit as quite possible. Familiar as he was with the Greek Psalter, he would have known the words of the repentant David, "Do not cast me away from your face, and do not take from me your Holy Spirit [*to pneuma to hagion*]" (LXX Ps 50:13; cf. v. 1, "A Psalm of David when Nathan the prophet came to him, after he had gone into Bathsheba"). Also relevant is King Saul's loss of the Spirit. "And the Spirit [*pneuma*] of the Lord departed from Saul, and an evil spirit from the Lord tormented him" (LXX 1 Sam 16:14).

> The seventy returned with joy, saying, "Lord, even the demons are subject to us in your name!" And he said to them, "I saw Satan fall like lightning from heaven. Behold, I have given [*didonai*] you authority [*exousia*] to tread [*patein*] upon serpents [*opheis*] and scorpions, and over all the power of the enemy; and nothing shall hurt you. Nevertheless, do not rejoice in this, that the spirits [*pneumata*] are subject to you; but rejoice that your names are written in heaven."

The "seventy," possibly meant to represent the seventy Gentile nations (cf. Genesis 10),[40] are able to conquer Satan's hosts when Satan has been dislodged from heaven.[41] They have gone out as Jesus' representatives, indeed, as his proxies (cf. Luke 10:1, 16). Verse 19 ("I give you authority to tread upon serpents") is probably based on Ps 91:13, "You will tread on the lion and the adder, the young lion and the serpent you will trample [*katapatein*] under foot." But the dominical tradition more closely reflects the language found in *T. Levi* 18:10-12.

> And he shall open the gates of Paradise and shall remove the threatening sword against Adam and shall give [*didonai*] to the saints to eat from the Tree of Life and the spirit of holiness shall be upon them and Beliar shall be bound by him and he shall give authority [*exousia*] to his children to tread [*patein*] on evil spirits [*pneumata*].

In this passage not only are the evil spirits subjugated but paradise is regained. The sword that prevents entry (cf. Gen 3:24) will be removed. The saints will be able to eat from the tree of life (cf. Gen 2:9; 3:22, 24), and the spirit of holiness, the power that successfully opposes the spirit of uncleanness, will be upon them. A related passage appears in *T. Dan* 5:9-12: "And there shall arise for you from the tribes of Judah and Levi the Lord's salvation. He will make war against Beliar. . . . And he shall take from Beliar the captives, the souls of the saints . . . and the saints shall refresh themselves in Eden." Again we find similar themes. The "souls of the saints" will be rescued from Beliar and they will enter and be refreshed in the garden of Eden. The eschatological agent described in the *Testaments of Levi* and *Dan* will lead the faithful back to the paradise lost by Adam when he yielded to the temptation of Satan (Beliar). Because of the paradise theme of these parallel passages, the "serpents" (*opheis*) of Luke 10:19 may be an allusion to the serpent of the garden of Eden, which in the LXX is translated *ophis* (cf. Gen 3:1-14; Rev 12:9; 20:2).[42]

---

40. See Marshall, *Luke*, 415; Fitzmyer, *Luke X–XXIV*, 846.

41. Fitzmyer (*Luke X–XXIV*, 862) plausibly suggests that behind this language is the image of Satan accusing the saints before God (cf. Job 1:6-12; 2:1-7; Zech 3:1-2). Satan has been defeated and expelled from heaven, thus ending his defamatory activity.

42. In the Targums Satan is often associated with serpents and scorpions; cf. P. Grélot, "Étude critique de Luc 10,19," *RSR* 69 (1981) 87–100, esp. 92–96.

As already noted, these texts are probably based on Ps 91:13. But Ps 91:11-12 was the very passage that Satan had quoted to Jesus in the third temptation: "He will give his angels charge of you, to guard you. . . . On their hands they will bear you up, lest you strike your foot against a stone" (Luke 4:10-11). Thus not only does Luke 10:17-20 speak of Satan and possibly allude to Eden traditions (as the clear allusions in the *Testaments* would indicate), but it may even echo the Lukan temptation narrative.

Temptation is another important aspect in Luke's Adam/Jesus typology. Because Jesus has successfully withstood temptation through the Holy Spirit (4:1-13; 22:40-46), so too can his followers, if filled with the Spirit, successfully withstand temptation. This is indicated by several passages, most of which are unique to Luke. For the Lukan evangelist temptation is a serious danger; because of it many will fall away, "And these have no root, who for a time believe, but in the time [*kairos*] of temptation [*peirasmos*] fall away" (Luke 8:13b). This language, most of which is Lukan (compare Mark 4:17; Matt 13:21), alludes to Luke 4:13, where Satan breaks off the temptation (*peirasmos*) of Jesus until an opportune time (*kairos*). At the last supper Jesus tells his disciples, "You are those who have continued with me in my temptations [*peirasmoi*]" (Luke 22:28). But because they have continued with him (and have not fallen away), they will be given the kingdom (Luke 22:29-30). Shortly before his arrest Jesus exhorts his disciples, "Pray that you do not enter into temptation [*peirasmos*]" (Luke 22:40). Luke has taken this saying from his Markan source where it occurs only once (Mark 14:38), but for emphasis he repeats it at the close of the scene (Luke 22:46). In the Lukan context the danger of losing faith and falling away is especially great, for Satan "demanded to have [Simon Peter], that he might sift [him] like wheat" (22:31; as he sifted Job?). But Jesus prayed for him, that his faith might not fail (22:32).

Second, Luke's Adam/Jesus typology is closely bound up with the evangelist's concern for the Gentiles. Adam was created by being given God's Spirit. But because of his sin and fall, he was not able to impart the Spirit to his posterity; as the first son of God, Adam failed. But Jesus, the second Son of God, succeeded and can now impart the Spirit of God to his disciples and generate more "sons of God." (This may be another parallel with Philo's exegesis.) Those who follow and obey Jesus will be "sons of the Most High" (Luke 6:35). This passage is apparently drawn from Q (cf. Matt 5:44-45) and may not represent a distinctive Lukan idea. But in the passage concerned with marriage and the afterlife (Luke 20:27-40; cf. Mark 12:18-27) the Lukan Jesus says, "They cannot die any more, because they are equal to angels and are sons of God, being sons of the resurrection" (Luke 20:36). The parallel in Mark reads only, "They are like angels in heaven" (Mark 12:25). When Luke declares that they can no longer die because they are sons of God, his redaction coheres with his Adam/Jesus typology. Adam, the first son of God, sinned and died, but Jesus, the second Son of God, obeyed and lived (as seen in his resurrection). Those who believe in Jesus will follow in his steps, no longer subject to death, as sons of God and sons of the resurrection. The idea that Christians are "sons of God" was of course common in early Christianity (cf. Rom 8:14-15; Gal 3:26; 4:5-6). Thus, whereas Adam failed to impart the Spirit and life to his posterity, Jesus, the second Son of God, was able to do so. Those who believe in him become "sons of God," never more to die.

The Adam/Jesus typology, when understood properly against Luke's pneumatology, sheds light on the evangelist's christology and on a problem with which he grapples thoughout his two-volume work: the Gentile question. In the Adam/Jesus typology he has found an important component of his solution. Just as the life of Adam, the first son of God, impacted humanity—Jews, Gentiles, and all—so the life of Jesus, the second Son of God, impacted all human beings. But unlike Adam, whose failure resulted in defeat and death at the hands of Satan, Jesus' success results in life (cf. 1 Cor 15:45).

— 4 —

FROM ISAIAH 61
TO LUKE 4

JAMES A. SANDERS

This chapter will sketch a history of the function of Isa 61:1-3 from its appearance in the Tanak to its role in the Lukan account of Jesus' appearance and sermon in the Nazareth synagogue. The method employed here is comparative midrash. (See definition and discussion above in Chap. 1.)

ISAIAH 61

The efforts of modern biblical scholarship have not rendered clear judgments about the meaning of Isa 61:1-3 at its first stages of formation. There are three major positions on its literary nature or form. But whether or not the pericope should be seen as the opening strophe of the fuller poem, 61:1-11, the first three verses are commonly seen as the basic small unit.[1] Some scholars view it as an Ebed Yahweh poem.[2] Otto Michel and others think it was influenced by the Ebed poems, an early poetic midrash

---

This chapter is a revision of my study, "From Isaiah 61 to Luke 4," in J. Neusner, ed., *Christianity, Judaism and Other Greco-Roman Cults* (M. Smith Festschrift; Leiden: Brill, 1975) 75–106.

1. James Muilenberg (*IB* 5.708–16) sees the basic poem as including 61:1-11 and having five strophes, of which vv. 1-3 form the first.
2. W. W. Cannon, "Isaiah 61:1-3 an Ebed-Jahweh Poem," *ZAW* 47 (1929) 284–88; O. Procksch, *Theologie des Alten Testaments* (Gütersloh: Bertelsmann, 1950) 290. Cf. Robert Koch, "Der Gottesgeist und der Messias (II)," *Bib* 27 (1946) 376–403, esp. 396–401, and J. Morgenstern, "Isaiah 61," *HUCA* 40–41 (1969–70) 109–21.

on the Ebed idea.[3] Still others believe that, form-critically, it presents the call of a prophet, perhaps 3 Isaiah.[4] Part of the reason for such diversity of opinion is the difficulty of determining the nature of Isaiah 56–66; much of what one thinks of the passage depends on a prior judgment about the larger body of material in which it is embedded.

Equally important in contributing to the uncertainty is content analysis of phrases in the text. As Bernhard Duhm pointed out, the author has mixed the figures of herald of good news and prophet.[5] Whether or not it is a confusion depends on one's understanding of either figure. Also, as Claus Westermann remarks, this pericope is surely the last example of a prophet freely and surely expressing the certainty that God had sent him or her with a message to the people. Such a view depends, of course, on the date one assigns to the basic unit. Another reason for scholarly uncertainty is that the author clearly draws on earlier material, especially Isa 42:3 and 7; Michel has seen this better than most. Isaiah 61 is a good instance of what Renée Bloch called biblical midrash in the Bible itself. Walther Zimmerli, who disagrees with Michel in part, concludes with a very similar view when he suggests the passage is the essence of an exilic sermon based on both Lev 25:10 and Deutero-Isaianic traditions![6]

Philologists have offered two suggestions about a difficult reading in the Masoretic Text, the verb *pqh*, in 61:1, which elsewhere in the Bible is used only of the opening of eyes or ears.[7] These suggestions are mutually exclusive—one bids us turn to Egyptian documents and the other to Babylonian. In 1947 the Egyptologist A. S. Yahuda cited the portion after the *maqeph* in the Isaiah text, *qôah*, as a loan word that in New Egyptian means "a wooden collar, especially used to be fastened tightly around the neck of the prisoners (*Aeg. Wb.* V 66)." He takes the phrase to mean "to open the

---

3. O. Michel, "Zur Eigenart Tritojesajas," *ThViat* 10 (1966) 213–30. See also W. Zimmerli, "Das 'Gnadenjahr des Herrn,'" in A. Kuschke and E. Kutsch, eds., *Archäologie und Altes Testament* (K. Galling Festschrift; Tübingen: Mohr [Siebeck], 1970) 321–32.

4. K. Elliger, "Der Prophet Tritojesaja," *ZAW* 49 (1931) 112–41; cf. C. Westermann, *Das Buch Jesaja, Kapitel 40–66* (ATD 19; Göttingen: Vandenhoeck & Ruprecht, 1966) 290–92. See also Zimmerli ("Das 'Gnadenjahr des Herrn,'" 321–32), whose position is rather complex but would not rule out the form-critical category of a prophetic call; cf. B. Duhm, *Das Buch Jesaja* (HKAT; Göttingen: Vandenhoeck & Ruprecht, 1892) 425–26.

5. Duhm, *Jesaja*; cf. Westermann, *Jesaja*, 290.

6. Cf. Zimmerli, "Das 'Gnadenjahr des Herrn,'" 330–32. This, I think, is right; see n. 7 below. R. Block, "Midrash," trans. M. C. Callaway, in W. S. Green, ed., *Approaches to Ancient Judaism* (Atlanta: Scholars, 1978) 29–50.

7. In Isa 42:20 it is used for opening ears. Note the same problem with respect to the Greek verb *dianoigo*, which although elsewhere used only for the opening of eyes or of the heavens (in a vision), signifies in Luke 24:32, after its normal use in 24:31, opening a scroll! This effective rhetorical device was used by Luke to stress that one can "see" (open the eyes) in the present only after one "sees" (opens) the scriptures. This point is more certain than the so-called proleptic eucharist celebrated in Emmaus: the breaking of bread as study of Torah is very ancient.

collars of the prisoners," and excuses the use of *pqh* instead of *pth* as a
purposive literary device of the author.[8] This is a very attractive explanation: biblical authors did precisely that sort of thing to score points by
such rhetoric.

But did they go to such extremes to accommodate an Egyptian word
that the first hearers or readers might not have known? The answer to that
question depends on a number of factors. In the meantime, an attractive
explanation has been advanced by the renowned Assyriologist Shalom
Paul.[9] Pointing out that Isa 42:7 has already equated opening the eyes with
liberation from prison, Paul suggests the prophet made *pqh-qh* parallel to
derôr and thus used it also to mean freedom. Paul cites a cuneiform
inscription in which Sargon declares that in liberating Dur-Yakin he
destroyed the prisons and "let the prisoners see the light." Such a phrase,
Paul states, was the equivalent of "I set them free." Paul translates Isa
61:1-2, then, "To proclaim liberty to captives and to prisoners freedom."
This explanation has the advantages of recognizing the import of Isa 42:7
for our passage and of suggesting a Mesopotamian idiom as an extra-
biblical parallel: it fits a broad view of the exilic or post-exilic Mesopotamian provenance of the passage.

EARLY WITNESSES

Early witnesses to the text betray patterns familiar in text criticism. They
all exhibit keen interest in the *pqh-qh* reading, clearly indicating to the
trained observer that they were struggling with the text (whether one
word or two) represented by the MT, and not with a genuine variant.
1QIsa[a] and 1QIsa[b] leave no space for a *maqeph*, suggesting perhaps a dupli-
cated form of the last letters of the root or perhaps indicating, with the
MT tradition, early uncertainty both about the form and the meaning.
Classical and traditional grammarians have most often taken the *pqh-qh* to be
a hapax noun form based on *pqh* with an intensive sense of eye-opening.[10]

---

8. A. S. Yahuda, "Hebrew Words of Egyptian Origin," *JBL* 66 (1947) 83–90, esp. 86–87.

9. S. Paul, "Deutero-Isaiah and Cuneiform Royal Inscriptions," in W. W. Hallo, ed., *Essays in Memory of E. A. Speiser* (AOS 53; New Haven: American Oriental Society, 1968) 180–86, esp. 182.

10. Most modern scholars have also taken it as a noun, as suggested by the ancient translators except the Targum; see BDB. P. Volz (*Jesaia II* [KAT 10; Leipzig: Deichert, 1932] 254) thought, on the basis of ten medieval manuscripts, that *qh* stood alone in an early text and was corrected above the line by the addition *pqwh*, the two of which then flowed together. Zimmerli ("Das 'Gnadenjahr des Herrn,'" 322) by contrast sees *pqhqwh* as a dittography of *pqwh*. Ibn Ezra, in contrast to both, had defended the MT grammatically by citing other verbs whose last two root letters are doubled, in the so-called *pe'al'el* form. Qimhi and Mezudat Zion admitted the possibility of a noun, but *Targum Jonathan*, Ibn Ezra, and Rashi are very clear about its being a verb in form if not in function.

Apparently the LXX understood it thus in translating it by the noun *anablepsis* and in translating the previous word by *tuphlois*, rendering the phrase *kai tuphlois anablepsin* continuing the predicate construction after the verb *keruksai/ liqro'*, which is precisely the text of Luke 4:18. Modern scholars have suggested that the LXX, and hence Luke, read *velassanverîm* instead of *vela'asûrîm*.[11] I think such a reading highly unlikely as Vorlage for the LXX. On the contrary, because of similar expressions in Hebrew Isa 42:7, 18, 22, and 43:8, the Greek translator had no difficulty whatever in understanding and conveying the metaphor of blindness for prisoners.[12] The burden of proof rests on those who defend a variant Vorlage behind the LXX reading. If I read Seeligmann correctly, this phrase in 61:1-2 is hardly surprising as an effort that the LXX translator understood as a metaphor in the Hebrew text.[13] Luke, as already noted, followed the LXX at this point, which is not surprising from what is known of First Testament quotations in Luke-Acts elsewhere. The Lukan citation reflects the LXX verbatim save for two variations: Luke omits the fourth of the six colons of 61:1 and reads *keruksai* instead of *kalesai* as the first word of 61:2. But we shall return to these and other observations about the Lukan citation.

When encountering a difficulty in the Vorlage, the LXX translator resolved it by translating the phrase (*vela'asûrîm peqahqôah*) metaphorically as the original author apparently had intended; and I think the translator would have based a defense on the same metaphors already cited in Isaiah 42–43. These chapters represent different authors in antiquity, indicated by the so called 2 and 3 Isaiahs. But as Walther Zimmerli has suggested, the later author may well have developed the earlier author's idea. It is even possible that in 61:1 an Isaianic disciple engaged in a very early midrashic reflection on the Deuteronomic/Isaian materials cited, and that the later LXX translator of Isaiah 61 understood quite well what the earlier one had done.[14]

Other points of interest arise when one compares the LXX with the Vulgate; almost invariably the latter follows the MT tradition where it differs from the LXX. The Vulgate follows the MT verbatim in the difficult opening phrases of v. 3, as compared to a translational attempt in some

---

11. Cf. first apparatus of *Biblia Hebraica*³ (>*BHS*).

12. Isaiah 29:18 and 35:5 apparently refer to actual healing (cf. Matt 8:1—9:34; Matt 15:31; Luke 7:22) and not, as in the Deuteronomic/Isaian passages, to prison blindness.

13. I. L. Seeligmann, *The Septuagint Version of Isaiah: A Discussion of Its Problems* (Leiden: Brill, 1948) 95–121. Seeligmann does not deal directly with Isa 61:1-3.

14. Translators may take advantage of a vertical reading of a biblical book, and the LXX translator of the later chapters of Isaiah in all likelihood translated 2 Isaiah as well; cf. Seeligmann, *Septuagint Version of Isaiah*. The translator would therefore have translated chap. 61 only a comparatively short time after chaps. 42 and 43. (The Syriac in this whole section seems to be a faithful daughter of the LXX.)

manuscripts of the LXX to facilitate the transfer into the receptor Greek: the inclusion of *Dominus* in v. 1b where the LXX lacks *kurios* for the MT tetragrammaton; and the inclusion of *Deo nostro* in v. 2b, after *diem ultionis*, where the LXX lacks *to theo hēmon* (most manuscripts) for the MT *le'lohenû*. One such point, however, is intriguing, and belongs, I am convinced, to the study of history of midrash rather than to textual criticism; this again as in v. 1f is the *pqah-qoah* difficulty. Here the Vulgate reads *clausis apertionem*,[15] which is just as interpretative in its own way as the LXX *tuphlois anablepsin*, but in a different tradition, represented later by Rashi and Qimhi: the opening of prisons instead of, with the LXX, the opening of eyes of the blind in prison. Of course, the rabbis often go on to interpret the prison as *galut*, which one cannot attribute to Jerome. Jerome probably did not have a variant Vorlage before him; he merely wanted to make sense in Latin of a cryptic Hebrew expression and in doing so showed himself a good student of the Bethlehem rabbinate.

In two cases the Latin appears to agree with the LXX rather than the MT. *Indulgentia* in v. 1e seems to stress a connotation of the LXX *aphesis* rather than the plain meaning of the MT *derôr*;[16] and *fortes iustitiae* in v. 3e is certainly closer to the LXX *geneai dikaiosunes* than to the MT *êlê hazzedeq*. However, it is very interesting to note that in this, too, Jerome seems to anticipate rabbinic interpretations recorded in Mezudat Zion and Mezudat David where "oaks of righteousness" are viewed as *gedolîm bema'aseh zedeq*— precisely *fortes iustitiae*.[17]

Some manuscripts and editors of the MT read *elê*, in Isa 61:3e, "gods," without the first *yod*. 1QIsaᵃ has the *yod* while 1QIsaᵇ has a lacuna and is therefore indeterminate. Josef T. Milik reads *elê* [*hazzedeq*] in 11Q Melch 14 (see below) as a citation of our passage. 11Q Melch, however, cannot be taken as textual witness since it is clearly a midrash and, according to the midrashic rules of the period, was perfectly free to read *elê* for *êlê*. In fact, no ancient witness is determinate for what the translator or the midrashist had as Vorlage; all the witnesses, including the Targum (see below), could as well have read the one as the other to derive the sense

---

15. Vetus Latina apparently had *vinctis apertionem* (understand *carceris*). Jerome in his commentary remarked that the sense of the Hebrew could be either that "the blind might see" (*caecis ut videant*) or that "prisons be opened" (*clausis apertionem*). Note that Aquila chose *diablepsin* (seeing clearly), Symmachus *apolusin* and *dianoiksin*. All ancient traditions except the Targum understood *peqah-qôah* as a verbal noun form.

16. *Aphesis* is, of course, correct for Hebrew *derôr* since the LXX here follows the practice of the LXX in Leviticus 25 and elsewhere (cf. Jer 34:8), but in those passages the Latin usually has *libertas* and not *indulgentia*. Cf. S. Daniel, *Recherches sur le vocabulaire du culte dans la Septante* (Études et Commentaires 61; Paris: Librairie Klincksieck, 1966).

17. Aquila, Symmachus, and Theodotion read *ischuroi tou dikaiou*, with variant *tou laou* [*sic*], which seems to be a mid-term understanding between LXX *geneai* and Latin *fortes*.

they convey. On the other hand one must leave open the possibility that *elê* was a very early, genuine variant, even, possibly, that the MT *êlê* is a hidden tiqqun or scribal correction for *elê*. The greater likelihood, nonetheless, is that the author fully intended "oaks of righteousness" as parallel to "a planting of Yahweh" but stylistically allowed for the possible poetic ambiguity: see *êlê ha-'arez* in Ezek 17:13 and 2 Kgs 24:15 (qere), where the meaning clearly is "powerful men."

The Targum Jonathan to Isaiah 61 is difficult to date, but it is interesting to compare the effort there with those of Qumran and the LXX to understand *peqah-qoah*.[18] The Targum reads *velid'asîrîn* for *vela'asûrîm* of the MT but for *peqah-qôah* offers in direct discourse the very words the herald is to proclaim to the prisoners: *'itgelû lenêhôr*, "Come forth to the light." Not surprisingly, the Targumist appears to reflect the tradition of the *maqeph*, and takes *peqah* to be a collective imperative, strengthened perhaps by the *qôah* enclitic. Then the Targumist simply throws in the towel. If one reads *peqah* as a verb, "Open the eyes," it may, in the context of prisoners, say to them what the Targum says, "Come out into the light."

But, in contrast to the LXX, there are other points of interest in the Targum for our study. The Targumist makes clear at the beginning of 61:1 that this passage was spoken by the prophet Isaiah, *'amar nebîya'*. The Targumist understands this passage as rabbinic Judaism later understood it (see below), as a reflection by the prophet on his vocation and hence on his source of authority. Scholarly discussions about the Ebed Yahweh, or about the office of *mebasser*, or about 3 Isaiah, would have been strange to the Targumist who saw Isaiah as saying something here about the prophet's vocation. That's the peshat; and there's an end of it.

For the Targumist *rûah 'adonay 'elohîm 'alay* becomes *rûah nebû'ah min qadam 'adonay 'elohîm 'alay*, which specifies the sense of the passage rather narrowly. A spirit of prophecy had gone forth from the presence of God to settle like a mantle on the prophet. In later rabbinic literature, this passage is cited to stress the peculiar authority of Isaiah as distinct from all other prophets. Although they do not, like the Targum, introduce the idea of a spirit of prophecy, the midrashim and the commentators do not depart far from this interpretation by the Targum. The elimination of the word *mashah* and the substitution of *derabbê yatî 'adonay*, "The Lord has appointed me," and reading it with the following, *lebassara' 'invetanayya'*, effectively eliminates the whole notion of anointing. "The Lord has appointed me to bear good news to the afflicted." Rashi and Mezudat

---

18. Editions used were the *Miqra'ot Gedolot* (Vilna: Romm, 1892; repr. New York: Pardes, 1951), and A. Sperber, *The Bible in Aramaic* (5 vols.; Leiden: Brill, 1959–68). Cf. J. F. Stenning, *The Targum of Isaiah* (Oxford: Clarendon, 1949) 202–5.

Zion say that it does not mean anointing but being made important or great.[19] Ibn Ezra and Qimhi cite Ps 105:15 (1 Chr 16:22; cf. 2 Sam 1:14-16) to insist that the passage refers to the prophet himself and none other.[20] The Targum uses the expression *qadam adonay* in interesting ways. The first as we have seen is in speaking of the spirit of prophecy *min qadam 'adonay*. The second instance is in the first colon of v. 2 where the text says *liqro' shenat razón la'donay*. The Targum translates the *lamed* by *qadam*, so that the sense of the colon becomes, "To proclaim the year of acceptance before the Lord and the Day of Puranut before our God." Here is a consistent picture of a *mebasser*, a herald-prophet, who goes forth from the presence of God to proclaim exactly what God wishes. All messianic overtones are eliminated, making the Targum possibly an indirect witness to earlier messianic interpretations. Whereas the LXX and Qumran indicate some interest in the *lameds* in v. 2,[21] the Targum shuts out all options with its *qadam 'adonay*. Finally, in v. 3 the Targum, in translating the phrase *êlê hazzedeq*, understands *rabrebê qushta'*, "princes of righteousness" instead of "oaks of righteousness."[22] As noted above, this is interesting in the light of the possibility that 11QMelch 14 read the phrase "Gods of Righteousness," or of Justice.[23]

THE RABBIS

Before turning to Qumran (where interest in Isa 61:1-3 was as great as in the Second Testament), we might for a moment look to the various rabbinic sources although the interest there was clearly not as great as among the sectarians. According to Aaron Mordechai Heimann, Isa 61:1 is cited nine times down through Ibn Bakudah, who includes 61:1 in his index, and Isa 61:3 five times.[24] About half these instances are mere passing

---

19. Mezudat Zion, like Rashi, uses the expression *'inyan gedûlah* but then cites Isaiah 45 and Cyrus to explicate. This seems to argue for an anti-Christian tendency as one tradition of Jewish interpretation. The Christian use of Isaiah 61 would have been the foil for this tradition.

20. "Do not touch my anointed ones; do my prophets no harm."

21. Cf. J. Ziegler, *Septuaginta: Vetus Testamentum Graecum: Isaias* (vol. 14; Göttingen: Vandenhoeck & Ruprecht, 1939) ad loc., where *eniauton kuriou dekton* has the variant *eniauton to kurio dekton*. At Qumran the reading becomes *shenat ha-razón lemalkî zedeq* in 11QMelch 9. See also the discussion in this Chap.

22. Targum reads *veyiqrôn* for the MT *veqora'* where 1QIsa^a has *veqare'û* or perhaps *yiqre'û*.

23. According to J. T. Milik, "Milkî-sedeq et Milkî-resa' dans les anciens écrits juifs et chrétiens," *JJS* 23 (1972) 95–144, quotes from 98 and 106. And I agree; see J. A. Sanders, "The Old Testament in 11QMelchizedek," *The Journal of the Ancient Near Eastern Society of Columbia University* 5 (T. Gaster Festschrift; 1973) 373–82. The original editors had read *êlê merômîm*. See also this Chap.

24. A. M. Heimann, *Sefer Torah ha-ketubah veha-mesorah 'al torah nebi'im veketubim* (3 vols.; Tel Aviv: Dvir, 1965) ad loc.

references with no real interest in Isaiah 61 except perhaps in asmakhta to something else quite different. These, except for the following one, I omit from consideration. In the Zohar (II 136b), the Sabbath is presented as the reflexion of the *'ôlam habba'*; on the Sabbath the souls of the just enter paradise on high and at a given moment, after a Sabbath promenade in paradise, recite either Isa 61:1 or Ezek 1:21. Both passages concern the activity of the spirit. The Ezekiel passage, so closely associated with the merkabah traditions, needs no explanation in the Zohar,[25] but it is interesting that our passage in Isaiah should be viewed in the same category. The Zohar is not an eschatological text but a mystical one; it nonetheless martials Isaiah 61 to support its speculations.

The *Mekilta* to Exod 20:21[26] claims that the text there, which speaks of Moses entering the *araphel* or deep darkness, really concerns Moses' humility. Isaiah 61:1 is cited alongside Num 12:3, Isa 66:2, and Ps 51:14 to establish Moses' great humility. In the same line is a passage in *b. 'Abod. Zar.* 20b, recorded as well in *Yalqut Shim'oni* and *Yalqut Mechiri*,[27] which, after providing in the name of Pinhas ben Ya'ir a scale of cause and effect in ascending ranks of piety and reward, states, in the name of Joshua ben Levi, that humility is the greatest of all these and cites as *dictum probantium* our passage, noting that the text does not say *lebasser hasîdîm* but *lebasser 'anavîm*. They are the *'anavîm* who will receive the good news; hence humility, *'anavah*, is *gedolah mikkulam*. The assumption is that *'anavah* earns the reward entailed in the message of the herald.

In *Lev. Rab.* 10.2 (on 8:1-4)[28] is recorded the familiar tradition, with slight variants in each, that in contrast to all other prophets, Isaiah alone received the Spirit of God, or as *Pesiqta* has it, "out of the mouth of God" (cf. 1 Kgs 22:20-23). While these do not stress, as does the Targum, a spirit of prophecy from God, they do not contradict the Targumic tradition. Isaiah 61:1 is at least twice cited along with Isa 32:14 and Isa 60:22 as one of the three passages that speak of the Holy Spirit in relation to the redemption of the end time. One is *Lam. Rab.* 3:49-50§9. In *Yalqut Mechiri,* ad loc., Lam 3:49 appears in the place of Isa 60:22. Finally, Isa 61:1 is linked in *Tg. Ps.-J.* Num 25:12 with Mal 3:1 in a view of the mission of Elijah when he announces the end time and the coming of Messiah.[29]

---

25. J. Neusner, "The Development of the *Merkavah* Tradition," *JSJ* 2 (1971) 149–60.

26. Par. *Jethro* §9. This same Midrash is recorded also in *Yalqut Shimoni* 2 §302, §485, §954.

27. The *Yalqut Shimoni* and *Yalqut Mechiri* references are ad loc., Isa 61:1.

28. Also in *Pesiq. R.* 33.3; *Yalqut Mechiri* ad loc.; *Yalqut Shimoni* 2 §443; *Pesiq. Rab Kah.* 16.4.

29. The phrase *pe'er tahat 'epher* in 61:3 is cited numerous times in the literature as proof text for the place the ashes of mourning for the temple should be put, i.e., on the same place on the forehead as the tefillin (*Midr.* Ps. 137.6; *b. Ta'an.* 16a; *Yalqut Shimoni* 2 §404 and §685).

In three of the six rabbinic traditions in which Isa 61:1-3 figures with any import at all, the passage is seen in relation to the eschaton: the mission of Elijah, final redemption by the *rûah haqqodesh*, and the exalted place of humility in receiving the good news of the final herald. In none of these is the passage interpreted strictly messianically, but clearly it was not unimportant in rabbinic discussions of the end time. An originally exilic text referring to a historical situation, in which in all probability an Isaianic disciple is thought to have the authority of God's Spirit to announce a jubilee release from the oppressive aspects of Diaspora, became in some rabbinic traditions an eschatological reference. This is, of course, especially the case at Qumran and in the Second Testament, to which we now turn.[30]

ISAIAH 61 AT QUMRAN

Until thirty years ago the importance of Isa 61:1-3 at Qumran was largely unrecognized. The use the Essenes made of these verses had gone virtually unnoticed except in an article by David Flusser.[31] Flusser here signaled allusions to Isa 61:1-2 in Matt 5:3-5; but he also pointed out an "enriching" juxtaposition of Isa 61:1 and Ps 37:11 in 1QH 18:14–15 and in 4QpPs 37. Flusser's translation of the former emphasizes his point:

> To (have appointed) me in Thy truth
> a messenger (of the peace) of Thy goodness,
> To proclaim to the meek the multitude of Thine mercies
> to let them that are of contrite spirit
> he(ar salvation) from (everlasting) source
> and to them that mourn everlasting joy. (1QH 18:14–15)

For those interested in literary style or later hermeneutics, there is a rare observation about rhetorical devices in 2 Isaiah; cf. *Pesiq. Rab Kah.* 16.4. Also there is quite a literature from the Middle Ages emanating from the *'avelê zîon*, who took their name from Isa 61:3.

30. The only passage I have so far been able to locate in (what used to be called) the Apocrypha and Pseudepigrapha is Sir 48:10-12 where it is said in the Greek that Elijah was filled with his spirit (certain MSS and Syro-Hexaplar have "holy spirit") and in the Syriac that Elijah received a double portion of prophecy. Unfortunately the Cairo manuscripts are mutilated or nonexistent at this point in chap. 48, and the Masada fragments do not extend this far. Ben Sira is probably not thinking either of Isaiah 61 or of the eschaton in this famous passage. H. L. Strack, *Die Sprüche Jesus', des Sohnes Sirachs* (Leipzig: Böhme & Deichert, 1903); R. Smend, *Die Weisheit des Jesus Sirach* (2 vols.; Berlin: Reimer, 1906) 1. 55–56, 461–63; M. Z. Segal, *Sefer Hakmat ben Sira ha-shalem* (Jerusalem: Bialik, 1953) 80; P. W. Skehan and A. A. Di Lella, *The Wisdom of Ben Sira* (AB 39; New York: Doubleday, 1987) 530–32.

31. D. Flusser, "Blessed are the Poor in Spirit . . . ," *IEJ* 10 (1960) 1–13. Cf. L. E. Keck ("The Poor among the Saints in the New Testament," *ZNW* 56 [1965] 108–29, and idem, "The Poor among the Saints in Jewish Christianity and Qumran," *IEJ* 57 [1966] 54–78), who criticizes Flusser. Keck's argument is unconvincing here.

Flusser's work on 4QpPs 37, however, was considerably complemented by the work of Hans Stegemann on the pesher (commentary) in 1963 and 1967, the full publication of the pesher in 1968, and John Strugnell's review of the latter in 1970.[32] But Flusser's essential observation is still valid: the pesher on Ps 37:11 clearly reflects Isa 61:1-2 by the midrashic technique of "enrichment common in all Judaism of the period."[33] A fresh translation of the pesher in the light of the work of Stegemann and Strugnell would read as follows:

> But the *'anawîm* shall inherit the earth and delight in abundant peace. Its pesher concerns the congregation of the *'ebyonîm* who accept the season of affliction but will be saved from the snares of Belial and thereafter all who inherit the earth will delight and luxuriate in all the delights of the flesh. (4Qp Ps 37 ii 9–10)

But the redemptive aspect of the *shenat razôn la'donai* is not the only facet of this passage reflected in Qumran thought. The *yôm naqam* of Isa 61:2 is stressed in 1QS 9:21–23 where the *maskîl*, or instructor at Qumran, is described as zealous for the *hôq*, law, and its time of fulfillment, which is paraphrased as the *yôm naqam* when the instructor will do nothing but *razôn* in that day.[34] This *razôn*, of course, means doing the pleasure of God, or doing what is *dektos* to God, at the end time. This passage alone makes clear the dual aspect of the *shenat razôn la'donai* of Isa 61:2 as understood at Qumran—bliss for the true Israel but utter damnation for Qumran's enemies.[35] The *yôm naqam* of Isa 61:2 also appears in 1QM 7:4–5; there the people of Qumran who are to fight with the holy angels in the great final battles are described as "volunteers, pure of spirit and flesh, and eager for the *yôm naqam*."[36] This line in 1QM immediately follows the passage that

---

32. H. Stegemann, "Der Peser Psalm 37 aus Höhle 4 von Qumran (4QpPs 37)," *RevQ* 4 (1963–64) 235–70, and idem, "Weitere Stücke von 4 Q p Psalm 37, von 4 Q Patriarchal Blessings und Hinweise auf eine unedierte Handschrift aus Höhle 4 Q mit Exzerpten aus dem Deuteronomium," *RevQ* 6 (1967–69) 193–227, esp. 193–210; J. M. Allegro and A. A. Anderson, *Qumrân Cave 4, I* (DJD 5; Oxford: Clarendon, 1968) plates 14–17; J. Strugnell, "Notes en marge du volume V des Discoveries in the Judaean Desert of Jordan," *RevQ* 7 (1970) 163–276, esp. 211–18. Cf. J. A. Fitzmyer, "Bibliographical Aid to the Study of the Qumran Cave IV Texts 158–186," *CBQ* 31 (1969) 59–71, esp. 65–67.

33. M. Gertner, "Terms of Scriptural Interpretation: A Study in Hebrew Semantics," *BSO(A)S* 25 (1962) 1–27, and idem, "Midrashim in the NT," *JSS* 7 (1962) 267–92. Cf. E. E. Ellis, "Midrash, Targum and New Testament Quotations," in E. E. Ellis and M. Wilcox, eds., *Neotestamentica et Semitica* (M. Black Festschrift; Edinburgh: T. & T. Clark, 1969) 61–69.

34. Cf. 1QH 10:19.

35. Mezudat David interprets the phrase *shenat* razôn* leyisra'el**.

36. Y. Yadin, *The Scroll of the War of the Sons of Light against the Sons of Darkness* (Oxford: Oxford University Press, 1962) 291.

lists those who are forbidden to come near the battlefield on that day, the halt, blind, lame, and those of impure or injured body.[37]

These uses of Isa 61:1-2 at Qumran were dramatically supplemented in 1965 in the publication of 11QMelch by Adam S. van der Woude.[38] Merrill P. Miller showed in an article published in 1969 that Isa 61:1-2 "stands behind the unfolding pesher material" of 11QMelch.[39] Isaiah is not just a part of the enriching biblical material but "is woven into the fabric of the commentary material and is in fact its formative element."[40] In his paper, Miller convincingly demonstrates that the citations in 11QMelch from Lev 25:13, Deut 15:2, Isa 52:7, and Pss 82:1-2 and 7:8-9[41] are all related to phrases from Isa 61:1-3, which link the citations so as to demonstrate the unity of the Scriptures. Words and phrases from Isa 61:1-3 appear in ll. 4, 6, 9, 13, 14, and 18–20 at points crucial to the fabric of the whole piece.[42] The words from Isaiah 61 are as follows:

> Line   4 *ha-shebûyîm* (*lishbûyim*)
> 6 *weqara' lahem derôr* (*liqro' lishbûyim derôr*)
> 9 *shenat ha-razôn lemalkê zedeq* (*shenat razôn la'donay*)
> 13 *noqmat mishpetê 'el* (*yôm naqam le'lohênû*)
> 14 *'elê* [*hazzedeq*] (*êlê hazzedeq*)
> 18 *hamebasser* (*lebasser*)
> 18 *meshîah ha-rü*[*ah*] (*mashah YHWH 'otî*)
> 19 [*lenahem kol 'abelîm lasûm la'abelê zîon*]
> 20 *lenah*[*em*] *ha'*[*abelîm*] (as above)

In 11QMelch, Isa 61:1-3 eschatologizes the Jubilee Year proclamation of Leviticus 25 and Deuteronomy 15 and shows the unity of Scripture, according to Miller.[43] In 11QMelch it is Melchizedeq, a heavenly judgment and redemption figure, perhaps the chief figure in the Qumran view of the heavenly council whom Milik calls "une hypostase de Dieu" (as over against

---

37. See Chap. 8 below, 116–20.
38. A. S. van der Woude, "Melchisedech als himmlische Erlösergestalt in den neugefundenen eschatologischen Midraschim aus Qumran Höhle XI," *OTS* 14 (1965) 354–73; M. de Jonge and A. S. van der Woude, "11QMelchizedek and the New Testament," *NTS* 12 (1966) 301–26; J. A. Fitzmyer, "Further Light on Melchizedek from Qumran Cave 11," *JBL* 86 (1967) 25–41; J. T. Milik, "Milkî-sedeq et Milkî-resa'," *JJS* 23 (1972) 95–144; P. J. Kobelski, *Melchizedek and Melchiresa'* (CBQMS 10; Washington: Catholic Biblical Association, 1981); E. Puech, "Notes sur le manuscrit de XIQMelkîsédeq," *RevQ* 12 (1985–87) 483–513.
39. M. Miller, "The Function of Isa 61:1-2 in 11QMelchizedek," *JBL* 88 (1969) 467–69.
40. Miller, "Isa 61:1-2 in 11QMelchizedek," 469, n. 13.
41. Isa 8:11 in l. 25 of 11QMelch should be added to the list.
42. See Sanders, "The Old Testament in 11QMelchizedek," 373–82.
43. Miller (n. 39 above) saw allusions to Isa 61:1-3, in 11QMelch ll. 4, 6, 9, 13, and in l. 18. See also Sanders, "The Old Testament in 11QMelchizedek." One of the remarkable aspects of Zimmerli's study ("Das 'Gnadenjahr des Herrn' "), is that he had seen Isa 61:1-3 as a reflection on Lev 25:10 and Isa 42:7 by the tradition-critical method without reference to Qumran or the rabbis. This suggests how complementary the two methods are if handled properly.

Melkiresha', his evil antagonist), who proclaims *shemittah* (l. 3) and *derôr* (l. 6) for the captive, that is for the Essenes, but proclaims the *yôm naqam* for the forces of Belial.[44] Melchizedeq proclaims or announces the end time (i.e., *melkî-zedeq* is the subject of the verb *qara'* of Isa 61:1 and 2), and executes God's judgment of the eschaton. Melchizedeq is identified as the evangelist or *mebasser* (ll. 16 and 18) who is anointed by the Spirit (l. 18). What Melchizedeq proclaims, in effect, is the "acceptable year of Melchizedeq" (l.9);[45] four times is Melchizedeq called the *'elohîm* (ll. 10, 16, 24, 25) or heavenly being[46] who on that day will reign and execute judgments against the forces of Belial but bring redemption for the "captives" (*shebûyîm*) or Essenes.[47] "Captives" in 11QMelch becomes an epithet for the convenanters like "poor" or "pure" or "good" in other Qumran texts.[48]

HERMENEUTICS

The quotation of Isa 61:1-2a is peculiar to Luke; it is lacking in the Mark 6 and Matthew 13 parallels.[49] Luke has made of the rejection pericope an important statement about the aspects of Jesus' teachings which offended his contemporaries. In Mark and Matthew, both of whom state that the folk at Nazareth *eskandalizonto en autō*, the offense is that of the prophet not honored in his own country nor by his own kin: his wisdom and his works seem pretentious for a hometown *tekton* (carpenter). In Luke, by contrast, we attend a synagogue service, see Jesus given an *'alîyah* to the *bîmah*, hear him read a *haftarah* portion from Isaiah, and hear him do

---

44. I agree with Milik ("Milkî-sedek et Milkî-resaʿ") against J. Carmignac ("Le document de Qumran sur Melkisédeq," *RevQ* 7 [1970] 343–78).

45. Recall that Rashi and Ibn Ezra interpreted 61:2a as *geʾûlah*, unlike Qimhi and Mezudat David who interpreted it to mean *shenat haggalût* and *shenat razôn leyisraʾel*. Rashi and Ibn Ezra could be messianic whereas the others appear political.

46. In 11QMelch he is the *'elohîm* of Ps 82:1 and the *'elohayik* of Isa 52:7.

47. The key word for the Essenes in 11QMelch is the *shebûyim* of Isa 61:1.

48. See 11QPs 154 for a significant clustering of such appellatives for the Qumran denomination: J. A. Sanders, *The Psalms Scroll of Qumran Cave 11 (11QPsᵃ)* (DJD 4; Oxford: Clarendon, 1965) 68–69, idem, *Dead Sea Psalms Scroll* (Ithaca: Cornell University Press, 1967) 108–9, and idem, "Psalm 154 Revisited," in G. Braulik et al., eds., *Biblische Theologie und gesellschaftlicher Wandel* (N. Lohfink Festschrift; Frieburg: Herder, 1993) 296–306.

49. Isa 61:1-2 in Luke has been treated by L. C. Crockett, *The OT in the Gospel of Luke with Emphasis on the Interpretation of Isa 61:1-2* (unpublished doctoral dissertation; Brown University, 1966). This fine work came to my attention only after the first draft of this study was completed; it is still available only through University Microfilms. See also Crockett, "Luke 4:25-27 and Jewish-Gentile Relations in Luke-Acts," *JBL* 88 (1969) 177–83. An important study which Crockett overlooks in this article is that of A. Strobel, "Das apokalyptische Terminproblem in der sogenannten Antrittspredigt Jesu, Lk 4:16-30," *TLZ* 92 (1967) cols. 251–54, which concerns itself with the relation of Isa 61:1-2 and Lev 25:10 in Luke 4:16-30. Neither Strobel nor Crockett saw the importance of Isaiah 61 (not to mention Lev 25:10) in 11QMelch, nor 11QMelch for Luke 4. For a more recent treatment of the peculiarities of the

biblical midrash on it based on Elijah and Elisha.[50] Luke makes it very clear, pace Jeremias,[51] that the faithful of Nazareth took offense at Jesus' midrash on the Isaiah passage enriched by the references to 1 Kings 17 and 2 Kings 5. What in Mark and Matthew is a rejection by Jesus of the people's *apistia*, in Luke is a rejection of Jesus by the people because of his sermon. The ambiguous reaction of the people after Jesus reads the passages from Isaiah 61 and 58:6 is shown in their single question (contrast parallels), "Is not this Joseph's son?" The people were both pleased and astonished by Jesus' acclamation that this very familiar and key passage of Scripture was being fulfilled on that very day. To say that this particular passage was being fulfilled was to proclaim the acceptable year of the Lord. The people would have been exceedingly pleased to hear that the great day had arrived but would have been puzzled that Jesus, a familiar local personage, would have arrogated to himself the role of *mebasser*, the herald of the great day, a role that at Qumran was, as we have seen, reserved for Melchizedeq, the chief *'elôhîm* of the heavenly council. That which in v. 22 is pleased astonishment, in v. 29, seven verses later, becomes threatening anger. Jesus' cousins and familiar friends turn from a puzzled but receptive audience into a lynching party. Luke forces us to ask what happened within vv. 23-27 that would cause a receptive congregation to turn into an angry mob. The same kind of question is forced upon us by Baruch when Jeremiah's cousins and familiar friends at Anathoth turned against him, stoned him, chased him out of town, and threatened to lynch him (Jeremiah 11:18-23). What had the man said that made them so angry?

In Luke it is not Jesus' general wisdom nor even his works that offend the people, as is apparently the case in Mark and Matthew: in Luke it is

---

quotation in Luke, see D. L. Bock, *Proclamation from Prophecy and Pattern: Lucan Old Testament Christology* (JSNTSup 12; Sheffield: JSOT, 1987) 105–11. See also Chap. 2 above.

In the classic source-critical mode H. Schurmann ("Zur Traditionsgeschichte der Nazareth Perikope Lk 4, 16-30," in A. Descamps and A. de Halleux, eds., *Mélanges bibliques en hommage au R. P. Béda Rigaux* [Gembloux: Duculot, 1970] 187–205) concludes that Luke 4:17-21 (23a) and 25-27 come from Mark, and 4:16, 22, 23b, 24, 28-30, from the *Redequelle* or sayings source: hence, one must not attribute to Luke everything not in Mark, nor build up a redaction-historical theology therefrom. The advice is cautionary and to some extent valuable, but the method exposes the need for a history of midrash approach. For an assessment of the critics see I. H. Marshall, *Commentary on Luke* (NIGTC; Grand Rapids: Eerdmans, 1978) 178–80, and J. A. Fitzmyer, *The Gospel according to Luke I–IX* (AB 28; Garden City, N.Y.: Doubleday, 1981) 526–28.

50. The critique of A. Guilding's theory (*The Fourth Gospel and Jewish Worship* [Oxford: Oxford University Press, 1960]) about a triennial lectionary cycle in the first century, by R. E. Brown, *CBQ* 22 (1960) 259–61 and other critics, should shift attention to the work of P. Billerbeck, "Ein Synagogengottesdienst in Jesu Tagen," *ZNW* 55 (1964) 143–61, which I have not seen mentioned by anyone dealing with this problem.

51. J. Jeremias, *Jesus' Promise to the Nations* (SBT 24; London: SCM, 1958) 44–45, following B. Violet, "Zum rechten Verständnis der Nazareth-Perikope," *ZNW* 37 (1938) 251–71.

the specific application Jesus makes of the Isaiah passage. There are many problems, as everyone knows, but the discovery of the importance of Isa 61:1-3 in 11QMelch focuses our attention on the question of the hermeneutics involved in this sermon at Nazareth as reported by Luke. The hermeneutic techniques which Luke used, however, are not as significant as the hermeneutic axioms underlying those techniques.[52] Before one can attribute true value to the hermeneutic techniques that an ancient midrashist used, one must first try to recover the hermeneutic axioms on which the techniques were based.[53] Recent work on midrash at Qumran suggests that two hermeneutic axioms were operative at Qumran.

The first was the principle that has been recognized by nearly all scholars who have worked on the Qumran pesharim but that was well expressed by Karl Elliger in 1953: "Der Ausleger hat ein ganz bestimmtes hermeneutisches Prinzip als Richtschnur. Und dieses lässt sich in zwei Sätzen zusammenfassen: 1. Prophetische Verkündigung hat zum Inhalt das Ende, und 2. die Gegenwart ist die Endzeit."[54] In other words, at Qumran prophecy had as its content the end time, and the present is the end time. B. J. Roberts extended this observation to show that the Qumran faithful believed that the Bible generally, and not just prophecy, had as its object the end time and that the covenanters believed they were to fulfill the role of the central *personae dramatis* of the end time. "The Bible was their concern and constituted their whole being. . . . What we have here (in the scrolls) is the literature, the actual self-expression, of a people who regarded themselves and everything surrounding them, as the embodiment of the fulfillable word of God."[55] They believed themselves the true Israel of the end time.

---

52. Gertner ("Midrashim in the NT," 270) lists six *midôt* employed by NT writers (*'al tiqrey*, *tartey mashma'*, enriching, *muqdam me'uhar*, syntactical inversions, and *midrash shemot*), and (idem, "Terms of Scriptural Interpretation," 1–27) the larger rubrics of midrash (*gezerah shavah*, *peshat* [*dianoigon*], *midrash haggadah*, etc.). W. H. Brownlee ("Biblical Interpretation among the Sectaries of the Dead Sea Sect," *BA* 14 [1951] 54–76) listed thirteen "presuppositions," or what we would now call hermeneutic technique at Qumran, evident in 1QpHab. A recent look at midrashic technique at Qumran has been offered by E. Slomovic, "Toward an Understanding of the Exegesis in the Dead Sea Scrolls," *RevQ* 7 (1970) 3–15 (*gezerah shavah*, *zeker ledaver*, and *asmakhta*). See Gertner's excellent caveat ("Terms of Scriptural Interpretation," 20–21), following Ben-Yehudah's Thesaurus, that the meaning of *peshat* is not "literal" but "contextual" or "widespread-meaning."

53. See my reviews of the work of M. Fishbane in *CBQ* 49 (1987) 302–5, and in *Theology Today* 47 (1991) 433–35.

54. K. Elliger, *Studien zum Habakuk-Kommentar vom Toten Meer* (BHT 15; Tübingen: Mohr [Siebeck], 1953) 275–87—a remarkable, early statement of Qumran ideology.

55. B. J. Roberts, "Bible Exegesis and Fulfillment in Qumran," in P. Ackroyd and B. Lindars, eds., *Words and Meanings* (D. W. Thomas Festschrift; Cambridge: Cambridge University Press, 1968) 195–207, esp. 195 and 199.

These are but different ways of expressing the first hermeneutic axiom at Qumran. The second has not been as clearly recognized but in my opinion is just as important as the first. One of my students expressed the axiom thus in a seminar paper, "All words of woe, curse, judgment, disapproval, etc., are to be directed against those outside the community, especially those in Jerusalem; but all words of blessing, praise, salvation, comfort, etc., are to be directed towards those inside the community."[56] Put more simply, the second hermeneutic axiom at Qumran required that Scripture be interpreted so as to show that in the eschaton God's wrath would be directed against an out-group and God's mercy toward the in-group. This does not mean that the covenanters viewed themselves as sinless or exempt from God's temporal judgments. The Qumran doctrines of humanity and sin were very high indeed, and the sect daily confessed and executed their ablutions. But in part because they viewed themselves as having an orthodox doctrine of sin and as judged betimes, they had faith that when the great day came they would be the objects of the blessings the Bible allowed. Put another way, the Essenes never in their commentaries interpreted Scripture as judgmental of themselves; there was no prophetic realism, in the form of a challenge from within their own self-conception, or prophetic critique at Qumran. No Scripture was ever interpreted as a judgment or challenge to their own theology or ideology, or to their confidence in their blissful destiny in the end time. They apparently had no prophet who interpreted the tradition as Jeremiah interpreted the Exodus covenant traditions so as to force his own people to face the essential and existential question of whether they really were the true Israel they claimed to be. Prophetic realism is that dimension within a community which challenges its identity, and challenges it on the basis and authority of the very tradition from which that identity springs. There was clearly no prophetic hermeneutic at Qumran but rather the hermeneutic tradition that John Bright calls the "official theology" as well preached by ancient court prophets and so-called false prophets who represented the normal, reasonable theology of their time. Prophetic critique does not simply challenge the ethics of a community but its very *ethos* or interpretation of the *muthos*—its self-understanding—without, however, rejecting the community.[57]

The first hermeneutic axiom at Qumran was eschatological. The second was constitutive; it marshaled scriptural authority in service of Qumran ideology. Only after the importance of these two hermeneutic axioms

---

56. J. Bresnahan, a Master of Sacred Theology candidate at Colgate Rochester Divinity School.

57. See J. A. Sanders, *From Sacred Story to Sacred Text* (Philadelphia: Fortress, 1987) 61–105.

is perceived do the various hermeneutic techniques at Qumran have any significance.

HERMENEUTICAL AXIOMS

When Jesus says in Luke 4:21, "Today this Scripture is fulfilled in your ears," he was saying what the good folk at Nazareth so much wanted to hear. He was observing, according to their "ears," the first hermeneutic axiom, but in doing so he went beyond anything we have in the Qumran scrolls. Near the end of 1QM occurs the famous prayer to be recited at the end of the seventh great battle against the forces of Belial when the final victory was won, but even there when *hayyôm* in the sense of "today" does occur the context is still a prayer, *hayyôm hôphia' lanû*, "Today, appear Thou to us." Like the Essenes the early Christians were convinced that Scripture was pertinent to the end time of their day, the *'et haqqez*; the Law and the Prophets and Psalms were subjected to the first hermeneutic axiom of Christian midrash which was the same as at Qumran. The early church also employed constitutive hermeneutics in order to demonstrate that Christ was the true Israel and in him the church was the new Israel of God.[58] In their belief, the truth of the First Testament was revealed only when contemporized to their day through the Christ figure as initial fulfillment of all that was there. To rephrase B. J. Roberts: what we have here (in the Second Testament) is the literature, the actual self-expression of a people who regarded Christ and everything surrounding him as the embodiment of the fulfillable Word of God.

So the first hermeneutic axiom in the Second Testament, like that at Qumran, is eschatological, but here it is intensified and heightened. The actual fulfillment had begun, and nowhere in the Second Testament is this more sharply put than in this hapax in Luke 4:21, *sēmeron peplērōtai hē graphē autē*. Following this, Luke omits the Markan report that the people were scandalized but suggests that they were amazed, as we have seen. Jeremias, following Violet, interprets this puzzlement or wonderment, by retroversion to Aramaic, as anger at Jesus for omitting the phrase "and day of vengeance for our God."[59]

Jeremias's point that Luke omits the phrase *kai hēmeran antapodoseōs* in Jesus' citation of Isa 61:2 is of great significance as we shall see in a

---

58. J. A. Sanders, "Habakkuk in Qumran, Paul, and the Old Testament," *JR* 39 (1959) 232–44; repr. in C. A. Evans and J. A. Sanders, eds., *Paul and the Scriptures of Israel* (JSNTSup 83; SSEJC 1; Sheffield: JSOT, 1993) 98–117; idem, "The Dead Sea Scrolls—A Quarter Century of Study," *BA* 36 (1973) 110–48, esp. 144–48; and idem, "Foreword," in C. A. Evans and D. A. Hagner, eds., *Faith and Polemic: Studies in Anti-Semitism and Early Christianity* (Minneapolis: Fortress, 1993) ix–xvii.

59. See n. 51 above.

moment, but not for the reasons that Jeremias cites! As mentioned above,
the second axiom in Essene hermeneutics was the belief that the end time
meant blessings for the Essenes but only woe for their enemies; this is
apparent in all Qumran literature, especially in 11QMelch, which maintains that Melchizedeq on that great and final day will wreak vengeance on
Belial and all other enemies. Jesus' omission of this all-important phrase
in his recitation of Isaiah is considerably more significant than his omitting
the earlier phrase in v. 1, "To bind up the brokenhearted," which has
synonymous parallels in the phrases preceding and following. The addition of the phrase, *apostelle tethrausmenous en aphesei*, from Isa 58:6, necessi-
tated the elision of one such colon for the dual purpose of establishing a
parallelism between the occurrences in Greek of *aphesin* in 61:1 and *aphesei*
in 58:6, and of emphasizing the idea of release, as 11QMelch also does.
The whole of the first half of 11QMelch is a midrash on the idea of release
in the jubilee texts of Leviticus 25, Deuteronomy 15, and Isaiah 61. Here,
11QMelch and Luke 4 are in striking harmony and seem both quite faithful to the ancient fabric of Isa 61:1-3 itself.[60]

Where they differ radically is in the Lukan Jesus' midrash on *who* the
poor, the captives, and the blind were. Whereas 11QMelch, by citing Lev
25:10 and Isa 52:7, reflects the second Essene axiom that the captives to be
released are the in-group or Essenes, Jesus' citation of the gracious acts of
Elijah and Elisha toward the Sidonian widow and the Syrian leper shows
that he does not subscribe to the Essene second axiom. Far from it, by this
enriching juxtaposition of Elijah, Elisha, and Isaiah 61, Jesus demonstrates
that the words meaning poor, captive, blind, and oppressed do not apply
exclusively to any in-group but to those to whom God wishes them to
apply. God sent (*elias epemphthē*) Elijah and Elisha to outsiders, the
Sidonian widow and the Syrian leper.

Luke's congregation would have known these stories very well if Luke's
two-volume theological history of what God had done in Christ and was
doing in the early church was the literary result of a theocentric program
of instruction in which narrative Scripture (LXX) was read (aloud by the
literate for all) in *lectio continua*. The remnant, who stayed in "the way"
after the fall of Jerusalem and the apparent failure of the parousia, would
have asked crucial questions about what kind of God was working in
Christ and through the church. Through such a program, Luke's community became knowledgeable about the One God of Scripture who had sent

---

60. See nn. 3 and 43 above. See also C. Perrot, "Luc 4:16-30 et la lecture biblique de
l'ancienne Synagogue," *RSR* 47 (1973) 324–40. Perrot has advanced the bold hypothesis that
the service in which Jesus read and preached may well have been Yom Kippur in Tishri. The
great value of Perrot's remarks is in his taking the Jubilee Year theme as key. Fitzmyer (*Luke
I–IX*, 530, 532) is aware of 11QMelch and its use of Leviticus 25, but he makes little of it.

the prophets and Jesus, the herald of God's good news. The widow and the leper, being outside ancient Israel, could lay no claims on divine promises nor on the blessings that Elijah and Elisha freely bestowed; God, as seen throughout biblical prophetic critique, was free to grant divine blessings where God willed.

Jesus' second axiom, if we read Luke correctly, is the contradiction of the Essene second axiom. Prophetic critique, so significantly lacking in the Qumran literature, is an integral part of Luke's Gospel or, perhaps, his Jesus sources. If the second axiom in the early church was largely the same as that at Qumran, as it surely was, then the church in its polemic with Judaism, about who was the true Israel, needed only to transmit Jesus' prophetic challenges to the Jews intact but to read them as acceptance of Gentiles and rejection of Jews. Thus the *ipsissima vox Jesu*, read by a diametrically opposed hermeneutic axiom (the constitutive rather than the prophetic), would say the opposite of what Jesus had intended. A simplified view of the operation of these two axioms would be as follows:

	Qumran	*Jesus and NT(?)*	*Early Church and NT(?)*
First axiom:	Eschatological	Eschatological	Eschatological
Second axiom:	Constitutive	Prophetic	Constitutive

It seems to me that the long-standing debate over the place and significance of the proverb in Luke 4:24 and parallels—that the prophet is either *atimos* or not *dektos* in his own *patris*—should be reviewed because the prophetic dimension of the hermeneutic second axiom underlying much of the Scripture by Jesus and Luke has now been recognized.[61] Two salient observations about the Lukan form of the proverb are necessary. First, only Luke, like Papyrus Oxyrhynchus 1 §6, has the adjective *dektos*; Mark and Matthew have *atimos*, and John in 4:44 has the noun *timē*. Second, Luke's citation of Isa 61:2 ends on the climactic *eniauton kuriou dekton—shenat razôn la'donai*—which, pace Jeremias, is the proper explanation for the omission of the following phrase about God's day of vengeance in Isa 61:2. Luke thus anticipated, by citing the Wisdom tradition about the nonacceptance of prophets, the exegesis that he would give to the Isaiah 61 lection by recalling the acts of grace of Elijah and Elisha: the year of the end time is determined by God alone. *Dektos* is normally used to express God's pleasure; in this proverb it is apparently used to speak of one person's acceptance of another. Just as *eudokia* in the *bat-qol* in the

---

61. See the review of the problem in a different light by H. Anderson, "Broadening Horizons: The Rejection at Nazareth Pericope of Luke 4:16-30 in Light of Recent Critical Trends," *Int* 18 (1964) 259–75, esp. 263–66.

Bethlehem theophany in Luke 2:14 expressed God's *razôn*, so the *dektos* of
Isa 61:2 refers to the *razôn* of God alone. By the midrashic technique
of *gezerah shavah*, the Lukan Jesus not only emphasizes the climactic position he had given to the concept of *dektos/razôn* in the Isaiah reading; he
also emphasizes that it is not what people have pleasure in or accept, but
what is acceptable to God that matters in the eschaton. The proverb in
Luke, "No prophet is *dektos* in his own *patris*" is not only much more likely
the original, as the Oxyrhynchus citation would indicate; it is a far stronger
and more offensive statement (if from Jesus) than the flaccid form of the
proverb in Mark and Matthew.

But the proverb in Luke has a greater function than to emphasize
God's will in the eschaton rather than human will. The proverb signals
which hermeneutic second axiom Jesus intended in his exposition of Isaiah
61 (and not only there, but in his whole ministry, which Luke claims
began with this midrash on Isaiah 61). No prophet, that is, no true prophet
of the Elijah, Amos, Isaiah, Jeremiah type is *dektos* by compatriots precisely
because the message always must bear in it a divine challenge to Israel's
covenantal self-understanding in any generation. In other words, a true
prophet of the prophet-martyr tradition *cannot* be *dektos* at home precisely
because of the hermeneutics. As the so-called true prophets of old cited
the ancient Mosaic and Davidic Torah traditions of Israel's origins not
only as the very authority of Israel's existence but as a judgment upon and
a challenge to the official ideology of their day, so the Lukan account of
the rejection pericope shows Jesus in that same prophetic tradition vis-à-vis
his contemporaries. By the prophetic-hermeneutic second axiom Jesus
turned the very popular Isaiah 61 passage into a judgment and a challenge to the definitions of Israel of his day. The proverb is true not only
because a hometown figure is overfamiliar and lacks the authority that a
measure of strangeness might bring, but also because a true prophet, in
an Elijah-type biblical tradition, must cast a light of scrutiny upon compatriots from the very source of authority on which they rely for their identity, existence, and self-understanding. It is in this sense of the word
"prophet" that I understand Otto Michel's dictum recently cited by Asher
Finkel: "Jesu Messianität ist prophetisch. Sie erhebt sich auf prophetischer
Grundlage, sie lebt von prophetischen Gesetzen. . . . Es liegt eine innere
Notwendigkeit in Jesu Gang zum Kreuz: Der Prophet ist Märtyrer."[62]

Larrimore Clyde Crockett asks if the controversy between Jesus and
John the Baptist, as reported in Luke 7:22-23, might not have occurred
because Jesus interpreted the crucial words "poor," "captive," "blind," and

---

62. See A. Finkel, "Jesus' Sermon at Nazareth (Luk. 4,16-30)," in O. Betz, M. Hengel, and
P. Schmidt, eds., *Abraham Unser Vater: Juden und Christen im Gespräch über die Bibel* (O. Michel
Festschrift; AGSJU 5; Leiden: Brill, 1963) 106–15, esp. 115.

"oppressed" to mean those whom the Essenes viewed as impure of spirit and flesh.[63] John, who would have gotten much of his own eschatological orientation at Qumran in his youthful years there, apparently disagreed with Jesus on this. Jesus' question *ti exēlthate idein* in Luke 7:24-25 is perhaps the vital one. What one looks for is axiomatic in how one reads a situation. The Jesus in Luke's sources apparently meant that if the word "poor" means poor, and the eschaton means good news whether the poor are in the in-group or not, then dwelling in the desert in sackcloth and ashes, fasting, or embracing poverty while rejecting the blemished victims of poverty, all miss the point. It would appear as though John had his doubts as to whether Jesus was indeed *ho erchomenos, ha-ba'*, and I suspect that the doubts arose precisely because John agreed with the Essene second axiom. If one expected the *mebasser* to come like Melchizedeq, in a blaze of glory with heavenly armies, then Jesus' point—that when Elijah comes he will act as he had previously and will bless outsiders—would have been offensive indeed.[64] "Blessed is he who takes no offense at me" (7:23) would mean that one's second axiom could not have been exclusivist, and *ptochoi/ 'anawîm* could not be in-group appellatives. If this construction of the encounter or controversy between Jesus and John is sound, then we may have grasped a pre-resurrection tradition.[65]

---

63. See n. 49 above.

64. Offensive to Jews, spoken to them by a fellow Jew who was an eschatological prophet, but encouraging to early Christians when later read (or misread) by constitutive hermeneutics to mean Judaism was rejected and the young church (mostly made up of Gentiles) was elect.

65. See J. Bajard, "La Structure de la péricope de Nazareth en Lc iv, 16-30," *ETL* 45 (1969) 165–71. This is a valuable study that coincides with my own at two essential points. After analyzing the so-called incoherencies in the Lukan material Bajard concludes (and this is his thesis) that Luke so transformed the structure of the account, as it appears in Mark, that the so-called incoherencies appear only if one sees Luke as taking Mark as his point of departure. On his own terms, Luke has precisely ordered his material to demonstrate that Jesus was rejected at Nazareth (contrast Mark and Matthew) at the beginning of his ministry for the same reason that he was put to death at its end—his refusal to limit salvation to his own homeland. Bajard correctly sees that the rupture between Jesus and his compatriots takes place in Luke only at v. 27 after the sermon and not at all at vv. 22-23. The bulk of Bajard's article is a study of the three key words in Luke's account, *marturein, thaumazein,* and *dektos*. These lead him to a view of vv. 22-23 that coincides with the one presented here, as well as to a view of the importance of *dektos* in vv. 19 and 24, gained by the word-study method. Bajard apparently knows nothing about midrashic techniques.

Another relevant article is D. Hill, "The Rejection of Jesus at Nazareth," *NovT* 13 (1971) 161–80; after reviewing the various problems presented by the Lukan account and the inadequacies of earlier studies, he correctly sees that *dektos* plays a crucial role in the pericope. Hill suggests that Luke here presents a programmatic prologue to Jesus' ministry and thereby makes two important points: (1) Jesus' gospel of "release" will achieve success outside the confines of Judaism; (2) Rejection by the Jews and acceptance by the Gentiles are not wholly matters of free choice but are phases in the overall purposes of God and essential stages in the Lukan theological history. After a review of the first-century synagogue lectionary problem (in which he cites L. C. Crockett, "Luke iv 16-30 and the Jewish Lectionary Cycle: A Word of Caution," *JJS* 17 [1966] 13–46, but not Crockett's dissertation, which no one seems to know), Hill draws six conclusions: (1) Jesus stresses, through Luke, that the prophetic

LUKE AND JESUS

In view of the comparisons available in the midrashic history of Isaiah 61 in the Second Temple Period, especially between Luke 4 and 11QMelch, can we any longer have confidence in a purely redaction-historical approach to the source of the midrash on Isaiah 61 reported in Luke 4? Who provided this prophetic dimension in the Nazareth sermon? Whose gift to the Second Testament was its prophetic second axiom—Luke's or the man Luke reports as having offended his compatriots to such an extent that they tried to lynch him? Why attribute this prophetic dimension to Luke? Is it not possible that Jesus used the Essene second axiom as a foil against which he gave his prophetic understanding of the judgments and grace of God in the end time—and thereby deeply offended some of his compatriots (was not *dektos* in his own *patris*)?[66] If we can recover the foil against which a Second Testament concept comes to full vitality, have

---

ministry that will win acceptance (with God) must transcend the limits of one's own land and people; (2) Luke's, similar to Paul's, theological history attempts to account for the failure of the gospel among Jews and its success among Gentiles; (3) One cannot reach back to Jesus by means of observations about lectionary cycles; (4) Nonetheless, it is fair to suggest that Jesus preached and taught in Nazareth and received less than enthusiastic reception (the rest is Luke's); (5) Jesus probably applied Isa 61:1 to himself at some time as seen by 11QMelch 18 *[sic]*; (6) The Beatitudes in Matthew 5 and the Nazareth pericope in Luke 4 indicate that both the first and the third evangelists put peshers on Isaiah 61 at the start of Jesus' ministry (Hill fails to cite Flusser [see n. 31 above]).

The works of Bajard and Hill are very encouraging. Both have seen the importance of *dektos* without using the method of comparative midrash, so that each fails to see its full importance (although Hill rightly sees the Lukan stress on divine will) in terms of Jesus' role in Luke as eschatological prophet. Each offers some suggestion about the contribution of Jesus to the Lukan account (and Hill rightly denies that either linguistic criteria or studies in the calendar will avail), but neither asks whether the point being scored in the episode better fits, or has a foil, in Jesus' or in Luke's time.

This all-crucial question cannot be put without engaging in comparative midrash. And if one attempts to trace a history of the function of Isa 61:1-3 one must, of necessity, emphasize its importance at Qumran for locating its significance in the Lukan story. Hill alone refers to 11QMelch in work to date on Luke 4, but, even so, misses its significance altogether: he cites l. 18 and comments that it is the only instance at Qumran of a single prophet being designated "anointed." Hill fails to see the basic position Isaiah 61 occupies in 11QMelch and fails to understand the basic similarity-yet-contrast to its function there and in Luke 4. He also does not see how the heavenly Melchizedeq as *mebasser* is a foil par exellence to the role of *mebasser* played by Jesus in Luke.

66. Recent studies clearly leave open the possibility that Jesus himself may have been responsible for the wordplays on *aphesis* and *dektos* in Greek; but what is important is not the origin of the hermeneutical technique but the source of the second, prophetic, axiom. See R. H. Gundry, *The Use of the Old Testament in St. Matthew's Gospel* (NovTSup 18; Leiden: Brill, 1967) 178–204; J. N. Sevenster, *Do You Know Greek? How Much Greek Could the First Jewish Christians Have Known?* (NovTSup 19; Leiden: Brill, 1968) 176–91; J. A. Fitzmyer, "Languages of Palestine in the First Century A.D.," *CBQ* 32 (1970) 501–31; J. A. Emerton, "The Problem of Vernacular Hebrew in the First Century A.D.," *JTS* 24 (1973) 1–23; S. Freyne, *Galilee from Alexander the Great to Hadrian: A Study of Second Temple Judaism* (Wilmington: Glazier; Notre Dame: Notre Dame University Press, 1980); H. C. Kee, "Archaeology in Galilee," *Bulletin of the Institute for Antiquity and Christianity* 18/1 (1991) 9–14, esp. 11 ("[In Palestine] most

we not satisfied one of the most rigorous criteria which make historical reconstruction of the thrust of Jesus' didache, his prophetic critique, possible? Whether or not we agree with Jeremias that the parables were directed by Jesus at his critics, we must concede that Jesus' prophetic critique of the common inversion of the Deuteronomic ethic of election was correctly understood by his critics and provoked reactions from them.[67]

This sketch of the history of the function of Isa 61:1-3 in the Second Temple Period provides a context for understanding its function in Luke 4,[68] and a breakthrough for understanding what are otherwise inconsistencies in Luke 4 as emphasized by source criticism.[69] It is the position of this chapter that none of these so-called inconsistencies actually exists in the text of Luke if approached using the method of comparative midrash as a supplement to other methods.

Whether Luke correctly understood Jesus' own second (prophetic) axiom and whether he shared the early church's second (constitutive) axiom, he clearly intended to stress the disproportionate earlier and later reactions of the congregation. He wanted to show that Jesus' exegesis of Isaiah 61 by means of the material from Kings on Elijah and Elisha disturbed his family and friends at Nazareth. Just after Jesus' reading from Isaiah 61, the people would have interpreted the passage as favorable to themselves; but when Jesus used the hermeneutic of prophetic critique the people were deeply offended.[70] One can hardly blame the congregation at Nazareth for expecting Jesus to interpret the *logoi tēs charistos* (Luke 4:22) or *divrê hesed*, which he had read from Isaiah 61, as favorable to

---

people, including Jews, spoke Greek") and 14 ("I cannot imagine, on the basis of archaeological evidence, anyone surviving in Galilee who did not speak Greek").

67. See Chap. 8 below.

68. Note, too, the symposium volume of four essays found in W. Eltester, ed., *Jesus in Nazareth* (BZNW 40; Berlin: de Gruyter, 1972). E. Grässer writes on "Jesus in Nazareth (Mc 6:1-6a)" (pp. 1–37); A. Strobel on "Die Ausrufung des Jobeljahres in der Nazareth-predigt Jesu; zur apokalyptischen Tradition Lc 4:16-30" (pp. 38–50); R. C. Tannehill on "The Mission of Jesus according to Luke iv:16-30" (pp. 51–75); and W. Eltester on "Israel im lukanischen Werk und die Nazareth-perikope" (pp. 76–147). Prof. Tannehill made some helpful comments on the occasion of the first exposure of my work on this subject at an annual Society of Biblical Literature meeting in New York in 1970, and I am very pleased to see his own work now available, especially his *The Narrative Unity of Luke-Acts*, Vol. 1, *The Gospel of Luke* (Philadelphia: Fortress, 1986); cf. my review in *Pacific Theological Review* 22 (1989) 79–81. The four studies in Eltester indicate great promise. Strobel deals at some length with 11QMelch and Tannehill with the Isaiah quotation, although none of the articles can be said to engage in comparative midrash.

69. See my effort with respect to the origins of the *Carmen Christi* of Philippians 2: "Dissenting Deities and Philippians 2:1-11," *JBL* 88 (1969) 279–90.

70. It is not necessary to belabor the point clarified by C. F. Evans ("The Central Section of St. Luke's Gospel," in D. E. Nineham, ed., *Studies in the Gospels* [R. H. Lightfoot Festschrift; Oxford: Blackwell, 1955] 37–53), that Luke viewed Jesus on a primary level as "the prophet like Moses" (Deut 18:15 reflected in Luke 9:51–53; 10:1; 11:27–28; 12:47–48 pass., and Acts 3:22; 7:37).

themselves, particularly when he had stressed *aphesis/ derôr* by the interpolation of Isa 58:6 (which also ends in *aphesis/ hophshîm*). He had moreover insisted, immediately upon sitting down, that the Isaiah passage should be understood in the eschatological or, at least, penultimate situation they, like the faithful at Qumran, believed themselves to be in.

The LXX indicates, as Seeligmann points out in discussing similar passages in Isaiah 9, 11, and 2 Isaiah, that the *derôr* of which the prophet spoke in chapter 61 pertained to the galut (Diaspora) that would walk from the darkness of dispersion to the light of life in Eretz Israel. Later the rabbinic traditions picked up the same interpretation and expanded it to the point of interpreting the *shenat razôn la'donai* as *shenat razôn leIsrael.* Although it is difficult to date the origins of the midrashic and talmudic passages in which Isaiah 61 figures with the same interpretation, Jerome's translation indicates they date at least from the fourth century C.E., and the LXX and Targum indicate a much earlier date. The uniqueness of Isaiah 61, which mentions prophetic authority directly from God rather than from prophetic predecessors, is also part of this tradition. The eschatological reinterpretation is indicated by the passages in *Midrash Lamentations* and the Palestinian Targum *(Ps.-J.)* to Numbers.

The material from Qumran, which provides ample evidence that all these interpretations were current in Jesus' day in Palestine and were fully held by the covenanters there, offers the necessary foil for understanding how Jesus' exegesis of Isaiah 61 would have shocked the people of Nazareth and angered them—and justifiably so. At Qumran the *mebasser* was interpreted as the Melchizedeq of Ps 110:4, a heavenly judging and redeeming figure who would come at the head of angelic armies to redeem the true Israel—that is, Qumran—and wreak vengeance and retribution on all its enemies, human and cosmic.

Jesus, by contrast, arrogates this passage of unique prophetic authority (which Qumran had already apotheosized to a heavenly figure, Melchizedeq) to himself and apparently insists that the *aphesis* of which it speaks will pertain in the end time to those outside Israel, and that what is *dektos, eudokia,* or *razôn,* is totally God's free choice. In the highly charged eschatological atmosphere of Qumran and the Second Testament, this would not simply have been divine largesse to outsiders on the way to final truth; it would be, as so often elsewhere in Luke (and in the prophetic corpus), a challenge to in-group meanings of election.

In Luke's effort to expand the petty opposition between Capernaum and Nazareth (which one gets more miracles?) to the tension between two early understandings of the mission of Jesus—that to Israel alone, that to the Gentiles—and to the prophetic tension that arises from that tension, far from there being an inconsistency in the pericope (between vv. 24 and

25-27) about who rejects whom, the Nazareth congregation rejected Jesus precisely because he preached Isaiah 61 in the way he did—by applying the hermeneutic axiom of prophetic critique even to the end time. Little wonder that the faithful at Nazareth rejected not only his interpretation but the preacher-interpreter as well. The offense was intolerable—it denied all they believed in, in the manner of earlier prophetic applications of precious identifying traditions.

The method of comparative midrash supplements other methods to clarify, perhaps for the first time, this Lukan pericope. From the perspective afforded by this method, there are no inconsistencies in the pericope but rather a text of introduction to Jesus' prophetic ministry in an eschatological age, which proleptically rehearses the end of that ministry at its beginning.

Often scientific exegesis is a search for the ancient question to which the text before us provided answers. The finding of the question or concern addressed unlocks the full significance of a text, and the "quest for the question" can be aided by (1) sketching a midrashic history of the passages of Scripture cited in that text so as (2) to recover the foil against which the midrash in the text comes alive. Luke's Nazareth pericope is the foundation stone of his Gospel, which he wrote largely to answer the embarrassing question of why Jesus was crucified. Jesus was the eschatological prophet anointed by the Spirit (Luke 3:21-22 where Ps 2:7 is interpreted in a midrashic complex with Isa 42:1 and 61:1); Jesus so challenged his compatriots' assumptions about divine election that he met the prophet-martyr's end. His message as *mebasser* was both a prophetic challenge to such assumptions and the announcement of the end time, not just one or the other. The combination was strange indeed. The angry reception his message received in Nazareth anticipated, according to Luke, the reception it would finally receive at its end.

Comparative midrash, seeking the foil to which a prophetic critique is directed, can be an aid in reaching behind Luke to Jesus himself. What may appear anti-Jewish or anti-Semitic in Luke, in Jesus would have been simply a challenge leveled at the theological ideology or political theology of his compatriots or *patris*. Hence, our final suggestion is that the Gospels and especially Luke, like the books of the prophets of old, if read out of context, appear anti-Jewish,[71] but read in full original context they are together part of the glory of a common past.

---

71. See N. A. Dahl, "The Story of Abraham in Luke-Acts," in L. E. Keck and J. L. Martyn, eds., *Studies in Luke-Acts* (P. Schubert Festschrift; Nashville: Abingdon, 1966) 139–58, and more recently J. Jervell, *Luke and the People of God: A New Look at Luke-Acts* (Minneapolis: Augsburg, 1972), as well as the dissertation by Crockett cited above in n. 49.

— 5 —

THE FUNCTION OF THE
ELIJAH/ELISHA NARRATIVES
IN LUKE'S ETHIC OF ELECTION

CRAIG A. EVANS

In a series of recent and significant studies, T. L. Brodie has offered convincing evidence of Luke's use of the Elijah/Elisha narratives (i.e., 1 Kings 17—2 Kings 9) in composing the two-volume work Luke-Acts.[1] Through paraphrase and imitation the evangelist, according to Brodie, "internalized" various themes, images, events, and vocabulary items found in these Old Testament passages.[2] Although Brodie eschews the designation "midrash,[3] his work will no doubt be warmly received by those interested in comparative midrash.[4]

This chapter is a revision of my study, "Luke's Use of the Elijah/Elisha Narratives and the Ethic of Election," *JBL* 106 (1987) 75–83.

---

1. T. L. Brodie, "A New Temple and a New Law: The Unity and Chronicler-Based Nature of Luke 1:1—4:22a," *JSNT* 5 (1979) 21–45; idem, "The Accusing and Stoning of Naboth (1 Kgs 21:8-13) as One Component of the Stephen Text (Acts 6:9-14; 7:58a)," *CBQ* 45 (1983) 417–32; idem, "Luke 7, 36-50 as an Internalization of 2 Kings 4,1-37: A Study in Luke's Use of Rhetorical Imitation," *Bib* 64 (1983) 457–85; idem, "Towards Unraveling the Rhetorical Imitation of Sources in Acts: 2 Kings 5 as One Component of Acts 8,9-40," *Bib* 67 (1986) 41–67; idem, "Towards Unraveling Luke's Use of the Old Testament: Luke 7.11-17 as an *Imitatio* of 1 Kings 17.17-24," *NTS* 32 (1986) 247–67; idem, *Luke the Literary Interpreter: Luke-Acts as a Systematic Rewriting and Updating of the Elijah-Elisha Narrative* (Rome: Pontifical University of St. Thomas Aquinas, 1987).

2. In addition to the items cited above, see esp. T. L. Brodie, "Greco-Roman Imitation of Texts as a Partial Guide to Luke's Use of Sources," in C. H. Talbert, ed., *Luke-Acts: New Perspectives from the Society of Biblical Literature Seminar* (New York: Crossroad, 1984) 17–46.

3. Brodie (*Luke the Literary Interpreter,* 59, 88) finds the term too general.

4. See the definition of "comparative midrash" above in the second part of Chap. 1 (4–13), and J. A. Sanders, *Canon and Community* (Philadelphia: Fortress, 1984) 62–67.

I have one principal reservation with respect to Brodie's work. I do not think that Luke

In his analysis of the opening part of the central section (9:51—10:20), which he compares to large sections of 1 Kings 19 and 2 Kings 1–3, Brodie comments that Christopher F. Evans's study, in which comparison of the entire central section (9:51—18:14) is made with Deuteronomy,[5] "lacks context and, above all, precision. For this reason it is very difficult to use it as the basis for argument."[6] Evans attempted to delineate parallels of substance and sequence between every pericope of Luke's central section and virtually all the contents of Deuteronomy 1–26. In answer to the question why the evangelist so edited and ordered his material, Evans could only suggest that Luke hoped to emphasize Jesus' identity as the "prophet like Moses" (cf. Deut 18:15-18). Brodie's criticism of Evans is justified, but he has dismissed the significance of the Deuteronomistic parallels too hastily. The more recent work of James A. Sanders, which Brodie cites in his dissertation but not in his discussion of Luke 9:51—10:20, seems to provide the "context" and "precision" lacking in Evans's earlier study.[7] Sanders concludes that the central section's unifying theme, like the primary theological concern of Deuteronomy, revolves around the question of *election* (i.e., who the people of God are; what God expects of the people; how God responds to the elect and non-elect).[8] Thus, the observation that the central section corresponds to Deuteronomy 1–26 may be understood as something more than a stylistic device intended to show that Jesus was the Deuteronomistic prophet; the observation also

---

creates narrative and dominical tradition from septuagintal materials, but rather he *edits* and *arranges* his narrative and dominical tradition reflecting the language and theology of the LXX. For an illuminating example of the problem see Brodie's "Not Q but Elijah: The Story of the Life-Giving Command (Luke 7:1-10) as a Systematic Adaptation of 1 Kings 17:1-16," which was read at the 1990 Society of Biblical Literature meeting in New Orleans and which will probably be published. Brodie thinks that it is more likely that Luke 7:1-10 was based on 1 Kgs 17:1-16 than on Q (see Matt 8:5-13). He prefers to view the LXX as Luke's source because the LXX, unlike the hypothetical Q, most certainly existed in the first century. True, but the parallel in Matthew, which does not appear to be a redacted version of Luke's pericope, as well as the similar story in John 4:43-54, suggests that Luke drew upon dominical tradition of some sort if not upon Q itself.

5. C. F. Evans, "The Central Section of St. Luke's Gospel," in D. E. Nineham, ed., *Studies in the Gospels: Essays in Memory of R. H. Lightfoot* (Oxford: Blackwell, 1955) 37–53. Evans begins his comparison at Luke 10:1.

6. Brodie, *Luke the Literary Interpreter,* 410–11, n. 317.

7. See Chap. 8 below.

8. See Chap. 8 below. For a criticial assessment of Evans and Sanders, among others, see C. L. Blomberg, "Midrash, Chiasmus, and the Outline of Luke's Central Section," in R. T. France and D. Wenham, eds., *Gospel Perspectives III: Studies in Midrash and Historiography* (Sheffield: JSOT, 1983) 217–61.

helps clarify a significant theological issue with which the evangelist grappled.[9] The issue is broadly ecclesiological.[10]

Other recent studies confirm the importance of viewing the Lukan portrait of Jesus against the background of Deuteronomy and Moses. For example, in a study that appeared in 1982, David P. Moessner argued that the evangelist "Luke portrays a Jesus who, like Moses, *must die* to effect the deliverance for his people."[11] A year later in another study Moessner argued that Luke 9:1-50 was composed as a preview of Jesus' impending journey as the prophet like Moses, as portrayed in Deuteronomy.[12] "What we discover," avers Moessner, "is a profound correspondence in the calling, execution, and fate of the calling of the one who is the prophet like Moses (Deut 18:15-19), effecting a new Exodus for a renewed people of God."[13]

Even in Craig L. Blomberg's recent attempt to argue for the presence of a chiastic parable source underlying Luke's central section, which the evangelist supplemented with material from Q, the writer concedes that many of the parallels with Deuteronomy are impressive and that this Old Testament book played a significant role in the theology of much of this part of the Lukan Gospel.[14] In this chapter the Deuteronomistic parallels identified by various scholars (such as Evans, Sanders, Drury,[15] Michael D. Goulder,[16] and John Duncan Martin Derrett[17]) will be assumed as valid, however they are identified. No further arguments will be advanced at this time.[18]

But it is not simply because the parallels with Deuteronomy *do* have a meaningful theological focus that they should not be ignored; there is also evidence that the theme of election is intrinsic to the Elijah/Elisha parallels themselves. That Luke may have internalized large portions of

9. For recent Lukan studies on this issue see J. Jervell, *Luke and the People of God* (Minneapolis: Augsburg, 1972), and D. L. Tiede, *Prophecy and History in Luke-Acts* (Philadelphia: Fortress, 1980).

10. See R. B. Hays, *Echoes of Scripture in the Letters of Paul* (New Haven and London: Yale University Press, 1989), and C. A. Evans and J. A. Sanders, eds., *Paul and the Scriptures of Israel* (JSNTSup 83; SSEJC 1; Sheffield: JSOT, 1993).

11. D. P. Moessner, "Jesus and the 'Wilderness Generation': The Death of the Prophet like Moses according to Luke," *SBLSP* (1982), 319–40, quotation on 339.

12. D. P. Moessner, "Luke 9:1-50: Luke's Preview of the Journey of the Prophet like Moses of Deuteronomy," *JBL* 102 (1983) 575–605.

13. Moessner, "Luke 9:1-50," 588. For a detailed discussion of the function of deuteronomistic Mosaic themes in Luke's central section see Moessner, *Lord of the Banquet* (Minneapolis: Fortress, 1989).

14. Blomberg, "Midrash."

15. J. Drury, *Tradition and Design in Luke's Gospel: A Study in Early Christian Historiography* (London: Darton, Longman & Todd, 1976) esp. 138–64.

16. M. D. Goulder, *The Evangelists' Calendar* (London: SPCK, 1978) esp. 95–101.

17. J. D. M. Derrett, *Law in the New Testament* (London: Darton, Longman & Todd, 1970) esp. 100, 126–55.

18. In a forthcoming study J. A. Sanders will offer a detailed exegetical analysis of these putative parallels. For now, see Chap. 9 below.

Kings[19] does not rule out the possibility that the evangelist made deliberate and meaningful use of Deuteronomy. On the contrary, the observation that Luke made extensive use of Kings only increases the probability that he utilized other portions of the Old Testament as well. (Indeed, Charles H. Talbert has recently pointed out that two, or even three, architectural patterns adopted and adapted by authors in antiquity were not at all unusual.[20]) By way of demonstration, those passages where allusion to Elijah/Elisha tradition is clearest will be examined (i.e., 4:25-27; 7:11-17; 9:52-55; 9:61-62).[21] Each example will be studied with this question in mind: What, if anything, does this passage have to do with election theology?[22]

ELIJAH AND ELISHA TRADITION
IN LUKE

Luke 4:25-27. References to Elijah and Elisha occur in the context of Jesus' sermon in the synagogue at Nazareth (4:16-30). This text is perhaps the clearest example of how the evangelist related the Elijah/Elisha tradition to the question of election. Not only do the references to Elijah and

---

19. Other studies suggest that the fourth evangelist might have done the same thing on a more modest scale; cf. D. G. Bostock, "Jesus as the New Elisha," *ExpTim* 92 (1980) 39–41; T. L. Brodie, "Jesus as the New Elisha: Cracking the Code," *ExpTim* 93 (1981) 39–42.

20. C. H. Talbert, *Literary Patterns, Theological Themes, and the Genre of Luke-Acts* (Missoula: Scholars, 1974) 13–14, n. 68; 64, n. 10.

21. These passages are cited by Brodie, "The Accusing and Stoning of Naboth," 420 and 420, n. 13. For more on the Elijah/Elisha tradition in Luke see P. Dabeck, "Siehe, es erschienen Moses und Elias," *Bib* 23 (1942) 175–89; R. E. Brown, "Jesus and Elisha," *Perspective* 12 (1971) 85–104; J. D. Dubois, "La figure d'Elie dans la perspective lucanienne," *RHPR* 53 (1973) 155–76. On the importance of Elijah in early Judaism see A. Wiener, *The Prophet Elijah in the Development of Judaism* (Boston: Routledge & Kegan Paul, 1978).

In a recent study M. M. Faierstein ("Why Do the Scribes Say That Elijah Must Come First?" *JBL* 100 [1981] 75–86) has argued that the idea that Elijah would immediately precede the Messiah is actually not to be found in first-century Judaism (or earlier) but is more likely a distinctively Christian interpretation. Against Faierstein, D. C. Allison ("Elijah Must Come First," *JBL* 103 [1984] 256–58) attempts to defend the traditional view. But the critical response of J. A. Fitzmyer ("More about Elijah Coming First," *JBL* 104 [1985] 295–96) makes it clear that the evidence is pretty much as Faierstein has assessed it. Malachi 4:5-6 ("Behold, I will send you Elijah the prophet before the great and terrible day of the Lord . . . "), especially if combined with 3:1-2 ("Behold, I send my messenger to prepare the way before me, and the Lord [Jesus?] whom you seek will suddenly come to his temple . . . "), as the redactor of Malachi no doubt intended, might have provided early Christians or Jewish apocalypticists with the understanding that Elijah was immediately to precede the Messiah. In any case, interpreting the Baptist as Elijah (cf. Mark 1:2-4 par.; 9:11-13 par.) is evidence that the Elijah traditions held special significance for the early Christians. Luke however does not view the Elijah tradition exactly the same as the Markan evangelist; see J. A. Fitzmyer, *The Gospel according to Luke I–IX* (AB 28; Garden City: Doubleday, 1981) 213–15.

22. Sanders in Chap. 8 below raises the same question about the central section and its relation to Deuteronomy.

Elisha concern election, but the opening text read by Jesus, Isa 61:1-2, may be seen as a "succinct restatement of election traditions" in which the oppressed and suffering are promised vindication and deliverance.[23] To whom Isaiah's promise of comfort applies depends, of course, on one's hermeneutic. According to the covenanters of Qumran, this prophetic passage promises comfort for them and judgment for their enemies (11QMelch 9–16; 1QH 15:15; 18:14–15).

But in the references to Elijah and Elisha the election issue comes into sharpest focus. In vv 25-26 the story of the famine and Elijah's assistance given to the widow of Zarephath is alluded to (1 Kgs 17:1-16). According to Kings, Elijah departed for Zarephath after telling Ahab of the coming drought. Although we are not explicitly told, Elijah probably left Israel to avoid persecution, even death. This is hinted at in 1 Kgs 17:3 ("hide yourself"), while the element of persecution is clearly seen elsewhere. According to 1 Kgs 18:4 Queen Jezebel had murdered many of Israel's prophets. Having defeated the prophets of Baal (1 Kgs 18:17-40), Elijah fled after being threatened by Jezebel (1 Kgs 19:2-3). Thus it was while fleeing that Elijah ministered to (and was ministered to by) a Gentile family; Elijah turned to the Gentiles because of rejection and persecution at home. Jesus too is unwelcome among his own (Luke 4:24) and, like Elijah, turns to outsiders and outcasts. Although this theme is only implied here, a major justification for turning to Gentiles later in Acts is Jewish rejection and persecution (Acts 13:46; 18:6; 28:28).

Another allusion (Luke 4:27) is to Elisha's healing of Naaman, the commander of the Syrian army (2 Kgs 5:1-14), at a time in Israel's history when Syria had the upper hand. Here the prophet did not leave Israel; the supplicant came to him. The healing of the leper demonstrates that "there is a prophet in Israel" (2 Kgs 5:8) and that "there is no God in all the earth but in Israel" (2 Kgs 5:15). To Luke, Jesus' healing ministry similarly proves that he is a prophet of God (see Luke 7:21-22). And Jesus, like Elisha, is willing to help a foreign soldier (Luke 7:1-10, note that this soldier has a faith greater than any Jesus finds in Israel; compare Acts 10). The allusion to the healing of an important soldier in the army of one of Israel's bitterest foes would have been particularly disturbing to a Jewish audience that, for the most part, resented and hated the Roman forces of occupation.

Larrimore C. Crockett has argued that Luke anticipates not only the Gentile mission but also the fellowship between Jews and Gentiles.[24] He

---

23. See Tiede, *Prophecy and History*, 44, and Chap. 4 above.
24. L. C. Crockett, "Luke 4:25-27 and Jewish-Gentile Relations in Luke-Acts," *JBL* 88 (1969) 177–83.

notes that Elijah was told to go to Sarepta of Sidonia, for God had a widow there to feed him (1 Kgs 17:9); in other words, a Gentile ministers to an Israelite (and not only the other way around as is usually assumed). Crockett thinks that Luke might have intended this biblical example to foreshadow the relief supplied by Gentile Christians to Jewish Christians of Judea (Acts 11:28),[25] and he interprets the Elisha-Naaman allusion similarly. Naaman, commander of the Syrian army, esteemed by his lord, brought gifts to Elisha (2 Kgs 5:1, 5, 15, 23). Crockett considers this proleptic of the episode of the Roman centurion Cornelius, a devout man respected by the Jewish people (Acts 10:1-8).[26] Just as Naaman was cleansed (*katharizein*) of his leprosy (2 Kgs 5:14), so too Cornelius and Gentiles are declared cleansed (*katharizein*) by God and should not be called common or unclean (Acts 10:15, 28; 11:9).[27] If Crockett's analysis is correct, Luke maintains that through Jesus the barrier preventing fellowship between Gentiles and Jews has collapsed. Not only will messianic blessings be extended to Gentiles, but they, no longer "unclean," will enjoy fellowship (esp. table fellowship) and reconciliation with Jews. This idea, of course, proves very controversial in Acts (esp. chaps. 8–15).

Sanders has sought to clarify the dynamic underlying the Lukan passage by noting that two basic hermeneutical axioms were assumed by, although not restricted to, the members of the Qumran community: (1) Each generation considered itself the "true Israel of the end time" and (2) in the end time God's wrath would be directed against Israel's enemies and his blessing generously bestowed upon Israel.[28] Whereas Jesus concurred with the first axiom (as seen in v. 21, "Today this Scripture has been fulfilled"[29]), his reference to and interpretation of the proverb ("Physician, heal yourself. . . ," v. 23) and the Elijah/Elisha narratives indicate his different interpretation of the second axiom. The difference lay in the understanding of who the "True Israel" was.[30] The references to the Elijah/Elisha stories indicate that even the Gentiles would receive the benefits and blessings of the Messianic era (such as later seen in the healing of the Samaritan leper in 17:11-19). Such an idea disagreed

---

25. Crockett, "Luke 4:25-27," 178.

26. So also C. F. Evans, *Saint Luke* (TPI New Testament Commentaries; London: SCM; Philadelphia: Trinity, 1990) 266.

27. Crockett, "Luke 4:25-27," 181–82. Another link between Luke 4 and Acts 10 is seen in the latter's reference to the anointing (*chriein*) of Jesus with the Spirit (Acts 10:38), probably an allusion to the former (*chriein*, 4:18); cf. Evans, *Saint Luke*, 269, and Chap. 3 above.

28. See Chap. 4 above.

29. Whether or not it can be demonstrated that Jesus uttered this saying, the belief that the Scriptures were at last fulfilled in Jesus' ministry certainly agrees with the eschatology criterion, one of the generally accepted criteria for determining the authentic sayings of Jesus. In any case, our concern here is with the evangelist's understanding.

30. See Chap. 4 above.

with prevailing views about who qualified for God's messianic blessings. The religiously upright assumed that Gentiles along with less devout Jews would be cast out. The upright, the true children of Abraham, anticipated God's blessings, but in Luke this thinking was challenged. This recalls the earlier poignant statement of the Baptist, "Do not begin to say to yourselves, 'We have Abraham as our father'; for I tell you, God is able from these stones to raise up children to Abraham" (3:8-9). Luke 4:16-30 provides a prophetic challenge to first-century assumptions about election, and central to this passage are the references to Elijah and Elisha.[31] Thus this pericope bears much affinity with the theological emphasis of the central section.

Since Luke probably intended this passage to have a programmatic or paradigmatic function for his Gospel,[32] later, less obvious allusions to the Elijah/Elisha tradition are no doubt meant to recall the lessons of the Nazareth sermon. These later allusions need not have the same meaning, but they must be seen in the context of Jesus' views on election as established in 4:16-30.

Luke 7:11-17. The account of the raising of the widow's son from Nain is unique to Luke. This miracle exemplifies Jesus' Elijah/Elisha-like ministry introduced earlier in the Nazareth sermon (4:25-27). In 4:25-26 the Lukan Jesus cited the story of Elijah's providing food for the widow and her son (1 Kgs 17:8-16). Although the present pericope (7:11-17) quotes no Old Testament passages, many of the story's details are probably intended to parallel the stories of Elijah raising the widow's son in 1 Kgs 17:17-24 and Elisha raising the woman's son in 2 Kgs 4:32-37. Seven parallels immediately suggest themselves: (1) "Nain" (Luke 7:11) may allude (rightly or wrongly) to the ancient city of Shunem where the woman of Elisha's miracle lived (2 Kgs 4:8). This name (from the Hebrew *Na' im* ["pleasant"] and/or Latin *Naim*) may represent an abbreviation of Shu*nem*. In any case, Nain was situated in the proximity of the ancient site.[33] (2) Both stories involve widows (Luke 7:12; 1 Kgs 17:9, 17). (3) Both stories involve the death of an only son (Luke 7:12; 1 Kgs 17:17; 2 Kgs 4:32). (4) Jesus meets the grieving widow at the "gate of the city" (Luke 7:12), as Elijah had met the widow (1 Kgs 17:10). (5) Both passages describe the speaking

31. Because he fails to take into account the hermeneutics at work in the pericope, Evans (*Saint Luke,* 267) thinks that the Old Testament precedents of Elijah and Elisha "hardly apply." He could not be more mistaken.

32. H. Conzelmann, *The Theology of St. Luke* (New York: Harper & Row, 1960) 31–37, and many commentators since.

33. S. T. Lachs (*A Rabbinic Commentary on the New Testament: The Gospels of Matthew, Mark and Luke* [New York: Ktav, 1987] 207–8) notes that modern Nain is an Arab village called Nein.

or crying out of the resuscitated son (Luke 7:15; 1 Kgs 17:22). (6) The clause, "He gave him to his mother" (Luke 7:15), follows 1 Kgs 17:23 verbatim. (7) Although the exclamation of the astonished crowd in Nain (Luke 7:16, "A great prophet has arisen among us") approximates the widow's exclamation (1 Kgs 17:24, "Behold, I know that you are a man of God"), it may not be a true parallel. The Targum's paraphrase of the exclamation in 1 Kgs 17:24, however, provides a very close parallel, "You are the prophet of the Lord."[34]

But does this Elijah/Elisha tradition utilized by the evangelist contribute anything meaningful to the theme of election? Yes, it does, if we recall that the prosperous and apparent righteous were regarded as blessed of God and the poor, the unfortunate, and apparent unrighteous were regarded as under God's judgment (cf. John 9:2). Jesus' compassion for and teaching about the poor, the defenseless (such as widows and orphans), the ostracized (such as tax collectors, "sinners," and Samaritans) are characteristic of the central section (see 10:29-37; 14:12-14, 15-24; 15:1-7, 8-10, 11-24; 16:19-31; 17:11-19; 18:9-14). In the pericope under consideration, the only son of a widow who is raised up by Jesus exemplifies the poor or defenseless receiving God's blessing.[35] This understanding receives added support in the subsequent pericope (7:18-23) where Jesus tells the Baptist's messengers " . . . The dead are raised up, the poor have good news preached to them" (v. 22), an unmistakable reference to Isa 61:1-2, which Jesus had read at the beginning of the Nazareth sermon. The inclusion of the clause "The dead are raised up" provides a close link between the miracle at Nain and the programmatic Nazareth sermon and so lends further support to the conclusion that election issues are present in this pericope as well.

Brodie furthermore sees Elijah tradition underlying the healing of the centurion's slave (Luke 7:1-10//1 Kgs 17:8-16) which would provide yet another example of a disenfranchised person (in this case the centurion) receiving God's blessing.[36] If Brodie is correct, and I think that he is, then the presence of additional Elijah/Elisha tradition in the immediate context would further support the contention of this chapter.

---

34. For more details see Brodie, *Luke the Literary Interpreter*, 134–53. Fitzmyer (*Luke I–IX*, 656) thinks that the reference to Jesus as a "great prophet" casts him in the role of *Elias redivivus*. Unlike Elijah, who had to stretch himself out on the child, Jesus needs only to speak the word.

35. Brodie (*Luke the Literary Interpreter*, 147) makes the important observation that the idea of God's vengefulness (cf. 1 Kgs 17:18) is carefully avoided by the evangelist (cf. Luke 4:18-19 [where Isa 61:2's "day of vengeance of our God" is omitted]; 7:6-7). The same avoidance is seen in Luke 9:54 as well (see Chap. 5 below).

36. Brodie, *Luke the Literary Interpreter*, 134–52. The possible parallel between Elisha's mercy on the Syrian captain (2 Kgs 5:1-14) and Jesus' mercy on the Roman centurion should also be considered.

Luke 9:52-55. When the Samaritans refuse to receive Jesus, whose destination is Jerusalem, the disciples ask their Lord (either realistically or rhetorically) if they should call fire down from heaven in order to destroy the Samaritans. Even without the textually uncertain clause, "As Elijah did," the allusion to 2 Kgs 1:9-16 is evident.[37] According to the story in 2 Kings, the dying Ahaziah, king of Samaria, sent messengers to inquire of Baalzebub, the god of Ekron, whether or not he would recover. Elijah met these messengers and sent them back to the king with the prophetic word that because he had inquired of a false god, he will die. The king then sent captains and companies of fifty who were destroyed by fire from heaven. Not until the third captain fell on his knees and showed the respect for Elijah as a "man of God" was judgment held back. This is the story to which Luke 9:52-56 alludes. When the "messengers" of Jesus are rebuffed by Samaritans, the disciples believe that they deserve the same fate that had overtaken their ancestors.

The pericope may parallel Luke 4:16-30; the former tells of Jesus' rejection at the outset of his Galilean ministry and the latter of Jesus' rejection at the outset of his journey to Jerusalem.[38] On the other hand, an ethnic parallel may be intended between the rejection by Jews at Nazareth (4:16-30), by Gentiles at Gerasa (8:37), and now by Samaritans in Samaria (9:52-55).[39] These interpretations are not necessarily mutually exclusive.

To first-century Jews, especially those favorably disposed to Christianity, the disciples' request would not seem wholly unwarranted. The Samaritans would have been viewed as deserving of judgment on at least two counts: (1) They had rejected Jesus, who as a prophet was on his way to Jerusalem. Such a rejection would probably have been interpreted as a rejection of Jerusalem and Judaism. (2) They were Samaritans, hated and despised by Jews for generations.[40] The anti-Samaritan sentiment among

---

37. No doubt because of the close verbal parallels with 2 Kgs 1:10 and 12, early scribes readily sensed the reference (A C D and numerous other MSS include the clause). J. M. Ross ("The Rejected Words in Luke 9:54-56," *ExpTim* 84 [1972–73] 85–88) has argued that the clause is original. There may also be an allusion to the contest on Mount Carmel in 1 Kgs 18:36-38, and compare the account of the destruction of Sodom and Gomorrah in Gen 19:24.

38. Evans, *Saint Luke*, 436.

39. E. E. Ellis, *The Gospel of Luke* (NCB; London: Oliphants, rev. ed. 1974) 151.

40. According to 2 Kgs 17:24-34 the people of Samaria were Gentiles, not Israelites, brought into the land from Cuthah (hence they are frequently called "Kutim" or "Cutheans"). The Samaritan claim of pure lineage was never accepted (*m. Qidd.* 4:3; *Gen. Rab.* 94.7 [on 46:8-13]). Samaritan acceptance of the law of Moses was regarded by Jews as insincere (*b. Qidd.* 75b; *b. B. Qam.* 38b) and imperfect (*m. Nid.* 4:1; 7:4; *m. Sheb.* 8:10; *Sipre Deut.* §56 [on 11:30]). Samaritans were accused of idolatry (*Gen. Rab.* 81.3 [on 35:4]; *y. Abod. Zar.* 2:1; 5:4), were regarded as fools (Sir 50:25-26; *T. Levi* 7:2), and were killed, it was believed with divine approval (*Jub.* 30:5–6, 23). Some rabbis believed that the Samaritans, excluded from the resurrection, would be burned up like cloth (*y. Kil.* 9:4).

In an earlier version of this study, I cited Ellis, (*Luke*, 151), who had in turn cited W. O. E.

first-century Jews is well known.[41] The most relevant point, however, is that in the passage in 2 Kings, to which the request of the disciples makes allusion, those upon whom fire fell were from Samaria. Thus, the correlation would have been readily perceived, adding scriptural justification to anti-Samaritan sentiment. In Jewish minds if any group was not elect but deserving of God's judgment, it was the Samaritan people. Utterly contrary to such expectation, Jesus rebuked his disciples and refused to permit such judgment. His attitude of clemency and mercy, coming where it does (i.e., in the central section itself, in which the theme of election is prominent—see 10:30-37 where the true neighbor proves to be a Samaritan, and 17:11-19 where only a Samaritan returns to give thanks) is yet one more prophetic challenge to assumptions about election theology.

Luke 9:61-62. This text represents a third encounter between Jesus and a person interested in following him. The first two encounters (see 9:57-60) occur in Matthew (8:19-22) and not in Mark and so presumably derive from Q. Because the third encounter is unique to Luke and has several verbal parallels with 1 Kgs 19:19-21, we may assume that once again the vocabulary and imagery of the LXX were exploited by the evangelist Luke for his own purposes.[42] The three calls concern what Jesus required of those who wish to take an active part in advancing the kingdom of God. Whereas in the pericopes discussed above Luke seems to correct false views of who are elect and why, in this pericope the evangelist positively sets forth what Jesus requires for participation. The third call, which echoes Elijah's call of Elisha, suggests that Jesus' demands are, as I. Howard Mar-

---

Oesterley (*The Gospel Parables in the Light of Their Jewish Background* [New York: Macmillan, 1936] 162), who years ago had claimed that the Samaritans were regularly cursed in the synagogue and that Jews offered up a prayer that no Samaritan enter paradise. E. Linneman (*Parables of Jesus: Introduction and Exposition* [London: SPCK, 1966] 54) made the same claim: "[The Jews] cursed the Samaritans publicly in the synagogues, and prayed God that they should have no share in eternal life." In a note (139, n. 8) she cites C. A. Bugge (*Die Haupt-Parabeln Jesu* [Giessen: Töpelmann, 1903] 395) who years earlier had stated essentially the same thing ("Der Samariter . . . der in den Synagogen öffentlich verflucht wurde; die Juden baten God, die Samariter möchten am ewigen Leben keinen Teil erhalten"). I have not, however, found primary documentation for this claim and suspect that it arose from the twelfth benediction of the *Amidah*, which in part reads, "Let the Nazarenes [Christians] and the Minim [heretics] be destroyed in a moment, and let them be blotted out of the Book of Life and not be inscribed together with the righteous." Samaritans were possibly understood to be included among the Minim. According to Justin Martyr (*Dialogue with Trypho* §95) Christians were cursed in the synagogue.

41. Josephus gives several illustrations of Jewish-Samaritan hatred and violence (e.g., *Ant.* 18.2.2 §30 [Samaritans reportedly scatter bones in Jewish temple]; 20.6.1–2 §118–130 [Samaritans attack and kill Jewish pilgrims; Jews retaliate]).

42. See Brodie, *Luke the Literary Interpreter*, 216-26; Evans, *Saint Luke*, 441, "It is plainly modelled on Elijah's summons of Elisha." With respect to the wider theological contexts of Luke and 1 Kings, Brodie points out several suggestive parallels.

shall has recently put it, "more stringent than those of Elijah."[43] Elijah permitted Elisha to return to his parents and to burn his plow, but Jesus does not permit one who would follow him to put a hand to the plow and then look back. This episode may anticipate the rejection of the self-righteous Pharisees (16:15; 18:9-14), the rich man (17:19-31), and the rich young ruler (18:18-30), persons whose fortune and apparent piety supposedly testified to God's blessing.

ASSESSMENT OF THE
ELIJAH/ELISHA TRADITION IN LUKE

In the four pericopes discussed above, the Lukan evangelist apparently shaped tradition to bring out parallels between Jesus and the prophets Elijah and Elisha. But there is also evidence that the evangelist Luke attempted to connect the Elijah/Elisha tradition with the Moses tradition (particularly that of Deuteronomy) underlying the central section. The opening verse of the section (9:51) contains the curious New Testament and the LXX hapax *analēmpsis* ("ascension" or "assumption"),[44] probably intended to echo the ascension traditions of both Elijah[45] and Moses.[46]

---

43. I. H. Marshall, *Commentary on Luke* (NIGTC; Exeter: Paternoster, 1978) 412; see also Fitzmyer, *Luke I–IX*, 834.

44. G. Lohfink (*Die Himmelfahrt Jesu: Untersuchungen zu den Himmelfahrts- und Erhöhungstexten bei Lukas* [SANT 26; Munich: Kösel, 1971] 212–17) argued that Luke 9:51 has both the death and ascension of Jesus in view. This is probably correct, since the evangelist earlier writes of Jesus discussing his *exodus* (see Luke 9:31). This "departure" surely entails death and ascension. Note also that the language of Luke 9:51 (*analēmpsis/poreuomai*) reappears in the description of Jesus' ascension in Acts 1:11 (*analambanein/poreuomai*).

45. Elijah's departure in the fiery chariot (2 Kgs 2:11) is of course the foundation of subsequent traditions about Elijah's ascension (1 Macc 2:58; Sir 48:9; *1 Enoch* 89:52; 93:8; Josephus, *Ant.* 9.2.2 §28, where Elijah's "disappearance" [*aphanizesthai*] is compared to that of Enoch's; *Apoc. Ezra* 7:6; *Sib. Or.* 2.187–89, where Elijah will return to earth in a chariot). For more on Elijah ascension tradition see Lohfink, *Die Himmelfahrt Jesu*, 57–59; J. Jeremias, "*El(e)ias*," *TDNT* 2.928–41.

46. Traditions about Moses' ascension begin with the mystery surrounding his death and burial, "So Moses the servant of the Lord died there . . . but no man knows the place of his burial to this day" (Deut 34:5–6). The idea of Moses' ascension might lie behind the *Assumption of Moses*, esp. in 10:12, "Keep these words and this book, Joshua of Nun, for from my death and burial [or ascension] until his coming there shall be 250 times." According to Pseudo-Philo, when Moses "was dying God established for him a platform and showed him then what we now have as witnesses, saying, 'Let there be as a witness between me and you and my people the heaven that you are to enter and the earth on which you walk until now' " (*Bib. Ant.* 32:9); trans. D. J. Harrington, "Pseudo-Philo," in J. H. Charlesworth, ed., *The Old Testament Pseudepigrapha* (vol. 2; Garden City: Doubleday, 1985) 346. Josephus is apparently aware of beliefs that at death Moses had been taken up to heaven, although he himself rejects the notion. Nevertheless, his description contributes to the mysteriousness of Moses' death, "While [Moses] bade farewell to Eleazar and Joshua and was yet communicating with them, a cloud of a sudden descended upon him and he disappeared [*aphanizesthai*]" (*Ant.* 4.8.48 §326); trans. H. St. J. Thackeray, *Josephus* (LCL 4; Cambridge: Harvard University

The evangelist probably combined traditions of the two great prophets of the past, both of whom were associated with the awaited eschatological drama (for Elijah, see Mal 4:5-6; for Moses, see Deut 18:15-19).[47] In his version of the transfiguration scene (9:28-36), Luke seems to have shifted

---

Press, 1961) 633. Note that Josephus also uses *aphanizesthai* in his description of the disappearance of Elijah (*Ant.* 9.2.2 §28, see n. 45 above). Thackeray (632–33, n. b) notes that Josephus's description of Moses' disappearance is reminiscent of legends of the assumptions of Aeneas and Romulus (see Dionysius of Halicarnassus, *Ant. Rom.* 1.64.4; 2.56.2). Josephus's description is somewhat similar to Luke's in Acts 1:9 where "a cloud took [Jesus] out of sight." Elsewhere Josephus says that when Moses delayed on the mountain (Exod 32:1) some of the people thought that he had been taken back to the deity (*Ant.* 3.5.7 §96). According to Philo (*Life of Moses* 2.51 §288, 291), the death of Moses was a journey to heaven in spirit. These speculations make it clear that at least some Jews in the first century believed that Moses had ascended to heaven, either on Sinai or at death. In fact, Moses' reception of the Law at Sinai is often portrayed as a heavenly ascent (*Frag. Tg.* and *Neof.* Deut 30:12; *Pesiq. R.* 20:4; according to Pseudo-Philo [*Bib. Ant.* 15:6] God said, in reference to Sinai, "I bent the heavens and descended").

In later writings the ascension of Moses is accepted. According to Clement of Alexandria (*Strom.* 6.15.132), Joshua saw Moses ascend with the angels. In what may be a reference to a portion of the *Assumption of Moses* no longer extant, Origen (*Hom. Josh.* 2:1) says that Moses was alive in the spirit but dead in the body. According to Jerome (*Hom. Amos* 9:6), "The Lord ascended in a cloud with Enoch, ascended with Elijah, ascended with Moses." *Acts of Pilate* 16:7 compares Moses with Enoch (who was widely thought of as assumed), "No one saw the death of Enoch or the death of Moses." Finally, according to *Sipre Deut.* §357 (on 34:5), some say that "Moses never died, and he stands and serves on high"; trans. R. Hammer, *Sifre: A Tannaitic Commentary on the Book of Deuteronomy* (Yale Judaica 24; New Haven: Yale University Press, 1986) 381; and *Midr. ha-Gadol* on Deuteronomy, "Three went up alive into heaven: Enoch, Moses, and Elijah"; trans. J. Jeremias, "*Moyses*," *TDNT* 4.855. For more on Moses ascension tradition see R. H. Charles, *APOT*, 2.422, esp. n. 12; Jeremias, "*Moyses*," 854–55, nn. 92–100; Lohfink, *Die Himmelfahrt Jesu*, 61–69; and Fitzmyer, *Luke I–IX*, 828. The evidence seems to indicate the belief that although Moses physically died and was buried, his soul was taken up into heaven. This idea is found in reference to other Old Testament worthies (*T. Abrah.* 14:6–7; *T. Job* 52:8–12; *T. Isaac* 7:1).

47. Elijah and Moses are together on the mount of transfiguration (Mark 9:2-8 par.). The two witnesses of Rev 11:3-12 could very well be Elijah and Moses (on Elijah cf. vv. 5-6 with 2 Kgs 1:10; on Moses cf. v. 6 with Exod 7:17, 19). (However, Elijah is sometimes paired with Enoch; see 4 Ezra 6:26; *Apoc. Elijah* 4:7–19; the latter seems dependent on Revelation 11). According to one midrash, God promises in the time to come to bring Moses with Elijah, "Moses, I swear to you, as you devoted your life to their service in this world, so too in the time to come when I bring Elijah the prophet to them, the two of you shall come together" (*Deut. Rab.* 3.17 [on 10:1]; cf. *b. Sota* 13b); trans. based on J. Rabbinowitz, *Midrash Rabbah: Deuteronomy* (London and New York: Soncino, 1983) 88. The rabbis compared Moses and Elijah at many points: "You find that two prophets rose up for Israel out of the tribe of Levi; one the first of all the prophets, and the other the last of all the prophets: Moses first and Elijah last, and both with a commission to redeem Israel. . . . You find that Moses and Elijah were alike in every respect. . . . Moses went up to heaven [Exod 19:3 is cited]; and Elijah went up to heaven [2 Kgs 2:1 is cited]. . . . Moses: 'And the cloud covered him six days' [Exod 24:16]; and Elijah went up in a whirlwind [2 Kgs 2:1 is cited]" (*Pesiq. R.* 4:2); trans. based on W. G. Braude, *Pesikta Rabbati* (2 vols.; Yale Judaica 18; New Haven: Yale University Press, 1968) 2.84–85.

The account of Jesus' ascension (Acts 1:2-11) is possibly related to both the Elijah and Moses ascension traditions. Just before the risen Christ ascends, his apostles ask, "Lord, will you at this time restore [*apokathistenai*] the kingdom to Israel?" This question probably echoes Elijah tradition (see Mal 4:5-6, where Elijah will "restore [*apokathistenai*] the heart of

the emphasis away from Elijah (whose name occurs first in Mark 9:4) to Moses.[48] Not only does the name of Moses first occur now (v. 30), but the heavenly figures discuss with Jesus his impending "exodus" (v. 31), which not only alludes to his departure but recalls the great event of salvation in biblical history.[49] In Jesus a new exodus is in preparation, and like the former one, salvation will result for the people of God. The command of the heavenly voice to "listen to him" (v. 35) probably echoes Deut 18:15 and strengthens the link to the Moses tradition.[50] The Lukan redaction of the transfiguration with its emphasis on Moses and the opening paragraphs of the central section (i.e., 9:51-62 and 10:1-20), with their significant Elijah tradition and probable allusion to Moses (seen in the reference to "assumption" in 9:51 and in the parallels between 10:1-3 and Deuteronomy 1:9-15, a passage that alludes to the appointment of the "seventy" in Exod 24:1; Num 11:16-25), provide evidence of the evangelist's attempt to weld together traditions of the two great prophets and to apply them to Jesus. Such redaction and composition on Luke's part provide a smooth transition into material (i.e., the central section) that has little to do with the Elijah/Elisha narratives, as Brodie himself readily acknowledges.

In conclusion, in those passages in Luke where the Elijah/Elisha references and allusions are clearest, the theme of election or ecclesiology is present if not paramount. Common to all four pericopes examined here is the question of requirements for membership and participation in the kingdom of God. These passages apparently emphasize that those assumed to be non-elect (Gentiles, Samaritans, the poor) may in fact be included in the kingdom and even serve as examples for others to follow, while those who assume their fitness for the kingdom (such as the pious and wealthy who say, "I will follow you") may actually be excluded. This theme parallels the ethic of election developed in the central section. The evangelist draws upon the LXX accounts of Elijah and Elisha as well as the

---

the father to the son"; and Mark 9:12, where Elijah is to "restore [*apokatastasis*] all things"); see M. D. Goulder, *Type and History in Acts* (London: SPCK, 1964) 148. According to Acts 1:2 Jesus "was taken up" (*analēmphthē*), the same expression used of Elijah when taken up by the chariot (2 Kgs 2:9; the cognate *analēmpsis* appears in Luke 9:51). When Moses ascended the mountain and entered the cloud, he was with God for "forty days" (Exod 24:15-18). Similarly, after forty days Jesus is taken up into a cloud (Acts 1:3, 9). If Luke 9:51 alludes to these ascension traditions, the passage undoubtedly anticipates Jesus' ascension which the evangelist later recounts (Acts 1:2, 9-11, 22; perhaps Luke 24:51).

48. Too much should not be made of this alteration in itself, for in Mark it reads, "Elijah with Moses appeared," while in Luke it reads, "Moses and Elijah . . . talked with him," thus suggesting perhaps no more than equality in the Lukan version.

49. Marshall, *Luke*, 380, 384–85; Fitzmyer, *Luke I–IX*, 794.

50. Fitzmyer, *Luke I–IX*, 803. For a much fuller discussion see Moessner's studies in nn. 11 and 12 above.

LXX Deuteronomy; both the LXX sources have been internalized. Brodie and others who see in Luke a reworking and adaptation of the Elijah/Elisha narratives should not therefore overlook the similar and closely related utilization of Deuteronomy. Luke does not borrow slavishly but freely modifies and adapts the LXX in creative ways. (For example, in Luke 7:11-17 Jesus does what Elijah did, but in 9:54 he does not.) In light of contemporary assumptions, Luke has redefined the grounds of election, and herein I believe lies the evangelist's chief contribution to New Testament theology.[51]

This exegesis is introductory; the question of exactly how Jesus and John are meant to relate to Elijah and Elisha in Luke is a difficult and complex issue.[52] My intent is to show that both Deuteronomy and Kings provided the evangelist Luke with some of the raw materials from which he was able to clarify certain aspects of his own distinctive views about the requirements for participation in the kingdom of God. By appealing to Israel's sacred tradition, the Lukan evangelist demonstrates that in Jesus' ministry the biblical story is continued and fulfilled.

---

51. For a comprehensive treatment of New Testament "redefinition" see J. K. Riches, *Jesus and the Transformation of Judaism* (London: Darton, Longman & Todd, 1980).

52. For a brief but concise assessment of the relationship of Elijah to John and Jesus, see Fitzmyer, *Luke I–IX*, 213–15 (which is preferable to that offered by H. Conzelmann, *The Theology of St. Luke* [New York: Harper & Row, 1961] 18–27). See also I. H. Marshall, *Luke: Historian and Theologian* (Exeter: Paternoster, 1970) 145–47; F. W. Danker, *Luke* (Philadelphia: Fortress, 1976) 29–31.

6

SINS, DEBTS, AND JUBILEE RELEASE

JAMES A. SANDERS

It has long been recognized that the Lukan account of the uninvited woman who shows extravagant love and devotion to Jesus, in Luke 7:36-50, is considerably different from the accounts of a similar episode related in Mark 14:3-9, Matt 26:6-13, and John 12:1-8.[1] Gospel synopses usually offer two titles for the same accounts, "The Anointing at Bethany" when the synopsis follows the other three accounts, but "The Woman Who Was a Sinner" or "The Woman with the Ointment" when the synopsis focuses on Luke.[2] Raymond Brown seems to lean, with Pierre Benoit, toward there having been two historical but similar episodes lying behind the differences.[3] Joseph Fitzmyer thinks of one tradition taking various forms in an early oral stage, a point Brown also allows.[4]

A third option needs to be kept open; Luke might possibly reflect primary contours of the episode that was interpreted by the others in terms of the beginnings of the passion account.[5] At least two points in

---

1. See R.E. Brown's very helpful summary comparison of the four accounts in *The Gospel according to John I–XII* (AB 29; Garden City: Doubleday, 1966) 450–52. See also J.A. Fitzmyer's comparative comments in *The Gospel according to Luke I–IX* (AB 28; Garden City: Doubleday, 1981) 684–86, and C. S. Mann's *Mark* (AB 27; Garden City: Doubleday, 1986) 555.

2. See K. Aland's *Synopsis Quattuor Evangeliorum* (Stuttgart: Württemburgische Bibelanstalt, 1964) 160–63, 361–63, 426–28, and A. Huck and H. Greeven, *Synopsis of the First Three Gospels* (Tübingen: Mohr [Siebeck], 1981) 79–80, 232–34.

3. A. Legault, "An Application of the Form-Critique Method to the Anointings in Galilee and Bethany," *CBQ* 16 (1954) 131–45.

4. Brown, *John*, 450–51; see Fitzmyer, *Luke I–IX*, 686.

5. R. Holst has argued that more rigorous form-critical method shows that Luke reflects the most primitive version; see "The One Anointing of Jesus: Another Application of the Form-Critical Method," *JBL* 95 (1976) 443, 446.

favor of this possibility are (1) slippage from anointing of the feet to anointing of the head is easier to explain than the reverse;[6] and (2) the abuse of the paraphrase of Deut 15:11 in Mark, Matthew, and John. The manner in which the latter is used to support the woman's anointing of Jesus (head in Mark and Matthew, feet in John) is totally divorced from its function in understanding the jubilee theme and does nothing to advance the Markan point about Jesus' acceptance of his anointing by the woman in preparation for his passion; by contrast, the theme of jubilee release of debts/sins is integral to the Lukan account, which lacks the paraphrase.

If Luke knew Mark or the others, he does not let knowledge of Mark's totally different points affect the power of meaning of jubilee for Jesus' ministry and teaching.[7] It is of course possible that Luke knew an early account similar to Mark's, and was encouraged by the paraphrase of Deut 15:11 to pursue his jubilee interpretation of events reported and transmitted about Jesus, giving this episode its distinctive jubilee cast and thus taking it completely out of the passion context of anointing. The two objections noted above are strong enough, however, to cause one to think rather that the traditioning movement was from a spontaneous act of adoration, cleansing Jesus' feet with tears and anointing them with oil, toward anointing his head with valuable oil made of pure nard in anticipation of his passion, with the jubilee cast of the whole reduced, in misunderstanding, to Jesus' patently proof-text defense of the woman's act by paraphrase of Deut 15:11.

Comparison of the four accounts shows that in Luke the woman's extravagance is expressed not in terms of the market value of the ointment but in terms of her spontaneous actions. In Luke there is no indignation shown on the part of others toward the woman's extravagance but rather toward Jesus' acceptance of her devotion.

Jesus' act of acceptance causes his host to question his authority as a prophet, a point Luke has carefully established by crowd and audience reactions to his teachings and miracles (4:32, 36, 37, 41, 44; 5:1, 15, 25, 26; 7:3, 6, 16, 17; cf. 8:1, 4, 34, 35, 39-40, 42; 9:43).[8] Jesus' quotation of the proverb, "No prophet is acceptable in his own country," in the Nazareth sermon (4:24), however, anticipates the negative reactions to this point by Pharisees and other leaders (4:28-29; 5:21-22; 6:7-8). As in our story the doubts harbored by scribes and Pharisees, in contrast to the Nazareth

---

6. See Holst, "One Anointing," 435–46; Brown supports the point (*John*, 451).

7. See Chap. 4 above (54–69). See also S. H. Ringe, *Jesus, Liberation, and the Biblical Jubilee* (Philadelphia: Fortress, 1985).

8. See R.C. Tannehill's insightful literary-redactional analysis of Jesus' quite different relations in the Lukan narrative to the oppressed, the crowds, the authorities, and the disciples, *The Narrative Unity of Luke-Acts.* I. *The Gospel according to Luke* (Philadelphia: Fortress, 1986) 101–274.

congregation, have not yet been voiced; they are perceived by Jesus, however (5:22; 6:8; 7:39, 49), thus underscoring for the reader/hearer Jesus'
prophetic power and authority.[9] The question of the Baptist concerning
Jesus' identity (7:20) contrasts with the certainty of the demons' knowledge of Jesus' identity (4:34, 41) and contributes to the atmosphere of
doubt created by the silent questioning of the leaders.

The narrational ploy of interjecting the leaders' doubts into the unfolding story of Jesus' perceived popularity permits Luke to underscore for
the hearer/reader Jesus' prophetic powers of knowing their unexpressed
thoughts; it is intensified in our story by the host's doubts about Jesus'
knowledge of the identity of the woman, when it is the host who doubts
Jesus' identity. Indeed, Jesus shows no interest in convincing Simon of his
own identity, in contrast to his later concern about the lack of faith by the
questioning disciples (8:25). If he did so, he might simply have to admon-
ish Simon not to tell, in the same manner in which he had rebuked the
demons; and that would not advance the flow of the narrative at all. In
fact, the host is probably to be understood as included in "those seated
together," in 7:49, who do not move from doubt to belief, but rather from
doubt to offense taken at Jesus' expression of authority to forgive the
woman's sins. This beautifully anticipates the very same move on the part
of the leaders generally as one moves through the central section into the
passion account.[10]

A marked difference between Luke's account of this episode and that
of the other evangelists is the abuse of Deut 15:11 in the latter and its total
absence in Luke; in its place is a parable about what a truly charitable
creditor might do when the Jubilee Year came around. The narrative of
the episode of the uninvited woman, as Luke recounts it, hinges on the
story within the story (7:40-43). The remarkable thing that the creditor
did is not even mentioned in the story. Verse 42 might have read at some
early point in the traditioning process, "Since they could not repay, the
creditor, instead of seeking a prosbul, graciously remitted both (debts)." It
is easily understood that, as the traditioning of the story moved into more
distinctly gentile settings, the technical detail of Jewish halakah would
easily be omitted since it would probably raise unnecessary legal questions

---

9. A point also stressed by D. A. S. Ravens in "The Setting of Luke's Account of the
Anointing: Luke 7.2—8.3," *NTS* 34 (1988) 282–92. I agree with Ravens that our story is well
placed in the flow of the Lukan narrative, but for more reasons than he offers; he is certainly
right however that part of Luke's thesis in this crucial section of the Gospel before the
journey to Jerusalem begins is that Jesus was the prophet expected and promised in Deut
18:15, 18. This latter point is stressed convincingly by D. Moessner, *The Lord of the Banquet*
(Minneapolis: Fortress, 1989) 45–79, 259–88.

10. One of the marks of Luke's literary style is that of "anticipation"; see Fitzmyer, *Luke I–
IX*, 207, 445, 518, 538, 632, passim.

and detract from the point understood in any cultural setting, the creditor's release of the debts. In the same process, reference to Deut 15:11 would possibly be dropped since its appearance in Mark, and perhaps his sources, was seen as impertinent and abusive of the jubilee legislation, and since the statement that the two debtors did not have the money to repay made the point about the presence of poor people in a pertinent way.

The verb used twice in the inner story is *echarisato* from *charizomai* meaning "freely remit or graciously grant." Luke had just used the verb (Matt 11:2-6) in 7:21 in narrative preparation of Jesus' response to the question of the Baptist about Jesus' identity, "and to many blind folk he graciously granted sight." Here Luke's Jesus says that the creditor "graciously granted or remitted to both (debtors)," "their debts" being understood. These are the three times Luke uses the verb in the Gospel. The other evangelists do not use it. He will use it four times in Acts, each time having the basic denotation of "remit" or "grant." In Acts 3:14 he uses it in reference to the remittance or release of Barabbas.

Charizomai does not appear in the LXX except in late texts; it undoubtedly came to be used in the place of the LXX *aphiēmi* which occurs with the noun *aphesis* five times in the jubilee legislation in Deut 15:1-3, and some fourteen times in the jubilee legislation in Leviticus 25. *Aphiēmi* is used in the LXX to translate both **shamaṭ* and its derivatives in Deuteronomy 15, and **darar* and its derivatives in Leviticus 25, the two passages establishing jubilee legislation. Whether it was also used in the early traditioning stages of the story in Luke 7:40-42 is difficult to say; but *charizomai* is a beautiful synonym for *aphiēmi* in these contexts and apparently came to be used for forgiveness of debts as well as sins.[11] Luke uses *aphiēmi* and derivatives four times in our passage but only in vv. 47-49 in terms relating to the forgiveness of sins—its most common usage in the New Testament.

Paraphrase of Scripture throughout early Jewish literature was very common, and *charizomai* in 7:40-42 is an appropriate synonym for *apiēmi* in vv. 47-49, which in the New Testament most often pertains to remission, release, or forgiveness of sins. The importance of jubilee themes to Luke's view of Jesus' mission and ministry was already signaled by Jesus' mixed citation of both Isa 61:1 and 58:6 in Luke 4:18.[12]

The legislation in Deuteronomy 15 includes exhortations to creditors to be generous toward fellow Israelites even and especially when the Jubilee Year approaches. While in 15:3-4 there is a promise that faithful remission of debts in the Jubilee Year would bring such divine blessings that there would be "no poor among you," considerably more space is given to

---

11. See Josephus, *Ant.* 6.7.4 §144, and the helpful note by Fitzmyer, *Luke I–IX*, 690.
12. See Chap. 4 above (62).

the exhortation not to be mean to a poor brother when the Jubilee Year draws near (Deut 15:7-11). Within the parenesis is the statement that there would always be the poor in the land (v. 11); this is in contrast to the promise in v. 4 that faithful obedience to the jubilee legislation about remission of debts would bring divine blessing "in the land which the Lord your God gives you by inheritance." Leviticus 25 includes considerably more exhortation than Deuteronomy concerning generosity to the poor and obedience to the principles and stipulations of the Jubilee.

When Jewish society moved into the more complex Hellenistic situations of an increasingly urban culture, loans became an intricate part of day-to-day commerce and not merely charitable sharing. Hillel is attributed with instigation of the institution of the prosbul (Hebrew *prozbul*, Greek *prosbolē*), a sort of waiver signed before a judge, in which a creditor could reserve the right to call in a loan regardless of the jubilee legislation.[13] Nearly every creditor would take advantage of the provision. Not to do so would have been rare indeed, but it could happen. Our inner story tells of a creditor who was generous and charitable enough to forgive two debts and hence not secure a prosbul.

Luke casts the story of the forgiveness of the sinful woman's many (*pollai*) sins in the light of the jubilee provision for the forgiveness of debts.[14] The woman did not have human creditors; at least we are told of none. On the contrary, she had means enough apparently to bring the myrrh with which she anointed Jesus' feet. Luke does not mention market value of the ointment, but one can imagine how she earned the money to buy it—a point lacking in the other Gospels where the woman's reputation is unmentioned. Possibly one or more of the *synanakeimenoi* about the table would have known.

Be that as it may, Jesus states that she loved *polu*. There has been a great deal of discussion about Jesus' description of the woman's activity. The force of Jesus' question to Simon after he had told the jubilee parable was to affirm that a heavy debtor would love the forgiving creditor more than one who had owed less (vv. 42-43); so Simon answered and so Jesus agreed. Commentators have puzzled, then, over Jesus' statement about how much the woman (had) loved. The exchange with Simon about the debtors would indicate that it was the woman's many "loves" indicated by *polu*; but it surely also refers to the love and devotion she has shown toward Jesus. All three of the verbs for "love" in the story are from *agapaō*, which in Koine Greek had taken on many shades of meaning. It seems to be pur-

---

13. *M. Shebi'it* 10:1–2, 3–4, 8–9.
14. The terms "sin" and "debt" are found in synonymous juxtaposition in 4QMess[ar]; see Fitzmyer, *Luke I–IX*, 223–24.

posefully ambiguous in the received text, however it might have been in the early traditioning process. One aspect of the multivalency might be that "little love" could refer to Simon's attitude or to the attitude of any of Jesus' antagonists in the fuller narrative Luke crafts.[15] Luke more than the other evangelists stresses Jesus' offensive behavior to the "righteous," in contrast to his great popularity and attraction for sinners and outcasts in society, such people as the uninvited woman. He indeed has just contrasted his behavior with that of the Baptist's (7:31-35); the woman in that sense was indeed one of Wisdom's children.[16]

The second suggestion of silent controversy, or offense taken by those at table, comes in v. 49. "And those reclining at table began to say among (to?) themselves, 'Who is this who even forgives (*aphiēsin*) sins?'" In contrast to Jesus' seeming acceptance by the crowds, the religious leaders, the tradents of all the traditions about God's grace, are the ones who must ask: "Who is this that speaks blasphemies? Who can forgive sins but God only?" (5:21). God alone forgives sins, but others are not infrequently commissioned by God to announce divine forgiveness, such as members of the heavenly council (MT Isa 40:2), or priests (LXX Isa 40:2), a herald (Isa 61:1-2), John the Baptist (Luke 3:3), and others.[17] Jesus' pronouncement of forgiveness in 7:48 is simply, "Your sins are forgiven (*apheōntai*)."[18]

The manner in which Jesus is presented as offending leaders elsewhere in the Gospel leads the reader and hearer to understand that Jesus here is viewed as something more than simply herald. The cultural and social history in which the persona of the sender is viewed as incarnate in the one sent is too extensive and well known to document here; this is especially the case where the one sent does not, with socially acceptable signs of humility, make the distinction clear. Luke leaves the whole scene pregnant with multivalency; he could not do otherwise, given the total story he must tell. In the multivalency, then, is room for sympathy for the sensibilities of the fellow guests, "Who is this fellow? He is popular as a teacher and healer. But does he think he is also God's herald?" The answer

---

15. See Fitzmyer, *Luke I–IX*, 692.

16. Moessner, *Lord of the Banquet*, 109.

17. See E. P. Sanders, *Jesus and Judaism* (London: SCM, 1985) 273. Ravens ("Setting"), citing Sanders, mistakenly assumes with LXX Isa 40:6 that 40:2-5 refers to the prophet. The MT of Isa 40:1-11 is a report of a meeting of the heavenly council, including God's commission to its members to pronounce forgiveness and salvation. The LXX re-signified the whole scene to include priests (40:2) and the prophet (40:6) as herald of the good news.

18. Undoubtedly a theological passive, "forgiven" by God. See Fitzmyer's discussion of the frequency of such theocentric expressions in Luke, *Luke I–IX*, 143–258. See also the study of passive forms in the Synoptic Gospels in D. S. Deer, *Les constructions à sens passif dans le grec des évangiles synoptiques* (Strasbourg: Université des sciences humaines de Strasbourg, Faculté de théologie protestante, 1973).

is yes; that role was established already at Nazareth in chapter 4, before the teaching and the healing started.

What Luke wanted to establish for the reader and hearer is that Jesus was indeed the one who was to come (7:20), the herald of the arrival of God's jubilee, God's acceptable year (Isa 61:2a; Luke 4:19) of release of sins. This was not simply a Jubilee Year indicated by the calendar; this was the introduction of God's jubilee, indeed God's kingdom of love, faith, salvation, peace, and forgiveness (7:50). Responsible religious leaders of any society would have to be cautious about and skeptical of those presenting themselves on their own authority (4:21, 32, 36) as heralds of God's jubilee, the long-awaited eschaton. Even modern religious leaders, academic or cleric, must in all honesty appreciate the multivalency of the passage and find some reflection of their own humanity in the thoughts of Simon and his *synanakeimenoi*.

Like the prophets of old, whose role Luke insists Jesus assumed in his day with his people, Jesus went about challenging powerful sinners, the leaders with social and institutional responsibility. But in all the Gospels, and Luke's especially, Jesus is portrayed in addition as going about forgiving powerless sinners like this marked woman. The prophets got into trouble enough with the authorities of their day; but Jesus' added role of herald of the release of all debts to God, pronouncer of the forgiveness of sins and the introduction of a new order, had to be a serious threat to those who had given their lives to being responsible to the established order, even when Jesus included the promises of hope that the new order would bring. Jesus presents a double offense to those who have tried most to be responsible. Like the prophets of old, he forces responsible folk to identify with those in the past whom Nathan, Isaiah, Jeremiah, Ezekiel, Hosea, Amos, and the others had addressed. That was bad enough, but he also makes the same responsible folk face up to what divine grace really means, the strangeness of it, and the threat it harbors to established institutions in society and to familiar modes of piety and practice.[19] The word Luke used to express the cancellation of the two debts in 7:42-43, is based on the same root as the word "grace," *charis*. Their debts were pronounced released, indeed graced out, and forgiven by the creditor. In like manner the sins of the uninvited woman Jesus pronounced released and forgiven by God. God's jubilee had arrived. "Go in (to) peace."[20]

---

19. See my "The Strangeness of the Bible," *USQR* 42 (1988), 33–37.

20. Most manuscripts read *eis eirēnēn* which was idiomatic and common enough; but D reads *en eirēnē*, which brings to mind the possibility that the other prepositional accusative expression bore with it the connotation of entering into peace, God's peace, not just into a momentary clear conscience, that might soon be sullied. Much of Luke's Gospel from this

By putting his version of this beautiful story at this point in his narrative, Luke makes several points crucial to his thesis. Jesus' identity as the herald of the Jubilee, the year acceptable to God (Luke 4:16-30, based on Isa 61:1-2), was already well established by the miracles and healings reported in Luke 4:31—7:17. "This report about him spread throughout Judea and all the surrounding country" (7:17). His identity as the one who was to come was accepted by the people at large, but the religious leaders were disturbed at his attitude toward the law (6:7, 11). Not long before the events recounted in this story, John the Baptist underscored the question of Jesus' identity by sending two disciples to ask Jesus pointedly if he was the one who was to come (7:19-20). Jesus' answer constitutes a review of what Luke reported about Jesus' healings and miracles in the Gospel narrative, a recital of fulfillment of the mission of the Jubilee herald of Isaiah 61, almost point by point (Luke 7:21-22).

In order to leave no doubt whatever in the reader's mind about Jesus' identity as a prophet, Luke reported that Jesus' host, Simon the Pharisee, said to himself that Jesus could not be a prophet because he apparently did not know who, and what sort of woman, was fawning over him. But he also reported that Jesus knew what Simon was thinking. Even if the Baptist and Simon were not sufficiently impressed by Jesus' works to accept his identity, the reader now knows that Jesus' prophetic powers extend to mind reading.

Clearly this is not just another Jubilee Year on the calendar of ancient Judaism. This is God's Jubilee, which Luke, after reporting more miracles and after describing the beginning of Jesus' and the disciples' journey to Jerusalem, identifies with God's kingdom to come. Luke's version of the dominical prayer (11:2-4) has several interesting differences from its counterpart in Matthew's Gospel (Matt 6:9-13), but the major difference is in Luke's phrase, "Forgive us our sins, for we ourselves forgive everyone indebted to us" (Luke 11:4), parallel to Matthew's "Forgive us our debts, as we also have forgiven our debtors" (Matt 6:12). Whereas Matthew reports the petition for forgiveness in purely Jubilee terms, that is, debts and debtors, Luke, through the telling of this beautiful Jubilee story, which parallels forgiveness of debts and forgiveness of the woman's sins, re-signifies debts to God as "sins." He then underscores the re-signification in his version of the dominical prayer, which follows three chapters after the story.

---

point on depends on the reader/hearer clearly understanding that Luke believed that in Christ's coming, God's jubilee or kingdom had been introduced. Because of this, a new hermeneutic had been introduced in Jesus' teaching for rereading and re-signifying familiar Scripture passages and traditions; see Chap. 8 below.

It does not require great imagination to perceive how meaningful this story on its simplest level would have been to Luke's congregation. One question it might have answered was whether there was anyone when Jesus was alive who loved him the way they obviously love him. To remain in the Way, and not to revert to Mithraism, the imperial cult, or even Judaism, particularly after the fall of Jerusalem in 70 C.E., the apparent failure of the parousia, and the increasing persecution and rejection on all sides, meant that the little Christian remnant of Luke's day must indeed have experienced a depth of faith that was undeniable and irrepressible. They would have many questions for a teacher like Luke. And some of those questions would surely have been something like the following. "Teacher, was there anyone back then who loved him the way we would like to? Do you know of anyone who expressed directly to him what we ourselves feel? Was it one of the disciples? Was it a religious leader of the time?" No, Luke would have had to respond, none of those. But there was one, also rejected and misunderstood in normal society, who loved him quite extravagantly because she had found in him true release and forgiveness.

— 7 —

"HE SET HIS FACE": ON THE MEANING OF LUKE 9:51

CRAIG A. EVANS

LUKE 9:51-56: A PRE-LUKAN CONTEXT?

Luke 9:51-61, a passage wholly unique to the Gospel of Luke, serves as the introduction to Luke's so-called travel narrative or central section (9:51—18:14). The passage presents interpreters with many problems, not the least of which is its curious blend of Hebraic and septuagintal style. My translation attempts to capture the Semitic flavor:

> [51] And it came to pass that when the days of his assumption were completed, he set his face to go to Jerusalem, [52] and he sent messengers before his face. And going they entered a village of Samaritans, to prepare for him. [53] But they did not receive him, because his face was going to Jerusalem. [54] And seeing this his disciples James and John said, "Lord, do you wish that we call fire to come down from heaven and consume them?" [55] But turning he rebuked them. [56] And they went to another village.

This concentration of Hebraisms and septuagintalisms gives the passage a distinct scriptural cast[1] and comports with H. F. D. Sparks's general conclusion that the evangelist Luke "deliberately copied the LXX language

---

This chapter is a revision of my studies, " 'He Set His Face': A Note on Luke 9, 51," *Bib* 63 (1982) 545–48; idem, " 'He Set His Face': Luke 9, 51 Once Again," *Bib* 68 (1987) 80–84.

---

1. D. L. Tiede, *Prophecy and History in Luke-Acts* (Philadelphia: Fortress, 1980) 55–63; idem, *Luke* (Augsburg Commentary on the New Testament; Minneapolis: Augsburg, 1988) 196–97; E. Schweizer, *The Good News according to Luke* (Atlanta: John Knox, 1984) 168; C. F. Evans, *Saint Luke* (TPI New Testament Commentaries; London: SCM; Philadelphia: Trinity, 1990) 435.

and consciously wrote in what he would call 'Biblical' style."[2] Luke 9:51-56 is a prime example of this procedure. Indeed, virtually all the essential syntactical components reflect Hebrew idiom and/or the Septuagint:[3]

"And it came to pass [*egeneto de*]." *Egeneto de* translates the Hebrew *wayyehi*, which the LXX often translates as *kai egeneto*. This construction occurs very frequently in Luke-Acts.

"when the days of his assumption were completed [*en tō symplerousthai tas hēmeras tēs analēmpseōs autou*]." The temporal *en tō* with infinitive clause is common in Luke (1:8, 21; 2:6, 43; 5:1, 12; Acts 2:1, "When the day of Pentecost had come [*en tō symplērousthai tēn hēmeran*]") and in the LXX (Gen 25:24; Lev 8:33; Jer 25:12, "When seventy years are completed [*en tō plerōthenai*]") and often accompanies *egeneto de* (or *kai egeneto*). Luke 3:21 offers an exact parallel. "And it came to pass [*egeneto de*] when all the people had been baptized [*en tō baptisthenai hapanta ton laon*]" (cf. Luke 6:1, 6, 12; 16:22). *Analēmpsis* is an unusual word that will be considered below.

"and/that he [*kai autos*]." Finite Greek verbs do not need personal pronouns. When pronouns are used, they are usually intensive. Luke's *kai autos* in this context is not intensive but unstressed, which is Hebraic. The idiom occurs approximately two dozen times: e.g., "And he [*kai autos*] will go before him" (1:17); "And he [*kai autos*] was making a sign to them" (1:22). Elsewhere in Luke all three of the aforementioned elements occur together, "And it happened [*egeneto de*], while the crowd was pressing upon [*en tō ton ochlon epikeisthai*] him hearing the word of God and he [*kai autos*] was standing on the shore . . . that he saw two boats" (5:1).

"set his face [*to prosōpon estērisen*]." This clause comes right out of the LXX, often translating *sum panim*, " 'Return to me, O dweller of Israel,' says the Lord, 'and I will not set my face [*ou stēriō to prosōpon mou*] against you' " (LXX Jer 3:12). "Son of man, set your face [*stērison to prosōpon sou*] against the mountains of Israel" (LXX Ezek 6:2). Its meaning will occupy us in the second part of this chapter.

"he sent messengers before his face [*apesteilen aggelous pro prosōpou autou*]." "Before one's face" is a septuagintalism (see LXX Exod 23:20; 33:2; 2 Kgs 6:32). The sending of messengers before his face echoes Mal 3:1,

---

2. H. F. D. Sparks, "The Semitisms of St. Luke's Gospel," *JTS* 44 (1943) 129–38; repr. in S. Jellicoe, ed., *Studies in the Septuagint: Origins, Recensions, and Interpretations* (New York: Ktav, 1974) 497–506, quote from 132 (500). Sparks (134 [502]) avers, "St. Luke himself was not a 'Semitizer,' but an habitual, conscious, and deliberate 'Septuagintalizer.' " See above, 14–25.

3. For a much fuller discussion, see J. A. Fitzmyer, *The Gospel according to Luke I–IX* (AB 28; Garden City: Doubleday, 1981) 114–25, 827–30.

"I send [*exapostellein*] my messenger [*aggelos*] to prepare the way before my face [*pro prosōpou mou*]." The subsequent identification of the messenger as Elijah (Mal 3:23 [ET: 4:5]) suits the Lukan context.

"because his face was going [*hoti to prosōpon autou ēn poreuomenon*]." The clause is another septuagintalism, perhaps based on 2 Sam 17:11, "And your face was going [*to prosōpon sou poreuomenon*] in their midst" (see also Exod 33:14-20). Using *eimi* with a participle instead of a finite verb form could be evidence of an Aramaism (cf. Luke 15:1).

"fire to come down from heaven and consume them [*pyr katabēnai apo tou ouranou kai analōsai autous*]." The disciples' request alludes to the actions of Elijah against the Samaritans. "And fire came down out of heaven and consumed [*katebē pyr ek tou ouranou kai katephagen*] him and his fifty" (LXX 2 Kgs 1:10, 12). Luke's clause does not follow the LXX exactly but may reflect the Hebrew.

Some think that this passage, with its concentration of Semitic elements, possibly derives from L, Luke's special written source.[4] Others have proposed more unusual origins. In the recent festschrift in honor of Bo Reicke, David Flusser argues that Luke 9:51-53 (and possibly also vv. 54-56) "was not invented [by Luke], but [the evangelist] copied it out of a written Vorlage, and at least vv. 51-53 were translated literally from the Hebrew to the Greek."[5] Flusser does not think that Luke himself translated this Hebrew fragment; someone before him did. The question is important, Flusser thinks, because if the fragment is translated back into Hebrew and carefully studied as such and against the history and tradition of Jewish pilgrimages to Jerusalem through hostile Samaria, a clearer understanding of the passage will be at hand. We cannot proceed to the second part of this paper until Flusser's provocative thesis is examined.

Flusser begins by reminding his readers of Josephus's account of the hatred and violence that occasionally broke out between Jews and Samaritans when the former, on their way to religious festivals in Jerusalem, attempted to pass through the territory of the latter (*J.W.* 2.12.3 §232; *Ant.*

---

4. R. Bultmann, *History of the Synoptic Tradition* (Oxford: Blackwell, 1968) 25–26, 385–86; J. M. Creed, *The Gospel according to St. Luke* (London: Macmillan, 1930) 140–41; see also Fitzmyer (*Luke I–IX*, 826), except that he is careful to note that vv. 51 and 56 are Lukan. H. Flender (*St. Luke: Theologian of Redemptive History* [Philadelphia: Fortress, 1967] 33–34) thinks that Luke has utilized an older tradition that portrayed Jesus as Elijah *redivivus*. This view is followed by I. H. Marshall, *Commentary on Luke* (NIGTC; Grand Rapids: Eerdmans, 1978) 404.

5. D. Flusser, "Lukas 9:51-56—Ein hebraisches Fragment," in W. C. Weinrich, ed., *The New Testament Age* (2 vols.; B. Reicke Festschrift; Macon: Mercer University Press, 1984) 1.165–79, quote from 167. He further explains (168–69) that whereas vv. 51-53 were translated literally, vv. 54-56 were either freely translated or restyled by the redactor. Flusser is not clear who this redactor was. Luke?

20.6.1 §118). Next he attempts to explain the meaning of the word
analēmpsis ("assumption" or "ascension"; Lat. *assumptio*) in 9:51. He notes
that this word occurs nowhere else in the Greek New Testament or in the
LXX. He thinks that the Hebrew word that underlies *analēmpsis* is *'lyh*, a
word that does not occur in the Hebrew Bible, but only in post-biblical
Hebrew texts, usually in reference to pilgrimage to Jerusalem (cf. *Sipre
Num* §89 [on 11:1-23]; *b. Pesahim* 8b).[6] He thinks that this was likely the
word that Josephus had in mind when he described the Jewish pilgrims
"going up" (*anabainein*) to the festival (*J.W.* 2.12.3 §232). But the Greek
translator of Flusser's putative Hebrew fragment misunderstood *'lyh* and
translated it *analēmpsis*, thinking that it referred to Jesus' ascent to heaven.[7] What originally in Hebrew had to do with a pilgrimage of Jesus, which
encountered Samaritan hostility (analogous to that described by Josephus),
was transformed into a christological statement.

The Greek translator misunderstood not only the meaning of "go up"
but also the Hebrew idiom "face." For the translator "face" signified the
hypostasis of divinity (cf. Exod 33:14-15, where God's "face will go with"
Moses) and approximated the "glory" associated with divinity.[8] Flusser
thinks that the translator got this idea from the christology attested in an
early form by Paul, who speaks of the "glory of Christ, who is the image of
God" (2 Cor 4:4; cf. 2 Cor 2:10; 4:6, where the "face of Christ" is mentioned. Paul's exegesis is a midrash on Exod 34:29-35, parts of which Paul
had alluded to earlier in 2 Cor 3:7-13). Paul has assumed that the "face of
Christ" is the same as the "glory of God." Thus, the face of Christ is an
early Christian hypostasis that the Greek translator of Hebrew Luke 9:51-
53 (and possibly 54-56) assumed. "When he says that the face of Christ
[*sic*] 'was going' . . . he alludes to Exod 33:14-15, where the going of the
face of God was spoken."[9]

Although not entirely without merit, Flusser's highly speculative reconstruction and interpretation encounter several serious difficulties: (1) The
septuagintalisms and Semitisms in Luke 9:51-56 occur in many other passages in Luke-Acts (as seen in the analysis above). Are we to suppose that
Hebrew *Vorlagen* underlie these passages as well? (2) Luke semiticizes
some passages that he has taken from his Greek sources, Mark and
Q (cf. Mark 1:27//Luke 4:36; Mark 1:40//Luke 5:12; Mark 12:4-5//Luke

---

6. Flusser, "Lukas 9:51-56," 167–68 and n. 8. Flusser (167, n. 6) notes with pleasure that
B. Reicke ("Instruction and Discussion in the Travel Narrative," *SE* 1 [TU 73; Berlin:
Akademie, 1959] 211) had suggested that *m'lyh*, which occurs in the superscriptions of
Psalms 120–134, might have lain behind Luke's *analēmpsis*. The LXX translates *anabathmos*.

7. Flusser, "Lukas 9:51-56," 170.

8. Flusser, "Lukas 9:51-56," 172.

9. Flusser, "Lukas 9:51-56," 174.

20:11-12; Matt 6:5-6, 32-33//Luke 11:1, 14).[10] If Luke can semiticize or septuagintalize Greek sources, is there any need to search for hypothetical Semitic sources lying behind those passages that evince Semitic and/or septuagintal elements? Sparks concludes that the materials special to Luke, where Semitic elements are often present, likely derive from the evangelist, who has composed his materials in his septuagintalizing manner.[11] Flusser himself notes that biblical Hebrew was sometimes imitated (e.g., Qumran).[12] He is correct, but would imitating the Septuagint be any more difficult? (3) Since Flusser makes no attempt to interpret 9:51-56 in its extant literary context,[13] he fails to appreciate the important contribution that this pericope makes to the evangelist's theology. Jesus' death and ascension, which were to be accomplished in Jerusalem, are distinctive Lukan emphases (cf. Luke 13:22, 31-35; 17:11; 18:31; 19:11, 28).[14] Moreover, v. 51 by all accounts was composed by Luke himself.[15] Although it is not impossible that by *analēmpsis* he meant nothing more than ascent to Jerusalem, the context (Jesus' "exodus" that he was about to "fulfill" in Jerusalem [Luke 9:31; cf. 13:32]; the use of the cognate *analambanein* in reference to Jesus' ascension [Acts 1:2, 11, 22]) argues for understanding the word as referring to the consummation of his ministry, which would include death[16] and probably the ascension as well.

In my judgment the most prudent position to take is that the evangelist probably did not compose out of whole cloth Luke 9:51-56. Rather, he inherited primitive tradition, whether or not it was part of what we might regard as an L source, which he then edited in his septuagintalizing style (as seen esp. in vv. 51, 53, 56).[17] This pericope was deliberately and consciously composed as the introduction to the travel narrative, a lengthy and significant Lukan arrangement that reaches its climax in Jerusalem, the city of Jesus' destiny. Interpretation of this pericope will therefore carry with it implications for the interpretation of the travel narrative as a whole. Any attempt at its interpretation must consider its context.

---

10. Sparks, "Semitisms," 130 (498).

11. Sparks, "Semitisms," 135–38 (503–6). For this reason, and for others, Sparks is skeptical of the existence of the L source.

12. Flusser, "Lukas 9:51-56," 169.

13. Flusser, "Lukas 9:51-56," 167, "We shall not occupy ourselves here with the position of the fragment in Luke and with its function."

14. See Fitzmyer, *Luke I–IX*, 826; Tiede, *Luke*, 197.

15. See Marshall, *Luke*, 405; Schweizer, *Luke*, 168; Fitzmyer, *Luke I–IX*, 826; Evans, *Saint Luke*, 435.

16. Flusser overlooks *Pss. Sol.* 4:18 where *analēmpsis* means death. Also overlooked are 4 Ezra 6:26; 8:20; and the *Assumption* (*analēmpsis*) *of Moses*. All of these texts were in circulation in the first century.

17. Although G. Dalman (*The Words of Jesus* [Edinburgh: T. & T. Clark, 1902] 30–31) thinks that Luke has not handled the phrase "set his face" correctly, especially in v. 53, he has no doubt that the phrase was known to the evangelist through the LXX.

LUKE 9:51-56 IN THE LUKAN CONTEXT

Flusser rightly called our attention to the importance of "face" in Luke 9:51 and 53, but he misinterpreted its meaning because he overlooked Luke's context. There might be a hint of divinity, since in the Old Testament we read of God's face being set (*stērizein to prosopōn*) against Jerusalem and the rebellious people (Jer 3:21; Ezek 14:8; 15:7). Yet that would be claiming too much, for there is nothing in this passage that hints at theophany, whether with reference to Sinai or whatever.[18] The biblical idiom might instead have in mind the prophets who were told to "set" their faces against God's people and against Jerusalem. If the Holy City is so important to Luke, perhaps here is the place to start.

In a study that investigates the evangelist Luke's interpretation of the destruction of Jerusalem, Charles H. Giblin sees awareness of the doom of Jerusalem emerge in the second and third major divisions of Jesus' adult ministry (i.e., 9:51—19:27 and 19:28—24:53; with 3:1—9:50 identified as the first division).[19] In his second division (9:51—19:27) Giblin argues that the fate of Jerusalem is only hinted at in a few passages (such as 10:10-16; 13:1-5, 31-35; 19:11-27). Jesus does not explicitly pronounce judgment upon the city until 19:41-45 (and again in 21:20-24 and 23:26-31). His analysis is helpful, and I think that in this respect his interpretation is essentially sound. However, with reference to 9:51, where the Lukan evangelist tells us that Jesus "set his face to go to [*autos to prosopon estērisen tou poreuesthai eis*] Jerusalem," Giblin concludes that Jesus announces only his intention to go to Jerusalem with no aspect of judgment hinted at,[20] even though such a hint, if there were any, would accord well with his overall interpretation of this portion of Luke's Gospel. Giblin avers that "the text demands and allows for nothing beyond an announcement of Jesus' firm intention to journey towards" Jerusalem.[21] However, Giblin's interpretation at this point may be unnecessarily limited.

All Lukan interpreters agree that at 9:51 ("When the days drew near for him to be received up, he set his face to go to Jerusalem") a major narrative shift takes place. The Galilean ministry is at an end; it is now time for

---

18. When Flusser ("Lukas 9:51-56," 175–77) suggests that Luke, or the "Greek translator," understood Jesus' "face" as his glory departing from him as he faced death (à la *Gospel of Peter* 5:19: "My Power, O Power, you have forsaken me!"), he leaves speculation behind and indulges in fantasy.

19. C. H. Giblin, *The Destruction of Jerusalem according to Luke's Gospel: A Historical-Typological Moral* (*AnBib* 107; Rome: Pontifical Biblical Institute, 1985). Giblin's overall thesis has not escaped serious criticism; see reviews by I. H. Marshall, *JTS* 37 (1986) 531–32; E. Richard, *JBL* 107 (1988) 329–31.

20. Here Giblin (*The Destruction of Jerusalem*, 31–32) sharply disagrees with my earlier study, "A Note on Luke 9, 51," 545–48.

21. Giblin, *The Destruction of Jerusalem*, 32.

Jesus to journey to Jerusalem to meet his fate.[22] But what exactly does the biblical expression "he set his face" imply? This expression is conveyed by a variety of verbs in the Hebrew: *shayt* (Num 24:1); *kun* (Ezek 4:3, 7); *shub* (Jer 3:12; Dan 11:18, 19); *nathan* (Lev 17:10; 20:3, 6; 26:17; Ezek 14:8; 15:7); and *sum* (Gen 31:21; Lev 20:5; 2 Kgs 12:18[17E]; Isa 50:7; Jer 21:10; 42:15, 17; 44:11, 12; Ezek 6:2; 13:17; 15:7; 21:2[20:46E], 7[21:2E]; 25:2; 28:21; 29:2; 38:2; Dan 11:17). The LXX uses a variety of verbs to translate the Hebrew: *apostrephein* (Num 24:1); *hetoimazein* (Ezek 4:3, 7); *tithenai* (Isa 50:7; Jer 49[42E]:17); *didonai* (Jer 49[42E]:15; Ezek 15:7; Dan 11:17, 18); *epistrephein* (Dan 11:18[θ], 19); *tassein* (2 Kgs 12:18; Ezek 14:4, 7; Dan 11:18[θ]); *ephistanai* (Lev 17:10; 20:3, 5, 6; 26:17; Jer 51[44E]:11); and *stērizein* (Jer 3:12; 21:10; Ezek 6:2; 13:17; 14:8; 15:7; 21:2[20:46E], 7[21:2E]; 25:2; 28:21; 29:2; 38:2). All of these occurrences have *to prosōpon* as the direct object.

Whereas one occurrence describes steadfast resolve (Isa 50:7), two describe flight (Jer 49[42E]:15, 17), and three others describe a human king's intention to wage war (2 Kgs 12:18[17E]; Dan 11:17, 18), the vast majority of the occurrences of this biblical expression have to do with prophesying judgment. None of these occurrences, however, parallels Luke 9:51 exactly, nor closely enough that we can say with certainty which text, if any, lies behind the evangelist. A few of the examples are found with words that describe travel. According to Dan 11:17 the king of the north (Antiochus III) "shall set his face to come [*dōsei* (θ: *taxei*) *to prosōpon autou epelthein*] with the strength of his whole kingdom." He will then "set his face to [*dōsei* (θ: *epistepsei*) *to prosōpon eis*] the coastlands" (Dan 11:18). Here the idea of travel is implied. In both instances the king has "set his face" to make war. The same idea is found in 2 Kgs 12:18(17E). "Hazael set his face to go up to [*etaxen Azael to prosōpon autou anabēnai epi*] Jerusalem." Again the context has to do with making war. Had *stērizein* been used (as it usually is when the Hebrew is *sum*), this passage would have been the closest verbal parallel to Luke 9:51. Only one other example uses the expression in reference to travel. Jeremiah warns the people of Judah who are contemplating flight, "If you set your face to [*dote to prosōpon hymōn eis*] Egypt, and go [*eiselthein*] there, the sword that you fear will overtake you in the land of Egypt" (Jer 49[42E]:15-16). Concerning those who fled to Egypt, the Lord says, "I am setting my face [*ephistēmi to prosōpon mou*] to destroy" (Jer 51[44E]:11-12).

---

22. The expression *en tō symplērousthai* signifies the arrival of a date, a time of fulfillment (and not the completion of a period of time). For Luke, it probably signifies the arrival of a very important date, for he uses the same expression to introduce his Pentecost narrative (Acts 2:1); see H. Conzelmann, *Acts of the Apostles* (Hermeneia; Philadelphia: Fortress, 1987) 13.

The parallels relevant to Luke 9:51 are those in which *stērizein* is found. All of these examples occur in Jeremiah and Ezekiel. Through Jeremiah, the Lord pleads, "Return to me, O house of Israel, says the Lord, and I will not set my face against [*ou stēriō to prosōpon mou eph'*] you" (3:12). But Israel does not repent, so the prophet says later: "For I have set my face against [*estērika to prosōpon mou epi*] this city for evil, and not for good. It will be delivered into the hands of the king of Babylon and it will be burned with fire" (21:10). The rest of the occurrences are found in Ezekiel. Concerning the wicked person, the Lord says through the prophet, "I shall set my face against [*stēriō to prosōpon mou epi*] that person" (14:8). The inhabitants of Jerusalem "will know that I am the Lord, when I have set my face against [*en tō stērisai me to prosōpon me ep'*] them" (15:7). The Lord's command that Ezekiel set his face becomes a virtual refrain. "Son of man, set your face towards [*stērison to prosōpon sou epi*] the mountains of Israel, and prophesy against [*epi*] them" (6:2; see also 13:17; 21:2[20:46E], 7[21:7E]; 25:2; 28:21; 29:2; 38:2). Of these occurrences, one parallels the Lukan context more closely than the others. "Prophesy, son of man, set your face toward [*stērison to prosōpon sou epi*] Jerusalem, and look toward [*epi*] their holy places, and you shall prophesy against [*epi*] the land of Israel" (21:2[20:46E]). With no exceptions, the expression *stērizein to prosōpon* is found in contexts threatening judgment.[23]

What does the evangelist Luke mean to say by using this biblical expression? Certainly the expression suggests resolute determination, as Giblin and most commentators readily agree.[24] The verb *stērizein* alone would connote this idea (lit. "to be strong"), while often the underlying Hebrew words mean about the same thing (e.g., the piel of *hazaq* means to strengthen or harden). The question, however, is whether or not the expression contributes to this section's sense of something ominous hanging over Jerusalem, as Giblin describes it. It has already been shown that the expression often connotes a sense of judgment (e.g., Jer 3:12; 21:10), especially in Ezekiel (e.g., 6:2; 13:17; 14:8; 21:2[20:46E], 7[21:2E]), the most likely source from which Luke derived this language.

---

23. G. Harder (*"Stērizo,"* *TDNT* 7.653–57, 655) is correct when he says that *stērizein* in the LXX expresses "the divine and prophetic turning to a place or person either to test or to judge." See also W. Grundmann, *Das Evangelium nach Lukas* (THKNT 3; Berlin: Evangelische Verlagsanstalt, 1961) 201.

24. Giblin, *The Destruction of Jerusalem*, 32; G. L. Hahn, *Das Evangelium des Lukas* (2 vols.; Breslau: Morgenstern, 1894) 2.6; M.-J. Lagrange, *Évangile selon Saint Luc* (Ebib; Paris: Gabalda, 1921) 284; A. Plummer, *The Gospel according to S. Luke* (ICC; Edinburgh: T & T Clark, 1922) 263; B. S. Easton, *The Gospel according to St. Luke* (New York: Scribner's, 1926) 152; F. Hauck, *Das Evangelium nach Lukas* (THKNT 3; Leipzig: Deichert, 1934) 135; Marshall, *Luke,* 405; Fitzmyer, *Luke I–IX,* 823.

In composing some of Jesus' oracles about the impending second siege and destruction, Luke utilized Ezekiel's prophetic language (as well as that of other prophets) describing the siege and first destruction of Jerusalem (compare Luke 19:41-44; 21:20-24 with Ezek 4:1-3; 21:6-12, 22). In fact, Giblin writes that Ezek 4:1-2 is alluded to in Luke 19:44,[25] Ezek 9:1 in Luke 21:20,[26] and Ezek 20:45—21:7 in Luke 23:31.[27] It is important to note that all of these passages are either unique to Luke or have been heavily redacted by him. Since the expression "set your face" occurs frequently in Ezekiel, an Old Testament book that contributed to various portions of Luke, especially those distinctively Lukan, it is not unreasonable to suspect that underlying the Lukan expression in 9:51, another passage unique to Luke, is once again Ezekiel. Furthermore, since these prophetic contributions from Ezekiel usually contribute to Luke's depiction of Jerusalem's grim fate, our suspicion that Ezekiel not only underlies Luke 9:51 but lends the passage a sense of the ominous, is strengthened. Moreover, the fact that Jesus' favorite self-designation is "Son of man," which occurs a few verses earlier in 9:44, and which is the most common designation for the prophet Ezekiel as well (e.g., 4:1; 8:17; 21:2[20:46E]; 21:7[2E], 11[6E], 14[9E]—note that this expression occurs in, or within close proximity to, those passages thought to have been utilized by the evangelist), adds conviction to our suspicion. The passage that Luke most likely had in mind is Ezek 21:7-11[2-6E]: "Son of man, set your face toward Jerusalem and preach against the sanctuaries; prophesy against the land of Israel and say to the land of Israel, Thus says the Lord: Behold, I am against you, and will draw forth my sword out of its sheath. . . . Sigh therefore, son of man; sigh with breaking heart and bitter grief before their eyes" (RSV).[28]

There are at least three reasons for suspecting that this passage (though not necessarily this passage alone)[29] underlies the expression "He set his face to go to Jerusalem" in Luke 9:51. (1) As in the passage from Ezekiel, the "setting of the face" refers to Jerusalem. (2) The Ezekiel passage falls

---

25. Giblin, *The Destruction of Jerusalem*, 56.
26. Giblin, *The Destruction of Jerusalem*, 87.
27. Giblin, *The Destruction of Jerusalem*, 102.
28. Tiede, *Prophecy and History*, 61; idem, *Luke*, 197.
29. F. W. Farrar (*The Gospel according to St Luke* [Cambridge: University Press, 1890] 195), J. Starcky ("Obfirmavit faciem suam ut iret Jerusalem: Sens et portée de *Luc*, ix, 51," *RSR* 39 [1951] 197–202), and E. E. Ellis (*The Gospel of Luke* [NCB; London: Nelson, 1966] 151) propose Isa 50:7, "I have set my face as a hard [*stereos*] rock." Plummer's exegesis (*Luke*, 263, ". . . The prospect of difficulty or danger") is clearly influenced by this possible parallel. The context is indeed suggestive; the words are spoken by the Lord's servant, who will carry on the task undaunted by adversaries. Although *stereos* occurs, we probably should look to a parallel that uses the verb *stērizein*.

within the larger passage (21:1-12 [20:45—21:7E]) that perhaps inspired the utterance found in Luke 23:31. If this is so,[30] Luke might very well have been acquainted with this particular passage. (3) Just as Ezekiel was grieved and spoke a word of judgment against Jerusalem and her sanctuaries, so Jesus, when he arrives at Jerusalem, weeps over the city (19:41; compare Ezek 21:11[6E]) and speaks a word of judgment (19:43-44; compare Ezek 21:7-11[2-6E], esp. v. 11[2E]).[31]

Another feature that may be relevant for our analysis is the question of whether this expression connotes a sense of dispatch. In the case of the expression as employed by Ezekiel, William H. Brownlee has so argued.[32] The fact that the expression in Luke occurs at the very beginning of Jesus' journey to Jerusalem, before he sends messengers on ahead (9:52) and only a few verses before the seventy-two are dispatched with a message and mission (10:1-12), may be only a coincidence, but the possibility that this expression might have been understood as having something to do with being dispatched with a message ought at least to be considered. Moreover, since Jesus' message for Jerusalem, like that of Ezekiel's, is essentially a negative one, the possibility becomes more suggestive.[33]

Giblin notes that the context suggests that no judgment is in view because of the clemency that Jesus shows the Samaritans, who had rejected Jesus "because his face was set toward Jerusalem" (9:53). He reasons, "If there were a judgmental tone regarding the Jewish capital in Luke's phraseology in v. 51, it would be very strange for Luke immediately to note the Samaritans' hostility to Jesus as he proceeds 'against' Jerusalem."[34] It would be strange, I agree, if the Samaritans opposed Jesus knowing fully well that he intended to pronounce a judgment upon the city. (And this I readily acknowledge to be Giblin's strongest point.) But their

---

30. See Ezek 21:3[20:47E]. Giblin (*The Destruction of Jerusalem*, 102–3) doubts that this passage best explains Luke 23:31. He finds in the rabbinic writings what he deems to be closer parallels.

31. Fitzmyer (*Luke I–IX*, 828) says this of the expression in 9:51: "Luke [may have been] thinking perhaps of the LXX of Ezek 6:2; 13:17; 14:8. . . . Here perhaps one should recall the mission of the prophet Ezekiel to the city of Jerusalem (Ezekiel 8–11)." Similarly, J. H. Davies ("The Purpose of the Central Section of St. Luke's Gospel," in F. L. Cross, ed., *Studia Evangelica*, vol. 2 [= TU 87; Berlin: Töpelmann, 1964] 164–69) believes that the expression is derived from Ezekiel and that the idea of judgment is present. Virtually every commentator cites these passages from Ezekiel.

32. W. H. Brownlee, "Ezekiel," *ISBE* 2 (1982) 254–55; idem, " 'Son of Man Set Your Face': Ezekiel the Refugee Prophet," *HUCA* 54 (1983) 83–110.

33. Harder ("*Stērizō*," 656), in reference to Luke 9:51, is correct when he says, "Jesus is announcing herewith both His own unalterable purpose and also the divine will not just that He should go to Jerusalem but that He should summon it to decision."

34. Giblin, *The Destruction of Jerusalem*, 32. I acknowledge in a study (" 'He Set His Face': A Note," 547) that the preposition *epi* (= '*el*), which is usually in the expression "set his face *against*" is of course not present in Luke 9:51 or 53. If it were, then the expression would not *connote* or *hint* at judgment, but would unambiguously *denote* such.

opposition is likely motivated by Jesus' interest in Jerusalem. They refuse him because he is perceived to be part of Judaism, a prophet whose destiny will be met at Jerusalem (13:33-35). The response of the disciples, who seem to be in a judgmental mood to say the least, is to call fire down upon the Samaritans. Obviously the element of judgment is present in this context, but what to make of it is the problem. Something seems to have suggested to the disciples that Jesus means business; any town that rejects him will face judgment. This we see in the instructions for the seventy-two and the later speeches concerning Jerusalem itself. Therefore, when confronted by the Samaritan rejection, the disciples expect a dramatic act of judgment. They do not think of a postponement of judgment[35] but expect the Samaritans to be treated as other Samaritans were treated in the stories of the Old Testament (e.g., 1 Kgs 18:36-38; 2 Kgs 1:9-14). Such a disposition on the part of the disciples becomes more intelligible if the expression in 9:51 was indeed meant to be ominous. As the passage now stands, the incident involving the Samaritans reveals that Jesus is merciful and does not wish judgment to fall upon anyone (compare his attitude of concern in 23:26-31).[36] In his later dispatch of the seventy-two (Luke 10:1-12), however, Jesus tells his disciples that it will "be more tolerable on that day for Sodom than for [the] town" that rejects his messengers (v. 12). Moreover, these instructions are followed by woes pronounced on the unrepentant cities of Chorazin and Bethsaida, in which warning of future judgment is made explicit (vv. 13-15). At its very outset, then, the journey to Jerusalem indeed appears to forebode ill for some of the cities to which Jesus goes.

It has been suggested that words from Mal 3:1 have been incorporated into Luke 9:52, "And he sent messengers before his face" (*kai apesteilen aggelous pro prosōpou autou*).[37] The relevant parts of Mal 3:1 read, "I send my messenger, and he will survey the way before my face" (*exapostellō ton aggelon mou, kai epiblepsetai hodon pro prosōpou mou*). Malachi goes on to say

---

35. As is taught by the parable of the Unproductive Fig Tree (13:6-9).

36. The reason that judgment will inevitably fall on Jerusalem (or any other city for that matter) is, as Giblin puts it (*The Destruction of Jerusalem*, 105), "surely not Jesus' personal hostility to the inhabitants of the city." This is an important observation, for it points to a crucial distinction between the compassionate prophet Jesus and the terrible judgment that God will bring upon the unrepentant city.

37. Easton, *Luke*, 152; I. de la Potterie, "Le titre *kyrios* appliqué à Jésus dans l'évangile de Luc," in A. Descamps and A. de Halleux, eds., *Mélanges bibliques en hommage au R. P. Béda Rigaux* (Gembloux: Duculot, 1970) 117–46, esp. 128; K. R. Snodgrass, "Streams of Tradition Emerging from Isaiah 40:1-5 and Their Adaptation in the New Testament," *JSNT* 8 (1980) 24–45, esp. 39; J. A. Fitzmyer, *The Gospel According to Luke X–XXIV* (AB 28A; Garden City: Doubleday, 1985) 828. The suggestion is likely, since in Mal 3:23(4:5E) the messenger is identified as Elijah, and in Luke 9:54 the disciples expect Jesus to react to the Samaritans as Elijah would have.

that the Lord will suddenly come to the temple in a way that none can endure or withstand, purifying and refining the sons of Levi (Mal 3:1-3). If Luke intends to allude to Mal 3:1, then he may have Malachi's judgmental context in mind as well.

The reference to the nearness of Jesus' time "to be received up" certainly anticipates the events of the passion, particularly the crucifixion and ascension.[38] In this final period of his life, of course, Jesus pronounces explicit words of judgment on the stubborn city (19:41-45; 21:20-24; 23:28-31). In killing the one sent to it the city has sealed its own fate. This constitutes only a minor, perhaps irrelevant, point, but it could add contextual support to my suggestion that 9:51 forebodes judgment.

In conclusion I find the meaning of Luke 9:51 not easily decided. In favor of understanding the expression as hinting at judgment would be the strong possibility that the phrase goes back to Ezekiel, which would make a judgmental tone most likely. If the phrase cannot be traced back to Ezekiel, however, the connotation of judgment, although by no means eliminated, is more remote. Moreover, the context itself is open to opposing interpretations. On the one hand, it is possible to see in the repetition of the expression in 9:53 an unlikelihood of any idea of judgment. On the other hand, however, the disciples' reaction and Jesus' instructions and sayings to the seventy-two seem to indicate that 9:51 forebodes judgment.

Giblin has contested my interpretation because it is, apparently, not "in line with Luke's forthright clarity of expression."[39] This is an important issue, for it concerns the whole question of Luke's use of the Old Testament. I tend to view the evangelist's use of the Old Testament as ranging from the obvious to the subtle, from explicit citation and/or comment to allusion. As an example of the subtle, in the infancy narrative Luke alludes to the rearing of Samuel in the temple (compare Luke 1:80; 2:40, 52 with 1 Sam 2:26), which would be clear only to those who knew their Old Testament stories well. Moreover, as an example closer to home, the exchange between Jesus and a would-be follower in Luke 9:61-62 surely is meant to allude to Elijah's call of Elisha (1 Kgs 19:19-20). But is such a subtle allusion forthrightly clear? Obviously not to all. I believe that the evangelist Luke writes with "forthright clarity of expression," but we moderns cannot always divine at what level of understanding his audiences lived.[40]

---

38. Fitzmyer (*Luke I–IX*, 827–28) seems undecided but appears to see *analēmpsis* as referring to more than Jesus' actual ascension. Given the full context, I think it difficult to understand otherwise.

39. Giblin, *The Destruction of Jerusalem*, 32.

40. See J. A. Sanders's discussion of this point above in Chap. 1.

Judging by its septuagintal language and numerous allusions to the Old Testament (both to individual texts and larger units), I think it fair to conclude that Luke wrote for an audience that was very familiar with its Septuagint, an audience expected to dig out of the Old Testament much about Christ and his church (see Luke 24:25-27, 45-56). Therefore, I think that it is quite possible if not probable (although admittedly not certain) that in using the expression in 9:51 "He set his face" the evangelist alludes to Ezekiel; and in alluding to this prophetic book he hints at the city's impending judgment. Luke uses this expression not simply to imply that Jesus has turned toward Jerusalem with steadfast resolve, but that Jesus' decision to go to the holy city is an event in continuity with the biblical story of the past. He implies that Jesus' ministry will affect the destiny of the city as surely as had the ministries of the great prophets before him, in a conscious attempt to align the story of Jesus at one more point with the canonical traditions of Israel's heritage.

—— 8 ——

THE ETHIC OF ELECTION IN LUKE'S GREAT BANQUET PARABLE

JAMES A. SANDERS

Much indeed has been learned from John Duncan Martin Derrett's treatment of the Great Supper parable, especially in its Matthean guise.[1] But although Derrett's vision of the problems posed in Matthew is largely convincing, it must be noted that he left aspects of the parable in Luke untouched.

My own work on the parable began while reflecting on the apparatus to Dominique Barthélemy's edition of the Qumran *Rule of the Congregation*. In the apparatus to 1QSa 2:6 Barthélemy has a simple one-line reference to Luke 14:21 but does not suggest his own thinking about it.[2] Yigael Yadin, in his masterful edition of the Qumran *War Scroll*, made no reference at all to the Lukan material despite obvious similarities between battles, banquets, and guests in the two.[3] The English publication of Joachim Jeremias's *Parables* in 1963 attempted no improvement of the German edition.[4]

This chapter is a revision of my study, "The Ethic of Election in Luke's Great Banquet Parable," in J. L. Crenshaw and J. T. Willis, eds., *Essays in Old Testament Ethics (J. Philip Hyatt, in Memoriam)* (New York: Ktav, 1974) 245–71.

1. J. D. M. Derrett, *Law in the New Testament* (London: Darton, Longman & Todd, 1970) 126–55. This chapter, in another form, constituted a portion of the Shaffer Lectures given at Yale Divinity School in April 1972.

2. D. Barthélemy and J. T. Milik, *Qumran Cave I* (DJD 1; Oxford: Clarendon, 1955) 177. See J. A. Sanders, "Banquet of the Dispossessed," *USQR* 20 (1965) 355–63.

3. Y. Yadin, *The Scroll of the War of the Sons of Light against the Sons of Darkness* (Oxford: Oxford University Press, 1962) 63–86, 290–93, 304–5.

4. J. Jeremias, *The Parables of Jesus* (London: SCM, 1963; based on the sixth edition of *Die Gleichnisse Jesu* [Göttingen: Vandenhoeck & Ruprecht, 1962]) 175–80, cf. 63–69. N. Perrin's *Rediscovering the Teaching of Jesus* (New York: Harper & Row, 1967) 110–16, follows Jeremias in

In 1966 Robert Funk published *Language, Hermeneutic and Word of God*. Central to his effort to make direct application of the so-called New Hermeneutic, or *Sprachereignis* (language-event) hermeneutic of Ernst Fuchs and Gerhard Ebeling, is a long section in two chapters on the parable of the Great Supper. These chapters, in the design of the book, bear much of the burden of Funk's argument about the validity of the New Hermeneutic. I have no quarrel with the New Hermeneutic as such. On the contrary, such an approach in its proper place, combined with the sociology of knowledge,[5] can be a valuable tool in exegesis and in the new efforts being launched to recover a valid sense of "canon" for our day.[6] But Funk had gleaned through the finest First Testament scholarship on the parable and still did not see the parable as I do.

The approach that I take here is that of comparative midrash; this method of exegesis has been discussed above in Chapter 1. As will be made clear below, the comparative approach to the study of the Great Banquet parable sheds light on the contexts of Jesus, the early Christian community, and the evangelist Luke. We begin with a discussion of prophetic criticism.

PROPHETIC CRITICISM

For some years now, my students and I have been diligently searching the available (and in some cases unpublished) Qumran literature to find evidence of the use there of the hermeneutics of prophetic criticism. So far we have been significantly unsuccessful. In no instance have we found a case at Qumran of contemporizing a First Testament tradition as a challenge to the in-group. Such an observation in no way mitigates the fact that the faithful at Qumran had a high doctrine of humanity and sin.

---

all important particulars in interpreting this parable. Other studies in the same time period which treat the parable include those by E. Linneman, "Überlegungen zur Parabol vom grossen Abendmahl," *ZNW* 51 (1960) 246–55; cf. her *Parables of Jesus* (London: SPCK, 1966) 89–91, 160–62; O. Glombitza, "Das Grosse Abendmahl," *NovT* 5 (1962) 10–16; E. Haenchen, "Das Gleichnis vom grossen Mahl," *Die Bibel und Wir* (Tübingen: Mohr [Siebeck], 1968) 135–55; and D. O. Via, Jr., "The Relationship of Form to Content in the Parables: The Wedding Feast," *Int* 25 (1971) 171–84. However, Glombitza and Via are purely form-critical studies, and all ignore the Old Testament and Qumran materials.

5. P. Berger, *The Social Construction of Reality: A Treatise in the Sociology of Knowledge* (New York: Doubleday, 1966).

6. Cf. B. S. Childs, *Biblical Theology in Crisis* (Philadelphia: Westminster, 1970); J. A. Sanders, *Torah and Canon* (Philadelphia: Fortress, 1972); and idem, "Adaptable for Life: The Nature and Function of Canon" in F. M. Cross, ed., *The Mighty Acts of God: Essays on the Bible and Archaeology in Memory of G. Ernest Wright* (New York: Doubleday, 1976); repr. in J. A. Sanders, *From Sacred Story to Sacred Text: Canon as Paradigm* (Philadelphia: Fortress, 1987) 11–39, esp. nn. 1–4 and 42–45 for bibliography. See also M. Smith, *Palestinian Parties and Politics That Shaped the Old Testament* (New York: Columbia University Press, 1971).

On the contrary, they apparently daily confessed their manifold sins and wickedness and unworthiness, in general confession, collectively and individually.[7] But, interestingly, every instance of interpretation of the First Testament is favorable to the denomination. Every blessing is seen as flowing toward themselves in the end time and every possible curse toward their enemies—whether the Hasmonaeans, the Romans, or the cosmic forces of evil. In other words, they were a normal denomination!

By contrast, when the above-outlined method is followed, one sees that, whereas the early Christians often followed just such in-group exegesis also, Jesus himself might have employed prophetic-critique hermeneutics in what he had to say to his in-group Jewish contemporaries. In the realm of canonical criticism, in fact, one reason the teachings of Jesus were so popular in the period after his death and especially following the fall of Jerusalem in 70 C.E., is that Jesus' prophetic strictures against his fellow Jews looked like the comfort and support the struggling Christian community thought they needed for their own view of themselves as the new Israel. As noted in earlier chapters, this false transfer of the Jesus traditions was effected by static analogy to their situation.

Obviously, in any attempt to reconstruct the second focus in the time of Jesus (as contrasted with the time of the evangelists) one needs extra-biblical material from Palestine of the earlier time period. And, in contrast to rabbinic literature, which is notoriously difficult to date and control, Qumran provides just such material[8]—dated pre-70 C.E. and, like the Second Testament, accepting as its acknowledged base of authority the First Testament. Sound methodic procedure would suggest looking for passages in both Qumran literature and the Second Testament that treat of the same First Testament material in order to compare the hermeneutics used in each. Fortunately, there is a plethora of such cases, one of which is provided by the Great Banquet parable in Luke 14 and by several passages in Qumran Cave 1 literature.

The central section of Luke's Gospel has been an enigma of Second Testament scholarship. Until Canon Streeter's *Four Gospels* this section was variously called the travel document, the Peraean section, the Samaritan document, and so on.[9] Since Streeter it has almost universally been designated by the term "central section." Even so, little headway has been made

---

7. As is quite clear in 1QH and CD; see Pss. 154 and 155 in 11QPs[a].

8. Cf. J. Neusner, *The Rabbinic Traditions about the Pharisees before 70* (3 vols.; Leiden: Brill, 1971) esp. 3.301–19. The Bar Ma'yan story in the Palestinian Talmud (Jeremias, *Parables*, 178–79; Perrin, *Rediscovering the Teaching of Jesus*, 114–20) is not only impossible to date but also impertinent.

9. B. H. Streeter, *The Four Gospels* (London: Macmillan, 1924). See also A. Wright, *The Gospel of St. Luke in Greek* (London: Macmillan, 1900) xix.

into probing its significance, the reason that Luke arranged his material in this way, and the ideas he wished to convey by so doing. In 1955, however, Christopher F. Evans, in a little-heralded article, showed that Luke had arranged his material parallel to Deuteronomy 1–26. Evans's article has received precious little attention, and the reason is, I think, that he failed to probe Luke's major purpose in doing what he had done.[10]

Evans rightly stresses that Luke presents Jesus in this section as the "prophet like Moses" fulfilling Deut 18:15. The substance of Evans's work is the observation that in Luke 9:51—18:43 the evangelist followed the order of LXX Deuteronomy by using catchwords. Though he does not make it explicit, Evans has shown clearly the midrashic technique of calling the reader's attention to a well-known First Testament authority. Luke, in excellent midrashic fashion, insists that to understand what Jesus said and did, to perceive the real truth about him, one must draw down, as a backdrop to his report of his words and deeds, the one authority needed to test the accuracy of the claims about Christ—the First Testament. Modern historians, in quest of answers to their needs, pull down a map or a chronological chart as a backdrop to test the truth of claims.[11] This approach, however, ignores Luke's own intention and presumes that he did not know Palestine at the time of Jesus and did not know Jesus very well. It is not that Luke knew Jesus very well, but that contemporary backdrops do not constitute a true control factor in making historical judgments about biblical materials.

If C. F. Evans is right that Deut 18:15, the promise of the prophet like Moses,[12] is at the heart of what Luke wants to say about Jesus in this section, and if he is right that the sequential pattern of Deuteronomy 1–26 lies behind this section, then special attention is drawn to what can readily be seen, in the light of Evans's work, as the heart of this central section of Luke's Gospel—the Great Banquet parable in Luke 14. That this parable

---

10. C. F. Evans, "The Central Section of St. Luke's Gospel," in D. E. Nineham, ed., *Studies in the Gospels* (Oxford: Blackwell, 1955) 37–53. Evans's thesis has been pursued in Acts by M. D. Goulder, *Type and History in Acts* (London: SCM, 1964). A student has called to my attention a popular, devotional-type presentation of Evans's thesis by J. Bligh, S.J., *Christian Deuteronomy (Luke 9–18)* (Langley: St. Paul, 1970). See also P. H. Ballard's excellent paper, "Reasons for Refusing the Great Supper," *JTS* 23 (1972) 341–50. It is encouraging to see increasing recognition of the importance of Deuteronomy in Luke.

11. One of the values of the sociology of knowledge is its ability to help us understand ourselves at those times we consider ourselves "objective." We are about ten generations into biblical scholarship and are now able to see that each generation in that noble procession was in basic ways responding to its own *Zeitgeist*. Qoheleth's observations, especially in 3:1–11, emerge as keenly pertinent after applying the sociology of knowledge to current research.

12. Cf. Luke 7:16; 9:8; and especially Acts 3:22; see also R. F. Zehnle, *Peter's Pentecost Discourse: Tradition and Lukan Reinterpretation in Peter's Speeches in Acts 2 and 3* (SBLMS 15; Nashville: Abingdon, 1971) esp. 71–94.

is at the heart of the whole section becomes clear when one realizes that the principal reason Luke arranged his material in this fashion was that he understood Jesus' teaching largely as prophetic critique of current inversions of the Deuteronomic ethic of election.

I tested this hypothesis by doing another vertical reading of the Gospel. Using the Greek *Synopsis* edited by Kurt Aland,[13] I read Luke and kept this question in mind: Is it possible that Luke was presenting Jesus as delivering a prophetic critique against false assumptions about election? And, *mirabile dictu,* while much of Luke preceding 9:51 but not much after chapter 18 may be so construed, everything in the central section *can* be so understood. If one takes Evans's lead, the purpose of the section and of the Great Banquet parable becomes evident.

DEUTERONOMY 20

In the Great Banquet parable the three excuses submitted by the *keklēmenoi,* who are unable to attend, are based on the four causes for deferment from serving in the army of the holy war of Yahweh given in Deut 20:5-8. Evans correctly sets Deuteronomy 20 parallel to Luke 14:15-35 in his schema.[14]

According to Deuteronomy 20, the four acceptable reasons for exemption from service in the army of the faithful are: (1) having built a house as yet not dedicated; (2) having planted a vineyard whose fruit has yet to be enjoyed; (3) having married and not yet consummated the marriage; and (4) being fainthearted. In the parable only three reasons are given: (1) having bought a field not yet inspected; (2) having bought five yoke of oxen not yet examined; and (3) having married recently.

Deuteronomy 20	*Luke 14*
Built house not yet dedicated	Bought field not yet inspected
Planted vineyard not yet enjoyed	Bought oxen not yet examined
Marriage not yet consummated	Recent marriage
Fainthearted	

The parable follows the first three stipulations in Deuteronomy rather closely. To put it another way, the distance between the first three stipula-

---

13. *Synopsis Quattuor Evangelium,* ed. K. Aland (Stuttgart: Württembergische Bibelanstalt, 1964).

14. By contrast note the recent judgments about the excuses by scholars who are unaware of the midrashic nature of the Lukan material and hence of the Old Testament roots: K. H. Rengstorf, "unrealistic"; G. V. Jones, "unrealistic"; E. Linnemann, "apologies for coming late"; G. Bornkamm, "fatuous"; J. Jeremias, "flimsy"! My own work on the parable indicated the pertinence of Deut 20:5-8, cf. Sanders, "Banquet of the Dispossessed"; and Derrett (*Law in the New Testament,* 135–37) perceives its relevance. I have found myself often in work on Luke

tions in Deuteronomy and the three in Luke 14 is no more or less than might be expected in a midrashic search of Scripture of this sort from this period.[15] The important point is that the parable follows the Deuteronomic holy war legislation in enumerating both economic and social reasons as a base for exemption from participation.

Important also is the fact that the fourth stipulation in Deuteronomy 20 is omitted from the parable. Interestingly enough it is the converse in 1QM 10:5–6. Only the fourth reason for exemption occurs in the *War Scroll*. But Yigael Yadin, the editor of the scroll in its definitive edition, explains that the members of the first three groups would have been eliminated on going forth from Jerusalem and those affected would simply remain at home.[16] The fourth group, however, the fainthearted, could, according to Yadin, be determined only at the battlefront when the army comes face to face with the enemy; 1QM 10:5–6 sets the process here and Yadin does not doubt that this was the actual procedure.[17]

By calling to the attention of the hearer or reader the holy war legislation of Deuteronomy 20, Jesus or Luke's Jesus, in excellent midrashic fashion, says one must have Deuteronomy 20 in mind in order to understand the parable's point. As Evans has demonstrated, this would have been no surprise to Theophilos or to any knowledgeable reader after him, since Luke 14 takes its place in the Deuteronomic sequence in the central section of the Gospel, a sequence already established as necessary to perceiving the theme being pursued.

That Deuteronomy 20 is concerned with a battle and Luke 14 with a banquet is no surprise either. Luke 14:14-15 has already established the parable as describing or dealing effectively with the great eschatological banquet. An astute hearer or reader would have expected the legislation of Deuteronomy 20 to be brought into the parable in 14:18-20. The holy war legislation is eschatologized at Qumran, as Yadin has shown from the *War Scroll;* and certainly the messianic banquet as anticipated in the *Rule of the Congregation* (1QSa) is eschatological.

Following the shift of emphasis from the this-worldly questions of lifestyle in the teaching on humility in Luke 14:7-14 (which occurs precisely

---

reverting to Deuteronomy despite the standard New Testament works on Luke. I called this to the attention of my colleague, R. H. Fuller, and he directed my attention to Evans. It was a felicitous confirmation in the sense that Evans approached the material along entirely different lines.

15. A comparative midrash study of the function of Deut 20:5-8 (cf. Isa 65:21-22) in later literature indicates that the first two excuses were not followed rigidly but indicated social preoccupation that might distract, whereas the last two were strictly adhered to—love commitment in betrothal and fear of death. See below n. 18.

16. Yadin, *Scroll of the War,* 65–70.

17. Yadin, *Scroll of the War,* 69.

at the end of that teaching [14:14] and in the transition comment from a guest at table [14:15]), the parable of the Great Banquet speaks directly of the guest list of the kingdom table in the eschaton. The relation of battle to banquet in the eschaton is discussed by Derrett[18] but needs elaboration.

Whereas Matthew used the word for wedding feast (*gamos*), Luke used the more general word for dinner or banquet, *deipnon*, which also meant "the Messiah's feast symbolizing salvation in the kingdom of heaven" (Rev 19:9, 17; cf. 1 Cor 11:20) according to Thayer's lexicon.[19] The call to feast in Luke's parable was to the victory banquet that would follow the holy war (cf. Ps 23:5; Isa 21:5). One needed but believe that the battle was already won, or in Lukan terms that the great jubilee or kingdom of God had been introduced by the coming of the Messiah/Christ. The failure to believe that the eschaton had been introduced in Christ induced "anger" in the host (Luke 14:21). To think that the battle was yet to be fought and that the deferments of Deuteronomy 20 still obtained—eliciting belief that God as holy warrior would traditionally not need many soldiers in that battle still to be waged (cf. Joel 4:9-12 [ET 3:9-12])—angered the host (God) who had in Christ effectively already fought the battle for all (cf. Luke 10:18, "I saw Satan fall like lightning from heaven") and was calling the *keklēmenoi* to celebrate the victory. All of Deuteronomy, indeed all of Scripture, had now to be read in the light of the new hermeneutic of the coming of Christ.

Only in Luke 14 and 15 and in 16:25 do we find forms of *kaleō* (and *parakaleō*) with other than the very neutral meanings of "named," "designated," "called," and the like. I have already pointed out the reason such a restricted use of *kaleō* is so interesting: a vertical reading of the central section of this Gospel with Deuteronomy 1–26 as backdrop clearly indicates Luke's great concern for abuses of Deuteronomy's theology and ethic of election.[20] It is surprising that Luke does not use this all-important word elsewhere (save in such cases as "You shall call his name John" [1:13]) to signify election, not even in Acts. Clearly he wants to underscore its use

---

18. Derrett, *Law in the New Testament*, 135, n. 2, and 136, n. 1; to his references add Ps 23:5. Because certain points are overlooked and others are confused, Derrett's work is vulnerable to criticism; cf. J. A. Fitzmyer, *The Gospel according to Luke X–XXIV* (AB 28A; Garden City: Doubleday, 1985) 1056. I. H. Marshall (*Commentary on Luke* [NIGTC; Grand Rapids: Eerdmans, 1978] 586) also raises some questions but concedes that "the series of excuses in Lk. may bear some relationship to Dt. 20:5-7." In his recent commentary C. F. Evans (*Saint Luke* [London: SCM; Philadelphia: Trinity, 1990] 574) has concluded that there is a relationship between the excuses of Deuteronomy and those of the Lukan parable. He detects "strong echoes" of Deuteronomy in Luke 14.

19. *A Greek-English Lexicon of the New Testament*, ed. J. H. Thayer (New York: American Book Company, 1896).

20. Among the recent studies see L. Perlitt, *Bundestheologie im Alten Testament* (WMANT 36; Neukirchen-Vluyn: Neukirchener Verlag, 1969).

in this core material of the central section of his Gospel. That *kaleō* (with *parakaleō*) serves Luke, in both the Great Banquet and the Prodigal Son parables, with the ambiguity of both meanings "invite" and "elect" is emphasized by the one exception, in 16:26, where it can only mean "comforted" or "entreated" in the sense of "elect": Lazarus is elect while the rich man at whose gate on earth he ate scraps is cursed or in pain. Lazarus is in heaven, the rich man in Hades—the final proof of election.

This is a major theme of the central section: the Deuteronomic ethic of election or ecclesiology has been subverted. Whereas Deuteronomy stressed that obedience brings blessings and disobedience curses, one cannot go on to assume (as many ever since Deuteronomy did assume—see the arguments of the friends in Job) that suffering indicates that one is not elect while riches or ease on earth indicates that one is elect. Clearly the theme reaches a climax in the parables of the Great Banquet, the Prodigal Son, and the Rich Man and Lazarus. This is why most discussions (nearly all negative) of whether *kaleō* in Luke 14–16 has to do with election are nowadays considered irrelevant and impertinent.[21] Interest has shifted to why Luke limited his use of *kaleō* to these three chapters. The answer is not difficult to secure. In the two parables in chapters 14 and 15, the center of attention is a banquet. *Kaleō* clearly means "invite" in the context of dinners and banquets, and only in such a context can Luke stress his major point that those who are confident that they shall be at the eschatological banquet, yet do not believe that the victory has proleptically been won, in all likelihood will not be.[22] This literary concept of double entendre serves his purposes admirably, and it is introduced by the apparently mundane discussion in 14:7-14 of a wisdom teaching on earthly practices of inviters and invitees. Luke thereby insists that we understand the meaning "invite" so that we do not think only of "elect" as we might otherwise. It is an excellent rhetorical device and well executed. Also, as Larrimore Clyde Crockett has admirably shown, Luke is intensely interested in table fellowship and centers his discussions of election and the relation of Jews and Gentiles in pictures of table fellowship.[23] *Keklēmenoi* in Luke means "apparently elect" or "those who consider themselves elected."

---

21. K. L. Schmidt ("*kaleō*," *TDNT* 3.487–536, esp. 487–91) is more nearly right in this regard than his critics, but even he did not, in my opinion, go far enough. Note, however, that his comment on Deut 20:10 and the use there of *ekkalein* for *qara'* (490) is not pertinent to our discussion.

22. See the similar conclusions of D. P. Moessner's study of the parallels between Deuteronomy and Luke in his *Lord of the Banquet* (Minneapolis: Fortress, 1989) esp. 289–325.

23. L. C. Crockett, *The OT in the Gospel of Luke with Emphasis on the Interpretation of Isa 61:1-2* (unpublished doctoral dissertation; Brown University, 1966). See the thesis of X. de Meeûs, "Lc XIV et le genre symposiaque," *ETL* 37 (1961) 847–70, to the effect that all of Luke 14 is a literary unit like the symposia of Plato, Xenophon, and Plutarch (apud J. Martin, *Symposium. Die Geschichte einer literarischen Form* [Paderborn: Schöningh, 1931] 33–148).

HOLY WAR AT QUMRAN

A number of links forge the intimate relation between the teaching of humility in 14:7-14 and the parable in 14:16-24. The principal ones are as follows:

1. The formulary introduction to the parable appears in v. 7 along with the introductory matter leading into the didache material of vv. 8-14, just as the mise-en-scène for both the teaching and the parable is provided at the head of the report of the deed (and challenge) of healing on the Sabbath which begins chapter 14. These are Lukan redactional techniques that cannot be overlooked.

2. The key word *keklēmenoi* (invited and "apparently elect") appears four times, twice in the teaching pericope (vv. 7-8) and twice in the parable itself (vv. 14 and 24).

3. The four-word listing "poor, maimed, lame, and blind" appears precisely in the two pericopes, at 14:13 and 14:21.

4. The exhortation that closes the pericope on humility ends on the same eschatological note that introduces the parables (vv. 14 and 15). Thus the "resurrection of the just" in v. 14 and "shall eat bread in the kingdom of God" in v. 15 both fix the focus of the parable on who is truly elect. The parable's ethical lesson apparently is given before the parable itself; that is, the challenge to the life-style of those who consider themselves *keklēmenoi* is leveled before the picture is painted of how it will actually be when the herald goes forth to proclaim that the kingdom table is prepared to receive those who have been "called" (*keklēmenoi*). The lesson is a challenge to the life-style of the *keklēmenoi* and the parable a challenge to their very identity.

The parable itself is in three parts. (1) Verses 16-17 describe the "invitation" and despatch of the herald. (2) Verses 18-20 give the excuses or the reasons the *keklēmenoi* "beg off" (*paraiteisthai*). (3) Verses 21-24 describe the reaction of the host who has freedom to alter the guest list at will, which allows the herald to "bring in" (v. 21) and "compel" (v. 23) others to come.

The herald is dispatched to call in the "many" (*kai ekalesen pollous*). Clearly *pollous* here means not crowds or the like but an in-group. As has been established on other bases, *polloi* is often the equivalent of the frequently used *ha-rabbim* at Qumran, a synonym of the elect.[24] The message

---

24. Cf. J. T. Milik, *Ten Years of Discovery in the Wilderness of Judea* (SBT 26; London: SCM, 1959) 101, and F. M. Cross, Jr., *The Ancient Library of Qumran and Modern Biblical Studies* (Garden City: Doubleday, 1961) 231; and see the comprehensive study by J. Carmignac, "HRBYM: Les 'Nombreux' ou les 'Notables'?" *RevQ* 7 (1971) 575–86.

of the herald is simple. "Come, for now all is ready."[25] The banquet table is prepared to receive those who will eat bread in the kingdom of God.

At this point, as might have been expected in the Deuteronomy sequence, the *keklēmenoi* begin to send in their reasons for not heeding the call. But Luke has not simply transferred the Deuteronomic material here out of context. The excuses applicable to the eschatological war are not pertinent to the eschatological banquet, which presupposes the eschatological victory and the introduction of the jubilee kingdom in the coming of the Messiah/Christ. The fact that the fourth reason for exemption from the eschatological scene, faintheartedness, is omitted from the parable underscores the reasoning developed by Yadin for the omission of the first three from 1QM 10:5–6,[26] all the more so since the victory is assured. This is precisely the point at which Qumran and the Second Testament differ: for the former the eschaton was at hand, for the latter it had already been introduced by God's victory in Christ.

Matthew's use of the banquet tradition is quite different from that of Luke's.[27] Matthew does not follow Deuteronomy at all but develops a midrash on Zephaniah 1. Hence, Matthew's presentation of the supper as a *gamos* (wedding banquet) given by the king for his son relates to the battle (because of Zephaniah 1) in quite a different manner from Luke's *deipnon* (banquet). Matthew cryptically summarizes the excuses as concern for farm and business and pictures an army in the place of Luke's servant or herald. Matthew describes the newly called guests as "all you can find" or simply as "both bad and good" and brings in the murder theme by picturing the *keklēmenoi* as unworthy and finally rejected by the king.[28] By contrast, central to the parable in Luke is the new list of guests specifically

---

25. Discussion of double invitations and the like, as by Jeremias followed by Perrin (both cited in n. 4), are impertinent; hence the relevance of *Lam. Rab.* 4:2 §2 to our passage is obviated.

26. Yadin, *Scroll of the War*, 69–71.

27. Derrett (*Law in the New Testament*, 126–55) fails at crucial junctures to distinguish between Matthew and Luke in their treatments of this material. This is generally the case with Derrett's work on the New Testament; he pays insufficient attention to either tradition criticism or redaction criticism. I admire his confidence in his attempt to reconstruct what Jesus himself said and did, and his approach is preferable to other treatments that in my opinion are too skeptical; but he is less than convincing when he pays little or no attention to the process intervening between Jesus and the Gospels. Derrett's astute observations about the importance of the Targum to Zephaniah 1 are limited to the Matthean guise of the parable.

28. The judgment of Perrin and others, that the *Gospel of Thomas*'s "version is nearer to the teaching of Jesus than either of the others" (*Rediscovering the Teaching of Jesus*, 112–13) is in my analysis of *Thomas* incorrect. From a synoptic study of Matthew 22, Luke 14, and *Thomas* §64 it is apparent that *Thomas*, as well as Matthew, is totally unaware of the Deuteronomy 20 basis of the excuses. The only serious question is whether Luke molded the

named as the poor, maimed, blind, and lame (as in 14:13). First, it must be noted that Luke uses no form of *kaleō* here. The new guests are simply brought in or compelled to come in, as though Luke wanted to be very careful in his use of this key word. He reserves it here to designate those who would consider themselves elect. Thus does he emphasize the freedom of the host to alter the guest list at will. "Blessed is he who shall eat bread in the kingdom of God" indeed! God can be angry at the "elect" (Luke 14:21) and execute the power and freedom in favor of whom God wishes, especially when belief in the new divine act, the final holy war victory, is spurned.[29]

In order to understand the list of new guests one must once more turn to the First Testament and to Qumran. The *Rule of the Congregation*, which specifically deals with those who may be admitted to the Qumran inner council and those who will sit at table when the Messiah comes, establishes an index of those forbidden access to either (1QSa 2:5–22). And the *War Scroll* establishes an index of those forbidden to approach the field of battle of the last great holy war when the holy angels will fight on the side of the faithful against their enemies (1QM 7:4–6). Both lists of the forbidden are drawn from the category of the sons of Aaron in Lev. 21:17-23, who are proscribed from approaching the veil or altar to offer the *lehem 'elohîm* (bread of God).

Lev 21:17-23	*1QSa 2:5–22*	*1QM 7:4–6*
blind	afflicted in flesh	(women and boys)
lame	crushed in feet or hands	lame
mutilated face	lame	blind
limb too long	blind	halt
injured foot	deaf	permanent defect in flesh
injured hand	dumb	afflicted with impurity of flesh
hunchback	defective eyesight	impure sexual organs
dwarf	senility	
defect in sight	(the simple—1:19–20)	
itching disease		
scabs		
crushed testicles		
any blemish		

Despite differences of terminology in the three lists, Leviticus 21 clearly

---

tradition he received to the Deuteronomic midrashic base or received it in the approximate form in which he reports it. My judgment is that Deuteronomy 20 is so integral to the parable that possibly it was this parable (at the heart of Luke's central section), received in a form close to what appears in Luke, which led Luke to construct his chaps. 9–18 as he did.

29. Much of the material in Luke stresses God's freedom to elect whom he wills: cf. his use of *dektos* in Luke 4:19, 24, and the meaning of *eudokia* in 2:14. See above Chap. 4 (63–69).

lies behind both proscriptions in the Qumran documents.[30] There can be little question that the twice-recorded "poor, maimed, blind and lame" in Luke 14 partly reflects such proscriptions. Qumran drew on the list in Leviticus 21 to clarify both who should not approach the field of eschatological battle and who should not be present at the messianic table. The Lukan list, however, seems to reflect the levitical only as refracted through such legislation as that of Qumran, and it is used with the opposite intention, as though the Great Banquet parable was specifically constructed to contradict the sort of membership or guest lists now known from the Qumran literature.

The *Rule of the Congregation,* just before and after the list of those forbidden access to the core of the community, gives two quite different kinds of lists. The first specifies those who are "invited" to the community council, and the second those "invited" to the community council when God will bring the Messiah for the messianic meal. The word "invited" occurs three times in this document (once as *niqra'im* and twice as *qeru'im*). (And, *mirabile dictu,* the other two occurrences of *qeru'im* in the Qumran literature are in 1QM 3:2 and 4:10—the other document from Qumran so important for understanding the Great Banquet parable!)[31]

> These are the men who will be invited (*niqra'im*) to the Community Council (from the age of twenty): all the wise men of the congregation, the understanding and the knowledgeable, the pure in piety, the men of great virtue with the leaders of the tribes, together with their judges and captains, commanders of thousands and commanders of hundreds, of fifties and of tens, and the Levites—each in his assigned place of duty. These are the men of renown called by the Assembly (*qeri'ê mo'ed*), appointed to the Community Council in Israel in the presence of the Priests, Sons of Zadoq. (1QSa 1:27–2:3)

Next comes the list of those forbidden to have membership in the community council. Then ensues one of the most interesting passages in the document for understanding the Great Banquet parable.

---

30. The midrashic relation between 2 Sam 5:8 and 6:19 and the Great Banquet tradition in the Second Testament needs to be studied now in light of the developing methods here indicated. Note that the texts 4QM[a] and 4QD[b] reflect the same proscriptions as those in the 1Q documents here cited. Cf. *m. Hag.* 2:7; *m. 'Abot* 2:6; *m. Bek.* 7; and *m. Tohar.* 7; but cf. *m. 'Abot* 1:5 and *'Abot R. Nat.* A 7.2. A related problem is that presented by 4QFlor 1:4 (the exclusion of the *mamzer, ben nekar,* and *ger*), but this stems from Deut 23:2-4 (1-3): cf. Ezek 44:6-9 as well as *m. Yebam.* 2:4, 6:1, 8:3; *m. Qidd.* 3:12, 4:1; *m. Ketub.* 3:1, 11:6; *m. Mak.* 3:1; *m. Sanh.* 4:2; *m. Hor.* 1:4; *Ps. Sol.* 17:28. See J. M. Baumgarten's excellent treatment of the *ger* at Qumran in "Exclusion of 'netinim' and Proselytes in 4QFlorilegium," *RevQ* 8 (1972) 87–96; and idem, *Studies in Qumran Law* (SJLA 24; Leiden: Brill, 1977) 75–87.

31. These expressions for the "elect" in 1QSa and 1QM are undoubtedly drawn from Num 1:16; 16:2; and 26:9.

This is the seating order of the men of renown, called (*or* invited) by the Assembly to the Community Council whenever God will bring the Messiah to be with them. The High Priest will come at the head of all of the Congregation of Israel. As for all the elders (fathers?) of the priests, sons of Aaron, called (*or* invited) by the Assembly, men of renown, they shall take their place under his primacy, each according to his status (*or* dignity). Thereafter shall the Messiah of Israel take his place. And then shall the heads of the thousands of Israel take their place under his primacy, each according to his status (*or* dignity) and according to the post that he occupies in their camps and on their marches. Thereafter shall all the heads of the elders (fathers?) of the Congregation as well as all the wise men of the Holy Congregation take their places under their primacy, each according to his status. When they shall be gathered about the table of the Community, or for drinking the wine, and when the table of the Community shall be ready (prepared) and the wine mixed so that it can be drunk, let no one touch the first bite of bread or touch the wine before the priest. For it is he who shall bless the first bite of bread and the wine; and he shall be first to touch the bread and then bless all the members of the united Congregation, each according to his status. (1QSa 2:11–21)

Thereafter it is provided that this messianic meal may be celebrated proleptically whenever a minimum of ten men are gathered to do so.

LUKE AND JESUS

It would be difficult to imagine more appropriate foils than these to what Luke reports that Jesus said, in both the teaching on humility and in the parable. He has completely inverted both the guest list and the seating arrangement as stipulated in the Qumran documents. People should assume neither where at table they will sit nor indeed that they will even have a place there. By focusing attention on the time of the "resurrection of the just" and on who "will eat bread in the kingdom of God," Luke makes it clear that Jesus is challenging the identity of those who consider themselves *keklēmenoi*. Like the classical prophets of the First Testament Jesus raises the question of Israel's identity and challenges assumptions about election.[32] "I tell you, none of the *keklēmenoi* shall taste my banquet" (14:24).

A final word is in order about the presence of the word *ptōchoi* in the two lists of substitute guests in Luke. This word, "poor," does not appear either in Leviticus 21 or in the two Qumran lists of those forbidden. And it is difficult to imagine that it would, for in both the First Testament and the Qumran literature all such words that might be rendered *ptōchoi*, the poor, the afflicted, and the humble, frequently appear as appellatives of

---

32. Cf. Sanders, *Torah and Canon*, 85–90.

Israel or the elect. At Qumran such words are used as self-designations of the sect: they considered themselves to be God's poor ones.[33] Throughout the First Testament such terms often appear in covenant formulations of the self-understanding of Israel. Israel in the First Testament is constantly reminded that the people had been slaves and must always be conscious of the poor and powerless in order to continue to be God's people in the full sense of the meaning of covenant people.[34] Luke's construction of these two pericopes constitutes Jesus' call to harken to this basic biblical concept. For this reason what is here proposed is an understanding of the parable, and the teaching on humility, as a prophetic critique of a common *inversion* of the Deuteronomic ethic of election. Deuteronomy may well say that God blesses the obedient and judges the disobedient. But it does *not* say that poverty, affliction, and lack of bodily wholeness are proof of God's disfavor.[35] On the contrary, these Lukan constructions appear to insist on a common First Testament theme that God has a kind of bias for those in apparent disfavor.

That common theme can sometimes seem to run counter to another, the pious desire of the faithful to practice purity out of reverence for God. In Leviticus 21 the afflicted are forbidden access to the veil and to the altar because of deep concern in the holiness code for purity in the community's cultic relations with God. At Qumran it is stated several times that the afflicted and impure are forbidden access to the council, to the eschatological battlefield, and to the messianic table, because of the *mal'akhê qodhesh* (the holy angels) who, it is feared, might be offended by such impurity.[36]

To recognize the possibility of conflict between two such prominent biblical themes is to engage in the necessary canons of historical research; for such conflict demonstrates the historical principle of ambiguity of reality without recognition of which no student can claim to be a historian. The historian cannot assume that one group is "good" and the other "bad," but must scrupulously describe what the sources lead us to perceive. This same principle must be recognized as well in working on the disputation sayings of the false prophets in the First Testament. We cannot

---

33. Cf. 1QH 2:34; 5:13–14; CD 6:16–21; 14:14; and Ps 154:18 (11QPsᵃ 18:15) and the notes thereto in J. A. Sanders, *The Psalms Scroll of Qumran Cave 11 (11QPsᵃ)* (DJD 4; Oxford: Clarendon, 1965) 66–67, and the ensuing discussion.

34. Deuteronomy designates Israel's concern for the poor, dispossessed, or powerless, by the terms sojourners, fatherless, and widows (cf. 14:29; 16:11-14; and 26:11-13).

35. In a sense, the books of Job and Ecclesiastes address themselves, in their time and way, to earlier inversions of the Deuteronomic ethic of election. Cf. Isa 56:3-7. In a broad sense, such a popular understanding of Deuteronomy's theology of election turned Jeremiah into its most insistent antagonist in the late seventh century B.C.E.

36. Most clearly in 4QFlor 1:4, 1QSa 2:8, and 1QM 7:6 and 10:11; but see also 11QMelch.

claim to have understood the so-called true prophets until every effort has been made to understand the best arguments of the so-called false prophets.[37] This is precisely what was meant above by the historical and literary foci of full context. The text before us can be understood only to the extent that we are aware of its spoken or written context. Only in this manner can points originally scored be recovered. We need not always assume a debate as such; but we must assume there was a reason for speaking or writing.

Is Luke alone responsible for such material that so vividly comes alive when seen as a prophetic critique of the in-group thinking of those who in the first century were confident they would be at the kingdom table? Any valid judgment of that question must finally depend on how crucial we view the Qumran materials for reconstructing the second focus, the foil to the parable, for surely they depict a Palestinian setting before 70 C.E.

Was Luke, in structuring this parabolic tradition as he did, attempting to say, "The Jews opted out and the Gentiles must be urged to come in"? It is possible, indeed, that such was his purpose—Matthew seems to intend such. Even so, a crucial question is in order. Is this not a good example of how a prophetic in-group critique of the earlier period (Jesus) can without malice aforethought be later subverted to say the opposite when contemporized by static transfer to fit the *later* second focus? In such a case, the original substance needed little change when the later focus was so utterly different.

Is it not possible that recognition of such dynamics of focus may lead to more optimism about recovering the teaching of the historical Jesus? The historian deals in probabilities, not certainties. Perhaps Luke's older reputation as a "historian" (reporting what was done and said by Jesus) should be as seriously entertained as his newer reputation as a "theologian" (making Jesus traditions relevant to his day). One need not make Luke an antiquarian to appreciate him as a gifted theological historian in the biblical sense.

---

37. As brilliantly demonstrated by A. S. van der Woude, "Micah in Dispute with the Pseudo-Prophets," *VT* 19 (1969) 244–60. See also Sanders, *Torah and Canon*, 85–90; idem, "Jeremiah and the Future of Theological Scholarship," *ANQ* 22 (1972) 133–45; and idem, "Hermeneutics in True and False Prophecy," in Sanders, *From Sacred Story to Sacred Text*, 87–105. Just such a positive approach based on "discussion literature" underlies the study of false prophecy by J. L. Crenshaw, *Prophetic Conflict: Its Effect upon Israelite Religion* (BZAW 124; Berlin: de Gruyter, 1971). See also F. Hossfeld and I. Mayer, *Prophet gegen Prophet: Eine Analyse der alttestamentlichen Texte zum Thema, wahre und falsche Propheten* (BibB 9; Fribourg: Schweizerisches katholisches Bibelwerk, 1973).

— 9 —

LUKE 16:1-18 AND THE
DEUTERONOMY HYPOTHESIS

CRAIG A. EVANS

THE DEUTERONOMY HYPOTHESIS

More than thirty years ago Christopher F. Evans proposed that Luke's central section (9:51—18:14) was patterned after the contents and order of LXX Deuteronomy 1–26.[1] His parallels can be distilled as follows (with a few larger groupings subdivided and other minor adjustments enclosed in square brackets):

Deuteronomy	Subject	Luke
1:19-25	sending of emissaries	10:1-3, 17-20
2:1—3:3	inhospitable kings and cities	10:4-16
[3:3-7, 23-27	conquest of evil	10:17-20]
4:5-8, 32-40	the source of wisdom	10:21-24
5:1—6:24	the Great Commandment	10:25-28
7:1-16	attitude toward foreigners	10:29-37
8:1-3	God's Word as food	10:38-42
8:4-20	God provides for the needs of people	11:1-13
9:1—10:11	God's enemies dispossessed	11:14-26
10:12-15; 11:26-28	blessings for the obedient	11:27-28
10:16—11:7	stubbornness and signs	11:29-36
12:1-16	clean and unclean	11:37—12:12
12:17-32	warning against selfishness/idolatry	12:13-34
13:1-5	time tests the faithful	12:35-48
13:6-11	faithfulness divides families	12:49-53
13:12-18	danger of judgment	12:54—13:5
[14:28	fruit every third year	13:6-9]

---

1. C. F. Evans, "The Central Section of St. Luke's Gospel," in D. E. Nineham, ed., *Studies in the Gospels* (R. H. Lightfoot Festschrift; Oxford: Blackwell, 1955) 37–53.

121

Deuteronomy	Subject	Luke
15:1-18	release from debt and slavery	13:10-21
[15:19-23	eating in God's presence	13:22-30]
16:1—17:7	feasts in Jerusalem	13:[31]22-35
17:8—18:22	justice and the law	14:1-14
20:1-9	excuses for exemption from holy war	14:15-24
20:10-20	terms of peace/counting cost	14:25-35
21:15—22:4	families and restoration of lost	15:1-32
23:15—24:4	slaves, usury, divorce	16:1-18
24:6—25:3	laws against oppressing the poor	16:19—18:8
26:1-19	tithes and obedience	18:9-14

Some scholars have enthusiastically endorsed Evans's study,[2] while others have not.[3] In what is probably the most thorough evaluation, Craig L. Blomberg has noted that the Deuteronomy hypothesis is weak in at least three important areas. (1) In ancient literature there are no parallels to what Luke supposedly has done. (2) Evans's alleged parallels are often vague and imprecise. In fact, at times better parallels may exist outside the sequence that Evans has proposed. (3) Not all of the content in Deuteronomy is paralleled. Omitted are Deuteronomy chapters 14; 19; 21:1-14; 22:5—23:14; 25:4-19.[4] Blomberg then raises another objection, one not leveled at Evans but certainly relevant to the debate as it has developed in recent years. He notes that many of Evans's followers have appealed to the method and genre of Jewish midrash to account for the imprecision in the parallels. He then surveys Jewish midrashim and finds nothing that remotely resembles Luke's central section in either form or method.[5] He accordingly concludes that beyond a few "suggestive" parallels, where themes from Deuteronomy may have been drawn upon, Evans's

---

2. J. D. M. Derrett, *Law in the New Testament* (London: Darton, Longman & Todd, 1970) 100, 126–55; J. Bligh, *Christian Deuteronomy (Luke 9–18)* (Langley: St. Paul, 1970); J. A. Sanders, "The Ethic of Election in Luke's Great Banquet Parable," in J. L. Crenshaw and J. T. Willis, eds., *Essays in Old Testament Ethics (J. Philip Hyatt, in Memoriam)* (New York: Ktav, 1974) 247–71 (see Chap. 8 above); J. Drury, *Tradition and Design in Luke's Gospel: A Study in Early Christian Historiography* (London: Darton, Longman & Todd, 1976) 138–64; M. D. Goulder, *The Evangelists' Calendar* (London: SPCK, 1978) 95–101; C. A. Evans, "Luke's Use of the Elijah/Elisha Narratives and the Ethic of Election," *JBL* 106 (1987) 75–83 (see Chap. 5 above); Robert W. Wall, " 'The Finger of God': Deuteronomy 9.10 and Luke 11.20," *NTS* 33 (1987) 144–50; idem, "Martha and Mary (Luke 10.38-42) in the Context of a Christian Deuteronomy," *JSNT* 35 (1989) 19–35.

3. J. A. Fitzmyer, *The Gospel according to Luke I–IX* (AB 28; Garden City: Doubleday, 1981) 826; C. L. Blomberg, "Midrash, Chiasmus, and the Outline of Luke's Central Section," in R. T. France and D. Wenham, eds., *Studies in Midrash and Historiography* (Gospel Perspectives 3; Sheffield: JSOT, 1983) 228–33; T. L. Brodie, *Luke the Literary Interpreter: Luke-Acts as a Systematic Rewriting and Updating of the Elijah-Elisha Narrative in 1 and 2 Kings* (Rome: Pontifical University of St. Thomas Press, 1987) 410–11, n. 317.

4. Blomberg, "Luke's Central Section," 223.

5. Blomberg, "Luke's Central Section," 223–25.

proposal does not stand.[6] Blomberg's criticisms are well-taken. He has clearly identified the problems and exposed the weaknesses in the methods of some of those who have followed Evans. A few comments on his objections are in order.

First, it is true that no exact literary parallels to Luke's proposed relationship to Deuteronomy can be adduced. The activity of rewriting biblical tradition, however, is to a certain extent cognate, and there are many examples of biblical rewriting. Deuteronomy is itself a rewriting of portions of Exodus, Leviticus, and Numbers. The Chronicler rewrites Deuteronomistic history (as found mostly in Samuel-Kings). The author of 1 Esdras rewrites biblical history from Josiah (2 Chronicles 35) to Ezra's public reading of the law (Nehemiah 7–8). *Jubilees* rewrites part of the Pentateuch (from Genesis 1 to Exodus 12), and Pseudo-Philo's *Biblical Antiquities* rewrites a much greater portion of biblical history (from Genesis to 2 Samuel). Similar activity is seen in the New Testament. Matthew and Luke incorporated and rewrote Mark, supplementing it from a collection of sayings. Ephesians incorporates and rewrites most of Colossians. Second Peter rewrites and incorporates most of Jude, placing much of the borrowed material in the middle part of the epistle.[7] In these cases, the order of the incorporated tradition is usually followed. But Luke has neither rewritten nor incorporated Deuteronomy. At most he has alluded to portions of it, followed the order of its contents, and selected dominical tradition that touches on larger theological issues (such as election) with which Deuteronomy and its interpreters were concerned. Are there other literary models that approximate what Luke may have done? The rabbinic materials, especially in the Mishnah and Tosefta, are often arranged topically by division and by tractate. But this factor is likely irrelevant to an analysis of Luke. The same probably should be said with regard to lectionary and calendar hypotheses.[8] The rabbinical midrashim likewise are not true analogues, and the lateness of these literary forms militates against such a comparison. However, literary imitation among Greco-Roman writers is somewhat cognate to what has been proposed of Luke's central section. In these cases the imitated material is only alluded to and not

6. Blomberg, "Luke's Central Section," 227–28.
7. See my study, "Luke and the Rewritten Bible: Aspects of Lucan Hagiography," in J. H. Charlesworth and C. A. Evans (eds.), *The Pseudepigrapha and Biblical Interpretation* (JSPSup; Sheffield: JSOT, forthcoming); and Evans, "The Genesis Apocryphon and the Rewritten Bible," in É. Puech and F. García Martínez, eds., *Mémorial Jean Carmignac* (*RevQ* 13; Paris: Gabalda, 1988) 153–65.
8. Goulder, *The Evangelists' Calendar*, 95–101. See the critical evaluation in L. Morris, *The New Testament and the Jewish Lectionaries* (London: Tyndale, 1964); idem, "The Gospels and the Jewish Lectionaries," in France and Wenham, *Studies in Midrash and Historiography*, 129–56.

rewritten in block. In fact, one scholar thinks that this is precisely what Luke has done in relation to 1 and 2 Kings (see below).[9] But Luke's parallels do not appear in the order of Kings. Consequently it must be admitted that if Luke has indeed followed the order and contents of Deuteronomy 1–26, he has done something, so far as we know, that no one else has done in quite the same manner.

But it is also fair to say that what has been proposed about the central section is not alien to the historiography and hagiography of the times. Ordering principles that are not necessarily chronological are often employed. Indeed, Blomberg himself has suggested that a chiastic parable source, which Luke edited and supplemented, actually underlies the central section.[10] There may be examples of ordering principles in the other Gospels. One scholar has suggested that Psalm 107 provides the "horizon" against which the collection of miracle stories in the first half of Mark (4:35—8:26) should be seen.[11] Psalm 107 may have influenced the evangelist, or earlier tradents, in the selection of traditions. As has often been pointed out, the Matthean evangelist may have arranged much of the dominical tradition into five major discourses (chaps. 5–7, 10; 13; 18; 24–25) in an effort to present Jesus' teaching in a form resembling that in which Moses' teaching is preserved.[12] Elsewhere I have suggested that

---

9. See Brodie, *Luke the Literary Interpreter.*

10. Blomberg, "Luke's Central Section," 240–48. The obvious advantage of appealing to chiasmus is that this literary device was popular in the first century, and abundant examples occur in the Old Testament. Blomberg's proposed chiastic parable source looks like this (247):

10:25-37	18:9-14	controversy
11:5-8	18:1-8	discipleship
11:11-13	17:7-10	discipleship
12:13-21	16:19-31	controversy
12:35-38	16:1-13	discipleship
13:1-9	15:1-32	controversy
14:1-6	14:28-33	controversy
	14:7-24	controversy

11. R. P. Meye ("Psalm 107 as 'Horizon' for Interpreting the Miracle Stories of Mark 4:35—8:26," in R. A. Guelich, ed., *Unity and Diversity in New Testament Theology* [G. E. Ladd Festschrift; Grand Rapids: Eerdmans, 1978] 1–13) has suggested that the miracles of Mark 4:35—8:26 roughly correspond to the order and themes found in Psalm 107. He finds correspondence in four categories: (1) deliverance from hunger and thirst in the wilderness (Ps 107:4-9; Mark 6:30-44; 8:1-10, 14-21); (2) deliverance from imprisonment (Ps 107:10-16; Mark 5:1-20; 6:13; 7:24-30); (3) deliverance from sickness (Ps 107:17-22; Mark 5:21—6:5, 13, 53-56; 7:31-37; 8:22-26); and (4) deliverance from peril at sea (Ps 107:23-32; Mark 4:35-41; 6:45-52).

J. D. M. Derrett's recent claim (*The Making of Mark: The Scriptural Bases of the Earliest Gospel* [2 vols.; Shipston-on-Stour: Drinkwater, 1985] 1.38) that Mark is a "gigantic midrash" on the Hexateuch and Lamentations, as well as on the "Jesus-material," is an example of "pan-midrashism" that knows no limits.

12. Drury, *Tradition and Design,* 141. The five Matthean discourses do not, of course, reflect the contents of the respective five books of Moses; nor is Matthew as a whole a midrash or lectionary, as has been claimed in Drury, *Tradition and Design,* 44, and in M. D. Goulder, *Midrash and Lection in Matthew* (London: SPCK, 1974) 4.

John 12 is composed in the light of Isa 52:7—53:12.[13] If Luke has arranged the central section to correspond to the contents of Deuteronomy, he has done nothing alien to the literary mentality that lies behind these other ordering principles.

Blomberg furthermore is certainly correct in his observation that many of the alleged parallels are vague and sometimes found outside the Deuteronomy sequence,[14] and that some extended sections of Deuteronomy are unparalleled altogether. In my judgment this observation militates against the view that Luke produced a midrash on Deuteronomy, that is, in the sense that Luke (or tradents before him) created or extensively redacted the materials in the central section according to what he found in LXX Deuteronomy;[15] but it does not militate against the view that Luke selected and arranged his materials according to the contents and order of LXX Deuteronomy. The theses of John Duncan Martin Derrett and Michael D. Goulder in particular have probably done more to damage the credibility of the Evans proposal than to commend it. James A. Sanders has rightly claimed that the place to go to understand the Lukan evangelist is the LXX, not rabbinica.[16] Hence the validity of the Evans proposal is not tied to whether or not Luke's central section should be considered a midrash in whole or in part; that is a separate question. The validity of the proposal is tied to the LXX version of Deuteronomy.

In all likelihood, Luke's central section does not parallel all the contents of Deuteronomy 1–26 for the simple reason that the evangelist did not possess dominical tradition corresponding to all the contents. Consider those parts of Deuteronomy for which Evans could suggest no parallel. Deuteronomy 14 consists of lists of animals that may or may not be eaten. With the possible exception of v. 28, which Luke might have intended to match with Luke 13:6-9, nothing in this chapter corresponds with Q or L, the materials from which Luke constructed the central sec-

---

13. C. A. Evans, "Obduracy and the Lord's Servant: Some Observations on the Use of the Old Testament in the Fourth Gospel," in C. A. Evans and W. F. Stinespring, eds., *Early Jewish and Christian Exegesis* (W. H. Brownlee Festschrift; Homage 10; Atlanta: Scholars, 1987) 221–36, esp. 232–36. G. W. Vander Hoek ("The Function of Psalm 82 in the Fourth Gospel," *SBL Abstracts* [1989] 155) has shown how Psalm 82 provided an organizing principle for John 10.

14. In this regard, Bligh's book (*Christian Deuteronomy*) hurts the credibility of the Deuteronomy hypothesis. Bligh follows the parallels only to Luke 12:54—13:5 (Deut 13:12-18). Thereafter he departs from the parallels proposed by Evans (at their most impressive juncture!) and, in my judgment, flounders. Goulder (*The Evangelists' Calendar*) also disagrees with Evans at several points. Because of the obvious subjectivity at work, Blomberg ("Luke's Central Section," 260–61) spoofs these proposed parallels by drawing up a list of several coincidental "parallels" between Psalms 1–10 and Luke 1:5—4:37.

15. This, I believe, is Blomberg's chief concern. If material is identified as "midrash," then it is unhistorical, and this he does not wish to concede; see Blomberg, "Luke's Central Section," 247.

16. J. A. Sanders, "Isaiah in Luke," *Int* 36 (1982) 144–55, esp. 146 (see Chap. 2 above).

tion.[17] Deuteronomy 19 has to do with cities of refuge for those who have commited manslaughter. What in the dominical tradition could parallel this? The first half of Deuteronomy 21, another part of Deuteronomy that finds no parallel in the central section, is concerned with the treatment of dead bodies and women captives. Again there is nothing in the dominical tradition that could conceivably be illuminated against these themes. Deuteronomy 22:5—23:14 consists of a variety of rules (e.g., about transvestites; mixing types of seed; tassles; virginity; rape; castration) that have no parallel in dominical tradition. Deuteronomy 25:4-19 is the only lengthy omission that at places could have been paralleled by dominical tradition, for example, the laws pertaining to justice (vv. 1-3), muzzling oxen (v. 4; cf. 1 Tim 5:18), and levirate marriage (vv. 5-10). But the best parallels with these portions of Deuteronomy 25 have in fact been employed by Luke elsewhere (compare v. 4 with Luke 13:15; 14:5; and vv. 5-10 with Luke 20:27-37).

In conclusion, Blomberg's criticisms increase the burden of proof on advocates of the Deuteronomy hypothesis, but do not eliminate the hypothesis. Vague parallels, a handful of verbal coincidences, and speculative reconstructions of lectionaries or midrashim will not bear up under critical scrutiny. For the Deuteronomy hypothesis to stand the parallels must be linked in exegetically and theologically meaningful ways. In short, if the hypothesis cannot shed light on the meaning of Luke, it ought to be abandoned.

FACTORS IN SUPPORT
OF THE DEUTERONOMY HYPOTHESIS

There are at least five factors that support the Deuteronomy hypothesis. They are as follows:

1. Literarily, the central section represents a major insertion of material into the Markan narrative that Luke has more or less followed. At 9:50 Luke breaks off from Mark 9:41, inserts his central section (or "travel narrative"), and returns in 18:14 to his source at Mark 10:13. Apart from Deuteronomy 1–26 or Blomberg's proposed chiastic parable source, the central section has no discernible order. Although I suppose it is not absolutely necessary to insist that Luke followed or developed some coherent ordering principle, the nature of his two-volume work suggests that

---

17. Luke omits Mark 7:14-23, which could have been a candidate for inclusion here, esp. v. 19b ("He declared all foods clean"), but the issue in Mark concerned washing the hands, not what kinds of food could be eaten. (The statement in v. 19b, of course, is a Markan editorial comment that directs the tradition toward a topic of interest to the Gentile church.) Peter's vision in Acts 10:9-16 is parallel but hardly appropriate for inclusion in the central section.

the evangelist was fond of progression and order.[18] If the central section is truly amorphous, it is the only passage of its kind in Luke-Acts. It is probably more prudent to assume that there is some ordering principle behind it. Theoretically, of course, a chiastic parable source could serve as such an ordering principle for the central section just as well as could Deuteronomy (or some other model).[19]

2. Contextual factors also support the Deuteronomy hypothesis. In recent and significant studies David P. Moessner describes Luke 9:1-50 as depicting Jesus in terms of a new Moses who is to lead his people on a journey to the promised land.[20] In this section of Luke, Jesus prepares himself and his followers for a new Exodus (see esp. vv. 30-31). Obviously if Moessner is correct, it is logical to view the central section following this preparation as a journey in which Jesus, the new Moses, delivers his final teaching. Moreover, the opening verse of the section (9:51) contains the New Testament hapax *analēmpsis* ("ascension" or "assumption"), which may allude to traditions about Moses' ascension, possibly even to the pseudepigraphal work *The Assumption of Moses*, where the great Lawgiver gives his final teaching before being taken up.[21] If the parallel with Moses is intended (remember that it is the Lukan evangelist who explicitly identifies Jesus as the "prophet like Moses"; cf. Acts 3:22-23; 7:37), then the plausibility of the Deuteronomy hypothesis is strengthened.

3. The theme of election runs throughout the central section, in an apparent attempt, as Sanders has argued, to correct a common inversion of the Deuteronomistic ethic of election.[22] Since "sinners," Samaritans,

---

18. The Gospel advances from ministry in Galilee (4:14–9:50), to ministry in transit (9:51—19:27), to ministry in Jerusalem (19:28—21:38). The book of Acts seems to follow the pattern of 1:8, as the gospel proclamation begins in Jerusalem (1:12—8:3) and spreads to Judea and Samaria (8:3—12:25) and to the Gentiles (13:1—28:31). In fact, the expression "to the end of the earth" (Acts 1:8) probably alludes to Rome (see *Pss. Sol.* 8:15), the very place where the Acts narrative ends (Acts 28:14-31).

19. Blomberg's chiastic solution is not the only one that has been proposed; see R. Mogenthaler, *Die lukanische Geschichtsschreibung als Zeugnis* (2 vols.; Zurich: Zwingli, 1948) 1.156–57; M. D. Goulder, "The Chiastic Structure of the Lucan Journey," *SE* 3 (=TU 87; 1964) 195–202; C. H. Talbert, *Literary Patterns, Theological Themes, and the Genre of Luke-Acts* (Missoula: Scholars, 1974) 51–52; K. E. Bailey, *Poet and Peasant* (Grand Rapids: Eerdmans, 1976) 80–82. Some of these proposed chiastic structures involve more of Luke than the central section alone. See Blomberg's critical assessment of these proposals ("Luke's Central Section," 235–40). Blomberg's proposed chiasmus must be restored by deleting several parables and sayings that allegedly had been added by the evangelist.

20. D. P. Moessner, "Luke 9:1-50: Luke's Preview of the Journey of the Prophet like Moses of Deuteronomy," *JBL* 102 (1983) 575–605. See also his related study, "Jesus and the 'Wilderness Generation': The Death of the Prophet like Moses according to Luke," *SBLSP* (1982) 319–40, and his recent major study, *Lord of the Banquet* (Minneapolis: Fortress, 1989). See also Evans, "The Central Section," 50–51, and D. L. Tiede, *Prophecy and History in Luke-Acts* (Philadelphia: Fortress, 1980) 60–61.

21. See Evans, "The Central Section," 51–52, and Chap. 5 above.

22. See Chap. 8 above. When the ethic is inverted, the poor and unfortunate are assumed

Gentiles, and other outcasts were usually assumed to be non-elect, it is not surprising that the Lukan evangelist, for whom this issue was of special significance, would have this theme serve as an ordering principle for his non-Markan dominical traditions. Obviously there is the danger here of arguing in a circle. If the central section is indeed ordered according to Deuteronomy, then one has a more solid basis for assuming the presence of election theology as reflected in Deuteronomy and its interpretation in contemporary traditions. But Luke's interest in election theology is not limited to the central section. He is interested in universal salvation throughout his two-volume work. This is seen most clearly in the Samaritan and Gentile missions in Acts 8–28, but there are also prime examples in his Gospel account (compare Luke 3:1-6 with Mark 1:2-3, where the quotation of Isa 40:3 is extended to v. 5; see also Luke 4:16-30; 7:11-17, 36-50).

There is evidence outside the central section itself that the evangelist has interacted with Deuteronomy in working out a view of election. According to LXX Deut 33:3-4; "And he spared his people, and all those sanctified [*hēgiasmenoi*] under your hands; and these are under you, and he received from his words [*logoi*] a law, which Moses commanded to us, an inheritance [*klēronomia*] in the synagogues of Jacob." This important passage is echoed in two places in Acts that give explicit expression to election theology. To the Ephesian elders the Lukan Paul says, "And now I commend you to God and to the word [*logos*] of his grace, which is able to build you up and to give you the inheritance [*klēronomia*] among all those who are sanctified [*hēgiasmenoi*]" (Acts 20:32). The Lukan Paul later testifies before King Agrippa: "The Lord said, 'I am Jesus. . . . I have appeared to you for this purpose, to appoint you to serve and bear witness to the things in which you have seen me and to those in which I will appear to you, delivering you from the people and from the Gentiles—to whom I send you to open their eyes, that they may turn from darkness to light and from the power of Satan to God, that they may receive forgiveness of sins and a portion [*klēros*] among those who are sanctified [*hēgiasmenoi*] by faith in me' " (Acts 26:18). The Gentiles are now numbered among the "sanctified," entitled to God's "inheritance." The Lukan evangelist has drawn upon the language of Deut 33:3-4 and applied it to the church in general (Acts 20:32) and to the Gentiles specifically (Acts 26:18). This allusion, as well as the explicit citations of portions of Deut 18:15-19, indicates that the evangelist's theology is informed in important ways by the language and concepts of Deuteronomy. Moreover, the expression in Acts 26:18, turning "from darkness to light," is, as Hans Conzelmann has

---

to be sinners and non-elect, while the wealthy and outwardly pious are assumed to be righteous and elect.

noted, the language of conversion.[23] The expression alludes to Isa 42:6 and 49:6 (but cf. Deut 33:2), which are quoted and alluded to elsewhere in Luke-Acts (cf. Luke 2:32; Acts 13:47; 26:23) and in other writings in reference to conversion (cf. Eph 5:8; 1 Pet 2:9; *Jos. Asen.* 8:9; 15:12).

4. Another factor supporting the Deuteronomy hypothesis is that it sometimes explains the rationale behind the evangelist's grouping of materials. Luke 16:1-18 presents the interpreter with an odd cluster of components. Commentators have freely admitted not understanding what principle, if any, the evangelist used to bring these materials together. The final part of this chapter will examine this part of the central section against the parallel passage from Deuteronomy that Evans first proposed. It will be shown that the parallel passage from Deuteronomy accounts for the combination of materials in Luke 16:1-18.

5. In the final analysis, the proof of the pudding is in the tasting. If the Deuteronomy hypothesis proves to be a true aid to the exegetical task, then it will have gone a long way toward verification. Some studies illuminate the Lukan text. Sanders has clarified the point that Luke is trying to make in the Great Banquet parable (14:15-24) by viewing it against Deut 20:1-9.[24] The exemptions from holy war in Deut 20:1-9 approximate the excuses offered by those who had been invited to the banquet, and the banquet itself symbolizes the feast of the eschaton after evil has been defeated in the final holy war—hence the relevance of holy war legislation for a parable about a victory banquet. The parable, however, reverses current election assumptions by having the apparently elect (*hoi keklēmenoi*) miss the feast, while the apparently non-elect (the lame, the poor, the blind) join it. In an analysis of another parallel, Robert W. Wall has argued that in Jesus' saying, "By the finger of God" (Luke 11:20), Luke intentionally echoes the Deuteronomistic narrative in which the covenant was written "by the finger of God" (Deut 9:10), in order to show that Jesus' ministry, like that of Moses, is also revelatory.[25] The two literary contexts are quite similar: the people are arrogant (Deut 9:4), stubborn (Deut 9:5-6), and in need of being reminded how God had been revealed in the past (Deut 9:7—10:11). The people must realize that they need One who is mightier than their foes (compare Deut 9:1-3 with Luke 11:21-22). In another study, Wall has suggested that the collection of material in the second half of Luke 10 (the encounter with the lawyer, vv. 25-28; the parable of the Good Samaritan, vv. 29-37; the Martha/Mary episode,

---

23. H. Conzelmann, *Acts of the Apostles* (Hermeneia; Philadelphia: Fortress, 1987) 211.

24. See Chap. 8 above, and Derrett, *Law in the New Testament*, 126–55. Sanders, in Chap. 8, suspects that this parable prompted Luke to construct the central section as he did. Derrett's discussion is focused on the Matthean version of the parable (cf. Matt 22:1-14).

25. Wall, " 'The Finger of God.' "

vv. 38-42) is illuminated by comparison with Deut 5:1—8:3.[26] When the lawyer asks how to "inherit eternal life," Deut 6:18 ("That . . . you should inherit") and 6:24 ("The Lord commanded us to do all things . . . that we should live") are echoed. Since the question alludes to Deuteronomy 6, it is not surprising that the correct answer to the question is Deut 6:5, quoted in Luke 10:27. The pericope ends with Jesus telling the lawyer, "Do this, and you will live" (v. 28). Similarly, the parable of the Good Samaritan, which illustrates what it means to love and so truly keep the law (in contrast to the legislation concerned with foreigners in Deuteronomy 7), ends with the admonition, "Go and do likewise" (v. 37). The section concludes with Mary listening to Jesus' teaching (Luke 10:39), an example of one who knows that "man does not live by bread alone, but . . . by everything that proceeds out of the mouth of the Lord" (Deut 8:3b). In contrast, Martha busies herself with the food that perishes (Luke 10:40; Deut 8:3a). As a final example, the three parables of Luke 15:1-32 form a related cluster that parallels much of the material in Deut 21:15—22:4. The parable of the Lost Sheep (Luke 15:3-7) parallels the instructions on returning a neighbor's lost oxen and sheep (Deut 22:1-4). The parable of the Prodigal Son (Luke 15:11-32) parallels the instructions on treating sons equally "when [the father] assigns his possessions as an inheritance for his sons" (Deut 21:15-17). The misbehavior of the prodigal son parallels the misbehavior of the disobedient son of Deut 21:18-21.[27] These studies exemplify the detailed analysis that must be undertaken if the validity of the Deuteronomy hypothesis is to be established.

DEFINING THE
DEUTERONOMY HYPOTHESIS

The appearance of close conceptual parallels and isolated verbal agreements argues for the Deuteronomy hypothesis but not in the form in which some have presented it. There is no evidence that the Lukan materials have themselves actually been shaped by Deuteronomy's contents—at least not in their Greek form. This claim is supported by a careful analysis of the very parallels that were surveyed in point 5 above and offered as support for the hypothesis. These parallels, certainly among the closest investigated to date, make it clear that neither the evangelist Luke nor earlier Christian tradents composed the contents of the central section as homilies (or midrashim) on the parallel passages from Deuteronomy. In all the examples the parallels could have been much closer; and indeed

---

26. Wall, "Martha and Mary."

27. J. A. Sanders, *Canon and Community: A Guide to Canonical Criticism* (Guides to Biblical Scholarship; Philadelphia: Fortress, 1984) 64–65.

we should have expected them to be closer if the Lukan materials actually were inspired by the contents of the parallels from Deuteronomy. Four examples reviewed above may help to clarify the problem.

1. According to Luke 10:39 Mary sat at the feet of Jesus, "listening to his word." The parallel in LXX Deut 8:3 reads, "Every word which proceeds through the mouth of God." "Word" in Deuteronomy is *rhema*, but in Luke it is *logos*. Now it is true that Luke's favorite designation for Jesus' teaching is *logos* (see 8:11). Should we not, nevertheless, expect him to depart from his preference in order to strengthen the connection to Deut 8:1-3, the passage that supposedly inspired the narrative that he recounts in Luke 10:38-42? If Luke or someone else created Luke 10:38-42 as a commentary on Deut 8:1-3, then why not use the exact word? Why settle for a synonym? As another example, had this Lukan pericope originated as a commentary on Deut 8:1-3, should we not expect the mention of "bread"? This word, as well as others, could have been worked into the narrative easily.

2. According to Luke 11:22 the "stronger" man "distributes [the] spoils" of the strong man whom he has conquered. This is paralleled in parts of Deut 9:1—10:11, where Moses reminds the Israelites that God has conquered nations that are "stronger," so that Israel could "inherit the nations" (Deut 9:1) and "inherit this good land" (Deut 9:4). If Luke has troubled to borrow "stronger" from his LXX, why not have the stronger man "*inherit* the spoils" or "distribute the *good* things"?

3. The three excuses offered in the parable of the Great Banquet (Luke 14:18-20) loosely parallel those of Deut 20:5-7. But if Luke created or redacted this parable as a commentary on Deuteronomy 20, why not have the discourteous guests offer the very same excuses? The first one could have said, "I have built a house, and it is not yet dedicated"; and the second, "I have planted a vineyard, and have not yet enjoyed it." Even the third excuse, which is the only one that truly parallels an excuse in Deuteronomy, is inexact. Had Luke followed the LXX, it should read, "I have betrothed a wife, but have not yet taken her." The three excuses of Deuteronomy 20 would have served the purposes of the parable just as well as the three that are actually found in the parable.

4. The same thing is observed in the parallels between the parable of the Prodigal Son and the instructions on inheritance and disobedient sons. According to Luke 15:12 the father "divided his living between them" (*dieilen autois ton bion*). The parallel in Deut 21:16 reads, "He should bequeath to his sons his possessions" (*kataklēronomē tois huiois autou ta hyparchonta autou*). Had the Lukan parable been inspired by this passage, why does it not pick up some of the septuagintal vocabulary? Three times in the Lukan parable property is referred to but never called *ta hyparchonta*. The misbehavior of the younger son is another area where more of Deu-

teronomy's language could have been easily exploited. According to Luke 15:13 the younger son "squandered his property in loose living" (*dieskorpisen tēn ousian autou zōn asōtōs*). Later in v. 30 the older son complains, "This son of yours . . . has devoured your living with harlots" (*ho huios houtos ho kataphagōn sou ton bion meta pornōn*). Deuteronomy 21:20 provides a very close conceptual parallel. "This our son is disobedient and contentious, he does not obey our voice, he revels and is a drunkard" (*ho huios hēmōn houtos apeithei kai erethizei, ouch hypakouei tēs phonēs hēmōn, symbolokopōn oinophlygei*). Had the language of the Lukan parable been inspired by Deuteronomy, we should have expected the older son's complaint to run more along these lines, "This son of yours has devoured your living in revelry and drunkenness."

I believe that the evidence requires us to understand the Deuteronomy hypothesis in the following terms:

1. Most of the materials in the central section originated without any reference to Deuteronomy. The parable of the Good Samaritan is a good example. In all likelihood the Scripture that lies behind the parable is 2 Chr 28:8-15 (esp. v. 15).[28] Nothing in Deuteronomy is likely to have inspired or influenced the creation of this parable.[29] There are of course exceptions. Luke 10:25-28 is obviously based on an interpretation of Deuteronomy 6. Not only is Deut 6:5 quoted, but vv. 18 and 24 are alluded to as well. Luke 14:15-24 may also have its roots in Deuteronomy 20 as well as in other passages and traditions.

2. The Lukan evangelist has arranged the contents of the central section to correspond to the order of contents in Deuteronomy 1–26 through parallel words and concepts. If the evangelist has redacted the materials according to the Deuteronomistic parallels, the redaction is infrequent and slight. Again, the parable of the Good Samaritan illustrates this point well. Although the parable in all likelihood originated without any reference to Deuteronomy, its placement opposite Deuteronomy 7 is quite meaningful. According to this chapter foreigners are to be hated (v. 2) and their holy places destroyed (vv. 5, 25). Association of Samaritans with a passage of Scripture which teaches Jews to hate foreigners and to destroy their holy places would not be without meaningful reference in Luke's time. Recall that one of the chief causes of the bitterness between Jews and Samaritans was the Jewish destruction of the Samaritan temple, an event that the first-century historian Josephus records (*J.W.* 13.9.1 §256).

---

28. See Derrett, *Law in the New Testament*, 209; F. S. Spencer, "2 Chronicles 28:5-15 and the Parable of the Good Samaritan," *WTJ* 46 (1984) 317–49.

29. Deutronomy has nothing to do with the parable, unless one can show that vv. 25-28 constitute the original introduction. In this case, the parable might have originated with Deuteronomy 7 in mind.

3. The evangelist has produced a "commentary" on Deuteronomy only in the most general sense. (In what sense this constitutes a "midrash" is another matter.) Apparently the evangelist wishes some of the main concepts of Deuteronomy to be refracted through the dominical tradition. It is also likely that Luke wishes his readers to study the materials of the central section in the light of the parallel passages and themes from Deuteronomy. Thus, the central section and Deuteronomy, set side by side, are mutually illuminating. For example, the gravity of the younger son's actions is brought out by Deut 21:18-21. His actions are worthy of death, but because of mercy he lives. In contrast to the requirement of Deut 7:2 ("Show no mercy [*eleein*] to [foreigners]") stands the parable of the Good Samaritan. Foreigners are to be destroyed because they will lead Israel into idolatry and the breaking of the covenant (Deut 7:4, 25). Ironically, according to Luke's parable it is the Samaritan who actually fulfills the requirement of the covenant, as the Jewish legist himself admits (Luke 10:37, "The one who showed mercy [*eleos*]"). Not all the parallels are this clear. Some have only the vaguest connection, and it is a mistake to read into Luke more than is there.

4. The question of "midrash" lying behind the Lukan materials is a separate issue. Some of the pericopes may be properly identified as instances of midrash even in the narrow sense that some scholars think is appropriate. Luke 10:25-28 is probably one of the clearest examples.[30]

LUKE 16:1-18 AND
DEUTERONOMY 23:15—24:4

Luke 16:1-18 is made up of several units of tradition whose relationship to one another is not at all obvious: the parable of the Dishonest Manager and appended lessons (vv. 1-13), criticism of the Pharisees (vv. 14-15), the saying about the law and the prophets (v. 16), the saying about the law's infallibility (v. 17), and the saying prohibiting divorce (v. 18). Because he has rejected the Deuteronomy hypothesis,[31] Joseph A. Fitzmyer is at a loss to understand Luke's rationale in grouping together these diverse materials. "It is . . . difficult to discern what thread . . . unites the chapter."[32] Indeed, apart from Deuteronomy, there is no thread that unites the chap-

---

30. Exegetical traditions not based on the LXX are likely pre-Lukan. But "midrashic" activity is not limited to pre-Lukan tradition. The evangelist's reshaping and contextualization of the tradition in the light of the Greek Scriptures are part of this midrashic activity.

31. Fitzmyer, *Luke I–IX*, 826.

32. J. A. Fitzmyer, *The Gospel according to Luke X–XXIV* (AB 28A; Garden City: Doubleday, 1985) 1095. Elsewhere Fitzmyer (*Luke the Theologian: Aspects of His Teaching* [New York: Paulist, 1989] 179–80) remarks, "Luke has made use of isolated utterances of Jesus, fashioning them

ter, as the following analysis will demonstrate. Luke 16:1-18 subdivides into three basic groupings.

Luke 16:1-13: The Parable of the Dishonest Manager and Appended Lessons. The parable of the Dishonest Manager has puzzled commentators since the publication of the Gospel of Luke. The basic problem has to do with interpreting the actions of the manager dismissed by the master. What does it mean when the manager reduced the bills of the master's debtors (vv. 5-7)? Some think that the manager, in a bid to gain favor with future potential employers, has cheated the master one last time. But this is unlikely, since the master commended the manager (v. 8). Following Derrett and others,[33] Fitzmyer thinks that the manager eliminated the interest added to the bills, interest that was in effect the manager's commission.[34] By eliminating the commission and so reducing the amounts that the debtors owed, the manager may hope to find new employment with these debtors (vv. 3-4). The Deuteronomistic parallel that illuminates this passage is Deut 23:15-16, 19-20. Fitzmyer, of course, cites Deut 23:19-20 but also notes that laws against usury are found elsewhere in Deuteronomy (15:7-8) and the Pentateuch (Exod 22:25; Lev 25:36-37). What draws our attention to Deuteronomy 23 is the presence of laws pertaining to the treatment of runaway servants (vv. 15-16). These servants are not to be oppressed but are to be allowed to dwell with the Israelites who take them in.

The parable has verbal and conceptual parallels with these passages from Deuteronomy 23, but the verbal parallels are not great. The "master" is *kyrios* in Luke 16:3 and Deut 23:15. The servant, however, is an *oikonomos* in Luke, a *pais* in Deuteronomy. The dishonest manager, expecting to be cast out soon, seeks to be received into the houses (*oikos*) of others (Luke 16:4). Similarly, the runaway servant is to be allowed to dwell (*oikein*) with the Israelites (Deut 23:16). The conceptual parallels are closer. The manager's action of eliminating the interest of the debtors' bills is in compliance with the laws against usury. The manager's plight resembles the plight of the runaway servant, who, after dismissal, must now look for a new master and a new house in which to be received. The Deuteronomistic parallel enjoins Israelites to take in and treat kindly slaves who are in need.

---

into a loose unit that does not hang well together." I agree with the first part of this statement; Luke has indeed made use of isolated utterances, most of which were probably gleaned from Q. It is with the second part of Fitzmyer's comment that I disagree.

33. M. D. Gibson, "On the Parable of the Unjust Steward," *ExpTim* 14 (1902–3) 334; J. D. M. Derrett, "Fresh Light on St Luke xvi: I. The Parable of the Unjust Steward," *NTS* 7 (1960–61) 198–219; repr. in Derrett, *Law in the New Testament*, 48–77.

34. Fitzmyer, *Luke X–XXIV*, 1098.

The appended sayings in vv. 8b-13 draw further lessons from the parable. Fitzmyer thinks that vv. 8b-9 had already been appended to the parable when Luke received the tradition.[35] Likewise, vv. 10-12 might also have been attached to these materials, linked by the catchword "mammon." By the same catchword Luke has added v. 13, a related saying that he found in Q (compare Matt 6:24). The presence of these sayings at this point in Luke has to do with the parable, not with Deuteronomy. The sayings were appended by early Christians in attempts to interpret and apply this puzzling parable. The presence of vv. 8b-13, therefore, is not problematic.

Luke 16:14-15. Reproof of the Greed of the Pharisees. The saying in v. 15 in itself does not necessarily have anything to do with greed but rather with the general theme that God sees through outward pretenses. It is Luke's introduction in v. 14 that makes the saying contribute to the subject of wealth, which had been the point of the preceding parable and appended sayings. Was there anything about the saying itself that led Luke to add it here?[36] There may be. In the proposed Deuteronomistic parallel the word "abomination" occurs twice (Deut 23:18; 24:6). Fulfilling one's vow by bringing the wages of a harlot or dog [Sodomite?] into the "house of God" is an "abomination [*bdelygma*] to the Lord your God" (Deut 23:18). Similarly, in Luke 16:15 what is exalted among people is an "abomination [*bdelygma*] in the sight of God." Making vows, of course, was an important part of Pharisaic religious practice (Matt 6:33-37; 23:16-22), and some of their vows had to do with money (see Mark 7:9-13). Elsewhere in Luke, Jesus is critical of the Pharisees who "devour widows' houses and for a pretense make long prayers" (20:47). Here avarice and hypocrisy are brought together. Since the abomination of Deuteronomy has to do with money, Luke might have felt that a saying describing Pharisaic love of money as an abomination was a suitable parallel. If Luke did not add this saying to Luke 16:1-13 for this reason, then it is hard to say why he did, especially if v. 14 is his editorial work.

Luke 16:16-18. Miscellaneous Sayings. Vincent Taylor thinks that these sayings make up a unit from Q which the Matthean evangelist has broken up (see Matt 5:18, 32; 11:12-13).[37] I. Howard Marshall and Fitzmyer agree.[38] If

---

35. Fitzmyer, *Luke X–XXIV,* 1106.

36. My question assumes that the evangelist composed v. 14, as Fitzmyer (*Luke X–XXIV,* 1112) thinks. If v. 14 were already attached to the saying in v. 15, then the evangelist would have joined it to Luke 16:1-13 because of its related theme.

37. V. Taylor, *The Formation of the Gospel Tradition* (London: Macmillan, 1935) 93.

38. I. H. Marshall, *Commentary on Luke* (NIGTC; Grand Rapids: Eerdmans, 1978) 626–27; Fitzmyer, *Luke X–XXIV,* 1114.

vv. 16-18 make up a unit, then this could explain why one or two of the sayings do not fit the context. That is, the evangelist made use of the whole unit even though only part of it suited his context. But does any one of the sayings fit the context? In fact, none of the sayings has anything to do with the theme of wealth and one's proper attitude toward it, which runs throughout Luke 16.[39] Why then did the evangelist insert this unit here? One would have expected Luke to move from v. 15 into the parable of the Rich Man and Lazarus (vv. 19-31). There is no clue in the Lukan context for the appearance of this unit here in the central section. In fact, Fitzmyer concedes, in reference particularly to v. 18, that "it is . . . puzzling why it has been introduced into this part of his travel account."[40] Ironically enough, it is v. 18 that explains the presence of the unit at this point in Luke 16. Deuteronomy once again clarifies the Lukan arrangement.

According to the Deuteronomy hypothesis Luke 16:18 parallels the law of divorce and remarriage in Deut 24:1-4. Whereas the law of Moses permits divorce, Jesus does not. That Deut 24:1-4 in all probability was understood to lie behind this dominical saying is seen in Matt 5:31-32 and Mark 10:2-12, two distinct passages in which this dominical tradition appears in the form of a response to explicit citations of Deut 24:4 (see Matt 5:31; Mark 10:4). I think it highly unlikely that this parallel is no more than a coincidence. Thus at every point, the major units of Luke 16:1-18 parallel significant portions of Deut 23:15—24:4 in meaningful ways.

ASSESSMENT

The characteristics of Lukan composition in Luke 16:1-18 comport with what has been observed elsewhere in the central section. Luke has arranged his materials to correspond with the contents of Deut 23:15—24:4. He has done this primarily through conceptual parallels although verbal parallels have played a part. There is no evidence, however, that he has rewritten his traditions in order to make them correspond to Deuteronomy more closely. As observed above, the Lukan evangelist passes up opportunities to bring the materials into closer verbal agreement. For example, at some point in the parable the dishonest manager could have been called a *pais* as the servant is called in Deut 23:15. The debtors might have had bills for "silver" and "food" as in Deut 23:19, instead of bills for "oil" and "wheat."

---

39. Fitzmyer (*Luke X–XXIV*, 1114) remarks that this unit "almost has nothing to do with" the rest of Luke 16.
40. Fitzmyer, *Luke X–XXIV*, 1121.

The Deuteronomy hypothesis is supported by the presence of frequent and meaningful parallels. These parallels not only clarify the meaning of given pericopes in the central section; they sometimes explain the presence and order of dominical tradition which would otherwise be a mystery. But the Deuteronomy hypothesis does not support some scholars' contention that much of the Lukan material in the central section originated as homilies or midrashim on Deuteronomy.

PROPOSED CRITERIA FOR EVALUATING
THE DEUTERONOMY HYPOTHESIS

The Deuteronomy hypothesis, by virtue of the length of the passages involved, runs the danger of subjectivity. With so much material, it is always possible to juggle things so as to produce some sort of correspondence. When scholars resort to explaining the order of the contents of the central section against hypothesized lectionaries and the contents themselves as products of very speculative and creative midrashic activity, there are no objective controls. Have bona fide parallels been discovered, or have they been created? To mitigate this concern by claiming that this is the way first-century Jews produced literature is gratuitous and really explains nothing;[41] objective controls are needed. In my judgment the proposed parallels between Deuteronomy 1–26 and Luke's central section should be evaluated against the following three criteria:

1. *Dictional Coherence.* Do the proposed parallel passages have common vocabulary? One should expect that, if Luke attempted to arrange the contents of the central section according to the topics and the order of the topics of Deuteronomy, common vocabulary would have been one of his criteria. Nevertheless, too much importance should not be attached to this criterion. In a comparison involving large passages common vocabulary often could be no more than coincidental. Meaningful parallels must involve more than common vocabulary.

2. *Thematic Coherence.*[42] Do the proposed parallel passages share common themes or topics? This is probably the most important criterion. If the Deuteronomy hypothesis is valid, one should expect Luke to arrange his

---

41. For example, see J. Drury, "Midrash and Gospel," *Theology* 77 (1974) 291–96, esp. 294.

42. The criteria of dictional coherence and thematic coherence have been suggested to me by B. Chilton in his study of Jesus and the Isaiah Targum; cf. B. D. Chilton, *A Galilean Rabbi and His Bible: Jesus' Use of the Interpreted Scripture of His Time* (Good News Studies 8; Wilmington: Michael Glazier, 1984).

materials according to common topics even more than according to common vocabulary.

3. *Exegetical Coherence.* Do the proposed parallel passages share a meaningful exegetical context? There are two aspects to this. First, there is the exegetical context of the respective passages of Deuteronomy. Does interpretation of Deuteronomy roughly contemporaneous to Luke cohere with the thrust of the parallel passage in the central section? That is to say, is there evidence that the proposed parallel passage in Deuteronomy was understood in a way that meaningfully coheres with the point made by the putative counterpart found in Luke's central section? Second, does comparison with Deuteronomy, in view of how it was interpreted in Luke's time, shed light on the Lukan pericope in question?

The parable of the Good Samaritan discussed above fulfills all three of these criteria. First is the important dictional coherence of the word "mercy." The punch line of the parable is the legist's admission that the man who proved to be the neighbor was "the one who showed mercy" (Luke 10:37). This coheres with Deuteronomy's repeated warning about not showing mercy (Deut 7:2, 16). Second, there is significant thematic coherence. Deuteronomy 7 speaks of Israel's relationship to foreign peoples. It commands Israelites to distrust and avoid making covenants with them. The parable of the Good Samaritan presupposes this thinking. Third, there is also important exegetical coherence. Deuteronomy 7 speaks of Hittites, Girgashites, Amorites, and others, but of course says nothing of Samaritans. To speak of Samaritans would be a gross anachronism; the setting of the Deuteronomistic story is centuries before the emergence of the Samaritan people. Is there any evidence in late antiquity of a connection between Deuteronomy 7 and Samaritans? There is. In Tosefta Deut 7:2 ("You shall make no covenant with them . . . and you shall show no mercy to them") is cited in the context of a discussion of Samaritans and Gentiles (cf. *t. 'Aboda Zara* 3:11-15), to affirm the teaching that a Samaritan may not circumcise an Israelite because this would be done "for the sake of Mount Gerizim" (i.e., for the Samaritan covenant, not for the Israelite covenant). To allow a Samaritan to circumcise an Israelite would therefore be a violation of the commandment found in Deuteronomy 7. This exegesis coheres with the point made in the parable of the Good Samaritan, especially when read against the background of Deuteronomy. The issue at the heart of Luke 10:25-29 has to do with fulfillment of the covenant. To fulfill it one must love God (Deut 6:5) and one's neighbor (Lev 19:18). But does "neighbor" exclude foreigners? The legist probably assumed that it did. One could read Deuteronomy in a static fashion and say that foreigners are excluded; they have no part in Israel's covenant. Therefore, they are to have no mercy shown them because they will lead Israel away from the covenant. But according to Luke, who read Deuteronomy with a different hermeneutic, a foreigner can fulfill the Law's principal commandment precisely by showing mercy. And by fulfilling it, the foreigner qualifies as a true child of the covenant.

In my judgment the Deuteronomy hypothesis must be worked out along these lines. Every pericope of Luke's central section must be examined in light of the above criteria. Only when that has been done shall we be in a position to make definitive statements about what relationship to Deuteronomy the central section may or may not have.[43]

43. I owe a word of thanks to C. L. Blomberg who read an earlier draft of this paper and offered several helpful criticisms.

A HERMENEUTIC FABRIC:
PSALM 118 IN LUKE'S
ENTRANCE NARRATIVE

JAMES A. SANDERS

The records of Jesus' "royal" entry into Jerusalem in the four Gospels have varying points of emphasis. But all four accounts agree on a major component for understanding the import of the entrance into Jerusalem: they all cite portions of Psalm 118, and Matthew and John cite also Zech 9:9. The confluence of these two First Testament passages signals a particular context of ideas whose importance for understanding the accounts should not be overlooked. According to the synoptics, the entry into Jerusalem would have marked the first time Jesus in the years of his ministry visited the historic city of David. The significance of the entry is thus heightened in the first three Gospels because it is presented as an event of unique import.

ZECHARIAH

All four Gospels force one's attention to the claim that Jesus was the king expected, the one who was to come; and the two First Testament passages here brought together emphasize the royal dimension of the claim. The Zechariah passage (9:9) points to the expectation that the messianic son of David will ride into Jerusalem on an ass and will claim the heritage of kingship. In the MT, the passage reads:

This chapter is a revision of "A New Testament Hermeneutic Fabric: Psalm 118 in the Entrance Narrative," in C. A. Evans and W. F. Stinespring, eds., *Early Jewish and Christian Exegesis: Studies in Memory of William Hugh Brownlee* (Homage 10; Atlanta: Scholars, 1987) 177–90.

> Rejoice greatly, O daughter of Zion!
>   Shout aloud, O daughter of Jerusalem!
> See, your king comes to you;
>   a righteous one and saved is he,[1]
> humble and riding on an ass,
>   on a colt, the foal of an ass.

And Psalm 118 points to the mode of entry of kings in antiquity, providing particulars on what was said and recited by the king, priests, and people when the royal procession approached the eastern gates of the city, passed through them, and went into the temple precincts. The four Gospels cite expressions from v. 26 of Psalm 118, and all but Luke the Hosanna of v. 25; but a full understanding of the psalm's function in the Gospel tradition depends on the reader's knowledge of the whole psalm to grasp the complete significance of the entry as a symbolic act.

A word of caution is in order. Modern readers of the Second Testament should not attribute their possible ignorance of Scripture, that is, the Scripture of the first-century church, to either the Second Testament writers or to their congregants. There is every reason to believe that common to all programs of instruction on conversion in the early churches was assiduous reading of Scripture, what we call the First (or Old) Testament, as well as Jesus traditions. Scripture was not so much Jewish as it was sacred, especially the Septuagint in the Hellenistic world; but other less formal-equivalent, more spontaneous translations such as those evidenced in some Second Testament literature as well as in much Jewish literature of the period were also studied. Such readings were typically done aloud in communities for the benefit of the illiterate, who were perhaps a majority of early Christians.

The synoptics make the point that Jesus reached Jerusalem from the east. This is quite significant because of the tradition that the Messiah

---

1. The citations of Zech 9:9 in Matthew and John exhibit the typical fluidity of the period in quotation of Scripture. Neither bothers with the second or fourth colon (stichos) of the six in the verse. The second is in synonymous parallelism to the first and is easily dropped. But the omission of the fourth, "A righteous one and saved is he," is interesting. The LXX translates it "righteous and saving," most witnesses reading the *auto* with the following (fifth colon). The re-signification in the LXX from "saved" to "saving" indicates lack of knowledge on the part of the LXX translators of the association of Zech 9:9 with the liturgical events expressed in Psalm 118. Matthew and John, who often reflect loose translations of a Hebrew text instead of the LXX, both omit any vestige of the fourth colon. They or their sources might not have known of the LXX re-signification of "saved" to "savior," or they might have wanted to continue with the image of the humble one riding. Matthew reflects a belabored literal translation of a (pre-MT) Hebrew text of the last two cola while John reflects a typically trimmed-down version. Neither seems to know the LXX. See B. Lindars, *New*

would approach Jerusalem from the area of the Jordan Valley.[2] But they also make it clear that Jesus did not ride the ass until he reached the eastern bounds of the city at Bethpage and Bethany. Riding the ass into Jerusalem is presented therefore as a symbolic act.[3] In ancient Israel the heir of David to be anointed rode the royal ass to coronation. Thus was Absalom's riding on the mule or ass, when he was hanged by the great tresses of the hair of his head, symbolic of his claim to the kingship he wished to wrest from his father, David (2 Sam 18:9). Thus was poor Mephibosheth's riding an ass as he approached the city a symbol of the claim he would have made for the old house of Saul if Absalom's insurrection had succeeded (2 Sam 19:26). Thus was it necessary for Solomon to ride on the royal mule or ass in the Kidron Valley to the sanctuary at Gihon in order effectively to counter Adonijah's claim to the throne and to secure his own accession (1 Kgs 1:33-37).

On the historical level Jesus apparently went out of his way to demonstrate his claim to fulfillment of these ancient royal traditions. On the Gospel level, however, the reader clearly is not to miss the royal claim established by the account of the trip to Jerusalem. Every gesture reported had a significance that traditionists would have understood very well indeed. The fact that all three synoptics include in the account the spreading of garments (*himatia*) in front of Jesus as he rode confirms the royal claim by its apparent allusion to the anointing of Jehu (2 Kgs 9:13) where it is said that after the young prophet from Elisha had privately anointed Jehu, the latter's lieutenants and close associates spread each a garment (LXX: *himation*) on the steps of the sanctuary, blew the trumpet, and exclaimed, "Jehu is king."[4]

Testament Apologetic (Philadelphia: Westminster, 1961) 113–14.

See other points discussed in J. D. M. Derrett, "Law in the NT: The Palm Sunday Colt," *NovT* 13 (1971) 241–58; H. Patsch, "Der Einzug Jesu in Jerusalem. Ein historischer Versuch," *ZTK* 68 (1971) 1–26; and O. Michel, "Eine philologische Frage zur Einzugsgeschichte," *NTS* 6 (1959) 81–82.

2. See the excellent study by J. Blenkinsopp, "The Oracle of Judah and the Messianic Entry," *JBL* 80 (1961) 55–64, especially on the importance of Gen 49:8-12 for understanding traditions of messianic expectation as well as for seeing how riding the ass would have been variously interpreted by the Romans on the one hand and by different Jewish groups on the other.

3. See J. D. Crossan, "Redaction and Citation in Mark 11:9-10 and 11:17," *BR* 17 (1972) 33–50. Crossan's discussion is the clearest I have seen to date on the necessity of seeing both the entry and the cleansing in the light of the prophetic symbolic acts recorded in the First Testament.

4. On the royal/messianic dimension of the entrance narrative see P. van Bergen, "L'Entrée messianique de Jésus à Jérusalem," *Questions liturgiques et paroissiales* 38 (1957) 9–24; A. George, "La Royauté de Jésus selon l'évangile de Luc," *Sciences eeclésiastiques* 14 (1962) 57–69; and R. Bartnicki, "Das Zitat von Zach ix, 9-10 und die Tiere in Bericht von Matthäus über dem Einzug Jesu in Jerusalem (Mt xxi, 1-11)," *NovT* 18 (1976) 161–66.

PSALM 118

In the time of Jesus Psalm 118 was recited at the Festival of Tabernacles or Booths in the fall, at Passover in the spring, that is, the fall and spring equinoctial festivals, and also at Hanukkah.[5] In pre-exilic times, however, Psalm 118 was a royal psalm that would have been recited at the annual enthronement of the king during the fall equinoctial celebration of the New Year.[6] In the first century during the fall celebration of Tabernacles, palm branches, probably marketed from sources in Jericho or elsewhere east and south of Jerusalem, would have been available to the inhabitants of Jerusalem for building the sukkah or booths. Unless the Jerusalem entry episode was somehow related in Gospel tradition to the Festival of Tabernacles in the fall, we must suppose either that Jesus and the disciples transported a considerable quantity of palm branches with them in the spring as they came up from the eastern valley (which seems unlikely), or that the symbols involved purposefully point to the ancient royal dimension of the reference.[7] The validity of the latter view seems confirmed by the fact that the citation from Zech 14:16 brings to mind the Festival of Tabernacles, during which the Lord, Yahweh, would appear on the Mount of Olives. "On that day Yahweh's feet shall stand on the Mount of Olives which lies before Jerusalem on the east" (Zech 14:4).

The admixture of the Zechariah and Psalm 118 passages and their citation in the entrance narrative (in Matthew and John) would have been as explosive as any such fusion could be. It is indeed significant that in all three synoptics the entrance narrative and temple-cleansing sequence are followed by a passage on the question of authority (Mark 11:27-33; Matt 21:23-27; Luke 20:1-8). Of all the acts attributed to Jesus either in the ministry materials or in the passion accounts, the entry into Jerusalem, with the royalist claims it implied, would have been taken as a challenge and even an offense to the establishment of the day, an establishment precisely represented by those who raised the question of authority—the priests, elders, and scribes. It would have been acceptable to recite Psalm 118 as one among many psalms in celebration of a festival, but it was blasphemous to reenact it with its original royal meanings to those not

5. See *m. Pesah.* 5:5 and 10:6; and *b. Pesah.* 117a, 118a, and 119a; *b. Sukk.* 45a; and *b. 'Arak* 10a. In the last mentioned reference Rabbi Yohanan (d. 279) noted the Hallel, Psalms 113–118, were recited on 18 days of the year in Palestine (8 days of Sukkoth, 8 days of Hanukkah, the first day of Passover, and the first of Weeks [*sic*]), and 21 days in the Diaspora (9 Sukkoth, 8 Hanukkah, 2 Passover, and 2 Weeks).

6. See the remarks by S. Mowinckel about Psalm 118 and its pre-exilic cultic function in *The Psalms in Israel's Worship* (2 vols.; New York: Abingdon, 1962) 1.118–21, 170, 180–81, 245; 2.30. See also M. Dahood, *Psalms III* (AB 17A; Garden City: Doubleday, 1970) 155; and E. E. Ellis, *The Gospel of Luke* (NCB; London: Nelson, 1966) 191.

7. See B. A. Mastin, "The Date of the Triumphal Entry," *NTS* 16 (1969) 76–82.

otherwise convinced of the claim. Such a reenactment would surely not occur until Messiah came to make a royal entry into city and temple, when the authorities would receive and acknowledge their messianic king.[8]

The fact that the evangelists or their sources expected their readers and hearers to have in mind the whole of Psalm 118, and more importantly to know its significance,[9] is indicated by the fabric of thought woven when the entrance narrative is taken seriously on its own scriptural or canonical terms. What the evangelists record might be thought of as the warp with the psalm and other scriptural allusions as the woof; together they make up the weftage of the Gospel accounts.

Hans-Joachim Kraus's discussion of the relationship between individual and communal elements in Psalm 118 demands a clearer answer than has heretofore been offered.[10] Rabbinic efforts to see in Psalm 118 a liturgical dialogue offer clues for the following suggestion as to how the psalm functioned in pre-exilic temple ritual.[11] As a hymn of royal entry Psalm 118 would have been recited in Iron Age Jerusalem when the king entered the city and the temple on the occasion of an annual rite of re-enthronement. After enduring the rite of humiliation, the king approached the city and gave an account of how the Lord God had delivered him from evildoers, the humiliators. The people would then have shouted, "Give thanks to the Lord, for his mercy [*hesed*, in royal theology meaning perhaps promise or providence] endures forever" (v. 1). In antiphony the people, the priests,

---

8. See again the discussions above in nn. 1, 2, and 4, and especially in Blenkinsopp, "Oracle of Judah," and van Bergen, "L'Entrée messianique."

9. See E. Lohse, "Hosianna," *NovT* 6 (1963) 113–19.

10. H.-J. Kraus, *Psalmen 64–150* (BKAT; Neukirchen-Vluyn: Neukirchen, 1972) 800–809.

11. There are three efforts, to my knowledge, in rabbinic literature to elaborate the liturgical aspects of Psalm 118: those in *b. Pesah.* 119a, the Midrash to Psalm 118, and the Targum to Psalm 118. English translations of the talmudic and midrashic texts may be consulted in I. Epstein, ed., *The Babylonian Talmud: Seder Mo'ed* (London: Soncino, 1938) ad loc., and in W. G. Braude, *The Midrash on Psalms* (2 vols.; Yale Judaica 13; New Haven and London: Yale University Press, 1959) 2.242–45. Those in the Talmud and Targum are historicizing, that is, they suggest who originally said or spoke the several parts of the psalm; the Midrash seems to suggest who should recite which parts in the future, perhaps at Messiah's arrival.

The Midrash indicates that the first halves of vv. 15, 16, 25, 26, 27, and 28 will be recited by "the men of Jerusalem inside the walls" while the second halves of those verses will be recited by "the men of Judah outside the walls." Then both groups will recite all of v. 29. Curiously the Midrash mentions that "David said" v. 19a. The Talmud and Targum scan the psalm in quite similar ways but with different people taking different parts. They agree, however, at two places: both see Samuel as having said v. 27b and David v. 28a. The Talmud notes that David said vv. 21a, 25b, and 28a; Jesse vv. 22a and 26a; David's brothers (priests, presumably?) vv. 23a and 25a; and "all of them" vv. 27a and 28b. The Targum notes that "the builders" said vv. 23a, 24a, 25a, and 26a; the sons of Jesse (priests?) vv. 23b and 24b; Jesse and his wife v. 25b; the tribes of Judah v. 27a; Samuel vv. 27b and 29; and David v. 28. These ancient perceptions of the dramatic/liturgical nature of Psalm 118 suggested the effort here elaborated. See again Mowinckel, *Psalms*, 180–81, and R. Press, "Der Gottesknecht im AT," *ZAW* 67 (1955) 90.

and the "Yahweh-fearers" would then sing in turn the refrain of vv. 2-4, "For his *hesed* endures forever." After an initial general recital of the humiliation experience (vv. 5-7), a chorus, perhaps, or the king and the people together would have sung forth the "It is better" affirmations of vv. 8 and 9.[12]

The king would have resumed the recital in vv. 10-13 but this time in the more specific terms of the "event" of humiliation. Thereupon the people or a chorus would join in the glad affirmation of v. 14.[13] Such an affirmation of faith would incite the following song, as recorded in vv. 15 and 16, sung by all present! One can almost hear the solo voice of, or for, the king in obbligato rise above the song with "I shall not die . . . " of vv. 17-18. After turning to face the temple gates, the king would intone v. 19, "Open to me. . . . " A select group of priests from within the temple would ponderously intone v. 20 to remind all that they were guardians of the gate of the Lord's house and had sole authority for granting admission.

In response the king would appeal directly to the saving act of God, which marked the salient day of ceremony, by engaging in the act of thanksgiving of v. 21. Thereupon would the chorus and perhaps all the people sing out about the wonder of divine election of the Davidic king, a wonder never ceasing to astound and amaze, generation to generation, even year to year—indeed the very marvel (*niphlat*, MT—*thaumastē*, LXX v. 23) being celebrated in the joyous ritual. It is difficult to determine if the traditional (LXX and ancient versions influenced by it) understanding of v. 24 is the correct one, that is, the affirmation of God's creation of that special day of celebration and reconfirmation of election; or if Mitchell Dahood is correct in seeing v. 24 as affirming that the day was indeed special since God had once more saved the king from death and reasserted the election.[14] The portion of the hymn sung by chorus and people (vv. 22-25) concludes with the stirring plea to God of the *Hoshi'ah-na'*, later in Greek to be called the hosanna (v. 25).

At the conclusion of the plea, which may in performance have been much longer, the priests, who had earlier fulfilled their role as gatekeepers (v. 20), now joyfully intoned the great "Blessed be he who enters . . . ," thereby officially recognizing and receiving the one arriving as the king. The climax of the ceremony has now been reached and the king once more affirmed as king. Yahweh's kingship may be in part expressed in the earthly Davidic king so that the king's very presence is the divine gift of

---

12. Psalm 118:1, 8, 9, 15, 16, 29 affords examples of common liturgical phrases that were adaptable to more than one hymn or song; cf. 11QPs[a] 17:1–6.

13. Ps 118:14 is found verbatim also at Exod 15:2a and Isa 12:2b, another example of common liturgical phrases used in different hymns.

14. See Dahood, *Psalms III,* 159.

light, and the chorus and people affirm this (v. 27).[15] Verse 27b indicates
the commencement of offering sacrifices of thanksgiving and may perhaps
have been intoned by the priests. The hymn concludes with the reaffirmation of faith by the king and all the people (v. 28) and finally the reverber-
ation of the incipit of v. 1 now as the refrain of the whole hymn *in inclusio.*

People	1. Give thanks to the Lord, for he is good; his *hesed* endures forever! 2. Let Israel say: his *hesed* endures forever. 3. Let the house of Aaron say: his *hesed* endures forever. 4. Let the Yahweh-fearers say: his *hesed* endures forever.
King	5. Out of distress I invoked Yah; Yah answered me with largesse. 6. When Yahweh is with me I have no fear. What could a mere mortal do to me? 7. When Yahweh is with me as my helper, then I look with confidence at my enemies.
People	8. It is better to take refuge in Yahweh than to trust in humans; 9. It is better to take refuge in Yahweh than to trust in princes!
King	10. All nations surrounded me; in the name of Yahweh I cut them off. 11. They surrounded me, they were all around me; in the name of Yahweh I cut them off. 12. They surrounded me like bees, they blazed like thorns on fire; in the name of Yahweh I cut them off. 13. I was hard pressed about to fall, but Yahweh helped me!
King and People	14. Yahweh was my strength and my song; he was with me as salvation.[16]
All	15. A shout of joy and salvation throughout the tents of the righteous: the right hand of Yahweh acts valiantly,

15. Ps 118:27 recalls the priestly benediction and the light of God's presence, here
expressed in the presence of the king as a gift of God.
16. The verse can, as has become customary, be translated in the present tense to emphasize God's ever-present strength and salvation. I have put it in the past tense here to show
that it may also be seen as the grand conclusion to the recital of vv. 10-13, a summation of the
presence of God in the event of humiliation.

| | 16. | the right hand of Yahweh is exalted, |
| | | the right hand of Yahweh acts valiantly. |

King   17. I shall not die but shall live
           to recite the deeds of Yah!
           18. Yah disciplined me sorely,
           but he did not hand me over to death.
           19. Open for me the gates of righteousness;
           I shall enter through them,
           I shall give thanks to Yah!

Priests   20. This is the gate that belongs to Yahweh;
           only the righteous may enter through it.

King   21. I give thanks to you for you answered me;
           you were with me a salvation.

People   22. The stone the builders rejected
           has become the cornerstone.
           23. This is Yahweh's own doing;
           it is a marvel in our eyes.
           24. This is the day on which Yahweh has acted;
           let us rejoice and be glad in him.
           25. Pray, O Yahweh, grant salvation;
           pray, O Yahweh, grant prosperity.

Priests   26. Blessed by the name of Yahweh be he who enters!
           We bless you from the House of Yahweh.

People   27. Yahweh is God and he has given us light!

Priests   Bind the festal sacrifice with ropes
           onto the horns of the altar.

King and   28. You are my God and I do give you thanks,
People   O, my God, I extol you.

All   29. Give thanks to Yahweh for he is good;
           his *hesed* endures forever!

The psalm thus would have been at the heart of the annual ceremony of the king's humiliation and exaltation, itself a liturgy of reaffirmation of Yahweh as God and King. The heart of the psalm is expressed in the two verses cited in the Gospel accounts: the hosanna plea of v. 25 which affirms the sovereignty of the acting, humbling, and exalting God, who has in this

New Year experience of the king demonstrated God's sovereignty by a new mighty act; and the welcome in v. 26 to the king expressed by the priests from the temple steps.

THE ENTRANCE

The warp and the woof weave a pattern that bears a message of barely subdued excitement. The Messiah has arrived and has been recognized as king by acclamation, not by those with power or authority but by a scraggly crowd of disciples and followers. Typical biblical themes abound in this pattern.

The approach to Jerusalem was traditionally from the east.[17] Bethphage and Bethany, modern Et-tor and Esariyeh, are located on the eastern slopes of the Mount of Olives, a location which none of the synoptics takes for granted but which all specify since, as we have seen, the Mount of Olives had eschatological meaning. The references in Zechariah 14 are important complements to the locales mentioned; they are probably more eschatological than geographic, though actual historicity is also highly possible. On the Gospel level, however, all history culminates here. The commission to fetch the colt depends on the glad expectation expressed in Zechariah 9 as well as on acquaintance with Scriptural traditions about coronation. The episode of the colt is as much eschatological as histori-cal[18] in dimension; the rhetorical mode of recounting the story heightens the mystery or divine dimension of the mission.

The references to the garments spread before the one riding the donkey provide a striking pattern of royal dimension. This is a king riding to coronation. "As he was drawing near, at the descent of the Mount of Olives, the whole multitude of the disciples began to rejoice and praise God with a loud voice for all the mighty works they had witnessed" (Luke 19:37). Subtly woven in is reference to the Kidron Valley in preparations for the recitation and enactment of Psalm 118. The phrase *peri pasōn dunameōn*, for all the mighty works, refers not only to the OT Gospel story of God's mighty acts toward the elect people Israel but more directly to God's election and traditional acts toward David and his heirs, traditional divine acts that are now contemporized in Christ's humiliation-exaltation story to be told in the passion account. Luke and John include the epexegetic *ho basileus*, the king, to clarify who was coming or arriving.

---

17. See Blenkinsopp, "Oracle of Judah."
18. See Patsch, "Der Einzug Jesu."

THE HOSANNA

It would be well at this point to trace the texture of the woof suggested in the hosanna (which Luke omits). First, it is a citation of Ps 118:25, which in the ancient royal use of the psalm was both the king's and the people's full recognition or confession of the kingship of Yahweh. Specifically, it was a plea for mercy and justice before the king. In the psalm it was a plea to God for salvation and prosperity for the following year; it was also ancient Israel's affirmation of the kingship or sovereignty of God even in the ceremony of the enthronement of the earthly Davidic king. But the *Hoshi'ah-na'* also has another context. It was the cry of the litigant as he or she entered the court of the king to submit a brief and plead a case (2 Sam 14:4 and 2 Kgs 6:26). The opening formula as the litigant entered the presence of the king who sat in judgment of cases in the city gate was the phrase *Hosha'-na'/Hoshi'ah-na'*. It was a cry for justice and mercy, but, more important, it was a formula spoken when entering the presence of the king as judge. In the psalm the people pronounced it when the humiliated, exalted king entered the temple gates of Yahweh, the Gates of Righteousness. Lohse is undoubtedly right that the psalm had attained a messianic meaning as a *Zuruf* in pre-Christian Judaism.[19]

In the Gospels, except Luke, the phrase was spoken by the disciples or the people before the temple after Jesus' entry into the city gate. It is repeated in the phrase "Hosanna in the highest" just after the recitation of Ps 118:26, the "Blessed be he . . . ," in both Mark 11:10 and Matt 21:9. Matthew uses it a third time just after the entrance when the people in the temple react to Jesus' healing of the blind and the lame by shouting, "Hosanna to the son of David." Luke omits the hosanna but has the epexegetic *ho basileus* in citing v. 26 of the psalm. Mark, who has the hosanna (11:9), adds after the citation of Ps 118:26, "Blessed be the coming kingdom of our father, David" (11:10). John, who also has the hosanna, further notes the royal dimension by adding "and the king of Israel" (12:13) after citation of the psalm.

In the synoptics this recognition and acknowledgment of the king as judge in the city gate is immediately followed by Jesus' proceeding into the city and entering the temple, as is indicated in Ps 118:25-26. In the Davidic royal entry, the king's arrival was marked by the exclamation of the priests from the temple steps, "Blessed by the name of Yahweh be he who arrives (or, comes); we bless you from the House of Yahweh." Thereafter follows in 118:27 the sacrifice of the festal victim(s) and the affirmation that Yahweh is El. This final event indicated in the psalm is reflected

---

19. Lohse, "Hosianna."

in Matt 21:12 and Mark 11:15 in the mention of "those who sold pigeons" for sacrifice. Even Luke has "drive out those who sold" also in the pericope on the cleansing of the temple.

STONES AND THE TEMPLE

The sequence of the disciples' recitation of Ps 118:26 and Jesus' first act of judgment as eschatological king within the temple against those who had made it into a den of robbers is interrupted in Luke by the intrusion of verbal exchange between Jesus and the establishment (which occurs in Matthew after the cleansing of the temple). Some Pharisees are reported to have chided Jesus to rebuke his blasphemous disciples. Jesus' reply was that if the disciples did not say the "Blessed be he . . . " (which the temple priests should have recited), then the very stones would recite it. Some students of the passage understand this pericope in Luke to be placed by the evangelist on the Mount of Olives overlooking the city and the stones to be those of the path or road from Bethany. Such a view puts geography above theology; here as in much of the rest of the Gospels, we have theological or eschatological geography.

From the fuller context of the Lukan warp and the woof from Psalm 118, the stones clearly refer not to pebbles of a rocky path but to the building stones of the temple, the destruction of which Jesus prophesies at the end of the intruding pericope. Luke 19:45, immediately following, indicates that Jesus was already in the city (contrast Mark 11:11 and Matt 21:10) and now enters the temple for judgment. What Jesus is saying to the Pharisees, according to Luke, is that the part of the royal entrance liturgy, which according to Psalm 118 the priests were supposed to have recited from the temple steps(namely the "Blessed be he . . . "), would have been recited by the stones of the temple if it had not at least been recited by the disciples (see a similar kind of theological affirmation in Luke 3:8). It is as though Jesus responded, "I'm sorry, friends, this event is happening, and the roles indicated have to be filled." Such high, objective theology is a Lukan characteristic.

A THEOPHANY

The fabric woven of the warp of the new act of God (*jeshu'ah–sotēria*) recorded in the Gospels, and the woof of the acts of God heralded in the psalm is canonical in texture and eschatological in design. According to the Gospel claim, Christ was the long-expected king unrecognized upon arrival by the authorities of the day. From them he won no credentials, and Gospel accounts faithfully reflect the understandable rejection by the authorities of the claims Jesus and the early church laid to the authority of the scriptural (First Testament) traditions. As the king uncrowned, Jesus passed judgment on the church and state of his day, very much as Yahweh had done through the prophets of old. And as with those prophets, the judgments and blessings went unheeded by contemporaries save for a few disciples and followers. On the one hand, Jesus' symbolic act was no more compelling or convincing than earlier prophetic acts had been. On the other, however, this later act, like its prophetic predecessors, was offensive to the responsible authorities, who were charged with the burden of the continuity of tradition. The claim to kingship was messianic, but the effect was a prophetic challenge.

Luke has two phrases emphasizing the claim to Davidic kingship as a reign of peace. Just after the citations from Psalm 118 by the disciples, Luke adds the expression, "Peace in heaven and glory in the highest" (19:38), similiar to the phrase he attributes to the heavenly chorus at the Bethlehem theophany (2:14), perhaps suggested to him by the *en tois hypsistois* in Mark/Matthew. In Jesus' lament over the city Luke employs the time-honored pun on the name of Jerusalem by reporting Jesus as saying of the city, "Would that you knew the things that make for peace!" The word *eirēnē*, peace, occurs more often in Luke than in any other New Testament book: it is apparently a Lukan interest.

In yet another sense Jesus' entry into Jerusalem is a theophany for Luke. Luke as much as any other Second Testament writer attributes to Jesus in the Second Testament what the First Testament says of Yahweh. The entry into Jerusalem seems more eschatological in dimension in Luke than in the other synoptics, all of which are eschatological enough. The stones of the temple might indeed welcome Jesus according to Luke, if no one else did. In light of the psalm the priests should have greeted Jesus from the temple steps after the disciples shouted the hosanna, but they did not; so the disciples shouted the "Blessed be he. . . . " Why did the priests not receive this "king" at his so-called triumphal entry? Because, as the prophetic intrusion says (Luke 19:41-45), Jerusalem did not know the time of its visitation, that is, the *kairos* of divine appearance. They could not recognize, they could not see that in this little parade the king had entered the gates of city and temple and thereby entered into judgment with his people. They simply did not believe that the time of judgment had arrived with the messianic king riding on the ass's colt from Bethany. They lacked the vision to which the disciples gave witness. This is not to say that on the historical level the disciples and followers knew what they were doing in terms of the eschatological significance of the enactment. On the contrary, there is a canonical dimension to God's re-signifying what humans otherwise do. What from the standpoint of the established institutions and recognized authorities of the day was a misguided, scandalous demonstration by a fringe group of society, in the divine economy, according to the Gospels, was a theophany, the arrival of a king and the presence of God.

Luke says that when "he entered the Temple and began to drive out those who sold," Jesus said to them, "It is written, 'My house shall be a house of prayer'; but you have made it a 'den of robbers' " (Luke 19:45-46). Matthew and Mark's picture of the arriving king's judgments in the temple is even more dramatic; according to Mark, Jesus "overturned the tables of the money-changers and the seats of those who sold pigeons, and he would not allow anyone to carry anything through the Temple" (Mark 11:15-16). The citations or authoritative references for Jesus' acts of judgment against the established authorities were significantly enough to Isaiah (56:7) and Jeremiah (7:11). According to the book of Isaiah the temple should be a house of prayer for all peoples, but, like Jeremiah, Jesus upon entering it found it a den of robbers.[20] The offense to the authorities was unmistakable. Jesus thrust the rapier of prophetic judgment to the heart of the cultus, and the reaction of the "chief priests and the scribes and the principal folk of the people" (Luke 19:47) was to bring charges against him later in the week, much as their predecessors had done against Jeremiah; both were charged with sedition and blasphemy (Jeremiah 7 and 38).

A CANONICAL REREADING

We cannot blame Jesus' contemporaries. On the contrary, we should identify with them. The enactment of the psalm as a prophetic symbolic act would have been no less blasphemous and scandalous to those responsible for Israel's traditions (and they would have known them well) than similar acts performed by the prophets in the late Iron Age. One thinks of Isaiah walking about in Jerusalem naked and barefoot for three years (Isa 20:3-4) to dramatize his message; or of Jeremiah's and Ezekiel's similarly dramatic acts in order to press the points of their messages (e.g., Jer 13:1-11; 16:1-9; 18:1-11; 19:1-13; Ezek 4:1-17; 5:1-4; 12:3-20). Such prophetic acts were also called "signs" (as in Ezek 12:11). They in all cases challenged the religious

---

20. On the question of corruption in the first-century temple see C. A. Evans, "Jesus' Action in the Temple: Cleansing or Portent of Destruction?" *CBQ* 51 (1989) 237–70; idem, "Jesus' Action in the Temple and Evidence of Corruption in the First-Century Temple," *SBLSP* (1989) 522–39; idem, "Opposition to the Temple: Jesus and the Dead Sea Scrolls," in J. H. Charlesworth, ed., *Jesus and the Dead Sea Scrolls* (Anchor Bible Reference Library; New York: Doubleday, 1992) 235–53.

and political authorities of the day and brought alienation, pain, and suffering upon the prophets who enacted them.

In all such passages modern readers who are responsible for the traditioning of Scripture, both preserving and presenting it, should by dynamic analogy identify with their appropriate counterparts in the scriptural narratives, so as to experience and hear the message conveyed. This is as much the case in reading the Gospel accounts of this prophetic enactment as in reading the prophets. With the priests, scribes, and elders in Mark 11:27, Matt 21:15 and 23, and Luke 20:1, we should be induced by our reading of this offensive act to ask by what authority Jesus did "these things." The precious psalm was not to be read and enacted in that way until Messiah came. Would there be a single judicatory of any Christian community today that would have been on those temple steps to recite the "Blessed be he . . ."? I dare say not. Not until Christians learn to monotheize when reading the Second Testament, to refuse to engage in good-people–bad-people hermeneutics, will they be able to read it for what it canonically says.

One of the remarkable things about the Gospel reports of the offense taken by the Pharisees and the other religious authorities at Jesus' teaching of Scripture and his various acts, symbolic and otherwise, was their continual willingness to dialogue with Jesus up to the point of being able to take no more. They knew very well the passages of Scripture he preached, taught, and re-presented by word and deed; they simply had a different hermeneutic for understanding them. One wonders how many modern Christians would be as tolerant of Jesus' scandalous interpretations and re-presentations of Scripture as the Pharisees were. "And some of the Pharisees in the multitude said to him, 'Teacher, rebuke your disciples.' " They were still willing even after this offense to discuss it with him.

But Jesus' response was in effect to say that although debating Scripture, indeed a very Jewish vocation, was important, this time it was not just a matter of debate; God was in fact bringing Scripture to fulfillment before their very eyes. The event was happening and that part of the liturgy (Ps 118:26) which should have been recited by the priests on the temple steps was at least being recited by the unauthorized followers of Jesus. And even then, should they have balked, the stones of the temple steps would have acted. Such is Luke's theocentric, objective theology.

At last, after Jesus' even more offensive act of daring to disrupt the customary temple procedures that facilitated the purchasing of animals so that the people, particularly those on pilgrimage, were able to offer sacrifices, the priests and scribes could not tolerate further offenses and still be responsible to their office. They had finally to take action themselves. And so on to the passion account.

—11—

THE TWELVE THRONES OF ISRAEL: SCRIPTURE AND POLITICS IN LUKE 22:24-30

CRAIG A. EVANS

In a significant study published some twenty years ago Jacob Jervell assessed Luke's understanding of the apostolate.[1] He argued that the Twelve, functioning as "eschatological regents," represent Israel's new leaders, Israel's former leaders having disqualified themselves by rejecting Jesus. Their apostolic task is to proclaim the fulfillment of God's promises to Israel, for the kingdom is soon to be restored (Acts 1:6). The resurrection of Jesus is the primary evidence for this claim (Acts 2:33-34; 3:19-21; 13:32-33). The resurrection, moreover, is the hope of Israel, a hope for which the twelve tribes yearn (Acts 26:6-7). Therefore, the apostles bear witness to the resurrection before the whole house of Israel (Acts 2:36; 10:42), a witness that constitutes their chief responsibility as Israel's new rulers. Even the Lukan Paul recognizes the priority of the witness of the Twelve (Acts 13:31). The awaited kingdom has been given to Christ (Luke 1:32-33; 22:29), who in turn has assigned it to his apostles (Luke 22:28-30). Through their preaching, the kingdom will be restored to Israel. But the restoration of Israel also requires the inclusion of a people from among the Gentiles (Acts 15:12-18). The Gentile mission is therefore a vital component in the restoration of Israel; indeed, it is Israel's task as the Lord's servant (Acts 13:47).

---

1. J. Jervell, "The Twelve on Israel's Thrones: Luke's Understanding of the Apostolate," in Jervell, *Luke and the People of God: A New Look at Luke-Acts* (Minneapolis: Augsburg, 1972) 75–112. For a similar analysis see G. Lohfink, *Die Sammlung Israels: Eine Untersuchung zur lukanischen Ekklesiologie* (SANT 39; Munich: Kösel, 1975) 63–84. The thesis of Jervell and Lohfink has influenced many scholars.

Without accepting every point of his thesis,[2] I think that Jervell has observed and described accurately an important feature in the Lukan evangelist's understanding of the apostolate. The reference to the apostles sitting on thrones judging the twelve tribes of Israel (Luke 22:30; cf. Matt 19:28) is part of an early eschatological concept, one that is based on Daniel 7 and Psalm 122.[3] Luke received it, of course, as a piece of dominical tradition most likely preserved in Q. But the way that the Lukan evangelist contextualized this tradition suggests that he was aware of the broader tradition underlying the dominical saying. The purpose of this chapter, therefore, is to explore further this background and to assess Luke's distinctive contribution.

DANIEL 7:9-27 AND PSALM 122:3-5 IN EARLY JEWISH AND CHRISTIAN INTERPRETATION

Daniel 7:9-27 and Ps 122:3-5 are quoted and alluded to frequently in Jewish writings. Both texts contribute to the general idea of Israel's restoration and the judgment of the nations. The present analysis of the history of interpretation will be limited to those interpretive traditions that speak of restoration, reigning, and judging, the ideas that are especially relevant for the dominical saying with which we are concerned.

The relevant portions of Dan 7:9-27 read:

> [9] As I looked, thrones were placed and one that was ancient of days took his seat. . . . [10] a thousand thousands served him, and ten thousand times ten thousand stood before him; the court sat in judgment, and the books were opened. . . . [13] there came one like a son of man. . . . [14] and to him was given dominion and glory and kingdom. . . . [18] the saints of the Most High shall receive the kingdom. . . . [22] and judgment was given for the saints of the Most High, and the time came when the saints received the kingdom. . . . [26] the court shall sit in judgment. . . . [27] and the kingdom . . . shall be given to the people of the saints of the Most High; their kingdom shall be an everlasting kingdom, and all dominions shall serve and obey them.

---

2. I disagree with Jervell when he concludes ("The Twelve," 92) that on the basis of Acts 15:12-18 (where Amos 9:11-12 is cited) "Israel's restoration is an established fact." Israel's restoration is in process as is indicated by the continuing mission to Israel throughout the remainder of Acts. To the very end, the Lukan Paul continues to preach the kingdom of God (Acts 28:31), the restoration of which Israel awaits (Acts 1:6). More will be said about this at the end of this chapter.

3. J. A. Fitzmyer (*The Gospel according to Luke X–XXIV* [AB 28A; Garden City: Doubleday, 1985] 1419) suspects that Ps 122:4-5 lies behind Luke 22:30, as do J. M. Creed, *The Gospel according to St. Luke* (London: Macmillan, 1930) 269, and I. H. Marshall, *The Gospel of Luke*

Ps 122:3-5 reads:

3   Jerusalem, built as a city
        which is bound firmly together,
4   to which the tribes go up,
        the tribes of the Lord,
        as was decreed for Israel,
        to give thanks to the name of the Lord.
5   There thrones for judgment were set,
        the thrones of the house of David.

Daniel 7 has made an important contribution to early Jewish and Christian eschatology. This passage is cited to support the view that the Messiah is to receive a throne,[4] and that the righteous (i.e., the "elect" or the "saints") will also sit on thrones. The "son of man" of Dan 7:13-14 was apparently understood in a messianic sense prior to Christianity. The passage is clearly alluded to in *1 Enoch* 69:29, "That Son of Man has appeared and has seated himself upon the throne of his glory" (see also 62:5; 69:27).[5] The similar references to the "Elect One" also probably reflect this Danielic tradition, "On that day, my Elect One shall sit on the seat of glory" (*1 Enoch* 45:3; 51:3; 54:3: "throne of glory").[6] Elsewhere we are told that the mighty kings of the earth will someday behold the Elect One sitting on his throne (*1 Enoch* 55:4; 62:3). The Elect One will judge "all the works of the holy ones in heaven above" (*1 Enoch* 61:8), and he will judge the kings and mighty ones of the earth (62:1-6).[7]

Early Christians also understood the passage as messianic, applying it to Jesus. This is seen in the eschatological discourse. "And then they will see the Son of man coming in clouds with great power and glory" (Mark 13:26 par.); at his trial before the Sanhedrin, "You will see the Son of man seated at the right hand of Power, coming with the clouds of heaven" (Mark 14:62 par., with influence of Ps 110:1); and in the opening saying of the

---

(NIGTC; Grand Rapids: Eerdmans, 1978) 818. R. H. Gundry (*Matthew: A Commentary on His Literary and Theological Art* [Grand Rapids: Eerdmans, 1982] 393) and Marshall (*Luke*, 818) cite several parallels with Daniel 7.

4. The passage appealed to most frequently to make this point is Ps 110:1, "The Lord says to my lord: 'Sit at my right hand, till I make your enemies your footstool' " (see Mark 12:36 par.; Luke 22:69; Acts 2:34-35; Heb 1:13; 10:12-13). It is interpreted messianically in the rabbis as well (see *Midr. Ps* 110.4 [on 110:1]; *b. Sanh.* 38b; *Gen. Rab.* 85.9 [on 38:18]; *Num. Rab.* 18.23 [on 17:21]).

5. Translation by E. Isaac, "1 (Ethiopic Apocalypse of) Enoch," in J. H. Charlesworth, ed., *The Old Testament Pseudepigrapha* (2 vols.; Garden City: Doubleday, 1983–85) 1.49. See also 69:27, "Judgment was given to the Son of the Man" (compare LXX Dan 7:22).

6. Translation by Isaac, "1 Enoch," 34, 37.

7. Translation by Isaac, "1 Enoch," 42.

Matthean discourse on the judgment of the nations, "When the Son of man comes in his glory, and all the angels with him, then he will sit on his glorious throne" (Matt 25:31).

The messianic interpretation of Daniel 7 continues in the rabbis. A particularly relevant midrash is attributed to Rabbi Aqiba (ca. 125 C.E.): "What is the explanation of 'until thrones were placed' (Dan 7:9)? One (throne) was for Him and one for David (i.e., the Messiah). This is the view of Rabbi Aqiba. Said Rabbi Yose (the Galilean) to him: 'Aqiba, how long will you profane the divine presence!' " (b. Sanh. 38b; see also b. Hag. 14a).[8] Elsewhere the rabbis apply Dan 7:13-14 to the Messiah (see b. Sanh. 96b–97a, 98a; Num. Rab. 13.14 [on 7:13]; Midr. Ps 21.5 [on 21:7]).[9]

Not only Messiah would reign and judge. Part of the eschatological hope was that the righteous in general will some day with God judge the wicked and reign over Israel and the nations. The LXX rendering of Dan 7:22 facilitated this concept, " . . . Judgment was given *to* the saints of the Most High" (my emphasis; compare MT, " . . . Judgment was given for the saints"). *1 Enoch* put it this way, "Behold, the Lord comes with ten thousand of his holy ones, to execute judgment upon all" (1:9; quoted in Jude 14–15). The idea was expressed clearly at Qumran. "God will judge all the nations by the hand of his elect" (1QpHab 5:4). Closely related is the belief that the elect were also to be given thrones. God promises in the last days, "I shall bring them out into the bright light, those who have loved my holy name, and seat each one by one upon the throne of his honor" (*1 Enoch* 108:12).[10] Apparently the patriarchs would receive thrones as well (*T. Isaac* 2:7). From these thrones "they will govern nations and rule over peoples, and the Lord will reign over them for ever" (Wis 3:8). To go along with their thrones, the elect will be given "crowns" (Wis 5:16; 1QS 4:7; 1QH 9:23–25), even royal garments (1QS 4:8). These ideas find frequent expression in the New Testament. Leaders of the elect will be given thrones (the apostles in Matt 19:28; Luke 22:30; the twenty-four elders in Rev 4:4); so also will those who "conquer" (Rev 3:21; see also *Mart. Isa.* 9:10, 18, 24–25). Christian "saints will judge the world" (1 Cor 6:2), receive a "kingdom," and "reign on earth" (Rev 5:10). They too will receive crowns

---

8. Translation based on J. Shachter and H. Freedman, *The Babylonian Talmud: Sanhedrin* (London: Soncino, 1935) 245. On messianic identification of "David" see 245, n. 6. Aqiba attempted to explain the significance of the plural reference to "thrones."

9. In *b. Sanh.* 96b–97a, Messiah is called "Bar Naphle." Behind this reference is a pun referring to the "fallen" tent of David (from the Hebrew *naphal*; Amos 9:11) and to the one who comes with the "clouds" (from the Greek *nephelē*; Dan 7:13). See Schachter and Freedman, *The Babylonian Talmud: Sanhedrin*, 654, n. 2.

10. Translation by Isaac, "1 Enoch," 89.

(2 Tim 4:8; Jas 1:12; 1 Pet 5:4; Rev 2:10; 3:11; 4:10; *Apoc. Elijah* 1:8, "Remember that he has prepared thrones and crowns for you in heaven").[11]

These motifs recur in the rabbis. "Because the people of Israel observe the Torah while among the nations, the Holy One, blessed be He, will in the future cause them to inherit a throne of glory; as you read, 'To make them . . . inherit the throne of glory' (1 Sam 2:8), which indicates that the Holy One, blessed be He, will at some future time restore to Israel its sovereignty; as you read, 'And the kingdom and dominion, and the greatness of the kingdoms under the whole heaven, shall be given to the people of the saints,' etc. (Dan 7:27)" (*Num. Rab.* 11.1 [on 6:3]; also *Midr. Tanh.* on Lev 19:1-2 [*Qed.* §1]; see further discussion below).[12] The Targum eschatologizes 1 Sam 2:8. "He raises up the poor from the dust, from the dunghill he exalts the needy one, to make them dwell with the righteous ones, the chiefs of the world; and he bequeaths to them thrones of glory, for before the Lord the deeds of men are revealed."[13] Note that the Targum reads plural "thrones."

Ps 122:3-5 contributes to the hope of the return of the twelve tribes, a hope that originated with the exilic and post-exilic prophets (Deut 30:3; Isa 49:6; 54:7; 56:8; 63:17; Jer 23:3; 29:14; 31:8, 10; 32:37; Ezek 11:17; 28:25; 34:13; 36:24; 37:19, 21, 24, 27; 39:27; 47:13) and continued in the later apocryphal and pseudepigraphal writings. Some texts make explicit reference to the regathering of the "tribes of Israel." According to Isa 49:6 the servant of the Lord is "to raise up the tribes of Jacob and to restore the preserved of Israel." Third Isaiah begs the Lord to return the tribes of God's inheritance (63:17). Ezekiel 37 predicts that someday the tribes of Israel and Judah will be reunited (v. 19), that "David will be king over them" (v. 24), and that God will dwell among them (v. 27). Later Ezekiel predicts that the "twelve tribes" will once again divide the land of their inheritance (47:13). Probably alluding to Ezekiel, Sirach prays that God "gather all the tribes of Jacob, and give them their inheritance as at the beginning" (36:11). Of Elijah, Sirach says, "You who are ready at the appointed time, it is written, to calm the wrath of God before it breaks out in fury, to turn the heart of the father to the son, and to restore the tribes of Jacob" (48:10, alluding to Mal 4:5-6).

The apocryphal and pseudepigraphal writings also make significant contributions to the hope of the regathering of Israel (Tob 13:5, 10, 13;

---

11. Christians will also receive special garments, but they usually have to do with righteousness (Rev 3:4-5; 7:14; 19:8, 14) or martyrdom (Rev 19:13). Compare Bar 5:2, "Robe of righteousness."

12. Translation based on J. J. Slotki, *Midrash Rabbah: Numbers* (vol. 1; London & New York: Soncino, 1983) 409.

13. Translation by D. J. Harrington and A. J. Saldarini, *Targum Jonathan of the Former Prophets* (Aramaic Bible 10; Wilmington: Glazier, 1987) 106.

14:5; Bar 2:34; 4:37; 5:5; 2 Macc 1:27; 2:7, 18; *Pss. Sol.* 8:28; 11:2; 17:26, 28, 44; *Jub.* 1:15; *1 Enoch* 90:33; *T. Benj.* 9:2; 4 Ezra 13:12-13, 39-49; *2 Apoc. Bar.* 77:6; 78:7). Several of these texts make specific reference to the "tribes." *Pss. Sol.* 17:44 says that the "tribes" will be reassembled in the days of the Messiah and that the Messiah will judge them (17:26). Moreover, Israel will once again be distributed in the land according to their tribes (*Pss. Sol.* 17:28). Fourth Ezra 13:39-49 foretells the regathering of the ten northern tribes (cf. 2 Kgs 17:1-6). According to *T. Benj.* 9:2, the dying patriarch says: "But in your allotted place will be the Temple of God, and the latter Temple will exceed the former in glory. The twelve tribes shall be gathered there and all the nations, until such time as the Most High shall send forth his salvation through the ministration of the unique prophet."[14] According to *T. Abrah.* 13:6 the wicked "will be judged by the twelve tribes of Israel."[15]

Although Qumran says nothing explicitly about the regathering of the twelve tribes, their social and military organization implies their restoration at least symbolically (1QS 8:11; CD 7:5; 1QSa 1:15, 29; 1QM 2:2–3; 3:14). However, anticipation of Messiah and the heads of the people (the twelve tribes?) assembled in the eschaton is given expression (1QSa 2:11–17):

> [Concerning the mee]ting of the men of renown [called] to assembly for the Council of the Community when [Adonai] will have begotten the Messiah among them. [The Priest] shall enter [at] the head of all the Congregation of Israel, then all [the chiefs of the sons] of Aaron the priests called to the assembly, men of renown; and they shall sit [before him], each according to his rank. And afterwards, [the Mess]iah of Israel [shall enter]; and the chiefs of [the tribes of Israel] shall sit before him, each according to his rank, according to their [position] in their camps and during their marches; then all the heads of fa[mily of the Congre]gation, together with the wise me[n of the holy Congregation], shall sit before them, each according to his rank.[16]

Unfortunately, it is not clear if the tribes are in view. The significance of this passage will be discussed below.

Josephus says nothing about the regathering of the twelve tribes, but he believes that they still exist, with the ten tribes living "beyond the Euphrates" (*Ant.* 11.5.2 §133). He also knows that the names of the twelve tribes

---

14. Translation by H. C. Kee, "Testaments of the Twelve Patriarchs," in Charlesworth, *The Old Testament Pseudepigrapha*, 1.827. Kee (827, n. 9b) correctly suggests that the "unique prophet" alludes to the prophet of Deut 18:15.

15. The passage in all probability was originally Jewish, with the phrase "at the second Parousia" representing a Christian interpolation.

16. Translation based on A. Dupont-Sommer, *The Essene Writings from Qumran* (Gloucester: Peter Smith, 1973) 108. For the Hebrew text, with pointing, see E. Lohse, *Die Texte aus Qumran* (Munich: Kösel, 1981) 50.

were inscribed on precious stones worn by the high priest (*J.W.* 5.5.7
§233–234). Christian interpretation essentially agrees. Paul believes that
when the "full number of the Gentiles come in . . . all Israel will be saved"
(Rom 11:25-26).[17] Paul's hope might have been based on Jewish eschatology in general or on specific dominical tradition and early Christian teaching, such as that behind the idea of the "twelve" disciples/apostles.

The idea of the "Twelve" in all probability originally had to do with the
hope of Israel's restoration and probably goes back to Jesus himself.[18]
(The meaning of Luke 22:30 [and Matt 19:28], which reflects this thinking, will be considered at greater length below.) The New Testament
affords other evidence of this perspective. In one case Christians are
addressed as the "twelve tribes in the Dispersion" (Jas 1:1; compare 1 Pet
1:1). In Revelation the saints are identified as twelve thousand from each
of the twelve tribes of Israel (7:4-8; 14:1, 3). The celestial mother of the
apocalypse wears a "crown of twelve stars" (12:1). On the twelve gates of
the new Jerusalem that descends from heaven are inscribed the names
of the twelve tribes of Israel (v. 12). The gates are later described as twelve
pearls (v. 21). On the twelve foundations of the new Jerusalem are
inscribed the names of the twelve apostles (v. 14). The city's length and
width measure twelve thousand stadia (v. 16), and its wall measures one
hundred and forty-four thousand cubits (v. 17).[19]

Rabbinic exegesis of Ps 122:3-5, emphasizing Israel's regathering, the
rebuilding of Jerusalem, the rebuilding of the temple, and judgment of
the nations, is in basic continuity with the exegesis of the earlier period:

1. The Regathering of the Tribes of Israel. According to *Midr.* Ps 122.4, Ps 122:4
looks to a time when God's presence will rest on Israel and will testify to
the twelve tribes that they are indeed God's people (see also *b. Qidd.* 70b).
This exegesis was meant to answer the question of whether or not the
twelve tribes were truly preserved through the time of exile. God will
testify to the tribes of "YH" (with the *yod* referring to the last letter, and

---

17. Aside from what Luke tells us that Paul said in Acts 26:6-7, Paul himself says nothing
about the twelve tribes. He does, however, note that he is from the tribe of Benjamin (Phil
3:5), which shows that tribal identity had some significance. It is likely, therefore, that "all
Israel" in Rom 1:26 implies all twelve tribes. Luke himself thinks it pertinent to note that the
prophetess Anna is of the tribe of Asher (Luke 2:36).

18. E. P. Sanders (*Jesus and Judaism* [Philadelphia: Fortress, 1985] 100) concludes that we
can be reasonably sure of "two facts: the existence of the twelve as a group . . . and the
betrayal by one of them." The Qumran community provides us with a similar group in its
council of "twelve perfect men" (1QS 8:1).

19. Interest in the symbolism of the number twelve fades in later Christian writings. See
Barn. 8:3; *Herm. Sim.* 9:17:1, where it is believed that there were twelve apostles as a testimony
to the twelve tribes. For further discussion see K. H. Rengstorf, "*Dodeka*," *TDNT* 2.321–28; C.
Maurer, "*Phule*," *TDNT* 9.245–50.

the *he'* referring to the first letter of some of the tribal names[20]), that they are truly God's. In the synagogue the hope of the regathering of the tribes and exiles of Israel was expressed in the tenth benediction of the *Amidah* and in the Aramaic paraphrases of Scripture. According to the Isaiah Targum the Lord's servant Messiah will bring the exiles back to Israel (53:8). Indeed, God will bring the exiles near (54:7). God scattered Israel; soon God will gather Israel (66:9). Paraphrasing and interpreting the "holy seed" of Isa 6:13, the Targum reads: "So the exiles of Israel will be gathered and they will return to their land. For the holy seed is their stump."[21] Similar expressions are found elsewhere in the Isaiah Targum (cf. 27:6; 35:10; 46:11; 49:6, 18; 51:11; 54:15; 60:4),[22] as well as in other Targums. "So Jerusalem . . . is to be filled with her exiled people" (*Tg. 1 Sam* 2:5; cf. *Tg. Jer* 31:23).[23] There is, however, some disagreement among the rabbis about the regathering of the ten northern tribes. "The Ten Tribes will neither live (in the world to come) nor be brought to judgment. . . . Rabbi Simeon ben Judah says: 'Even as the day departs and does not return, so shall they not return.' Rabbi Aqiba says: 'Even as the day is now overcast and now bright again, so shall their darkness be made bright' " (*'Abot R. Nat.* 36:4).[24] But in another place we are told that Aqiba holds the opposite view: "The Ten Tribes shall not return again. . . . as this day goes and returns not, so do they go and return not. So Rabbi Aqiba. But Rabbi Eliezer says: 'As the day grows dark and then grows light, so also after darkness is fallen upon the Ten Tribes shall light hereafter shine upon them' " (*m. Sanh.* 10:3).[25] However, as has already been seen in the earlier Jewish tradition, there is every expectation that all twelve tribes will be regathered.

2. The Rebuilding of Jerusalem. Ps 122:3-5 was appealed to as evidence that Jerusalem would some day be rebuilt: "Rabbi Aha taught: Jerusalem will be rebuilt for the sake of the tribes of Israel, for directly after it is said 'Jerusalem, which is (re)built' (Ps 122:3) there follow the words 'whither

---

20. See Num 26:7 (*hr'wbny*: "the Reubenites"), 14 (*hshshm'ny*: "the Simeonites"), 27 (*hzzbwlny*: "the Zebulunites"); W. G. Braude, *The Midrash on Psalms* (Yale Judaica 13; 2 vols.; New Haven: Yale University Press, 1959) 2.517, n. 10.

21. Translation by B. D. Chilton, *The Isaiah Targum* (Aramaic Bible 11; Wilmington: Glazier, 1987) 15.

22. For further discussion see B. D. Chilton, *The Glory of Israel: The Theology and Provenience of the Isaiah Targum* (JSOTSup 23; Sheffield: JSOT, 1982) 25–33; and idem, *The Isaiah Targum*, xv, 15, 52–56, 101–11.

23. Translation by Harrington and Saldarini, *Targum Jonathan of the Former Prophets*, 106.

24. Translation based on J. Goldin, *The Fathers according to Rabbi Nathan* (Yale Judaica 10; New Haven: Yale University Press, 1955) 150.

25. Translation based on H. Danby, *The Mishnah* (London: Oxford University Press, 1933) 398.

the tribes go up. . . . There they will set thrones for judgment' (Ps 122:4-5)"
(*Midr.* Ps 122.6 [on 122:3-5]).[26]

3. The Rebuilding of the Temple. Psalm 122:3-5 was also appealed to as evidence that the temple would some day be rebuilt: "You find that all the
miracles which the Holy One, blessed be He, did for Israel and will do for
them are for the sake of the tribes. Even the Temple is to be rebuilt for the
sake of the tribes, as is said, 'Jerusalem which is to be (re)built' (Ps 122:3).
And what follows in the text? 'Because there the tribes go up' (Ps 122:4)"
(*Pesiq. R.* 4.1).[27]

4. Judgment of the Nations. The rabbis were careful to explain that the
"thrones of judgment" are not for judging Israel, but for judging "the
nations of the world" (*Midr.* Ps 122.6 [on 122:5]; also *Midr. Tanh.* on Lev
19:1-2 [*Qed.* §1]).[28] In the Targum the idea of judgment drops out altogether, perhaps to avoid the impression that Israel was to be judged.[29] "For
there thrones will be set in Jerusalem, thrones in the Temple for the kings
of the house of David."

In *Midrash Tanhuma* the related passages (Daniel 7 and Psalm 122)
intersect in what may be a very illuminating parallel. Tractate *Qedoshim* §1
(on Lev 19:1-2), containing tannaic tradition, offers the following midrash
on the holiness of God:[30]

[71.1] And Yahweh spoke to Moses, saying: "Speak to the sons of Israel and
say to them: 'Be [2] holy [because I the Lord your God am holy]' " (Lev
19:1). This is what the passage says: "Yahweh of hosts will be exalted [3] in
judgment [and the holy God will make himself holy in righteousness]" (Isa
5:16). When will the Holy One, blessed be He, be exalted in this world? [4]
When he passes sentence and makes judgment on the peoples of the world,

---

26. Translation based on Braude, *The Midrash on Psalms*, 2.301.

27. Translation based on W. G. Braude, *Pesikta Rabbati* (Yale Judaica 18; 2 vols.; New
Haven: Yale University Press, 1968) 1.83. Although Ps 122:3 in the MT is usually translated
"built," *banah* can also mean "rebuilt." For more on the rebuilding of the temple see *Tg. Isa*
53:5; *b. Pesah.* 5a; *Amidah* §14.

28. Translation based on Braude, *The Midrash on Psalms*, 2.301.

29. Later Christian interpreters understand Matt 19:28 as predicting the punitive judgment of Israel. After citing Matt 19:28, Origen (*Com. Matt.* 15:24) says that "the just will judge
the twelve tribes of Israel which have not believed." Chrysostom (*Hom. Matt.* 64:2) asks:
"What is the meaning of 'judging the twelve tribes of Israel'? It means 'condemning them.' "
He supports his interpretation by appealing to Matt 12:41-42, saying that just as the Ninevites
and the queen of the South will condemn Israel, so also will the twelve apostles who will sit
upon twelve thrones.

30. The translation is mine and is based on the text in S. Buber, *Midrash Tanhuma* (Vilna:
Romm, 1912) 71–72. Part of the material in the square brackets is supplied by Buber himself;
the rest I have added from other editions of *Midrash Tanhuma*. For the reader's convenience,
I have numbered the lines of the translation to correspond with the Hebrew lines of Buber's
text (i.e., p. 71, ll. 1–7; and p. 72, ll. 1–12).

as it says: "Yahweh has stationed himself for the litigation; He stands to judge peoples" (Isa 3:13). [5] And it says: "I kept looking until thrones were set up" (Dan 7:9). What does "thrones" mean? [6] Why are there many thrones? But it is written: "I saw Yahweh sitting upon a throne [high and lifted up" (Isa 6:1); and it is written: "A king sits on a throne of judgment" (Prov 20:8).] [7] What then does "thrones" mean? Rabbi Yose the Galilean and Rabbi Aqiba [discussed this question]. One said: " 'Thrones'—this refers to the throne and to the throne's footstool." [72.1] The other said: "These are the thrones that belong to the people of the world, which the Holy One, blessed be He, is about to overthrow, [2] as it says: 'I will overthrow the throne of kingdoms and I shall destroy the strength of the kingdoms of the nations' (Hag 2:22). You should know [3] that 'thrones are placed' is not written here, but 'were cast down'; as it is written: 'Horse and rider he cast into the sea' " [4] (Exod 15:1). Our rabbis say: "What does 'thrones' mean in the world to come? The Holy One, blessed be He, will sit and the angels will give [5] thrones to the great ones of Israel, and they will sit. And the Holy One, blessed be He, will sit with them [or: with the elders] as presiding Judge. They will judge the peoples [6] of the world, as it says: 'Yahweh comes in judgment with the elders of his people and his princes' (Isa 3:14). Here it is not written [7] 'against,' but 'with' the elders [and his princes], teaching that the Holy One, blessed be He, sits with the elders and princes of Israel to judge the peoples [8] of the world. And whose are these thrones? (They belong to) the house of David and to the elders of Israel, as it says: 'There sit thrones [9] for judgment, thrones for the house of David' " (Ps 122:5). Said Rabbi Phineas in the name of Rabbi Hilkiah [10] in the name of Rabbi Reuben: "When you say, 'there sit thrones for judgment, thrones for the house of David,' what can 'The ancient of days sat down' (Dan 7:9) [11] mean, if not that He sits between them as presiding Judge and with them judges the peoples? [12] Therefore, it is written: 'until thrones were placed' " (Dan 7:9).

The reference to the holiness of God in Lev 19:1 leads to the citation of Isa 5:16, where the holy God will be exalted in judgment. God will be exalted when judging the "peoples of the world" (71.3–4; citing Isa 3:13). Isaiah, however, does not refer to the "peoples of the world" (the Gentiles), but to the "peoples" of Israel, as the Isaianic context makes quite clear; the midrashist has exploited the ambiguity of the plural "peoples" (*'ammiym*; RSV reads "people"). The midrash then goes on to ask why Dan 7:9 refers to "thrones" in the plural, in contrast to Isa 6:1 and Prov 20:8, which refer to only one throne (71.5–7). We have seen this question raised before with respect to Dan 7:9. In traditions already considered, Aqiba had thought that the plural referred to divine and messianic thrones (*b. Sanh.* 38b; *b. Hag.* 14a). But that option is not entertained here, even though Aqiba is one of the authorities. One rabbi (Yose?) suggests that the plural refers to two parts of the throne, the seat and the footstool (71.7). The other rabbi (Aqiba?) suggests that "thrones" refers to the thrones of Gentile nations, thrones that will be overthrown[31] (72.1–3; citing Hag 2:22 and Exod 15:1; see the same interpretation of Hag 2:22 in *Midr. Ps* 47.2 [on 47:4]). The eschatological interpretation that follows (72.4–12) is particularly relevant for our concerns. Still alluding to Dan 7:9,[32] the midrash explains that when God sits on the throne, other "thrones" will be given to the "great ones of Israel" (72.5). Then they with God who sits as a presiding judge "will judge the peoples of the world" (72.5–6). Isa 3:14a is cited as scriptural proof but not without an important re-signification of the text. The midrashist notes that the preposition is not "against" (*'al*), but "with" (*'im*) (72.6–8). Consequently God does not come *against* the people in judgment, but *with* the people in judgment. Once again, the ambiguity of the Hebrew text, ambiguous only when viewed atomistically, is exploited.[33] The midrashist goes on to ask who will sit on these thrones of judgment (72.8). We are told that the thrones belong to the house of David and to Israel's "elders," as can be inferred from Ps 122:5 (72.8–9). Dan 7:9 is thus interpreted in light of Ps 122:5. When the "ancient of days sat down" (72.10), he sat on the throne in the midst of the thrones that belong to Israel's elders. Therefore, in the time to come God, with the elders of Israel, will sit as a presiding judge and judge the peoples of the world (72.11; as *Midr. Ps* 122.6 [on 122:5] had also concluded).

The rabbinic exegesis preserved in *Midrash Tanhuma* closely parallels the expectations of Qumran (cf. 1QSa 2:11–17 quoted above). Although obviously different at points, this exegesis to a great extent also reflects the concepts that lie behind Luke 22:24-30.

LUKE'S TRADITION

By assembling a few components from Mark and Q, the Lukan evangelist produces a speech for the Passover setting (Luke 22:24-38). We are concerned with the first part of it:

> [24] A dispute also arose among them, which of them was to be regarded as the greatest. [25] And he said to them, "The kings of the Gentiles exercise lordship over them; and those in authority over them are called benefactors. [26] But not so with you; rather let the greatest among you become as the

---

31. Again the ambiguity of a word has been exploited to bring out the desired meaning. In this instance *rmy* in Dan 7:9 is understood as "throw down" instead of "set up."

32. Here *rmy* is understood as "set up," not "thrown down."

33. The Hebrew text actually says exactly the opposite. Isaiah is threatening judgment against Israel's elders and princes for devouring God's vineyard and looting the poor (cf. Isa 3:14b). He is not foretelling a time when God will sit with Israel's leaders and judge the nations.

youngest, and the leader as one who serves. [27] For which is the greater, one who sits at table, or one who serves? Is it not the one who sits at table? But I am among you as one who serves. [28] You are those who have continued with me in my trials; [29] and I assign to you, as my father assigned to me, a kingdom, [30] so that you may eat and drink at my table in my kingdom, and sit on thrones judging the twelve tribes of Israel."

Luke's opening verse (v. 24) summarizes Mark's account of the dispute among the disciples which resulted from the request of James and John (Mark 10:35-41). Portions of Luke 22:25-27 derive from Mark 10:42-44, while v. 30 parallels Matt 19:28.[34] These parallel materials are found in diverse contexts, and will be considered individually.

MARK

The material from Mark (10:35-45) is found in the context of the journey to Jerusalem (see v. 32), where James and John request to be allowed to sit on Jesus' right and left in his "glory" ("kingdom" in Matt 20:21). When the other disciples learn of this request, they become indignant (Mark 10:41). The dominical tradition that follows (vv. 42-45) parallels what we find in Luke.

> [35] And James and John, the sons of Zebedee, came forward to him, and said to him, "Teacher, we want you to do for us whatever we ask of you." [36] And he said to them, "What do you want me to do for you?" [37] And they said to him, "Grant us to sit, one at your right hand and one at your left, in your glory." [38] But Jesus said to them, "You do not know what you are asking. Are you able to drink the cup that I drink, or to be baptized with the baptism with which I am baptized?" [39] And they said to him, "We are able." And Jesus said to them, "The cup that I drink you will drink; and with the baptism with which I am baptized, you will be baptized; [40] but to sit at my right hand or at my left is not mine to grant, but it is for those for whom it has been prepared." [41] And when the ten heard it, they began to be indignant at James and John. [42] And Jesus called them to him and said to them, "You know that those who are supposed to rule over the Gentiles lord it over them, and their great men exercise authority over them. [43] But it shall not be so among you; but whoever would be great among you must be your servant, [44] and whoever would be first among you must be slave of all. [45] For the Son of man also came not to be served but to serve, and to give his life as a ransom for many."

The Matthean evangelist (20:20-28) follows the Markan account more closely than does Luke. He does not omit the request of the disciples that

---

34. See Fitzmyer's discussion, *Luke X–XXIV*, 1411–14. Luke 22:29-30a is probably Lukan. Part of v. 28 ("You are those who have continued with me") may echo Matt 19:28 ("You who have followed me").

occasioned the dispute. He does, however, modify the Markan account by having the mother of James and John, instead of James and John themselves, make the request.[35] The object here is probably to avoid portraying the disciples as evincing the very characteristics that Jesus criticizes in his teaching about willingness to serve rather than be served. Luke probably omitted Mark 10:35-40 for the same reason.

Q

Matthew's version of the judging of the twelve tribes (19:28) is inserted between Peter's saying about leaving everything to follow Jesus, and Jesus' promise that those who follow him will receive back one hundredfold in this world and eternal life in the world to come (Matt 19:27-29; cf. Mark 10:28-30). The saying reads:

> Jesus said to them, "Truly I say to you, in the new world, when the Son of man shall sit on his glorious throne, you who have followed me will also sit on twelve thrones, judging the twelve tribes of Israel."

Luke's version (22:28-30) parallels the second half of the saying:

> [28] "You are those who have continued with me. . . . [30] that you may eat and drink at my table in my kingdom, and sit on thrones judging the twelve tribes of Israel."

Since this passage is verbally quite close to Mark's saying and is inserted by the Matthean and Lukan evangelists into two different locations in the Markan narrative (Matthew shortly after the interview with the wealthy young man; Luke during a last supper discourse),[36] the saying very likely does indeed derive from Q. Both evangelists have contributed to the passage. Matthew probably added "Son of man" and "in the new world" (lit. "in the regeneration"). Luke dropped the "Amen, I say to you," inserted vv. 29-30a (v. 30a is probably a Lukan equivalent for the first part of the saying about sitting on the throne of glory), and omitted the "twelve" in Q's "twelve thrones." He omitted the "twelve" because he had earlier dis-

---

35. Matthew makes other changes as well. Before making her request in v. 20, the mother of James and John kneels. Because it is the mother who makes the request, Jesus responds in v. 21 in the second person singular ("What do you want?"). He allows, however, the rest of the dialogue to remain in the plural (see vv. 22, 23, 24). In v. 21 he substitutes "kingdom" for "glory." In v. 23 the Matthean Jesus says "my cup" and at the end of the verse adds "by my father."

36. The saying in the Matthean context is an obvious intrusion. Peter reminds Jesus that he and the disciples had left everything to follow Jesus (19:27) and asks what will happen to them. Verse 29 gives the answer, v. 28 does not. In the Lukan context the saying fits better; here it is reworded to speak of eating and drinking at Jesus' table in his kingdom, and thus is appropriate for the last supper.

qualified Judas from the apostolate (Luke 22:3, 22); hence there are not twelve true apostles at the time that Jesus speaks.[37] (Judas's replacement will be added in Acts 1:15-26.) The saying in Q probably originally read something like this, "Truly I say to you, when I sit on my glorious throne, you who have followed [*or* continued with] me will also sit on twelve thrones, judging the twelve tribes of Israel."

The original meaning of "judging [*krinein*] the twelve tribes" was probably akin to the OT sense of "ruling."[38] There is no indication that the saying carries a punitive sense in either Matthew or Luke.[39] According to *Pss. Sol.* 17:26, Messiah "will gather a holy people whom he will lead in righteousness; and he will judge the tribes of the people."[40] We have here a close parallel, in which *krinein* appears, and it is clearly in the sense of ruling.[41] The saying, both in its original sense and in its later adaptation by the evangelists Matthew and Luke, probably connotes the sense of rule and not that of punitive judgment.[42] Moreover, *Pss. Sol.* 17:26 clearly implies that judging the tribes of Israel can only take place after their regathering and restoration. In this case, the saying not only does not threaten punishment, but anticipates Israel's restoration.[43]

---

37. Jervell, "The Twelve," 85–86; Fitzmyer, *Luke X–XXIV*, 1419.

38. Fitzmyer, *Luke X–XXIV*, 1419. Fitzmyer cites 1 Sam 8:20 where *shapat* is used to describe the authority of Israel's new king. Although the word literally means "to judge," the context demands that it be understood in the sense of "ruling." In LXX Judg 3:10 *krinein* translates *shapat* but again with the meaning of ruling; see also Dan 9:12. R. A. Horsley (*Sociology and the Jesus Movement* [New York: Crossroad, 1989] 119) translates "liberating the twelve tribes."

39. Both the rabbis and church fathers stray from the original idea of Ps 122:3-5/Matt 19:28 (Luke 22:30) when they interpret it in a punitive sense and apply it against each other.

40. Translation by R. B. Wright, "Psalms of Solomon," in J. H. Charlesworth, ed., *The Old Testament Pseudepigrapha* (vol. 2; Garden City: Doubleday, 1985) 667.

41. Note also *Pss. Sol.* 17:29, "[Messiah] will judge [*krinein*] peoples and nations in the wisdom of his righteousness." Trans. Wright, "Psalms of Solomon," 667. Even in this instance where Messiah is described as judging the Gentiles, it is in the sense of rule, not punishment or destruction.

42. Luke's understanding of the twelve as "witnesses" may bear some relationship to this saying. P. H. Menoud ("Jesus and His Witnesses: Observations on the Unity of the Work of Luke," in Menoud, *Jesus Christ and the Faith* [PTMS 18; Pittsburgh: Pickwick, 1978] 149–66, esp. 152–56) has noted that *martys* in Luke-Acts means one who understands and is in a position to evaluate. He notes, for example, that Josephus describes Titus as an "eyewitness and judge" (*autoptes kai martys*) of the capture of the temple (*J.W.* 6.2.5 §134). Whereas *autoptes* means no more than to be an observer, *martys* here connotes a stronger idea. The implication is that Titus not only had firsthand knowledge of what took place but was in a position to reward or punish his men according to their actions on the field of battle. Accordingly, Luke refers to the apostles as *autoptai* (Luke 1:2) and *martyres* (Luke 24:48; Acts 1:8). Menoud suggests that Luke's use of *martyres* should be understood in the stronger sense. The apostles have not only observed, they are now in a position to assess the significance of what has happened. If this is how Luke understands *martys*, then he has strengthened the apostles' qualification to act as Israel's "judges."

43. Although not citing *Pss. Sol.* 17:26, Lohfink (*Die Sammlung Israels*, 83) correctly concludes that Luke portrays Jesus as regathering Israel.

Did the passage originate with Jesus? Rudolf Bultmann believes that it is a saying of the risen Lord, "deriving from the early Church, for it was there the Twelve were first held to be judges of Israel in the time of the end."[44] He further says that the tradition later came to be universalized, as seen in Rev 3:21.[45] This latter point is likely correct, but the form of the tradition in 1 Cor 6:2 ("Do you not know that the saints will judge the world?") is also universal, and it is earlier than the synoptic tradition. Contrary to Bultmann's claim, there really is no evidence that the early community thought that the twelve apostles would judge Israel. Since the tendency in the early church was to give the tradition universal application, the particular, and unparalleled, application of the saying in Q argues for its authenticity. Moreover, the fact that the saying is not applied in an anti-Jewish sense in Gospels which contain polemical materials also argues for the authenticity of the saying.[46] It would appear then that Jesus expected the Twelve, along with himself, to rule Israel.

LUKE'S DISTINCTIVE CONTRIBUTION

The significant feature about Luke 22:24-30 is seen in the materials that have been combined.[47] The Markan story of the request to sit on Jesus' right and left and Q's saying about the disciples sitting on thrones judging the twelve tribes of Israel make up a total picture that is mirrored in Jewish traditions. In isolation, the components parallel Jewish interpretation at many points. (1) The disciples' request to sit on Jesus' right and

---

44. R. Bultmann, *The History of the Synoptic Tradition* (New York: Harper & Row, 1963) 158–59.

45. Bultmann, *History of the Synoptic Tradition*, 159, n. 4.

46. The disciples' request to sit on Jesus' right and left (Mark 10:35-40) is probably also authentic, for it paints an uncomplimentary picture of the petitioners; see V. Taylor, *The Gospel according to St. Mark* (London: Macmillan, 1966²) 439. Jesus' deference to God in Mark 10:40 probably did not derive from the early church. If it had, Jesus would have assumed the prerogative of granting specific places at the table. Because Mark 10:35-40 is cognate to Q's saying about sitting on thrones and judging the tribes of Israel, these related sayings might once have comprised a single passage. Perhaps it originally read something like this: "The sons of Zebedee said to him, 'Grant us to sit, one at your right hand and one at your left, in your glory.' But Jesus said to them, 'You do not know what you are asking. To sit at my right hand or at my left is not mine to grant, but it is for those for whom it has been prepared. Truly I say to you, when I sit on my glorious throne, you who have followed [*or* continued with] me will also sit on twelve thrones, judging the twelve tribes of Israel.'"

47. In a recent study W. S. Kurz ("Luke 22:14-38 and Greco-Roman and Biblical Farewell Addresses," *JBL* 104 [1985] 251–68) compared Luke 22:14-38 to Greco-Roman (e.g., Plato, *Phaedo*; Diogenes Laertius, *Epicurus* 10:16–18) and biblical (e.g., 1 Kgs 2:1-10; 1 Macc 2:49-70) farewell addresses. (He rightly maintains [253, n. 7] that Luke's composition stands closest to the biblical materials.) His comparative analysis to a great extent clarifies the form and function of Jesus' farewell address in Luke 22:14-38 but he does not explain the theological significance of the combination of certain elements in vv. 24-30. My study, without competing with or contradicting Kurz's analysis, attempts to explain the significance of this combination.

left probably reflects concepts illustrated by Jewish interpretation of Dan 7:9. Thrones will be set up for God and the Messiah and/or Israel's elders and princes. From the Christian perspective, of course, Jesus and his disciples will be among those who qualify. (2) When Jesus says that assigning places to sit is not his prerogative, again there is coherence with Jewish interpretation. According to *Midr. Tanh.*, *Qed.* §1 (72.4–5) the "angels will give thrones to the great ones of Israel, and they will sit." Neither Messiah nor his agents have this prerogative. (3) The discussion of who is "greatest" presupposes the interpretation just noted. The "great ones of Israel" will sit on the thrones. But what defines greatness? Jesus' saying in Mark 10:42-43 (adapted in Luke 22:24-27) defines it. The one who is great is the one who serves. (4) When the Matthean Jesus says that the Son of man will sit on his throne of glory, portions of Daniel 7 (esp. vv. 9, 13-14) are recalled, portions also interpreted messianically in Jewish sources. (5) Finally, the last part of the saying that the disciples will sit on thrones judging the twelve tribes again alludes to Daniel 7 (esp. vv. 18, 22, 26-27) and to Ps 122:3-5; and again the understanding coheres with tendencies in Jewish interpretation.

These parallels are impressive, but they derive from two distinct sources: Mark (parallels 1-3) and Q (parallels 4-5). In Luke, remarkably, the essential elements from both synoptic sources are combined. It is even more striking that these elements are combined in at least one Jewish midrash as well. In *Midrash Tanhuma,* Dan 7:9 is interpreted, and various explanations are offered to account for the plural "thrones." The solution is finally found in the reference to thrones in Ps 122:5: thrones will be given to Israel's "great ones" and "elders," and from these thrones judgment against the Gentiles will be given. A similar point is made in the Lukan discourse, when a dispute arises as to which of the disciples was to be regarded as the "greatest." Paradoxically Jesus says that the "greatest" is to "become as the youngest, and the leader as one who serves" (Luke 22:26). To these the kingdom will be assigned (Luke 22:29). They will eat and drink at the banquet table in the kingdom,[48] and they will sit on thrones judging the twelve tribes of Israel (Luke 22:30).

Although not obviously commenting on any particular scriptural precedent, 1QSa 2:11–17, quoted above, may very well illustrate a longed-for eschatological picture based on the same principles. According to this passage the "men of renown" (lit. "men of the name") shall sit in the presence of the Messiah "each according to his rank." The disciples'

---

48. Luke often describes the kingdom of God in the language of eating and drinking at the banquet table (Luke 13:29; 14:7-11, 12-14, 15-24; 15:21-24); cf. D. P. Moessner, *Lord of the Banquet* (Minneapolis: Fortress, 1989).

request to sit at Jesus' right and left reflects this picture; so does Jesus' teaching about how to qualify for the seats of honor in the time of the messianic banquet (cf. Luke 14).

But how is one's "rank" determined? Evidently Jesus held to views on this question which were at variance with conventional wisdom. His redefinition of the "great ones" (i.e., those who serve, rather than those who are served), or what Qumran calls the people of renown, spoke to Luke's concern about the question of election.[49] The challenge to prevailing assumptions of who will qualify for the seats of honor, and on what basis, coheres with Jesus' hermeneutic of prophetic critique. And to Luke that hermeneutic was especially dear.

There is no question that Luke 22:30 (//Matt 19:28) is based on Daniel 7 and Psalm 122. Not only is this dominical saying ultimately based on these scriptural traditions, but I think that it also reflects the essential aspects of their interpretation in early Judaism. Luke's combination of dominical materials suggests that he understood and agreed with this interpretation. He not only anticipates Jesus' enthronement but the enthronement of the apostles (twelve apostles when Judas is replaced by Matthias) who with Jesus will rule over the restored house of Israel.

If this analysis is sound, a major part of Jervell's thesis receives confirmation. But this study does not support his conclusion that Israel's restoration is achieved by the time that the narrative reaches Acts 15 and that therefore the twelve apostles are allowed to fade from view.[50] According to Luke 22:28-30 and the interpretive tradition against which it should be understood, the apostles will reign over the tribes of Israel some time in the future. This is the clear implication of the passage. In no sense is this reign achieved in Acts. The restoration of the kingdom has been initiated, but the apostles have not yet eaten and drunk at Jesus' kingly table (Luke 22:30). Luke's use of this tradition strongly implies that Israel has a future, but it is a future inextricably bound up with Christ's reign, guaranteed by his resurrection, to which the apostolic preaching gives witness.

---

49. See Chap. 8 above.

50. Jervell, "The Twelve," 92–93. This mistake leads Jervell to conclude in another essay ("The Divided People of God," in Jervell, *Luke and the People of God*, 63–64, 68–69) that the final scene in Acts (28:17-28) is meant to bring the Jewish mission to a close. For better assessments see E. Franklin, *Christ the Lord: A Study in the Purpose and Theology of Luke-Acts* (Philadelphia: Westminster, 1975) 114–15; R. L. Brawley, *Luke-Acts and the Jews: Conflict, Apology, and Conciliation* (SBLMS 33; Atlanta: Scholars, 1987) 74–78.

PROPHECY AND POLEMIC: JEWS IN LUKE'S SCRIPTURAL APOLOGETIC

CRAIG A. EVANS

For years scholars have recognized that the Jews in Luke-Acts play a major role in the evangelist's narrative and theology. What to make of this role, however, has been another matter. Opinions are diverse, ranging from the conclusion that Luke views Jews with great sympathy, to the opposite conclusion that he hates them.[1] A major factor in this discussion is the function of Scripture in Luke-Acts,[2] for the manner in which the evangelist applies the Scriptures to the Jews should to a significant extent reveal his true perspective. Jack T. Sanders (not to be confused with James A. Sanders, the coauthor of this book) agrees. Recently he has argued that Luke's use of the prophetic Scriptures is primarily intended to show that God has rejected the Jews and that they no longer have any hope of salvation.[3] According to Sanders, the evangelist is thoroughly anti-Semitic

---

1. For a recent assessment see R. L. Brawley, *Luke-Acts and the Jews: Conflict, Apology, and Conciliation* (SBLMS 33; Atlanta: Scholars, 1987).

2. T. Holtz, *Untersuchungen über die alttestamentlichen Zitate bei Lukas* (TU 104; Berlin: Akademie, 1968); M. Rese, *Alttestamentliche Motive in der Christologie des Lukas* (SNT 1; Gütersloh: Mohn, 1969); G. D. Kilpatrick, "Some Quotations in Acts," in J. Kremer, ed., *Les Actes des Apôtres* (Gembloux: Duculot, 1979) 81–87; E. Richard, "The Old Testament in Acts," *CBQ* 42 (1980) 330–41; J. Jervell, "The Center of Scripture in Luke," in Jervell, *The Unknown Paul* (Minneapolis: Augsburg, 1984) 122–37; H. Ringgren, "Luke's Use of the Old Testament," *HTR* 79 (1986) 227–35; D. L. Bock, *Proclamation from Prophecy and Pattern: Lucan Old Testament Christology* (JSNTSup 12; Sheffield: JSOT, 1987); J. B. Tyson, "Scripture, Torah, and Sabbath in Luke-Acts," in E. P. Sanders, ed., *Jesus, the Gospels, and the Church* (W. R. Farmer Festschrift; Macon: Mercer University Press, 1987) 89–104.

3. J. T. Sanders, "The Prophetic Use of the Scriptures in Luke-Acts," in C. A. Evans and W. F. Stinespring, eds., *Early Jewish and Christian Exegesis* (W. H. Brownlee Festschrift; Homage 10; Atlanta: Scholars, 1987) 191–98.

and does not merely oppose the Jewish religion but actually hates the Jewish people.[4]

It is the purpose of this chapter to assess the function of every Old Testament Scripture in Luke-Acts which has any bearing on the question of the evangelist's view of the Jewish people. Since Sanders has offered the most recent and comprehensive treatment of this subject, his publications will frequently serve as the point of departure. My intention, however, is not to engage in undue polemic. Although I disagree with his conclusions, I believe that Sanders's work has brought certain issues into sharp relief and so in some ways has advanced the discussion.

The analysis that follows is in two sections. The first treats the function of Scripture in the Lukan Gospel. The second treats the function of Scripture in Acts. Our concern is to observe patterns or indications of development. The chapter will conclude with an assessment.

THE FUNCTION OF SCRIPTURE IN LUKE

The Birth Narrative

Luke 1:14-18. "He will be great before the Lord, and he shall drink no wine nor strong drink, and he will be filled with Holy Spirit, even from his mother's womb. And he will turn many of the sons of Israel to the Lord their God, and he will go before him in the spirit and power of Elijah, to turn the hearts of the fathers to the children, and the disobedient to the wisdom of the just, to make ready for the Lord a people prepared" (vv. 15-17). The angelic announcement of John's birth echoes several biblical passages. The clearest allusions are to Num 6:3; Judg 13:4 (v. 15); Mal 2:6 (v. 16); Mal 3:1; 4:5-6; Sir 48:10; 2 Sam 7:24 (v. 17); and Gen 15:8 (v. 18). The allusion to the Baptist's preparatory work, described chiefly in terms of Malachi's image of the eschatological Elijah (cf. Mark 1:2; 9:11-12),[5] has been enriched by allusions to the Nazarite vow and to Abraham's question about God's promise. Allusions to these traditions only heighten the reader's expectation that something good is in store for Israel. Indeed, the birth of John will occasion joy (v. 14), and his ministry will "turn many of the sons of Israel to the Lord their God" (v. 16).[6]

---

4. J. T. Sanders, *The Jews in Luke-Acts* (Philadelphia: Fortress, 1987) xvi–xvii, 47, 310, 317; idem, "The Parable of the Pounds and Lucan Anti-Semitism," *TS* 42 (1981) 660–68; idem, "The Salvation of the Jews in Luke-Acts," in C. H. Talbert, ed., *Luke-Acts: New Perspectives from the Society of Biblical Literature Seminar* (New York: Crossroad, 1984) 104–28.

5. This interpretation of Malachi and its reference to Elijah is not uniquely Christian; see *Pesiq. R.* 4.2; 33.8; *Seder Eliyyahu Zuta* §1 (169); *Pirqe R. El.* §40 (56a.i–ii); §43 (61b.i); *m. 'Ed.* 8:7; *Sipre Deut.* §342 (on 33:2); *Midr.* Ps 3.7 (on 3:6); Pss. 42/43.5 (on 43:2).

6. For further details see J. A. Fitzmyer, *Luke I–IX* (AB 28; Garden City: Doubleday, 1981) 325–27; Bock, *Proclamation from Prophecy,* 57–60.

Luke 1:32-33. "He will be great, and will be called the Son of the Most High; and the Lord God will give to him the throne of his father David, and he will reign over the house of Jacob forever; and of his kingdom there will be no end." The angelic announcement of Jesus' birth likewise echoes various Scriptures. Being given the throne of David "his father" alludes to the Davidic covenant (2 Sam 7:12, 13, 16) and to the Isaianic promise (Isa 9:7), while the promise of Jesus' eternal reign and kingdom alludes to Israel's messianic hopes (Mic 4:7; Dan 2:44; 7:14). Throughout the birth narratives Jesus' Davidic descent is emphasized (1:69; 2:4, 11).[7]

Luke 1:36-38. "For with God nothing will be impossible." The angelic announcement to Mary that her kinswoman Elizabeth had conceived in her old age and that nothing is impossible for God is a clear allusion to the promise given Abraham regarding Sarah (cf. Gen 18:14). Not only is Jesus' birth a fulfillment of the promise to David, in itself highly significant; it is also presented as an event that parallels one of the greatest events preserved in the sacred story.[8] Mary's humble identification as the "Lord's handmaid" echoes Hannah's words of devotion (1 Sam 1:11).

Luke 1:46-55. "He has helped his servant Israel, in remembrance of his mercy, as he spoke to his fathers, to Abraham and to his posterity for ever" (vv. 54-55). The Magnificat is modeled after Hannah's song of thanksgiving (1 Sam 2:1-10)[9] and is replete with scriptural allusions. Of special interest are vv. 54-55, acknowledging God's aid (Isa 41:8-9), God's abiding mercy (Ps 98:3), and the fulfillment of God's promises to Abraham (Gen 12:1-3; 17:6-8; Mic 7:20) and his descendants (2 Sam 7:11-16). These verses give eloquent expression to Israel's fondest hopes.[10]

Luke 1:68-79. "To grant us that we, being delivered from the hand of our enemies, might serve him without fear" (v. 74). The Benedictus, like the Magnificat, praises God for keeping his promises to Israel. Virtually every line resonates with biblical language. Alluding to several Scriptures,

---

7. See further Fitzmyer, *Luke I–IX*, 347–48; Rese, *Alttestamentliche Motive*, 185; Bock, *Proclamation from Prophecy*, 60–69.

8. See J. A. Sanders, "Annunciations," *Scripture in Church* 18/69 (1988) 115–20.

9. In the Targum 1 Sam 2:1-10 has been refashioned into an apocalypse foretelling the eventual triumph of Israel's Messiah; see further D. J. Harrington, "The Apocalypse of Hannah: Targum Jonathan of 1 Samuel 2:1-10," in D. M. Golomb, ed., *"Working with No Data": Semitic and Egyptian Studies* (T. O. Lambdin Festschrift; Winona Lake, IN: Eisenbrauns, 1987) 147–52. For an English translation of the passage see S. H. Levey, *The Messiah: An Aramaic Interpretation* (Cincinnati: Hebrew Union College, 1974) 34; D. J. Harrington, *Targum Jonathan of the Former Prophets* (Aramaic Bible 10; Wilmington: Glazier, 1987) 107–8.

10. For further details see Fitzmyer, *Luke I–IX*, 366–69; Bock, *Proclamation from Prophecy*, 69–70.

Zechariah blesses God because "he has visited and redeemed his people [cf. Ps 111:9], and has raised up a horn of salvation for us [cf. Ps 18:2] . . . that we should be saved from our enemies and from the hand of all who hate us [cf. Ps 18:17; 2 Sam 22:18] . . . which he swore to our father Abraham [cf. Gen 26:3] . . . " (vv. 68-73). It would be singular hypocrisy indeed if the evangelist Luke in fact hated the Jews. Again the ministry of John is anticipated in the allusion to Mal 3:1 in v. 76.[11]

Luke 2:29-32. "Mine eyes have seen thy salvation which thou hast prepared in the presence of all peoples, a light for revelation to the Gentiles, and for glory to thy people Israel." The Nunc Dimittis contains important allusions to Isa 40:5 (which will reappear in Luke 3:6) and Isa 42:6; 49:6 (which will reappear in Acts 13:47; 26:23).[12] The references to salvation, all the peoples, and the Gentiles certainly contribute to Luke's emphasis of the Gentile mission. But the significance of the concluding line, "and for glory to thy people Israel," must not be underrated. The relationship of this line with the one that precedes is significant. Whereas God's salvation will become a light that gives revelation to the Gentiles, it will also give glory to Israel (see LXX Isa 46:13). Israel's priority over the Gentiles is here hinted at.[13] These are the positive words, however; negative ones follow. In v. 34 Simeon tells Mary that Jesus will occasion the "fall and rising of many in Israel." Correctly sensing that this verse mirrors the whole of the story in Acts, Sanders applies the "rising" to Acts 1–5 and the "fall" to the remainder of Acts.[14] But this runs opposite to Luke's order. He does not say the "rising and fall," but the "fall and rising." Moreover, Luke's point is likely not temporal at all. He implies that some will fall and some will rise, that Israel will be divided in its response to Jesus. This theme recurs throughout Luke-Acts and is the main point in the concluding scene of Luke's second volume (Acts 28:24-25). It is also the meaning of the sword that will pierce Mary's soul (Luke 2:35). Jesus, who will be "spoken against" (*antilegomenon*), will become the cause of division, even within families (see Luke 8:21; 11:27-28; 12:51-53).[15]

The pro-Jewish stance of the infancy narratives is obvious. Sanders acknowledges this fact but argues that these narratives are intended to show that Jesus and Christianity had a legitimate beginning in "good Jew-

---

11. See further Fitzmyer, *Luke I–IX*, 382–89; Rese, *Alttestamentliche Motive*, 178–83; Bock, *Proclamation from Prophecy*, 70–74.

12. Isa 42:6 is interpreted messianically in the Targum; see Levey, *The Messiah*, 59–60.

13. Fitzmyer, *Luke I–IX*, 428.

14. J. T. Sanders, *The Jews in Luke-Acts*, 161.

15. Fitzmyer, *Luke I–IX*, 429–30; Rese, *Alttestamentliche Motive*, 184; Bock, *Proclamation from Prophecy*, 89–90.

ish piety."[16] Luke's point, according to Sanders, is to show that in rejecting Jesus, Judaism has deviated from the path of biblical faith and piety. No doubt there is an element of truth in this. Luke certainly does wish to show that Christianity had its origin in the best of Jewish piety. But if that was his main point, why does the evangelist over and over again say that Israel's fondest hopes have been realized when in fact they have not? In what sense does Jesus' advent lead to glory for Israel (2:32) if in fact it leads to rejection and damnation? How have the descendants of Abraham been delivered from their enemies (1:73-74)? How has Israel been helped (1:54) if Luke views Jesus' advent as resulting in Israel's destruction and eternal separation from God? It is revealing that Sanders avoids discussing these passages in detail. In fact, the one passage that he does discuss, he misconstrues (2:34-35). In my judgment, the presence of so much pro-Jewish material, with its allusions to biblical traditions that give expression to Israel's nationalistic hopes, militates against the thesis that Luke is anti-Semitic and sees Israel's final and total ruin prophesied in the Scriptures. The infancy narratives seem to me to stress that in Jesus the messianic promises are fulfilled and that in their fulfillment salvation will be extended to the Gentiles. A somewhat more complicated picture emerges in the function of Scripture throughout the remainder of Luke-Acts.

Ministry in Galilee

Luke 3:4-6. "As it is written in the book of the words of Isaiah the prophet, 'The voice of one crying in the wilderness: Prepare the way of the Lord, make his paths straight. Every valley shall be filled, and every mountain and hill shall be brought low, and the crooked shall be made straight, and the rough ways shall be made smooth; and all flesh shall see the salvation of God'" (cf. Isa 40:3-5). Luke has derived this citation from Mark 1:2-3. He has omitted Mal 3:1 (which will appear later in 7:27) and has extended the citation of Isa 40:3 to v. 5.[17] The reason for this extension is obvious: Luke understands the "way of the Lord" to have a universal application. "All flesh shall see the salvation of God." This idea certainly lays the groundwork for the later Gentile mission, but there is no reason to think that the Jewish people are thereby excluded.[18] This important Isaianic text was earlier alluded to in the infancy narratives, in passages about John (1:17, 76-79), which anticipate Israel's forgiveness and restoration. But the text is alluded to in passages about Jesus as well. It is found in the Nunc

---

16. J. T. Sanders, *The Jews in Luke-Acts*, 161.

17. For textual discussion see Holtz, *Über die alttestamentlichen Zitate bei Lukas*, 37–39; Bock, *Proclamation from Prophecy*, 93–99.

18. J. T. Sanders ("The Prophetic Use of the Scriptures," 194–95) seems to imply that Isa 40:5 has in mind only Gentiles.

Dimittis (lit.), "My eyes have seen your salvation which you have prepared in the face of all peoples" (2:30-31) and at the beginning of Jesus' journey to Jerusalem (lit.), "He sent messengers before his face . . . to prepare for him" (9:52). The allusion in the infancy narrative suggests that the theme of Isaiah 40 applies to the whole of Jesus' anticipated ministry as much as it does to John's, while the allusion in 9:52 provides a specific example of this theme's actualization. Jesus is now on his way to Jerusalem and has sent messengers ahead to prepare his way. In applying Isa 40:3-5 to Jesus as well as to John, the evangelist is saying that whereas preparation is John's task (an idea rooted firmly in Christian tradition), "the salvation of all flesh" is Jesus' task.[19]

Luke 4:16-30. "The Spirit of the Lord is upon me, because he has anointed me to preach good news to the poor. He has sent me to proclaim release to the captives and recovering of sight to the blind, to set at liberty those who are oppressed, to proclaim the acceptable year of the Lord" (vv. 18-19; cf. Isa 61:1-2 + 58:6).[20] Luke's account of Jesus' Nazareth sermon is a reworking and expansion of Mark 6:1-6a. By placing this pericope at the beginning of Jesus' public ministry (rather than near the midpoint, as it is in Mark [and Matthew]), the evangelist no doubt wishes to show at the outset what Jesus' ministry will entail.[21] Jesus' announcement that messianic blessings are to be extended to Gentiles (as illustrated by the examples of 1 Kgs 17:1-16; 2 Kgs 5:1-14) is met with Jewish indignation and hostility. Most interpreters see Jesus' rejection and death, as well as the Gentile mission, foreshadowed in this episode.[22] This seems clear enough. But Sanders also believes that the final rejection of the Jews is anticipated (as he believes is seen in Acts 28:26-27).[23] This seems to be reading a little too much into the text. The point of the passage is not that messianic blessings are to be withheld from Jews, much less that the Jewish people are to be rejected. The evangelist maintains, rather, that the assumption held by many Jewish people of Luke's time that such blessings are for Jewish people exclusively is wrong, and that challenging this assumption is

---

19. For further discussion see K. R. Snodgrass, "Streams of Tradition Emerging from Isaiah 40.1-5 and Their Adaptation in the New Testament," *JSNT* 8 (1980) 24–45.

20. For textual discussion see Holtz, *Über die alttestamentlichen Zitate bei Lukas*, 39–41; Rese, *Alttestamentliche Motive*, 143–44; Bock, *Proclamation from Prophecy*, 105–11.

21. See H. Conzelmann, *The Theology of St. Luke* (New York: Harper & Row, 1960) 31–37.

22. R. C. Tannehill, "The Mission of Jesus according to Luke IV 16-30," in E. Grässer, ed., *Jesus in Nazareth* (BZNW 40; Berlin: de Gruyter, 1972) 51–75, esp. 62–63; S. G. Wilson, *The Gentiles and the Gentile Mission in Luke-Acts* (SNTSMS 23; Cambridge: University Press, 1973) 40–41.

23. J. T. Sanders, *The Jews in Luke-Acts*, 165–68; idem, "The Salvation of the Jews," 116. E. E. Ellis *(The Gospel of Luke* [NCB; London: Oliphants, rev. ed., 1974] 98) misinterprets the passage the same way.

a major factor in Jewish rejection of Jesus.[24] The evangelist believes that election is not based upon physical descent from Abraham (Luke 3:8)[25] but upon response to the Christian message. We see this clearly in Luke 8:19-21, where Jesus' true family is made up of "those who hear the word of God and do it"; these will enjoy the messianic blessing announced at Nazareth. This presentation of election, which admittedly serves the evangelist's Gentile interests, is no more anti-Semitic in Luke than it is in Paul (see Rom 9:6).

Luke 8:10. "To you it has been given to know the secrets of the kingdom of God; but for others they are in parables, so that seeing they may not see, and hearing they may not understand" (cf. Isa 6:9-10). According to Mark 4:11-12 all things are parabolic (i.e., enigmatic) to "outsiders," in order that they may see but not perceive; and may hear but not understand; lest they repent and be forgiven (see discussion of Acts 28:25-27 below). This saying, coming where it does, implies that Jesus tells parables in order to prevent comprehension, repentance, and forgiveness. Luke, however, substitutes "others" for "outsiders" and omits Mark's "lest they repent and be forgiven." Luke's redaction removes much of Mark's sting (compare Matt 13:11-15). If anything, Luke appears to be trying to avoid the impression that Jesus' teaching is esoteric and exclusive.[26]

Journey to Jerusalem

Luke 10:25-37. "What is written in the law? How do you read?" (v. 26). After hearing the lawyer recite the Great Commandment (Deut 6:5 [10:12;

---

24. This point is made clear by J. A. Sanders, "From Isaiah 61 to Luke 4," in J. Neusner, ed., *Christianity, Judaism and Other Greco-Roman Cults* (M. Smith Festschrift; Leiden: Brill, 1975) 75–106, esp. 96–104; see Chap. 4 above. The omission of the phrase "And the day of vengeance of our God" (Isa 61:2b) from Jesus' quotation (cf. Luke 4:18-19) is curious, if Luke intends the passage to be understood in a vindictive sense (compare the interpretation of Isa 61:1-2 in 11QMelchizedek 9–16). But the omission is in keeping with the evangelist's challenge to assumptions about election, for example, that the Messiah has not come to bless the apparent elect nor to punish the apparent non-elect. For further details, see B. D. Chilton, *God in Strength: Jesus' Announcement of the Kingdom* (Studien zum Neuen Testament und seiner Umwelt 1; Freistadt: Plöchl, 1979) 123–77; idem, "Announcement in Nazara: An Analysis of Luke 4:16-21," in R. T. France and D. Wenham, eds., *Studies of History and Tradition in the Four Gospels* (Gospel Perspectives 2; Sheffield: JSOT, 1981) 147–72. Moreover, L. C. Crockett ("Luke 4:25-27 and Jewish-Gentile Relations in Luke-Acts," *JBL* 88 [1969] 177–83) argues that Luke's use of the Elijah/Elisha traditions in Luke 4:25-27 and elsewhere was intended to show that Gentiles are now acceptable to God and that Jews and Gentiles can be reconciled in fellowship. See also C. F. Evans, *Saint Luke* (TPI New Testament Commentaries; London: SCM; Philadelphia: Trinity, 1990) 275.

25. This idea also finds expression in the words of the Lukan Peter, "I perceive that God shows no partiality" (Acts 10:34). Such sentiment contradicts anti-Semitism.

26. For further discussion see C. A. Evans, *To See and Not Perceive: Isaiah 6.9-10 in Early Jewish and Christian Interpretation* (JSOTSup 64; Sheffield: JSOT, 1989) 123–26.

Josh 22:5]; Lev 19:18), Jesus admonishes the legist to keep the commandment and live (10:28, echoing Lev 18:5).[27] The lawyer, "desiring to justify
himself" (a pejorative expression in Luke; cf. Luke 16:15), then asks who
his neighbor is (10:29). Sanders correctly perceives that Luke understands
the parable that follows to be an illustration of what it means to keep the
commandment to love one's neighbor. According to the parable, the
Samaritan fulfills the commandment; the priest and Levite do not. Sanders
believes that this parable contributes to Lukan anti-Semitism, since "by no
Jewish prescribed practice, but by behaving like a Samaritan, can salvation
be obtained. . . . Jesus' final words mean not only that the hearer should
behave in a certain way, but that the legist should behave like a Samaritan,
not like the Jewish religious leaders."[28] Again Sanders seems to be reading
into the parable an element that is not present.[29] The parable's point is
that anyone (even a Samaritan), not just a religious expert, can show love
and so keep the Great Commandment, not that it is necessary to avoid
being Jewish and to attempt to imitate a Samaritan.[30] Indeed, since the
parable is based on the story of the merciful Samaritans in 2 Chronicles
(28:15), one should not suppose that the parable enjoins behavior contrary to Jewish traditions.[31]

Luke 13:35. "Behold, your house is forsaken. And I tell you, you will not
see me until you say, 'Blessed is he who comes in the name of the Lord!' "
(= Matt 23:37-39; cf. Ps 118:26). The opening line echoes Jer 12:7; 22:5,
prophetic passages that speak of God deserting the sinful people. Because
Jerusalem has refused Jesus (Luke 13:34), judgment will befall the city.
This seems clear enough, but the meaning of the second line of v. 35 is
less clear. Because of the allusion to Ps 118:26, the triumphal entry may be
in view (Luke 19:38).[32] But this is not likely, since it is the disciples of
Jesus, not the inhabitants of Jerusalem, who cry out, "Blessed is the King
who comes in the name of the Lord!" (see 19:37). Moreover, such an
interpretation makes little sense, for the inhabitants of Jerusalem *will* see

---

27. On pre-Christian usage of these OT texts in combination, see J. A. Fitzmyer, *The Gospel
according to Luke X–XXIV* (AB 28A; Garden City: Doubleday, 1985) 879.

28. J. T. Sanders, *The Jews in Luke-Acts*, 183–84 (his emphasis).

29. Fitzmyer (*Luke X–XXIV*, 885) says that to read the parable in an anti-Semitic way "is
just another subtle way of allegorizing it."

30. E. Franklin (*Christ the Lord: A Study in the Purpose and Theology of Luke-Acts* [Philadel-
phia: Westminster, 1975] 158) maintains that "it is probably a mistake to see the main point
of this in its commendation of a particular way of life." See also S. G. Wilson, *Luke and the
Law* (SNTSMS 50; Cambridge: University Press, 1983) 16.

31. See J. D. M. Derrett, "The Parable of the Good Samaritan," in Derrett, *Law in the New
Testament* (London: Darton, Longman & Todd, 1970) 210–11.

32. See F. Danker, *Jesus and the New Age* (St. Louis: Clayton, 1972) 162; J. T. Sanders, *The
Jews in Luke-Acts*, 193.

Jesus. They will see him and reject him. The saying, therefore, likely alludes to the parousia,[33] at the time when the kingdom is finally restored to Israel (Acts 1:6, 11); then stubborn Jerusalem will finally bless the Messiah. But not until then will the inhabitants be gathered together under the wings of Messiah's care and protection. The expectation is that someday, but not now, the Jewish nation will respond and be reconciled to the Messiah.[34]

Ministry in Judea and Jerusalem

Luke 19:41-44. "And when he drew near and saw the city he wept over it, saying, 'Would that even today you knew the things that make for peace! But now they are hid from your eyes . . .'" (v. 41). Verses 43-44 constitute an oracle replete with prophetic language about Jerusalem's first destruction (Isa 29:3; Jer 6:6, 15; 10:15; Ezek 4:2).[35] What was hinted at in Luke 13:35 is now made explicit. Jerusalem has not known "the things that make for peace," and it has not recognized "the time of [its] *visitation*" (v. 44). Now the city faces destruction, and for this reason Jesus weeps. Whether or not Luke is the author of the oracle of vv. 42-44 is not certain, but there is little reason to doubt that v. 41, which describes Jesus' lamentation, is from the evanglist himself.[36] How Sanders can say that there is present no element of sadness in this pericope is curious, for it appears that this is the very element that Luke himself has added.[37]

Luke 19:46. "It is written, 'My house shall be a house of prayer'; but you have made it a den of robbers" (cf. Isa 56:7; Jer 7:11). Luke omits Isaiah's "for all the nations" (as does Matthew, cf. 21:13). Sanders attaches significance to this omission although he does not clearly describe the sig-

---

33. See J. M. Creed, *The Gospel according to St. Luke* (London: Macmillan, 1930) 187; I. H. Marshall, *The Gospel of Luke* (NIGTC; Grand Rapids: Eerdmans, 1978) 577; Fitzmyer, *Luke X–XXIV*, 1035. The rabbis understood Ps 118:26 in reference to the day of redemption; see *Midr. Ps* 118.22 (on 118:24-29). Many of the Hallel Psalms were regarded as eschatological; see J. Jeremias, *The Eucharistic Words of Jesus* (London: SCM, 1966) 256–57; Str-B 2.256; Bock, *Proclamation from Prophecy*, 118.

34. Bock (*Proclamation from Prophecy*, 118) comments: "In the context of the Lucan portrait of Jesus' ministry the Pharisees are called upon to respond to Jesus and acknowledge him as Messiah. Until this recognition is given, their house is abandoned." Although contingent upon repentance, the same idea is present in Acts 3:19-21: "Repent therefore, and turn again, that your sins may be blotted out, that times of refreshing may come from the presence of the Lord, and that he may send the Christ appointed for you, Jesus, whom heaven must receive until the time for establishing all that God spoke by the mouth of his holy prophets of old."

35. See C. H. Dodd, "The Fall of Jerusalem and the 'Abomination of Desolation,'" *JRS* 37 (1947) 47–54; repr. in Dodd, *More New Testament Studies* (Grand Rapids: Eerdmans, 1968) 69–83.

36. Marshall, *Luke*, 718; Fitzmyer, *Luke X–XXIV*, 1257.

37. J. T. Sanders, *The Jews in Luke-Acts*, 210. For better assessments see D. L. Tiede, *Prophecy and History in Luke-Acts* (Philadelphia: Fortress, 1980) 65–96; Fitzmyer, *Luke X–XXIV*, 1255–57.

nificance. Fitzmyer and others are probably correct in noting that since the temple no longer stands as Luke is writing, and since the "nations" are entering the church, not the temple, the omission is not unexpected[38] and probably does not reflect an anti-Semitic tendency. Moreover, Luke's double omission of the cursing of the fig tree (Mark 11:12-14, 20-21) and Jesus' exertion to expel the vendors (Mark 11:15b-16) mitigates the severity of the Markan portrait.

Luke 20:17-18. "What then is this that is written: 'The very stone which the builders rejected has become the head of the corner'? Every one who falls on that stone will be broken to pieces; but when it falls on any one it will crush him" (cf. Ps 118:22; Isa 8:14-15 + Dan 2:34).[39] Mark's version of the parable of the Wicked Vineyard Tenants (Mark 12:1-12) concludes with a quotation of Ps 118:22-23. Luke, however, has replaced v. 23 ("This was the Lord's doing, and it is marvelous in our eyes") with a saying whose first part is probably an allusion to Isa 8:14-15. "And [the Lord] will become . . . a rock of stumbling . . . and many shall stumble thereon; they shall fall and be broken. . . . " Underlying the second part is probably Dan 2:34, "A stone was cut out by no human hand, and it smote the image on its feet of iron and clay, and broke them in pieces."[40] The latter text is messianic,[41] the former clearly judgmental of Israel. The combination implies disaster for those who oppose God's Messiah.[42] Because Jesus speaks to the "people" (v. 9), who respond with "May it not be!" Sanders believes that Luke really intends the parable to apply to the entire nation and not just to the religious leaders (as, contrary to Sanders, is made explicit in v. 19).[43] The

---

38. Creed, *St. Luke*, 242; Marshall, *Luke*, 721; Fitzmyer, *Luke X–XXIV*, 1261.

39. On the form of the citation see Bock, *Proclamation from Prophecy*, 126–27.

40. See Creed, *St. Luke*, 246–47; Marshall, *Luke*, 732; Fitzmyer, *Luke X–XXIV*, 1282. B. Lindars (*New Testament Apologetic: The Doctrinal Significance of the Old Testament Quotations* [Philadelphia: Westminster, 1961] 184) notes that the rescension of Theodotion parallels Luke's paraphrase more closely and may reflect an early exegetical tradition.

41. The "stone" is probably in reference to the nation of Israel, but the symbolic event described is probably to be understood as messianic.

42. Str-B 1.877 cites an instructive rabbinic parallel. Commenting on Haman's plan to destroy the Jews, Rabbi Simeon ben Jose ben Lakunia says: "In this world Israel is likened to rocks, as it says, 'For from the top of rocks [i.e., the patriarchs] I see him' (Num 23:9); 'Look unto the rock whence ye were hewn' (Isa 51:1). [The Israelites] are compared to stones, as it says, 'From thence the shepherd of the stone of Israel' (Gen 49:24); 'The stone which the builders rejected' (Ps 118:22). But the other nations are likened to potsherds, as it says, 'And he shall break it as a potter's vessel is broken' (Isa 30:14). If a stone falls on a pot, woe to the pot! If a pot falls on a stone, woe to the pot! In either case, woe to the pot! So whoever ventures to attack [the Israelites] receives his deserts on their account" (*Esth. Rab.* 7.10 [on 3:6]); translation based on M. Simon, *Midrash Rabbah: Esther* (London and New York: Soncino, 1983) 85. This midrash also cites Dan 2:34.

43. J. T. Sanders, *The Jews in Luke-Acts*, 211–13. In his "The Prophetic Use of the Scriptures" (196) Sanders comments that the Lukan Peter's reference to "you builders" (Acts 4:11,

people's response probably means nothing more than that they hope that what Jesus described will not befall their religious leaders and institutions.[44] And Luke's explicit reference to the people in v. 9 reflects what had already been implied in Mark (cf. Mark 12:12).

Luke 21:20-24. "But when you see Jerusalem surrounded by armies, then know that its desolation has come near. . . . for these are days of vengeance, to fulfill all that is written" (vv. 20, 22). The references to "days of vengeance" (v. 22), "wrath upon this people" (v. 23), and the trampling of Jerusalem (v. 24) underscore the judgmental nature of this oracle that is loosely based on Mark 13:14-20. Again Old Testament imagery is echoed (Hos 9:7; Sir 28:18; Deut 28:64; Zech 12:3).[45] Sanders rejects the interpretation that the phrase "until the times of the Gentiles" implies restoration of Jerusalem.[46] In itself it probably does not,[47] but statements in the following pericopes suggest that restoration of some sort is in view. When the times of the Gentiles are fulfilled, various cosmological signs will take place (vv. 25-26, alluding to Isa 34:4). The Son of man will come with power and great glory (v. 27, alluding to Dan 7:13). When these things take place, Jesus enjoins his audience, "Look up and raise your heads, because your redemption is drawing near" (v. 28). After the parable of the Fig Tree (vv. 29-30), Jesus concludes, "When you see these things taking place, you know that the kingdom of God is near" (v. 31). In view of the question that the disciples put to Jesus in Acts 1:6 ("Lord, will you at this time restore the kingdom *to Israel?*" [my emphasis]), the saying in Luke 21:31 certainly leaves open the possibility of Israel's restoration. Another indication is the way that Luke has contextualized the apocalyptic discourse. Whereas in Mark 13 this discourse is held in private with the disciples so that one might argue that Mark intends it to apply only to Christians, in Luke's context it is uttered publicly in the temple. After cleansing the temple (19:45-46), Jesus "was teaching daily in the temple" (v. 47; cf. 21:37). In 20:1 we are told that "one day, as [Jesus] was teaching the

---

alluding to Ps 118:22) includes "all the people of Israel" (Acts 4:10). This is not the case. Peter wants "all the people" to know that the lame man was healed by Jesus. The "builders" refers only to the Jewish religious leaders (in a negative sense, CD 4:19; 8:12, 18; in a positive sense, *Tg.* Ps 118:22-29; *b. Shab.* 114a; *b. Ber.* 64a; cf. 1 Cor 3:10). Peter has been addressing the religious leaders, as Acts 4:5-8 makes clear.

44. Marshall, *Luke*, 731–32; Fitzmyer, *Luke X–XXIV*, 1285.

45. For further parallels see Marshall, *Luke*, 773; Fitzmyer, *Luke X–XXIV*, 1344–47.

46. J. T. Sanders, *The Jews in Luke-Acts*, 218.

47. The expression may, however, imply a limit to Gentile domination; see Dan 2:44; 8:13-14; 12:5-13; 1QS 4:18–19; Rom 11:25-27. Brawley (*Luke-Acts and the Jews*, 125) finds "uncanny verbal resemblances" between Luke 21:24, Ezek 39:23, and Zech 12:3, passages that foretell national restoration (see Ezek 39:24-29; Zech 12:4-9). If these resemblances are significant, the concluding verse of this Lukan oracle may indeed imply Israel's restoration.

people in the Temple. . . . " There is no indication throughout the remainder of chapter 20 and on through chapter 21 that the context has changed. (In 20:45 he speaks in the "hearing of all the people"; cf. 21:38.) With regard to the prediction of the temple's destruction, Jesus' prophecy in Mark 13:1 is occasioned by a comment by "one of his disciples." In Luke's version, however, Jesus' prophecy is occasioned by "some" (21:5), presumably some of the people in the temple whom Jesus had been teaching. Thus when Jesus says "your redemption is drawing near" and the "kingdom of God is near," he is speaking to the people and not only to his disciples. If the whole of chapter 21 is taken into consideration,[48] the evangelist seems to be saying that the destruction of Jerusalem is a necessary (and prophetically predicted) prelude to the events that lead up to Israel's redemption and kingdom. Since Luke has Jesus addressing these oracles and admonitions to the Jewish people as a whole and since Acts 1:6 clearly implies expectation that the kingdom at some time will be restored to Israel, one cannot conclude that the judgmental oracle in 21:20-24 implies the destruction of all Jews or the end of Jewish eschatological hopes.

Passion

Luke 23:26-31. "And there followed him a great multitude of the people, and of women who bewailed and lamented him. But Jesus turning to them said, 'Daughters of Jerusalem, do not weep for me, but weep for yourselves and for your children. For behold, the days are coming when they will say, "Blessed are the barren, and the wombs that never bore, and the breasts that never gave suck!" Then they will begin to say to the mountains, "Fall on us"; and to the hills, "Cover us" ' " (vv. 27-30, cf. Hos 10:8; Rev 6:16). These are the words of Jesus as he is led away to be crucified. With the exception of the opening verse (v. 26, cf. Mark 15:20b-21), the pericope is unique to Luke. The citation of Hosea is appropriate to the Lukan context. In Hos 10:7-8 the prophet predicts the destruction of Israel's high places and altars (i.e., places of worship). Moreover, the expression "The days are coming" echoes similar prophetic warnings about impending disaster (Jer 7:32; 16:14).[49] Sanders comments that this episode "dramatically brings [Jewish] guilt into view."[50] True, Jerusalem's guilt in executing Jesus is implied, but the main point of the passage seems to consist in Jesus' warning. The women should weep for them-

---

48. J. T. Sanders (*The Jews in Luke-Acts*, 389, n. 77) offers no commentary on vv. 25-36, explaining that these verses do "not concern us here."

49. See D. L. Tiede, *Luke* (Augsburg Commentary on the New Testament; Minneapolis: Augsburg, 1988) 414–15.

50. J. T. Sanders, *The Jews in Luke-Acts*, 226.

selves, as Jesus earlier had wept (19:41-44), for catastrophe will befall the city. The pathos of the scene belies an anti-Semitic orientation (see also 23:48).

Luke 23:34. "And Jesus said, 'Father, forgive them; for they know not what they do.' "[51] While being crucified, Jesus asks that the people (probably the Jewish people as well as the Roman executioners[52]) be forgiven on the grounds of ignorance, a theme that recurs later in Acts. The biblical idea behind this sentiment is found in Num 15:25-31. If a person (or the entire nation of Israel) sins unwittingly, atonement is possible; but if a person sins deliberately (or defiantly), there is no atonement (for either Israelite or Gentile).[53] By uttering this prayer, which is unique to Luke, Jesus makes atonement possible, according to Old Testament law, for those who have opposed him and have condemned him to death.[54] The same point is made by Peter to the Jews of Jerusalem (Acts 3:17), by Paul to the Jews of the Diaspora (Acts 13:27), and by Paul to the Gentiles (Acts 17:30).[55] The implication is that atonement is possible for all, Jews and Gentiles alike. Sanders's explanation that the prayer is intended only to set the stage for the "Jewish springtime" of the first five or six chapters of Acts is inade-

---

51. J. T. Sanders (*The Jews in Luke-Acts*, 227, 359–60, n. 159) accepts the prayer of forgiveness as textually genuine, as do M.-J. Lagrange, *Évangile selon Saint Luc* (Études bibliques; Paris: Gabalda, 1941⁵) 587–88; C. S. C. Williams, *A Commentary on the Acts of the Apostles* (Black's New Testament Commentaries; London: Black, 1957) 79, 112; M. Dibelius, *From Tradition to Gospel* (Cambridge and London: James Clarke, 1971) 203, n. 2; B. M. Metzger, *A Textual Commentary on the Greek New Testament* (London and New York: United Bible Societies, 1971) 180; Ellis, *Luke*, 267–68; G. Schneider, *Das Evangelium nach Lukas* (2 vols.; Gütersloh: Mohn, 1977) 2.483; Marshall, *Luke*, 868 (with caution); but see Fitzmyer, *Luke X–XXIV*, 1503–4.

52. Marshall, *Luke*, 867. It is not clear, however, that Luke implies the Romans here. Having omitted Mark 15:16-20, which describes the abuse that Jesus suffered at Roman hands, Luke says that Pilate delivered Jesus up to "the will of the Jews" (23:25) and "they [the Jews?] crucif[ied] him" (23:26). Jesus' prayer of forgiveness may be intended to apply only to the Jews.

53. In the targumic tradition Num 15:25-31 has an eschatological application (with italics showing significant departures from the Hebrew): "Let the priest make atonement before the Lord for the person who has sinned through ignorance, to atone for him; that it may be forgiven him. . . . But a man who transgresses with presumption, whether of the native-born or strangers, who does not turn away from his sin before the Lord, causes anger and will perish from among his people. . . . with destruction in this world shall that man be destroyed, *and in the world to come he will give account of his sin at the great day of judgment*" (*Tg. Ps.-J.* Num 15:28-31). The passage is thus interpreted in the rabbis as well. According to Rabbi Aqiba, Num 15:31 means that the sinner will be "cut off in this world and in the next" (*b. Sanh.* 64b; cf. 90b; 99a). Elsewhere it is taught that the "any person" of Num 15:27 may include laymen, rulers, even the high priest (*b. Hor.* 7b).

54. C. G. Montefiore (*The Synoptic Gospels* [2 vols.; New York: Ktav, 1968²] 2.625) notes that Jesus' prayer fulfills Isa 53:12, "For the transgressors he made intercession." Nothing, however, points specifically to Isaiah 53.

55. The three major theologians of Luke-Acts (Jesus, Peter, and Paul) excuse the Jews on grounds of ignorance.

quate.[56] Not only is the ignorance theme applied to the Jews after the first six chapters of Acts, it is applied to the Gentile mission as well. Furthermore, Stephen's similar prayer of forgiveness (7:60) comes *after* the Jewish spring. If Jesus' prayer is meant to set the stage for the Jewish spring, what does Stephen's similar prayer accomplish? Does it not imply that despite fierce Jewish opposition, the proper Christian attitude is one of forgiveness? If Jesus' prayer of forgiveness made continuation of the Jewish mission possible, why would not Stephen's prayer do the same? Finally, these Lukan prayers of forgiveness stand in stark contrast to scriptural traditions themselves. Consider Isaiah's angry imprecation, "Forgive them not!" (Isa 2:6, 9), or the vengeful utterances of the martyred sons of 2 Maccabees (a book with which Luke was apparently familiar, cf. 2 Macc 3:26 and Luke 24:4; 2 Macc 9:8-10 and Acts 1:18; 12:23): "For you [Antiochus IV] there will be no resurrection to life!" (7:14); "Keep on, and see how [God's] mighty power will torture you and your descendants!" (7:17); "Do not think that you will go unpunished for having tried to fight against God!" (7:19; compare the embellished version of these prayers in 4 Macc 9:9, 32; 10:11, 21; 12:12, 14, 18; cf. 5 Macc 5:17, 23, 46-51). Nothing is more out of step with anti-Semitism than the Lukan prayers of forgiveness, prayers uttered by the only Christians (as Luke would surely regard Jesus, as well as Stephen) portrayed in Luke-Acts to have been put to death by the Jews.[57]

Luke 23:46. "Then Jesus . . . said, 'Father, into thy hands I commit my spirit!'" (cf. Ps 31:5). Psalm 31, attributed to David, is a prayer of lamentation and thanksgiving. The psalmist had been ill (vv. 9-10), the object of lies and traps (vv. 4, 18, 20), scorned by enemies and abandoned by friends (v. 11), and had sought refuge in God in the face of death (vv. 5, 13). The suitability of this psalm for Jesus' passion is obvious: Jesus, the son of David, has been falsely accused, entrapped, scorned, betrayed, and now, hanging on the cross, faces death. Rabbinic interpretation of this psalm, emphasizing messianic and eschatological themes (cf. *Midr. Ps* 31.2-3, 5-7 [on 31:1], 8 [on 31:24]), further clarifies why such a psalm would be utilized in the passion tradition. The specific verse that the Lukan Jesus has quoted was employed as a prayer before going to sleep (cf. *Num Rab.* 20.20 [on 23:24]; *Midr. Ps* 25.2 [on 25:1]; *b. Ber.* 5a). It was a prayer that God protect one's spirit until one awakens. The idea of "sleep" was proba

---

56. J. T. Sanders, *The Jews in Luke-Acts*, 63. References to the early chapters of Acts as the "Jewish spring" or "Jerusalem springtime" are found on 69–71, 243, 283, 303, and elsewhere. This expression is also applied to the early chapters of the Gospel (161).

57. James was put to death by Herod Agrippa I, grandson of Herod the Great (Acts 12:2). Agrippa was of partial Jewish descent, but that is not at issue in Luke-Acts.

bly understood to refer either to literal sleep or to death (note Acts 7:59-60, where the dying Stephen prays, "Lord Jesus, receive my spirit" [alluding to Luke 23:46 and Ps 31:5], and then "falls asleep"). In this sense the psalm is particularly suitable for the dying Jesus, for it speaks of opposition and danger from fellow Israelites. Applied to Jesus, the psalm implies that Jesus, like David, faced opposition from his own people, and, like David, entrusts his spirit to God.[58]

THE FUNCTION OF SCRIPTURE IN ACTS

Jewish Mission

Acts 1:20. "For it is written in the book of Psalms, 'Let his habitation become desolate, and let there be no one to live in it'; and 'His office let another take'" (cf. Pss 69:25; 109:8). Scripture foretold Judas's act of betrayal and the need for him to be replaced. That these prophecies should be found in Psalms 69 and 109 is particularly appropriate, since early Christians applied details of these psalms to Jesus' passion (Ps 69:21 in Matt 27:34, 48; Mark 15:23, 36; Luke 23:36; John 19:29; Ps 109:25 in Matt 27:39; Mark 15:29).[59] The replacement of Judas points to Luke's sense of the need to maintain the Twelve, the core around which restored Israel would be formed.[60] During Jesus' ministry the Twelve are appointed (Luke 9:1-6) and are later told that they will someday sit on thrones judging the twelve tribes of Israel (Luke 22:30), a passage that clearly implies the realization of Israel's kingdom hopes.[61] The replacement of Judas is necessary (Acts 1:21-26), so that the reconstituted "Twelve" may begin its ministry of testifying to Jesus' resurrection (Acts 1:22b; 2:32; 10:39-41). Peter urges his fellow Israelites to repent so that "times of refreshing may come" and that God "may send the Christ" who is waiting in heaven until God establishes all that the prophets had proclaimed (Acts 3:19-21). James quotes the promise of Amos 9:11-12 (that the fallen and ruined "dwelling of David" will be rebuilt) as having been fulfilled in Jesus and the apostolic ministry (Acts 15:16). Later, Paul tells Herod Agrippa II that "our twelve tribes hope to attain" to God's promise of the resurrection (Acts 26:6-7). These passages and others give strong indication that

---

58. For more details see Lindars, *New Testament Apologetic*, 93–95; Fitzmyer, *Luke XX–XXIV*, 1519; Rese, *Alttestamentliche Motive*, 200–201; Bock, *Proclamation from Prophecy*, 147–48.

59. See Lindars, *New Testament Apologetic*, 102–10.

60. See J. Jervell, "The Twelve on Israel's Thrones," in Jervell, *Luke and the People of God: A New Look at Luke-Acts* (Minneapolis: Augsburg, 1972) 75–112; Fitzmyer, *Luke I–IX*, 188–89.

61. See Chap. 11 above. Luke 22:30 has no negative connotation (as it does in later patristic exegesis).

Luke believes that Israel will be restored and that this restoration will come about through the witness of the twelve apostles. This emphasis is indeed strange, if Luke intended to dispense with, or hated, Israel.[62]

Acts 2:16-21. " . . . But this is what was spoken by the prophet Joel: 'And in the last days it shall be, God declares, that I will pour out my Spirit upon all flesh, and your sons and your daughters shall prophesy. . . . And it shall be that whoever calls on the name of the Lord shall be saved'" (cf. Joel 2:28-32 [Hebr. 3:1-5]).[63] When the Twelve, who represent the reconstituted Israel (as argued above), receive the Spirit and begin to prophesy (or speak in tongues; Acts 2:3-4), we probably have an allusion to Num 11:16-30, where Moses gathered seventy men who were given the Spirit and enabled to prophesy.[64] We are told that the "Spirit rested upon them [Eldad ānd Medad]" (Num 11:26, cf. *Frag. Tg.* Num 11:26). This phrase closely resembles Luke's description, "Resting on each one of them . . . the Holy Spirit."[65] Jewish tradition views Numbers 11 as eschatological in some respects. In one tradition the prophecy of Eldad and Medad is recast as an apocalypse predicting Messiah's victory at the end of time (*Frag. Tg.* Num 11:26). But even closer to the point of the Joel citation is the exclamation of Moses, "Would that all the Lord's people were prophets, that the Lord would put his Spirit upon them!" (Num 11:29; cf. *Sipre Num.* §96 [on 11:26-30], " . . . Would that the entire people of God be prophets!").[66] This passage is taken up and made part of Jewish eschatology, sometimes in conjunction with the very passage that Luke has cited from Joel. Consider this midrash: "[The Lord] said: 'Oh that they had such a heart as this always, to fear Me, and keep the commandments' [Deut 5:29; Hebr. 5:26]; and . . . the disciple Moses . . . said: 'Would that all the Lord's people were prophets' [Num 11:29]. Neither the words of the [Lord] nor the words of the disciple [Moses] are to be fulfilled in this world, but the words of both will be fulfilled in the world to come: The words of the [Lord], 'A new heart also will I give you and you shall keep My ordinances' [Ezek 36:26], will be fulfilled; and the words of the disciple, 'I

---

62. One might argue that Luke thought of Christians as constituting a "new Israel." J. T. Sanders (*The Jews in Luke-Acts,* 48–50) and others have, however, rightly rejected this interpretation.

63. For discussion of textual details see Holtz, *Über die alttestamentlichen Zitate bei Lukas,* 5–14; Rese, *Alttestamentliche Motive,* 46–52; Bock, *Proclamation from Prophecy,* 156–69.

64. F. F. Bruce, *Commentary on the Book of the Acts* (NICNT; Grand Rapids: Eerdmans, 1954) 68; D. J. Williams, *Acts* (NIBC 5; Peabody: Hendrickson, 1990) 50. On the possibility that Isa 28:7-13 lies behind the Pentecost story, see the discussion in Chap. 13 below.

65. See M. Wilcox, *The Semitisms of Acts* (Oxford: Clarendon, 1965) 101–2.

66. Joel is probably based on Num 11:29; see Bruce, *Acts,* 68; W. S. Prinsloo, *The Theology of the Book of Joel* (Berlin and New York: de Gruyter, 1985) 90 n. 51.

will pour out My Spirit upon all flesh; and your sons and your daughters shall prophesy' [Joel 2:28], will also be fulfilled" (*Midr.* Ps 14.6 [on 14:7]).[67] In other words, Joel 2:28 is understood as the specific fulfillment of Moses' wish in Num 11:29: all of the Lord's people will become prophets when God pours out the Spirit. Similar interpretations are found elsewhere. One midrash, commenting on the seventy chosen to receive the Spirit (Num 11:16-17) and on Joshua who received the Spirit (Deut 34:9), has God explain, "In this world only a few individuals have prophesied, but in the world to come all Israel will be made prophets; as it says, 'I will pour out my Spirit . . . '" (*Num. Rab.* 15.25 [on 11:17], quoting Joel 2:28).[68] Another midrash explains that God has withdrawn the divine presence from this world but in the world to come will remove the stony heart (quoting Ezek 36:26), will pour out the Spirit on Israel (quoting Joel 2:28), and once again will allow the divine presence to dwell among Israel, so that the people (quoting Isa 54:13) will be taught of God (*Deut. Rab.* 6.14 [on 24:9]). The passage from Joel is cited in messianic discussions as well. In the days of Messiah and in the world to come, the righteous will be seated in the presence of God, for God will pour out the Spirit upon them (*Seder Eliyyahu Rabbah* §4 [19]). "The signs in the heavens and on the earth" (Joel 2:30) will be fulfilled in Rome's destruction (*Pesiq. Rab Kah.* 7.11 and *Pesiq. R.* 17.8). Israel's enemies will be vanquished and her temple rebuilt, and then God (quoting Joel 2:28) will pour out the Spirit upon all flesh (*Midr.* Ps 138.2 [on 138:2]). Luke's citation and application of this prophetic passage cohere with Jewish interpretation, and it is likely that he sees in this prophecy yet another instance of the fulfillment of Israel's hope. The pouring out of God's Spirit of prophecy on the Twelve (and the other disciples) is evidence that the Twelve represent Israel and that their eschatological message has been confirmed. Since it is the eschatological hour and repentance is a prerequisite for eschatological blessings,[69] Peter, as had the prophet Joel before him (Joel 2:13), calls

---

67. Translation based on W. G. Braude, *The Midrash on Psalms* (Yale Judaica 13; 2 vols.; New Haven: Yale University Press, 1959) 1.186.

68. Translation based on J. J. Slotki, *Midrash Rabbah: Numbers* (2 vols.; London and New York: Soncino, 1983) 2.672.

69. Repentance is required for national redemption. R. Eliezer (ca. 90 C.E.) said: "If Israel repent, they will be redeemed; if not, they will not be redeemed" (*b. Sanh.* 97b; trans. H. Freedman, *The Babylonian Talmud: Sanhedrin* [London: Soncino, 1935] 660; cf. *y. Ta'an.* 1:1). "Rabbi Jehudah said: If Israel will not repent they will not be redeemed. Israel only repents because of distress, and because of oppression, and owing to exile, and because they have no sustenance. Israel will not do a great repentance until Elijah comes, as it is said [Mal 4:5-6], 'Behold, I will send you Elijah, the prophet, before the great and terrible day of the Lord come. And he shall turn the heart of the fathers to the children, and the children to their fathers'" (*Pirqe R. El.* §43 [61b.i]; trans. G. Friedlander, *Pirke de Rabbi Eliezer* [New York: Sepher-Hermon, 1981] 344). ". . . That his name be called upon until the day of repentance [*paenitentiae*] when the Lord will surely visit his people" (*T. Moses* 18:1). Repentance is also

for repentance (Acts 2:38-40). Luke has of course grounded the demand for repentance not only in the belief that such was an eschatological requirement but also in the fact that the people were responsible for the death of Jesus (compare Acts 2:22-23, 36; Joel 4:19). By stressing that the Jews were directly responsible (and the Romans only indirectly involved, as is probably implied by v. 23), the need for repentance is clearly established and its reference clearly defined. Ultimately repentance is required not just to bring in the kingdom but to bring about reconciliation with the King. Repentance cannot simply be general (i.e., for sins), but must have a christological reference; otherwise, Christianity in the context of Judaism is superfluous.[70] If general repentance is all that is required, then why be a Christian?[71] This is Christian apologetic, not anti-Semitism. Throughout Acts, Gentiles and Jews alike are admonished to repent for the forgiveness of their sins (3:19; 10:43; 11:18; 17:30; 26:18, 20).[72]

When the people realize that they have shed the blood of an innocent man (compare Acts 2:22-23, 36; Joel 4:19), they cry out to Peter and the apostles. The people must repent and become Christians (Acts 2:38). This is what is required to receive the "promise" of forgiveness and the gift of the Holy Spirit (Acts 2:21, 39; cf. Joel 2:32; Isa 57:19). The promise idea, like the repentance idea, is here defined christologically. The restoration, which will come about after national repentance, is now presented in a Christian light. Although this offer has Christian strings attached and so is opposed to any form of Judaism that excludes belief in Jesus, it is not in itself anti-Semitic. We must remember that becoming a Christian in the first century did not mean ceasing to be Jewish (as is often thought today).

---

the condition for the appearance of the Messiah. ". . . Until you return to the Lord in integrity of heart, penitent and living according to all the Lord's commands. Then the Lord will be concerned for you in mercy and will free you from captivity under your enemies" (*T. Judah* 23:15). A "star from Jacob" (cf. Num 24:17) will arise (*T. Judah* 24:1), on whom the Spirit will be poured out (24:2; cf. Isa 11:2; 61:1), and then God "will pour the Spirit of grace" on Israel (*T. Judah* 24:3; cf. Joel 2:28) to "judge and save all that call on the Lord" (*T. Judah* 24:6; cf. Joel 2:32). "If all Israel together repented for a single day, redemption through the Messiah would follow" (*Pessiq. R.* 37.2 [trans. R. H. Charles, *APOT* 2.415]). For further discussion see R. F. Zehnle, *Peter's Pentecost Discourse: Tradition and Lukan Reinterpretation in Peter's Speeches of Acts 2 and 3* (SBLMS 15; Nashville: Abingdon, 1971) 72–73.

70. In this regard Luke is part of the early Christian effort to recast Jesus the proclaimer as Jesus the proclaimed. Jesus' eschatologically based demand for repentance (Mark 1:15) is deleted in Luke (cf. Luke 4:14-15), because it will become the disciples' message about Jesus.

71. Note Acts 19:1-7 (esp. v. 4), where John's baptism of repentance is interpreted christologically.

72. It should be noted that in his address to the Athenians (17:16-31), the Lukan Paul makes the same point made earlier in the speeches addressed to Jews, "The times of ignorance God overlooked, but now he commands all men everywhere to repent, because he has fixed a day on which he will judge the world . . ." (vv. 30-31; compare 3:17; 13:27).

Acts 2:25-28 (and 13:35). "For David says concerning him, 'I saw the Lord always before me, for he is at my right hand that I may not be shaken. . . . For thou wilt not abandon my soul to Hades, nor let thy Holy One see corruption'" (cf. Ps 16:8-11). The quotation is based upon the LXX, which more readily accommodates the text's application to Jesus' resurrection. But this interpretation is not limited to the Greek version, nor is it exclusively Christian. Some rabbinic tradition understands this verse (in the Hebrew) as promising resurrection (*Midr.* Ps 16.10–11 [on 16:9-10]; *b. B. Bat.* 17a), and Psalm 16, moreover, is understood as messianic (*Midr.* Ps 16.4 [on 16:4]). Luke's interpretation is therefore in essential agreement with Jewish interpretation. The major difference, of course, lies in his application of the text to Jesus.[73] Later in the sermon at Antioch of Pisidia (13:16-41), where Ps 16:10 is again quoted, the Lukan Paul argues that Jesus' resurrection fulfills the promises that God had made to the Jewish fathers and "fulfilled to us their children" (v. 33). The argument here is not meant to show that Jesus has fulfilled Scripture but that Jesus' resurrection fulfills the Davidic covenant and lays the foundation for Israel's restoration (see further discussion below).

Acts 2:30. "Knowing that God had sworn with an oath to him that he would set one of his descendants upon his throne" (cf. Ps 132:11; 2 Sam 7:12-13). The Lukan Peter alludes to the Davidic promise, itself an important part of messianic expectation (see *Midr.* Ps 43.5 [on 43:3]; *Tg.* Ps 132:10-18, esp. v. 17). This promise had appeared earlier in the angelic annunciation in Luke 1:32-33. In being resurrected and made to sit at God's right hand (Acts 2:31-35, quoting Ps 110:1), Jesus fulfills the Davidic promise.[74] Although the Davidic promise is applied to Jesus and so is distinctively Christian, there is nothing anti-Semitic in its application. Claiming that Jesus was none other than the awaited Davidic Messiah is a calculated appeal to Jews.

Acts 2:34-35. "For David . . . himself says, 'The Lord said to my Lord, Sit at my right hand, till I make thy enemies a stool for thy feet'" (Ps 110:1). Drawing upon a passage understood messianically and as promising hope of restoration (see Luke 20:41-44 par.; Heb 1:13; 10:12-13; *Midr.* Ps 110.4 [on 110:1]; *b. Sanh.* 38b [Rabbi Aqiba, ca. 125 C.E.]; *Gen. Rab.* 85.9 [on 38:18]; *Num. Rab.* 18.23 [on 17:21]),[75] the Lukan Peter presents Jesus as

---

73. For more details see Rese, *Alttestamentliche Motive*, 55–58, 89–93; Bock, *Proclamation from Prophecy*, 169–81.

74. For more details see Bock, *Proclamation from Prophecy*, 177–81.

75. For a survey of early Jewish interpretation of Ps 110:1 see D. M. Hay, *Glory at the Right*

the Jewish Messiah and exalted Lord now sitting at God's right hand. This important text completes the argument of the Pentecost sermon. The Jesus who has been rejected and crucified was not only guiltless but is Israel's Messiah and Lord.[76]

Acts 3:22-23. "Moses said, 'The Lord God will raise up for you a prophet from your brethren as he raised me up. You shall listen to him in whatever he tells you. And it shall be that every soul that does not listen to that prophet shall be destroyed from the people'" (Deut 18:15-16, 19; cf. Lev 23:29).[77] There is some evidence that prior to Christianity Deut 18:15-19 was interpreted eschatologically if not messianically. The passage is probably alluded to in 1 Macc 14:41 ("Until a trustworthy prophet should arise"), where *anistemi* is employed (as also in Deut 18:15, 18 and Acts 3:22; 7:37). First Maccabees 4:46 ("Until there should come a prophet") may also be an allusion to this text. *T. Ben.* 9:2 ("Until the Most High send his salvation in the visitation of the unique prophet") might be relevant (see also *T. Levi* 8:15, "A prophet of the Most High"). Qumran's anticipated prophet was based on this passage (1QS 9:11 ["Until the coming of the prophet"]; 4QTest 1:5–8 [Deut 18:15-18 is quoted]). Similarly, Samaritans awaited a *taheb* ("restorer"), a prophet like Moses who would reveal the truth (*Memar Marqah* 4:12; John 4:19, 25, 29; cf. Josephus, *Ant.* 18.4.1 §85–86).[78] In the New Testament, the text may be alluded to in the transfiguration account (Mark 9:7 par.); it is alluded to often in the Fourth Gospel (1:21, 25, 45[?]; 5:46[?]; 6:14[?]; 7:40). Luke's application of the text to Jesus is most explicit. In rabbinic sources Deut 18:15-19 is applied to various prophets but not to messianic figures (*Sipre Deut.* §176 [on Deut 18:16]; *Midr.* Ps 1.3 [on 1:1]; *Seder Eliyyahu Rabbah* §17 [85], "Moses our teacher . . . father of prophets"; *Pesiq. R. Kah.* 13.6; Philo, *On the Special Laws* 1.11 §65).[79] In what may reflect anti-Christian polemic, *Sipre Deut.* §175 (on 18:15) specifically states that the prophet whom God will raise up will not

---

Hand: Psalm 110 in Early Christianity (SBLMS 18; Nashville: Abingdon, 1973) 21–33. There is evidence that this psalm was understood messianically prior to Christian usage (probably beginning with the Hasmonaean rulers). The Targum, possibly in reaction to Christian interpretation, has Ps 110:1 refer specifically to David.

76. For more details see Rese, *Alttestamentliche Motive,* 58–66; Bock, *Proclamation from Prophecy,* 181–86.

77. For discussion of textual details see Rese, *Alttestamentliche Motive,* 66–71; Bock, *Proclamation from Prophecy,* 191–94.

78. The basic proof texts for the Samaritan *Taheb* are Deut 18:15-19 and Num 24:17 (probably alluded to in Matt 2:2). The Samaritans attached such great importance to the Deuteronomic passage that it was appended to the tenth commandment.

79. Joshua *might* be understood as the fulfillment of Deuteronomy 18 in *T. Moses* 10:15.

go to the Gentiles. This may explain why Deuteronomy 18 is not interpreted messianically in the rabbis.[80]

Josephus provides accounts of first-century messianic claimants who asserted that they were prophets and who probably saw themselves as fulfillments of the promise of Deut 18:15, 18. The first mentioned is one Theudas (ca. 45 C.E.) who claimed that he was a prophet and could command the river to part (*Ant.* 20.5.1 §97).[81] The allusion to Moses is unmistakable.[82] A few years later a man from Egypt (ca. 56 C.E.) claimed to be a prophet at whose command the walls of Jerusalem would fall down (*Ant.* 20.8.6 §169–70; *J. W.* 2.13.5 §261–63). This hoped-for sign was probably inspired by the story of Israel's conquest of Jericho, led by Joshua the successor of Moses.[83] Finally Josephus tells us of yet another "impostor" who promised salvation and rest, if the people would follow him into the wilderness (*Ant.* 20.8.10 §188).[84]

In reference to Deut 18:19 (a portion of which is paraphrased in Acts 3:23) the rabbis taught that disregarding the words of a prophet placed one's death "in the hands of heaven" (*m. Sanh.* 11:5, quoting part of Deut 18:19 ["I will require it of him"]; see further discussion in *b. Sanh.* 89a–b). The warning of Deut 18:19 is illustrated by the judgment that befell the prophet of 1 Kgs 20:35 who had disobeyed the word of another prophet (*Sipre Deut.* §177 [on 18:19]). For Luke, of course, Jesus is the prophet like Moses whom God had raised up. If failure to heed the words of any other prophet was dangerous, failure to heed the messianic prophet was even more so. Since Luke understands Jesus to be this promised prophet, we should hardly be surprised that he makes use of the warning of Deut 18:19. This warning, or threat, is part of Luke's evangelistic appeal; by

---

80. Rabbinic tradition, however, compares Messiah with Moses: "R. Berekia [ca. 350 C.E.] said in the name of R. Isaac: As the first redeemer [Moses] was, so shall the latter redeemer [Messiah] be. What is stated of the former redeemer? 'And Moses took his wife and sons, and set them upon an ass' (Exod 4:20). Similarly will it be with the latter redeemer, as it is stated, 'Lowly and riding upon an ass' (Zech 9:9). As the former redeemer caused manna to descend, as it is stated, 'Behold, I will cause to rain bread from heaven for you' (Exod 16:4), so will the latter redeemer cause manna to descend, as it is stated, 'May he be as a rich cornfield [*or* 'pieces of bread'] in the land' (Ps 72:16). As the former redeemer made a well to rise (cf. Num 20:11; 21:17-18), so will the latter redeemer bring up water, as it is stated, 'And a fountain shall come forth of the house of the Lord, and shall water the valley of Shittim' (Joel 3:18)" (*Eccl. Rab.* 1:9 §1). Trans. from A. Cohen, *Midrash Rabbah: Ecclesiastes* (London and New York: Soncino, 1983) 33. Briefer comparisons are also found in *Pesiq. R.* 1.7; *Midr.* Ps 90.17 (on 90:15).

81. This may be the same Theudas whom Luke mentions in Acts 5:36.

82. Either to the crossing of the Red Sea (Exod 14:21-22), or to the crossing of the Jordan River (Josh 3:14-17), led by Joshua, Moses' successor, or to both.

83. See Josh 6:20. This messianic claimant may be the person alluded to in the question put to Paul in Acts 21:38.

84. The warning about not heeding a messianic summons to the wilderness (Matt 24:26) likely reflects this messianic wilderness theme.

making use of it, he wishes to attract Jews, not drive them away (see discussion of Acts 13:41). Its usage is not an expression of hatred, and the threat itself (3:23) is particular, not universal.

Acts 3:25. " . . . Saying to Abraham, 'And in your posterity shall all the families of the earth be blessed'" (Gen 12:3; 22:18; 28:14; cf. 17:4, 5; 18:18; 26:4).[85] Josephus, Philo, the Pseudepigrapha, and rabbinic haggadah pass on and develop traditions illustrating how Abraham and his achievements had been a blessing to all humanity. We are told that Greeks, Chaldeans, and Egyptians learned philosophy, mathematics, science, astrology, and monotheistic religion from Abraham. Obviously this aspect of the Abrahamic covenant is important to Luke's interest in the Gentile mission. For Luke, it is the salvation offered to Gentiles through Israel's Messiah that fulfills the promise of blessing through Abraham's descendants. Possibly in response to Christian exploitation of this promise, some Jewish interpretation carefully qualifies this theme. The Gentile families of the earth are blessed, as Gen 12:3 says, but they are blessed for Israel's sake (*b. Yebam.* 63a). Another tack is to see the blessing in a negative light. The Gentiles are blessed in Abraham's seed in that they exploit Israel. Commenting on Gen 22:17-18 one midrash explains: "In this world [Israel is] compared to dust, but in the days of the Messiah they will be compared to the sand of the sea. As sand spoils the teeth, so will Israel in the days of the Messiah destroy all the nations persecuting them" (*Num. Rab.* 2.13 [on 2:32]; also *Pesiq. R.* 11.5).[86] In other words, Israel does not intend to bless the Gentiles; the nation does so only because strong Gentile nations take advantage of it. Eventually, however, this "blessing" will come to an end through the Messiah. Thus, Jewish interpretation at this point could not be more at variance with Christian interpretation. According to Christian interpretation (see Gal 3:8, commenting on Gen 12:3 par.), the Messiah is himself an important aspect of the Abrahamic blessing for the Gentiles (see the pre-Christian interpretation of the Abrahamic covenant in Sir 44:21-23). Through the Messiah Gentiles have an opportunity to participate in the Abrahamic covenant. Although Luke's (and Paul's) use of this part of the Abrahamic covenant is meant to open the door to Gentiles, it is not intended to exclude Jews.

Acts 4:25-26. " . . . Who by the mouth of our father David, thy servant didst say by the Holy Spirit, 'Why did the Gentiles rage, and the peoples imag-

85. For discussion of textual details see Rese, *Alttestamentliche Motive,* 71–78; Bock, *Proclamation from Prophecy,* 194–97.
86. Translation by Slotki, *Midrash Rabbah: Numbers,* 1.46.

ine vain things? The kings of the earth set themselves in array, and the rulers were gathered together, against the Lord and against his Anointed' " (Ps 2:1-2). In Peter's speech Jesus is the "Anointed"[87] (or Messiah) whom various adversaries have opposed. By referring to David and Jesus as God's "servant" (*pais*, vv. 25, 27, 30), the evangelist strengthens the link between the two figures. What was foretold by David's inspired utterance has been fulfilled by what has recently happened to Jesus and what is now happening to his apostles.[88]

We know little about how Ps 2:1-2 was interpreted prior to Christian usage. 4QFlor 1:18–19 quotes Ps 2:1-2, but little of the exegesis is extant. The interpretation is clearly eschatological ("At the end of days"), but whether or not it is messianic is difficult to tell. According to its exegesis, "The kings of the nations will rise against the elect [pl.] of Israel. . . . and a re[mnant] will be left."[89] In *1 Enoch* (a document well represented at Qumran) the Messiah is frequently called "the elect one."[90] There is also a reference to "Moses" (4QFlor 2:3), which may have something to do with Deut 18:15-19 (cf. 4QTest 1:5–8; 1QS 9:11), but not enough text remains to be sure. (See below for further discussion of pre-Christian interpretation of Psalm 2.) Aside from Acts, the only other New Testament writing that makes use of Ps 2:1-2 is Revelation, where parts of these two verses are echoed in 6:15; 11:15 ("Our Lord and his Anointed"); 11:18 ("The nations raged"); 17:18; 19:19 ("The kings of the earth"). As in 4QFlorilegium, Ps 2:1-2 contributes to the seer's vision of the establishment of the messianic kingdom, which from the seer's perspective is still to come. In Acts, however, the psalm is understood as already fulfilled in the experience of Jesus and his apostles.

In post–New Testament rabbinic interpretation, however, Psalm 2 is cited frequently and is consistently interpreted eschatologically and messianically. Some rabbis believed that Ps 2:1-2 would be fulfilled in the eschatological battle of Gog and Magog described in Ezekiel 39 and foreseen by David: "Yet, even in the time-to-come, Gog and Magog will set themselves against the Lord and His anointed, only to fall down. David, foreseeing this, said: 'Why do the heathen rage? . . . ' "[91] (*Midr.* Ps 2.2 [on 2:1-2]; cf. *b. Ber.* 7b; *b. 'Abod. Zar.* 3b). Resistance against Israel in the time to come will

---

87. Jesus' anointing by the Spirit is a prominent theme in Luke (Luke 3:22; 4:1, 14, 18; Acts 10:38).

88. For more details see Holtz, *Über die Alttestamentlichen Zitate bei Lukas*, 53–56; Rese, *Alttestamentliche Motive*, 94–97; Bock, *Proclamation from Prophecy*, 201–8.

89. A. Dupont-Sommer, *The Essene Writings from Qumran* (Oxford: Blackwell, 1961) 314.

90. See 40:5; 49:2, 4; 51:4; 52:6, 9; 53:6; 55:4. In 45:3 the Messiah is called "my [i.e., God's] elect one."

91. Translation by Braude, *Midrash on Psalms*, 1.35.

be futile. All the nations will bow down to the "lord Messiah" (*Midr. Ps* 2.3 [on 2:2]; see *Pss. Sol.* 17:32 where the same messianic epithet is employed).

Luke's application of Ps 2:1-2 to the Jews as well as to Gentiles, is unique. The verse following the quotation (Acts 4:27) identifies the Anointed's opponents. Most commentators agree that Herod represents the citation's "kings of the earth," Pontius Pilate the "rulers," the Gentiles the "Gentiles," and the peoples of Israel the "peoples." The latter is plural only because the corresponding word of the quotation is plural. The original reference, of course, was to the Gentile "peoples," not to the people of Israel.[92] This re-signification casts the Jews themselves into the role of opposing the Messiah. Nevertheless, the Lukan evangelist views the Gentiles and their rulers as equally opposed to Jesus and Christianity. Sanders, however, thinks that when Luke says that the Gentiles and peoples of Israel have gathered together "against" Jesus (where the evangelist uses *epi* instead of *kata*, the preposition found in the citation itself) he intentionally obfuscates the sense of the passage, probably to diminish the role of the Gentiles as opponents of Christianity.[93] Luke may have done this elsewhere,[94] but in this passage *epi* can mean only "against" (a meaning that it has elsewhere in Luke and the New Testament). The Gentiles are just as opposed to Christianity as are the Jews. Luke's point is that all opposition to Christianity, whether of Gentile or Jewish origin, fulfills Scripture and is in accordance to the divine will (Acts 4:28).

Acts 7:42-50. Stephen's speech (Acts 7:2-53) summarizes biblical history, alluding to and quoting a number of passages, and is intended to answer the charges in 6:13-14, "This man never ceases to speak words against this holy place and the law; for we have heard him say that this Jesus of Nazareth will destroy this place, and will change the customs which Moses delivered to us." These charges are said to be "false," and they clearly echo the charge brought against Jesus (Mark 14:57-58). Interpreters are confronted by two basic problems. (1) The speech apparently contains irrelevant material and does not seem to be in the form of an apology. (2) The speech seems to confirm the truthfulness of the charges even though they have been described as false. In the analysis that follows, it is assumed that a source of some sort has been used,[95] one that has been adapted as

---

92. Lexically *'ummim* could include Israelites (see Ps 117:1). But the parallelism of Ps 2:1-2 makes it likely that only Gentiles are opposed to the Lord and his Anointed.

93. J. T. Sanders, *The Jews in Luke-Acts*, 13–14.

94. Compare Luke 23:25-26 with Mark 15:15-21. Luke may mean that the Jews, rather than the Romans, crucified Jesus; for more on this see J. T. Sanders, *The Jews in Luke-Acts*, 9–13.

95. Recitations of biblical history are not uncommon to Jewish and Christian writers (see Ps 105:12-45; Heb 11:4-40; cf. Acts 13:17-25). Some such recitation probably lies behind Stephen's speech.

Stephen's reply. It is this factor that accounts for the first problem. As the analysis will further show, however, the speech actually does answer the charges, and, from a Christian perspective, shows them to be false.

The first half of the recitation is essentially irenic. Abraham is called, promised a new land, and is told that some day his descendants will worship God at the place of revelation (Sinai). In Egypt, God remembers the promise and raises up Moses. Here we encounter the only negative item in this part of the recitation. Moses senses that God is to deliver the people through him, "but they did not understand" (v. 25); and Moses' offer is rebuffed (vv. 26-29). The idea of not understanding is part of Luke's ignorance theme (see Luke 23:34; Acts 3:17; 13:27). This initial rejection of Moses, however, only proves to be a foretaste of things to come. In vv. 30-34 Moses' sense of calling is confirmed by the theophany of the burning bush. God is identified to Moses as the "God of Abraham, Isaac, and Jacob" (v. 32; cf. Exod 3:6). Reference to Abraham recalls the beginning of the recitation (v. 2). Luke probably intended this, for he has inverted the order of Exod 3:5-6, citing v. 6, then v. 5. Moses is told that the place where he stands is holy ground (v. 33; cf. Exod 3:5). Here Israel will worship, thus fulfilling the promise to Abraham.

The second half of the recitation, however, is quite polemical. According to vv. 35-43 worship at Sinai proved to be a disaster. Although God had sent Moses to Israel as a "ruler and deliverer" (v. 35), the people "refused to obey him" (v. 39), despite the "wonders and signs" (v. 36; cf. 6:8), preferring not to worship as God had commanded (vv. 40-43). They rejected Moses (and by implication rejected the prophet who would succeed him, v. 37),[96] making and worshiping a golden calf, one of the "works of their hands" (vv. 39-40).[97] For this reason God "gave them over to worship the host of heaven" (v. 42a), a tragedy that anticipates the quotation from Amos in vv. 42-43: "Did you offer to me slain beasts and sacrifices, forty years in the wilderness, O house of Israel? And you took up the tent of Moloch, and the star of the god Rephan, the figures which you made to worship; and I will remove you beyond Babylon" (Amos 5:25-27). Luke follows the LXX but with two significant variants. First, he has inserted the phrase "to worship them" (v. 43). This insertion recalls the promise made to Abraham at the beginning of the speech. The people have been led to a holy place to worship God, but when there they wor-

---

96. For discussion of the christology of Acts 7:37 see Rese, *Alttestamentliche Motive*, 78–80; Bock, *Proclamation from Prophecy*, 215–25.

97. In Jewish interpretation the calf incident (Exod 32:1-14) was viewed as an extremely serious sin. The story is mentioned dozens of times in the Talmud and midrashim. The rabbis ponder why God, able to foresee Israel's grievous sin, nevertheless chose to make a covenant with this people; see *Exod. Rab.* 42.1 (on 32:7).

shiped idols, not God. This insertion thus makes the citation more appropriate for its present usage. Second, the Lukan citation reads "Babylon" instead of "Damascus" as in the Hebrew. This change suggests that the Babylonian exile of Judah is in mind rather than the earlier exile of the northern kingdom of Israel (of which the original oracle spoke). Such a rendering makes this prophetic text more suitable to Stephen's speech, for he is addressing the descendants of those who returned from the Babylonian exile.[98] An allusion to the Babylonian captivity moreover carries with it a reminder of the fate of the First Temple. The application of this prophetic text to the calf incident offers a poignant criticism of Israel. The whole of Israel's negative history from idolatry at Sinai to idolatry that led to defeat and exile is summarized (see Ps 106:19-41 for a similar summary).

The final part of the speech begins with a positive emphasis (vv. 44-46). In possession of a tent that had been constructed according to heavenly design (v. 44; cf. Exod 25:8), the people, led by Joshua ("Jesus" in the LXX),[99] were successful in "gaining possession of the Gentiles."[100] This success continued until the time of David (v. 45b). In v. 46 we are told that David "found favor in the sight of God and asked leave to find [*heuriskein*] a habitation [*skēnōma*] for the God of Jacob." We have here an allusion to Ps 132(131):5, " . . . Until I find [*heuriskein*] a place for the Lord, a

---

98. The other changes are probably to be accounted for in this way. Since Damascus dropped out, so have the references to the Assyrian deities "Sakkuth" and "Kaiwan." The substitutes, "tent of Moloch" and "star of the god Rephan," are largely based on revocalization of the Hebrew consonants. The *Damascus Document* offers an interesting adaptation of this passage from Amos. According to CD 7:13–19 the text has been fulfilled by the sect's withdrawal from the Jerusalem religious establishment. In Damascus the sect will establish the truth of the Law and the Prophets, "whose words Israel has despised" (7:18; translation by Dupont-Sommer, *Essene Writings*, 134). The Lukan Stephen makes a similar point at the conclusion of his speech (Acts 7:53). Although these exegeses are obviously different, they both find in Amos 5 prophetic criticism of the religious establishment, their common opponent. At least one rabbinic interpretation views Amos 5:25 differently. After quoting Num 9:5 ("They kept the passover in the first month . . .") the midrash goes on to comment: "Scripture records the disgrace of Israel, for they observed only this passover alone. And so Scripture states, 'Did you even offer to me [plural] sacrifices and meal-offerings in the wilderness' (Amos 5:25) [with the answer, no, only that one]" (*Sipre Num.* §67 [on 9:5]; translation by J. Neusner, *Sifré to Numbers* [vol. 2; Atlanta: Scholars, 1986] 25. The bracketed words are Neusner's.) It is unlikely that Amos originally meant this, nor does it seem to be Luke's point. As the subsequent verses suggest, Luke maintains that, for all their religious activity in the wilderness, Israel failed to realize that God is transcendent and is not confined to a human-made house.

99. R. P. C. Hanson (*The Acts* [Oxford: Clarendon, 1967] 101) suggests that Joshua/Jesus is a deliberate wordplay. As obedient Israel once succeeded in gaining control of the Gentiles under the leadership of Joshua, it may do so again if it is obedient and follows Jesus. But if Luke has this parallel in mind, he makes nothing of it. (Indeed, in the speech itself he makes little of the reference in v. 37 to the prophet like Moses.)

100. The RSV reads, "They dispossessed the nations." The word *kataschesis*, however, literally means "taking possession."

tabernacle [*skēnōma*] for the God of Jacob." Most commentators assume that the Lukan Stephen refers to David's desire to build the temple (2 Sam 7:2-7),[101] but Luke may have no more in mind than David's desire to take the ark of the covenant to Jerusalem (2 Sam 6:17, where David places the ark in a *skēnē*). In any case, Luke does not expressly say that David desired to build the temple.

In v. 47 the Lukan Stephen notes that it was David's son Solomon who actually built a "house" for God. Although there is nothing in itself negative in this verse, the verse that follows is clearly critical, "Yet the Most High does not dwell in houses made with hands" (v. 48). Alluding to Gospel tradition (Mark 14:58), Luke says "house(s),"[102] instead of "temple." This deliberate rephrasing of the tradition accommodates the citation in vv. 49-50: "Heaven is my throne, and earth my footstool. What house will you build for me, says the Lord, or what is the place of my rest? Did not my hand make all these things?" (vv. 49-50; cf. Isa 66:1-2).[103] Many have concluded that Luke is saying that the construction of this temple was in some way wrong, in which case the charge brought against Stephen had a legitimate basis.[104] The point of criticism might lie in the idea that unlike the wilderness tabernacle, the Solomonic Temple was constructed without divine instructions. This may be so, but in the tradition to which the Lukan Stephen has been alluding the temple is not criticized (see esp. 2 Sam 7:13; 1 Kgs 8:18-21; 2 Chr 7:1-3), nor is there evidence of such a stance elsewhere in Luke-Acts.[105] Indeed, in 1 Kgs 8:27 Solomon gives expression to what is basically the same point as the passage from Isaiah. Thus we should probably understand the criticism exactly as v. 48 states it,

---

101. Brawley's paraphrase of the verse illustrates this assumption well, "David's desire for a temple is a sign of God's favor" (*Luke-Acts and the Jews*, 121; see also H. Conzelmann, *Acts of the Apostles* (Hermeneia; Philadelphia: Fortress, 1987) 56. However, the text does not say this.

102. The plural may refer to both tabernacle and temple, but I doubt it. The evangelist probably has in mind all temples, Jewish and pagan alike (cf. Acts 17:24).

103. The rabbis link Isa 66:1-2 to the tabernacle: "When the Holy One, blessed be he, said to [Moses], 'Let them make me a sanctuary, that I may dwell among them' [Exod 25:8], Moses thought: 'Who is in a position to make a sanctuary in which he can dwell? "Behold, heaven and the heaven of heavens cannot contain thee" [1 Kgs 8:27]!' Furthermore, it says, 'Do not I fill heaven and earth?' [Jer 23:24]. It also says, 'The heaven is my throne, and the earth is my footstool' [Isa 66:1]. The Holy One, blessed be he, told him: 'I do not ask for a sanctuary in accordance with my capacity, but in accordance with theirs. For should I desire it, the whole world could not hold my glory, nor even a single one of my attendants'" (*Num. Rab.* 12.3 [on 7:1]); translation by Slotki, *Midrash Rabbah: Numbers*, 1.452. Rabbinic interpretation stresses that the temple could not contain God (*Pesiq. R.* 4.3; *Seder Eliyyahu Zuta* §9 [188]; *b. Sanh.* 7a).

104. M. Simon, "Saint Stephen and the Jerusalem Temple," *JEH* 2 (1951) 127–42; idem, *St. Stephen and the Hellenists* (London: Longmans, Green, 1958) 45; Conzelmann, *Acts*, 56; I. H. Marshall, *The Acts of the Apostles* (Tyndale New Testament Commentaries; Grand Rapids: Eerdmans, 1980) 146; D. J. Williams, *Acts*, 128–29. For a different assessment see Brawley, *Luke-Acts and the Jews*, 120–23.

105. Brawley, *Luke-Acts and the Jews*, 118–20.

"The Most High does not dwell in houses made with hands." Nothing is wrong with the temple itself nor with building it, but it is wrong to believe that it (and perhaps it alone) is the habitation of God. Moreover, allegiance to a temple built with human hands could place Israel in danger of repeating its earlier wilderness sin, for the golden calf had also been made by "their hands" (v. 41). Although it is not certain, the repetition of this phrase might have invited such comparison. The temple "not made with hands" could refer to the church (as in 1 Cor 3:16-17; Eph 2:19-22; 1 Pet 2:4-7), to heaven where Christ is seated (as in Heb 8:2; 9:24), or to Christ himself (as in John 2:19-22; Rev 21:22). In any case, it implies the Christian alternative to the temple at Jerusalem; the Lukan Paul makes the same point in Acts 17:24. In this light, the charge against Stephen was indeed without foundation. Stephen did not speak against the temple but against a false view of the temple, a view that precluded Christian messianology.

In the wake of the destruction of the temple, the issue of its replacement was a live one. The Christian view, probably rooted in something that Jesus had originally said (part of his idea of restoring the "true" Israel) and to a degree paralleling ideas found among the Essenes (see below), is at issue here. The claim that the true temple is "not made with hands" is construed as an attack against the one that is "made with hands." Such an attack is contrary to the law of Moses, since it attacks, by association, the tabernacle also. Stephen agrees that the tabernacle and temple were of God, but argues that despite these gifts, God's people did not always worship God properly. They did not in the wilderness, when the law was given and when the tabernacle was first erected, nor have they now (vv. 51-53).

Luke's view of the temple and of correct Mosaic custom obviously reflects a thoroughly Christian viewpoint. But his criticism of the religious establishment, as vehement as it is, is not an attack on Jews themselves (no more than is Qumran's similar criticism of the religious establishment). Moreover, this criticism must be viewed in light of the post-70 C.E. situation. The Jewish nation had been defeated and its temple destroyed. These facts demanded explanation. Luke believes that these things happened because Jesus had been rejected.[106] But with the temple gone, an alternative is needed, and the Christian temple "not made with hands" is that alternative. When Luke proposes this Christian alternative, he has not taken an anti-Semitic stance; instead, his position to an extent parallels Jewish belief that true worship can take place without a physical temple.[107]

---

106. See C. H. Giblin, *The Destruction of Jerusalem according to Luke's Gospel: A Historical-Typological Moral* (AnBib 107; Rome: Pontifical Biblical Institute, 1985).

107. Consider the following statements from Philo, "But it is not possible genuinely to

Luke believes that true worship not only can take place apart from the physical temple but that it can take place only in relationship to the temple not made with hands. The restoration of Israel will come about through allegiance to this new heavenly temple, not through allegiance to a temple "made with hands."[108]

Gentile Mission

Acts 8:32-33. "Now the passage of Scripture which he was reading was this: 'As a sheep led to the slaughter or a lamb before its shearer is dumb, so he opens not his mouth. In his humiliation justice was denied him. Who can

---

express our gratitude to God by means of buildings and oblations and sacrifices, as is the custom of most people, for even the whole world were not a temple adequate to yield the honour due to Him" (*On Noah's Work as a Planter* 30 §126; translation by F. H. Colson and G. H. Whitaker, *Philo* [LCL 3; Cambridge: Harvard University Press, 1930] 277). "The highest, and in the truest sense the holy, Temple of God is, as we must believe, the whole universe. . . . There is also the Temple made by hands. . . . for he judged that since God is one, there should be also only one Temple" (*On the Special Laws* 1.12 §66–67; translation by F. H. Colson, *Philo* [LCL 7; Cambridge: Harvard University Press, 1937] 137, 139). "What house shall be prepared for God the King of kings, the Lord of all, who in His tender mercy and loving-kindness has deigned to visit created beings and come down from the boundaries of heaven to the utmost ends of earth, to show His goodness to our race? Shall it be of stone or timber? Away with the thought, the very words are blasphemy" (*On the Cherubim* 29 §99–100; translation by Colson and Whitaker, *Philo* [LCL 2; Cambridge: Harvard University Press, 1927] 69). "One worthy house there is—the soul that is fitted to receive Him. Justly and rightly then shall we say that in the invisible soul the invisible God has His earthly dwelling-place" (*On the Cherubim* 29–30 §100–101; translation by Colson and Whitaker, *Philo* [LCL 2] 69). According to Josephus, the Jews were given the chance to put this philosophy to the test during the war with Rome. When Titus asked the inhabitants of Jerusalem to surrender for the sake of their city and temple, he was told that "the world was a better temple for God than this one" (*J. W.* 5.11.2 §456–458). This sentiment is not without parallel. Baruch, written ca. 100 B.C.E., ostensibly to console the people shortly after Jerusalem was destroyed (1:2), explains that the temple was destroyed because of human wickedness (2:24-26) but that God nevertheless still possesses a house: "O Israel, how great is the house of God! And how vast the territory that he possess!" (3:24). The universe itself is God's temple.

Qumran conceived of a form of Judaism that could worship God properly without access to the Jerusalem temple. In fact, some passages seem to suggest that the Qumran community regarded itself as the true "temple." Consider the following, "It [the community] shall be a Most Holy Dwelling for Aaron" (1QS 8:8–9; translation by G. Vermes, *The Dead Sea Scrolls in English* [New York: Penguin, 1962] 85). "[The community] shall atone for guilty rebellion and for sins of unfaithfulness that they may obtain lovingkindness for the Land without the flesh of holocausts and the fat of sacrifice. And prayer rightly offered shall be as an acceptable fragrance of righteousness, and perfection of way as a delectable free-will offering" (9:4–5; translation by Vermes, *Dead Sea Scrolls*, 87; compare Josephus, *Ant.* 18.1.5 §19, "[The Essenes] fulfill their sacrifices among themselves"). "He has commanded a Sanctuary of men to be built for Himself, that there they may send up, like the smoke of incense, the works of the Law" (4QFlor 1:6; translation by Vermes, *Dead Sea Scrolls*, 243–44). For further discussion see B. Gärtner, *The Temple and the Community in Qumran and the New Testament* (SNTSMS 1; Cambridge: University Press, 1965) 22–46.

108. Since rebuilding the temple was being seriously considered during the latter part of the first century, Luke's polemic is even more understandable. In his view, rebuilding the temple would constitute a major challenge to Christian claims. I cannot therefore agree with Brawley (*Luke-Acts and the Jews*, 118–32) that Luke envisions the rebuilding of the temple as part of the restoration of Israel (Acts 1:6).

describe his generation? For his life is taken up from the earth'" (cf. Isa 53:7-8).[109] This citation is one of a few explicit New Testament citations of Second Isaiah's Servant Songs (42:1-4; 49:1-6; 50:5-11; 52:13—53:12) that are applied to Jesus. The first song is cited once and the fourth five times (Isa 42:1-4 in Matt 12:18-21; Isa 53:1 in John 12:38; Isa 53:4a in Matt 8:17; Isa 53:7b-8a in Acts 8:32-33; Isa 53:12 in Luke 22:37; Isa 52:15 in Rom 15:21). There are many other possible allusions, especially in Luke-Acts (e.g., Isa 42:1 in Luke 23:35; 49:6 in Luke 2:32; 52:13 in Acts 3:13; 4:27, 30; 53:12 in Luke 11:21-22).[110] Before considering how the Lukan evangelist understood this particular passage or the other Servant Songs, it is necessary to determine how these passages and the expression "servant" were understood prior to his writing.

"Servant" and "servant of the Lord" are used to refer to a variety of Old Testament worthies including the Messiah.[111] This fact alone militates against the claim that the servant epithet is a technical reference to the Servant Songs or to the Messiah. Moreover, the evidence that Second Isaiah's Servant Songs were viewed as messianic prior to Christianity is meager. Some of the messianic references in *1 Enoch* may reflect such an understanding,[112] but in the absence of explicit references much doubt remains. The LXX appears to understand the fourth song as referring to an individual (not necessarily to a messianic figure) but sees the first one as referring collectively to Israel (42:1: "Jacob is my servant"). The Isaiah Targum considers the first and fourth songs messianic (cf. Isa 42:1; 52:13; also note 43:10). But is this targumic tradition pre-Christian? The Messiah of the Isaiah Targum is quite different from that of the MT. The Aramaic Messiah will build the sanctuary (53:5); he will deliver up his enemies to be slaughtered like sheep (53:7); he will deliver Israel (53:8); he will cast the wicked into Gehenna (53:9); and he will teach Israel the law (53:10-12). Bruce D. Chilton has concluded, and I think rightly, that this tradi-

---

109. See Rese, *Alttestamentlich Motive*, 97–104; Bock, *Proclamation from Prophecy*, 225–30.

110. For many more allusions, see C. H. Dodd, *According to the Scriptures: The Sub-Structure of New Testament Theology* (London: Nisbet, 1952) 88–96; Lindars, *New Testament Apologetic*, 77–88, 144–52. For more on the general topic, see W. Zimmerli and J. Jeremias, *"Pais Theou,"* *TDNT* 5.654–717, in which it is argued that the Servant Songs have made a major contribution to NT christology; and M. D. Hooker, *Jesus and the Servant: The Influence of the Servant Concept of Deutero-Isaiah in the New Testament* (London: SPCK, 1959), in which it is argued that the influence of the Servant Songs on NT christology has been exaggerated.

111. It is used of the patriarchs (2 Macc 1:2), Moses (Deut 34:5; Josh 1:13; Wis 10:16; *b. Sot.* 14a), David (1 Kgs 11:36; Isa 37:35; 1 Macc 4:30), Zerubbabel (1 Esdras 6:27), and Messiah (Zech 3:8; *Tg.* Zech 3:8; 4 Ezra 7:28, 29; *2 Apoc. Bar.* 70:9), among others (see *Sipre Deut.* §27 [on 3:24]).

112. *First Enoch* calls the Messiah the "Elect" (39:6; 40:5; etc.; cf. Isa 42:1); the "Righteous" (38:2; 39:6; cf. Isa 53:11); the "light of nations" (48:4; cf. Isa 49:6; 42:6); and "hidden" (48:6; cf. Isa 49:2).

tion largely derives from the period between Jerusalem's two wars with Rome (70 C.E. to 135 C.E.).[113] The messianic claimant of the second war, Simon ben Kosiba, could very well have been seen as the fulfillment of the Aramaic version of Second Isaiah's fourth Servant Song. The messianic identification itself, however, probably originated earlier, as the New Testament usage testifies.[114]

The Gospel of Mark may allude to the Servant Songs (Isa 50:6 in Mark 14:65; 15:15; Isa 53:11-12 in Mark 10:45; 14:24);[115] no allusions appear in Q, however. Thus, the evangelist Luke had little to draw upon in his tradition. If the Markan passages are true allusions to the Servant Songs, especially to the fourth one, then the vicarious element had become part of early christology. But has Luke taken over this element? It seems not. Although the suffering Messiah idea occurs in Luke-Acts (see Luke 24:26, 46; Acts 3:18; 17:3; 26:23), it is not directly linked to Isa 52:13—53:12.[116] Indeed, the passage presently under consideration (Acts 8:32-33) cites most of Isa 53:7-8 but omits the very lines that contribute to the idea of vicarious suffering (53:6b: "The Lord has laid on him the iniquity of us all"; 53:8b, "He was cut off out of the land of the living, stricken for the transgression of my people"). If the evangelist has an interest in Jesus as the servant who suffers vicariously, these omissions are not easily explained.[117] Luke's real interest in the Servant Songs seems to lie in his effort to vindicate Jesus. His other explicit citations and clear allusions contribute to this, for example, Luke 22:37, where a portion of Isa 53:12 is cited, "And he was reckoned with transgressors."[118] Being classed with criminals is part of Jesus' humiliation. When the Lukan Peter proclaims to the people that "God . . . glorified [*doxazein*] his servant [*pais*] Jesus" (Acts 3:13a), he has probably alluded to Isa 52:13 ("Behold, my servant [*pais*]

---

113. B. D. Chilton, *The Glory of Israel: The Theology and Provenience of the Isaiah Targum* (JSOTSup 23; Sheffield: JSOT, 1983) 95–96.

114. The Suffering Servant Song is rarely interpreted messianically in the rabbis (for references to Messiah's vicarious suffering, based on Isa 53:5, see *Sipra Lev.* 12.10 [on 5:17]; *Ruth Rab.* 5.6 [on 2:14]; *Midr. Sam.* 19:1; the references to Messiah as a "leper" or "sick one" are based on Isa 53:3, e.g., *b. Sanh.* 98b). Many rabbinic interpreters rejected altogether the messianic interpretation of this song. For a convenient compilation of Jewish interpretation, see A. Neubauer and S. R. Driver, *The Fifty-Third Chapter of Isaiah according to the Jewish Interpreters* (2 vols.; Oxford and London: James Parker, 1876–77; repr. New York: Ktav, 1969).

115. These passages are accepted as allusions by V. Taylor, *The Gospel according to St. Mark* (London: Macmillan, 1966²) 444–45, 546.

116. Fitzmyer (*Luke I–IX*, 211–12) cautiously concludes, probably correctly, that Luke's use of *pais* alludes to the servant of 2 Isaiah's songs, and that the suffering Son of man theme inherited from the Jesus tradition (Mark 8:31; Luke 9:22) became fused with the servant concept.

117. Hooker, *Jesus and the Servant*, 113–14.

118. For more details see Rese, *Alttestamentlich Motive*, 154–64; Bock, *Proclamation from Prophecy*, 137–39.

. . . will be glorified [*doxazein*] ").[119] Although Jesus had been "delivered up and denied in the presence of Pilate" (Acts 3:13b), he has now been vindicated. The citation of Isa 53:7-8 is part of this theme.[120]

Acts 13:33. " . . . This he has fulfilled to us their children by raising Jesus; as also it is written in the second psalm, 'Thou art my Son, today I have begotten thee' " (Ps 2:7). In his sermon at Antioch of Pisidia, the Lukan Paul cites Ps 2:7 as fulfilled in the resurrection of Jesus. The passage is variously applied to Jesus' baptism (Mark 1:11), transfiguration (Mark 9:7),[121] and ascension (Heb 1:5). Parts of this psalm are quoted or alluded to elsewhere (vv. 1-2 in Acts 4:25-26 [see above]; v. 1 in Rev 11:18; v. 2 in Rev 6:15; 11:15; 17:18; 19:19; v. 5 in Rev 11:18; v. 7 in John 1:49; Rom 1:4; Rev 12:5;[122] v. 8 in Heb 1:2; vv. 8-9 in Rev 2:26-27; v. 9 in Rev 12:5; 19:15; v. 11 in Phil 2:11; and v. 12 in Rev 11:18).

There is some evidence that Ps 2:7 was understood in a messianic sense prior to Christianity.[123] E. Earle Ellis has argued that the references to "my son the Messiah" in 4 Ezra 7:28-29 provide some evidence,[124] but were these actually inspired by Psalm 2? 1QSa 2:11–12 may allude to Ps 2:7 ("When [Adonai] will have begotten the Messiah among them"[125]), but the text is uncertain.[126] In reference to the "Lord Messiah" there are some vague allusions to Ps 2:9 in *Pss. Sol.* 17:24-26 and 18:7, but we are in no position to draw any conclusions about the understanding of v. 7. Parts of 2 Sam 7:11-16 closely related to Ps 2:7 are cited in 4QFlor 1:10–12. George J. Brooke translates: " 'And the Lord declares to you that he will build you a house. And I will raise up your seed after you, and I will establish the throne of his kingdom for ever. I will be to him as a father, and he will be

---

119. See further Rese, *Alttestamentlich Motive*, 111–13; Bock, *Proclamation from Prophecy*, 188–90.

120. See the recent study of D. L. Jones, "The Title 'Servant' in Luke-Acts," in Talbert, *Luke-Acts: New Perspectives*, 148–65. It might be added that the Servant Songs are not cited in reference to Jesus alone (see Isa 49:6 in Acts 13:47, in reference to Paul and Barnabas).

121. Some have argued that only Isa 42:1 lies behind the baptism and transfiguration traditions; see Lindars, *New Testament Apologetic*, 139–40; Fitzmyer, *Luke I–IX*, 485. According to Codex D, Ps 2:7 is actually quoted in Luke's version of the transfiguration (9:22). In the *Gospel of the Ebionites* §4 (cf. Epiphanius, *Haer.* 30.13.7–8), the heavenly voice at the baptism says, "Today I have begotten thee." Psalm 2:7 is probably alluded to also in the baptismal account of the *Gospel of the Hebrews* §2 (cf. Jerome, *Commentary on Isaiah* §4 [on 11:2]), "Thou art my first-begotten Son that reigneth forever."

122. Lindars (*New Testament Apologetic*, 143) suspects that the redundant use of *huios* in Rev 12:5 (lit. "she bore a male son") echoes Ps 2:7. The apocalyptic application of Psalm 2 parallels, but does not reflect, rabbinic interpretation (cf. *Midr.* Ps 2.2–3 [on 2:1-2]; see discussion in text above).

123. As noted by Fitzmyer, *Luke I–IX*, 485.

124. Ellis, *Luke*, 91–92.

125. Translation by Dupont-Sommer, *Essene Writings*, 108.

126. See Fitzmyer, *Luke I–IX*, 339.

to me as a son:' he is the shoot of David. . . . "[127] Dale Goldsmith and Brooke think that the passage is a pesher that has in mind Ps 2:7 and not 2 Samuel 7 only, and that such a pesher underlies Acts 13:33-37.[128] If this is correct, then Ps 2:7 was understood messianically prior to Christianity.

In the rabbis, however, the messianic interpretaion of Ps 2:7 is quite clear (see *b. Sukk.* 52a; *Midr. Ps* 2.9 [on 2:7], where Isa 42:1; 52:13; Ps 110:1; and Dan 7:13-14 are also cited and interpreted messianically).[129] This fact provides some evidence that Christian interpretation of Ps 2:7 was not entirely original unless we assume that the rabbis borrowed from Christian exegesis or independently arrived at the same interpretation.[130]

The significant point in Luke's use of Ps 2:7 is that it is cited as having fulfilled the promise to the "fathers" (Acts 13:32) and to "us their children" (v. 33). If the Lukan evangelist intends to write off the Jews, then it is strange that he once again emphasizes the fulfillment of God's promises to Israel (Luke 1:54-55, 68-72). Not only is the resurrection of Jesus presented as the fulfillment of Jewish expectation, the implication is that this fulfillment is to the advantage of the Israelites. The good news promised to us, the Lukan Paul proclaims to his fellow Jews, has been fulfilled in the resurrection of Jesus. The citations that follow in vv. 34-35 complete this line of argument.

Acts 13:34. "And . . . he spoke in this way, 'I will give you [pl.] the holy and sure blessings of David'" (cf. Isa 55:3).[131] The Lukan citation abbreviates and slightly paraphrases its septuagintal source, which itself differs from the Hebrew.[132] The only odd feature about the LXX's version is the translation of *hesed* ("steadfast love") as *hosios* ("holy").[133] But this rendering

---

127. G. J. Brooke, *Exegesis at Qumran: 4QFlorilegium in Its Jewish Context* (JSOTSup 29; Sheffield: JSOT, 1985) 92.

128. D. Goldsmith, "Acts 13:33-37: A *Pesher* on 2 Samuel 7," *JBL* 87 (1968) 321–24; Brooke, *Exegesis,* 209.

129. *Tg.* Ps 2:7 is probably not messianic. Levey (*The Messiah,* 105) translates, "You are as dear to Me as a son is to a father; you are as meritorious as though I had created you this day." The point seems to be the innocence of the Lord's favorite.

130. It is hardly likely that the rabbis borrowed from Christian exegesis or arrived at a similar understanding independently. They do not deny the messianic application of Ps 2:7, but do argue against Christianity's claim of Jesus' divine sonship. Commenting on Exod 20:1 ("I am the Lord thy God") Rabbi Abbahu (ca. 300) is reported to have said, "A human king may rule, but he has a father and a brother; but God said: 'I am not thus; I am the first, for I have no father, and I am the last, for I have no brother, and besides me there is no God, *for I have no son*'" (*Exod. Rab.* 29.5 [on 20:1], alluding to Isa 43:10-11 and 44:8, my emphasis; see also *y. Ta'an.* 2:1).

131. The citation literally reads, "I will give you the holy, faithful things of David."

132. The LXX reads, "I will make with you an eternal covenant, the holy, faithful things of David." The MT reads, "I will make with you an eternal covenant, my steadfast, sure love for David."

133. *Hosios* often translates *hasid* (Deut 33:8; 2 Sam 22:26; and some twenty-four times in the Psalms), but only here in Isa 55:3 does it translate *hesed.* In the LXX *eleos* usually trans-

serves Luke's purposes by enabling the evangelist to link Isa 55:3 to the
subsequent citation of Ps 16:10 in v. 35, where reference is made to
the Lord's *hosios* ("Holy One") who will not see corruption (see earlier
discussion of Ps 16:10).[134] The context suggests that the Davidic covenant[135] has been fulfilled in Jesus' resurrection. But the Isaianic context is
significant as well. Isaiah 55:3 is part of a passage in which the exilic
community is offered renewal and restoration; if the people will listen,
they will live and the Davidic covenant will be remembered (vv. 3-4). Just
as David was a testimony to the Gentiles, the day will come, the prophet
predicts, that the Gentiles will come running to Israel, "because of the
Lord your God, and (because) of the Holy One of Israel" (v. 5). Therefore
Israel is exhorted to forsake wickedness and to return to the Lord (vv. 6-7)
so that restoration will follow (vv. 8-13). According to the Lukan Paul, the
resurrection of Jesus, the Lord's Holy One, guarantees this promised restoration of Israel.[136]

Acts 13:40-41. "Beware, therefore, lest there come upon you what is said in
the prophets: 'Behold, you scoffers, and wonder, and perish; for I do a
deed in your days, a deed that you will never believe, if one declares it to
you'" (Hab 1:5). Again Luke follows the LXX, which differs somewhat
from the Hebrew.[137] The citation serves two functions. First, it is
apologetic, forestalling questions about why few Jews have believed the
Christian message (and, in the immediate context, why "the Jews" in v. 45
reject Paul's preaching). Second, it is a warning not to fall into the unbelief and judgment that the citation mentions. Sanders misconstrues this
second function and believes that the citation is a threat, not a warning.[138]

---

lates *hesed*. Possibly the Isaiah translator either mistook *hesed* for *hasid* or found the latter
reading in the text.
   134. Luke's *doso* ("I will give") also parallels *dosei* ("you will give") of Ps 16:10. Conzelmann (*Acts*, 105) wonders if Luke is drawing from a source in which Isa 55:3 and Ps 16:10
had been combined.
   135. It is likely that the expression *ta hosia David ta pista* refers to the Davidic covenant, in
which David is promised that his throne will be established (MT *'aman*; LXX *pistousthai*)
forever (2 Sam 7:16); see Bock, *Proclamation from Prophecy*, 253.
   136. For more details see Rese, *Alttestamentliche Motive*, 86–89; Bock, *Proclamation from
Prophecy*, 249–54.
   137. The MT reads: "Look among the nations, and see; wonder and be astounded. For I
am doing a work. . . ." The LXX translator might have read *bwgdym* ("traitors" or "scoffers"),
instead of *bgwym* ("among the nations"). The fragmentary text 8HevXIIgr 16:22–25 indicates
a reading different from the LXX. Although Hab 1:5 is not extant in 1QpHab 1:16–17, the
exegesis that follows (2:1–3, "[The explanation of this concerns] the traitors who are with
the man of lies; for [they have] not [believed the words] of the teacher of righteousness . . .
and (it also concerns) the trai[tors who have betrayed the] new [covenant]") might be based
on a version that reads "traitors" instead of "nations."
   138. According to J. T. Sanders (*The Jews in Luke-Acts*, 261): "One might . . . expect some
encouragement to believe . . . , but this does not occur. Instead, a threat follows: 'Watch
out. . . .'"

In fact, he thinks that the Lukan Paul is actually trying to *prevent* the conversion of those Jews who favorably respond to his preaching (vv. 42-43).[139] Such an interpretation flies in the face of the narrative itself, since the Lukan Paul anticipates belief (v. 39). After his sermon "the people begged" to hear more on the following Sabbath (v. 42), and "many *Jews* and devout converts to Judaism followed Paul and Barnabas" (v. 43, my emphasis). There are so many sympathetic hearers, in fact, that he refers to them as "multitudes" (v. 45). The Lukan Paul admonishes his audience to believe; he does not discourage belief.

Acts 13:47. "For so the Lord has commanded us, saying, 'I have set you to be a light for the Gentiles, that you may bring salvation to the uttermost parts of the earth'" (cf. Isa 49:6). Luke tells us that "the Jews" were jealous and contradicted Paul (v. 45). Their jealousy might have been because of Paul's success or because of resentment at the idea of sharing with Gentiles their privileged relation to God, more likely the latter. Because of this rejection, Paul announces his intention to turn to the Gentiles (v. 46). For scriptural justification he quotes Isa 49:6, a text that describes the task of the servant Israel.[140] This text is part of a tradition that looks to the time when the nations will see the glory of Israel and "walk in her light."[141] But in Luke-Acts, Isa 49:6 is not applied exclusively to Gentiles. The text is alluded to in Luke 2:32 ("A light for revelation to the Gentiles, and for glory to thy people Israel") and, more importantly, at the end of Acts (26:23) it is again found. "... By being first to rise from the dead, he would proclaim light to the people [i.e., Israel] and to the Gentiles."[142] In

---

139. J. T. Sanders, *The Jews in Luke-Acts*, 261–62. Sanders bases his interpretation on a questionable understanding of the phrase "to abide in grace." He argues (261) that it means to "remain fixed in their accustomed religious development," i.e., their non-Christian faith. This is hardly what Luke is trying to say; see E. Haenchen, *The Acts of the Apostles: A Commentary* (Philadelphia: Westminster, 1971) 413.

140. There are indications elsewhere that Luke might have viewed the apostolic witness as the fulfillment of Israel's task as the servant of the Lord. The risen Christ tells the apostles, "You are my witnesses ... to the end of the earth" (Acts 1:8). This commission may echo two of the servant passages where the Lord enjoins Israel, "Become my witnesses ... and my servant" (LXX Isa 43:10) and "Be salvation to the end of the earth" (LXX Isa 49:6). The two main components of Acts 1:8 are found in these servant passages in 2 Isaiah. When the Lukan Paul says, "For thus the Lord has commanded us" (Acts 13:47a) and then quotes Isa 49:6, a passage addressed to Israel as the Lord's servant, Luke seems to see the servant's task as that of the apostles. The task of Isa 49:6 is also to "establish the tribes of Israel and to return the dispersed of Israel" (see Luke 22:28-30 and Chap. 11 above). On the link between Acts 1:8 and Isa 43:10 I am indebted to P. H. Menoud, "Jesus and His Witnesses: Observations on the Unity of the Work of Luke," in Menoud, *Jesus Christ and the Faith* (PTMS 18; Pittsburgh: Pickwick, 1978) 156. See also Dodd, *According to the Scriptures*, 90; Wilcox, *Semitisms*, 80.

141. See Isa 42:6; 60:3; *1 Enoch* 48:4; *Gen. Rab.* 59:5 (on 24:1); *Exod. Rab.* 15.21 (on 12:2); 36.1 (on 27:20); *Num. Rab.* 21.22 (on 28:2); *Song Rab.* 1:3 §3; 1:15 §4; 4:1 §2; *b. B. Bat.* 75a.

142. Acts 26:18 also does not support the notion that the Jews are banished. "I send you

both cases Israel is included in the blessings that result from the advent of Jesus, but in the Antioch sermon the passage is quoted specifically to justify Paul's Gentile missionary efforts. Upon hearing Paul's pronouncement, an undetermined number of Gentiles believe and the Christian message spreads throughout the region (vv. 48-49), which provokes further Jewish resentment. After Paul and Barnabas are driven out of the city, "they [shake] off the dust from their feet" (vv. 50-51). This action does not categorically reject the Jews; it only symbolizes a protest against a given town or region (see Luke 9:5; 10:11; Acts 18:6).[143] Nowhere in Luke-Acts does this gesture have universal significance. Although Jewish unbelief at Antioch of Pisidia makes Paul turn to the Gentiles, which is the main concern of the passage, the apostle continues to go to Jews (see 14:1; 17:1, 10; 18:4, 19; 19:8).

Acts 15:15-17. "And with this the words of the prophets agree, as it is written, 'After this I will return, and I will rebuild the tabernacle of David, which has fallen; I will rebuild its ruins, and I will set it up, that the rest of men may seek the Lord, and all the Gentiles who are called by my name,'

[to the Gentiles] to open their eyes . . . that they may receive forgiveness of sins and a place among those who are sanctified by faith in me." Since "those who are sanctified" stand in contrast to the "Gentiles," the text probably refers to Jews, or rather, Christian Jews, understood here as partners with the Gentiles.

143. J. T. Sanders's misunderstanding of Paul's declarations to turn to the Gentiles leads him to say (*The Jews and Luke-Acts*, 276) that Luke's "narrative [does not] immediately conform to the principle of Paul's declaration," that is, of having Paul say one thing (no longer going to Jews), but doing another (continuing to go to Jews). This is faulty analysis, and if these declarations are correctly interpreted, the putative discrepancy disappears. When Paul says that he will turn to the Gentiles (whether in Antioch or Corinth), he turns to the Gentiles of the city. When he leaves that city, he once again turns to the Jews.

A related issue requires comment. Sanders frequently appeals to Acts 18:6 ("And when they opposed and reviled him, he shook out his garments and said to them, 'Your blood be upon your heads! I am innocent. From now on I will go to the Gentiles'"), thinking that it implies that the Jews of Corinth are just as responsible for Jesus' death as the Jews of Jerusalem and that all Jews will be destroyed (*The Jews in Luke-Acts*, xvii, 53, 276, 317, 355, n. 102). His interpretation could not be further from the truth. First, as argued above, Paul's declaration does not have universal application. Second, the expression about blood being on one's head is an idiom that probably derives from Ezek 33:2-9, where the "watchman" (i.e., the prophet) is enjoined to warn the people when danger approaches. If the people ignore the prophetic warning, their blood is upon their own heads; if the prophet fails to warn them, then he is responsible. Thus Paul says that he is "innocent." As Brawley (*Luke-Acts and the Jews*, 73) correctly says, Paul's declarations "warn the Jews of their responsibility and absolve Paul of his." When the Lukan Paul applies this idiom to the Jews of Corinth, he is not implying that they are guilty of Jesus' death, but only of rejecting the apostolic preaching. In Acts 20:26-27 (a passage that Sanders does not discuss) the same idiom recurs. "I testify to you this day that I am innocent of the blood of all of you, for I did not shrink from declaring to you the whole counsel of God." Now Paul speaks to the elders of the church of Ephesus, who are mostly, if not all, Gentiles. Obviously this idiom does not have universal application, nor does it have anything to do with guilt. It means only that when the messenger has faithfully fulfilled the mission, responsibility remains not with the messenger but with the people (whether they believe the message or not).

says the Lord, who has made these things known from of old" (cf. Amos 9:11-12). This citation is a paraphrase of the LXX, which has not followed the Hebrew exactly. What the LXX translates as "that the rest of men may seek the Lord" reads in the Hebrew, "That they may possess the remnant of Edom."[144] Once again the LXX serves Luke's purposes better than the Hebrew. The citation is enriched by a few words from Jer 12:15 ("I will return") and Isa 45:21 ("Things known from of old"), passages which also speak of Israel's restoration. (Luke is probably aware of these contributions, hence the plural reference to "the words of the prophets.") The passage from Amos has been cited because "God . . . visited the Gentiles, to take out of them a people for this name" (Acts 15:14). Although Luke does not say so explicitly, the implication seems to be that inclusion of Gentiles is vital to the restoration of the "tent of David."[145] This is not at Israel's expense but to its glory (Luke 2:32).[146]

Since Jewish interpretation is based on the Hebrew, there is no parallel to Luke's understanding of Amos 9:12. Jewish interpretation of Amos 9:11, however, does to a degree parallel Luke's usage. According to CD[A] 7:16, Amos 9:11 was fulfilled when the Essenes restored the correct interpretation of the Law.[147] In 4QFlor 1:11–13 the text is understood in a messianic sense: "This is the branch of David [=Messiah, cf. 4QpIsa^c; Jer 23:5; 33:15; Zech 3:8; 6:12] who will arise with the Seeker of the Law and who will sit on the throne of Zion at the end of days; as it is written, 'I will raise up the tabernacle of David which is fallen.' This 'tabernacle of David which is fallen' (is) he who will arise to save Israel."[148] This finds an interesting parallel in the rabbis. According to b. Sanh. 96b–97a, the Messiah will be called Bar Naphle, that is, "Son of the Fallen [Tabernacle]." The passage reads: "Rabbi Nahman asked Rabbi Isaac: 'Have you heard when Bar Naphle will come?' 'Who is Bar Naphle?' he asked. 'Messiah,' he answered . . . 'as it is written, "In that day I will raise up the tabernacle of David that is fallen." ' "[149] Under the influence of Amos 9, one midrash of

---

144. The LXX translator probably read *yidresu* for *yiresu*, and vocalized *'dm* as "man" (making it the subject), rather than as "Edom" (the object). See Lindars, *New Testament Apologetic*, 35, n. 3.

145. See Jervell, "The Twelve on Israel's Thrones," 93. On the basis of the citation of Amos 9:11-12, Jervell (92) thinks that "Israel's restoration is an established fact." I disagree; Israel's restoration is under way but is far from accomplished.

146. See D. L. Tiede, "'Glory to Thy People, Israel': Luke-Acts and the Jews," in J. Neusner, P. Borgen, E. S. Frerichs, and R. A. Horsley, eds., *The Social World of Formative Christianity and Judaism* (H. C. Kee Festschrift; Philadelphia: Fortress, 1988) 327–41.

147. See Dupont-Sommer, *Essene Writings*, 134, n. 2.

148. Translation by Dupont-Sommer, *Essene Writings*, 313.

149. Translation based on Freedman, *The Babylonian Talmud: Sanhedrin*, 654. "Naphle" comes from the Hebrew *naphal* ("to fall"). Freedman notes (654, n. 2) that Bar Naphle is generally assumed to represent the Greek *huios nephelōn* ("son of the clouds"), inspired by Dan 7:13, "there came with the clouds of heaven one like a son of man."

Ps 76:1-2 reads the verses as a question and answer: "When will God be known in Judah [v. 1]? When God raises up his tabernacle [v. 2], as it says in Amos . . ." (*Midr.* Ps 76.3 [on 76:3, and 1]; see also *Gen. Rab.* 88.7 [on 40:23]). Restoration is clearly in view, possibly even the rebuilding of the temple. The Targum of Amos 9:11 presents a similar emphasis. "At that time I will reestablish the fallen kingdom of David, and will rebuild their cities and repair their synagogues; and it (the Davidic dynasty) shall rule over every kingdom, and shall put an end to and destroy great armies, and it shall be rebuilt and firmly established on its foundations as in the days of old."[150] The hope for a restored kingdom is plainly evident.

Acts 28:25-27. "The Holy Spirit was right in saying to your fathers through Isaiah the prophet: 'Go to this people, and say, You shall indeed hear but never understand, and you shall indeed see but never perceive. For this people's heart has grown dull, and their ears are heavy of hearing, and their eyes they have closed; lest they should perceive with their eyes, and hear with their ears, and understand with their heart, and turn for me to heal them'" (cf. Isa 6:9-10). The Lukan Paul has quoted the LXX verbatim[151] in order to provide an explanation of the disputatious and divided Jewish response to Paul's preaching at the close of Acts (28:17-25). Sanders believes that by this concluding scene and citation Luke intended to close the door on the Jews once and for all.[152] But the passage does not do this for at least two reasons. First, "some" Jews are "persuaded" by Paul's preaching (v. 24). By this Luke surely means that these people are converted, for elsewhere in Acts "persuaded" ones are called "brethren" (17:4, 10),[153] a designation that the evangelist uses for Christians (1:15; 10:30; 11:1, 12, 29). The concluding scene thus depicts some Jews believing, some not. Since Paul continued to evangelize Jews after his earlier declarations to turn to the Gentiles (13:46; 18:6), the same pattern must

150. Translation by Levey, *The Messiah*, 157, n. 116. The expression "firmly established" probably alludes to the Davidic covenant (2 Sam 7:16).

151. The Hebrew and Aramaic versions are somewhat different. Isa 6:9-10 was a passage widely used in early Christian circles to explain the rejection of Jesus and unbelief in the Christian gospel (cf. Mark 4:12; Matt 13:13-15; Luke 8:10; John 12:40; Rom 11:7). Whereas early Christians exploited the critical emphasis of this prophetic text, Jewish interpreters either ignored it or applied it in innocuous ways. For further discussion see Evans, *To See and Not Perceive.*

152. J. T. Sanders, *The Jews in Luke-Acts,* 53, 298–99; idem, "The Prophetic Use of the Scriptures," 198; idem, "The Salvation of the Jews," 111–12. In reference to v. 28, Haenchen (*Acts,* 724) thinks that the saving proclamation has been transferred "from the Jews to the Gentiles." Elsewhere ("The Book of Acts as Source Material for the History of Early Christianity," in L. E. Keck and J. L. Martyn, eds., *Studies in Luke-Acts* [Philadelphia: Fortress, 1966] 258–78, quote from 278) Haenchen says, "Luke has written the Jews off."

153. Haenchen (*Acts,* 507) understands the persuaded of Acts 17:4 as converts, but not (*Acts,* 723–24) those of Acts 28:24; see also Conzelmann, *Acts,* 227.

hold here in chapter 28 as well. Surely the "all" of v. 30 is not meant to exclude any group, Jewish or Gentile. Second, Isa 6:9-10 is not quoted to show that God has rejected Israel; the passage simply does not say this. Rather, it explains why the nation of Israel in general ("this people") has failed to believe the Christian message and why the gospel is extended to the Gentiles (Acts 28:28).[154] In this passage Luke's prophetic and apologetic stance comes to clearest expression; Luke is dealing not with a Jewish problem but with a Gentile one. He is trying to show, on empirical and scriptural grounds, that the Gentile mission is legitimate, not that the Jewish mission will be terminated.[155]

In the Gospel Jesus had promised the kingdom of God (Luke 9:27; 12:32; 22:29). Since the kingdom had not yet come, when would the promise be fulfilled? It is therefore not surprising that at the outset of Acts the risen Christ is asked, "Lord, will you at this time restore the kingdom to Israel?" (Acts 1:6). The disciples did not ask if the kingdom was to be given to them or to the church, but when it would be restored to Israel. Nothing in Jesus' reply indicates that the kingdom was not for Israel. The question and answer had to do with when, not if or to whom. Acts ends with Paul still preaching the kingdom of God (Acts 28:31), and the kingdom has not yet been restored to Israel because Israel has not yet believed in Jesus as the Messiah. Israel's opinion of him remains divided; thus the prophecy of Isa 6:9-10 remains in force and the restoration is unfulfilled.

ASSESSMENT

Broadly speaking, five functions of Scripture have been detected in Luke-Acts:

1. *Christological.* Many of the citations are christological and often linked to

---

154. Brawley's assessment (*Luke-Acts and the Jews,* 76–77) is correct. See also D. P. Moessner, "Paul in Acts: Preacher of Eschatological Repentance to Israel," *NTS* 34 (1988) 96–104.

155. J. A. Sanders ("Isaiah in Luke," *Int* 36 [1982] 144–55, esp. 147–48; rev. and repr. as Chap. 2 of the present volume) compares Acts 28:30-31 ("And [Paul] lived there two whole years at his own expense, and welcomed all who came to him, preaching the kingdom of God and teaching about the Lord Jesus Christ openly and unhindered") with 2 Kgs 25:29-30 ("So Jehoiachin put off his prison garments. And every day of his life he dined regularly at the king's table; and for his allowance, a regular allowance was given him by the king, every day a portion, as long as he lived"). Sanders's proposal is intriguing. Although defeated and imprisoned, Jehoiachin comes to enjoy the favor of the world power of his day. By implication God's work is continuing; the people have a future. Luke may be making a similar point. Although encountering setbacks, even failure (such as the delay of the parousia and widespread Jewish rejection of the gospel), and now under house arrest, the apostle Paul is still favored by a world power—a sign that God's work is continuing. Such a comparison, if intended, may suggest that setbacks are only temporary. The Jewish people as a whole will come to faith, the kingdom will be restored to Israel, and the king will return.

Israel's hopes for restoration through a Davidic Messiah (throughout infancy narratives; Ps 2:7 in Acts 13:33; Ps 16:10 in Acts 2:25-28; 13:35; Ps 110:1 in Acts 2:34-35; Ps 132:11 in Acts 2:30; Isa 53:7-8 in Acts 8:32-33; Isa 55:3 in Acts 13:34; Amos 9:11-12 in Acts 15:15-17; Joel 2:28-32 in Acts 2:17-21).

2. *Soteriological.* Some citations stress universal salvation (Isa 40:3-5 in Luke 3:4-6; Isa 49:6 in Acts 26:23; Isa 61:1-2 in Luke 4:18-19). Some stress the salvation of Gentiles (Isa 49:6 in Acts 13:47).

3. *Apologetic.* Some texts explain lack of comprehension (Isa 6:9-10 in Luke 8:10), or unbelief (Ps 2:1-2 in Acts 4:25-26; Isa 6:9-10 in Acts 28:26-27; Hab 1:5 in Acts 13:41). Some underscore respect for Jewish Law (Exod 13:2, 12 and Lev 12:2-8 in Luke 2:22-24, 39; Deut 6:5 in Luke 10:27-28; Exod 22:28 in Acts 23:5), which may be part of Lukan apologetic, although I suspect that there is a genuine respect for Israel's Law and heritage.

4. *Minatory.* Some texts threaten and warn (Deut 18:19 in Acts 3:23; Ps 118:22; Isa 8:14-15 + Dan 2:34 in Luke 20:17-18; Hab 1:5 in Acts 13:41). Where the Lukan Jesus alludes to prophetic Scriptures to predict Jerusalem's destruction, sorrow is usually expressed (Luke 19:41-44; 23:26-32).

5. *Critical.* Some texts criticize Israel for past and present failings (Amos 5:25-27 in Acts 7:42-43; Isa 66:1-2 in Acts 7:49-50). The emphasis here is chiefly christological and restorative. Even the minatory citations are intended to warn Israel to accept Jesus as Messiah and so bring on restoration. Thus it it would seem that the function of Scripture in Luke-Acts simply does not support Sanders's conclusion that the Lukan evangelist hates the Jews and foresees no restoration of Israel.

J. T. Sanders's interpretation is based upon a serious misreading of the relevant passages. As I see it, he has failed to distinguish intramural polemic from racial hatred. The Lukan evangelist is a participant in a late first-century struggle to define the people of God, the heirs of the biblical promises. In the aftermath of Jerusalem's destruction and the continuing delay of the parousia, the conflict was brought to a boil.[156] Luke believes that Christians make up the true people of God, for they have believed in Jesus the Messiah, the one who has fulfilled Scripture. Those who reject the Messiah reject the purposes of God and so stand under the judgments of Scripture. Obviously this means that Luke understands these judg-

---

156. See Tiede, *Prophecy and History,* 1–7.

ments to apply to all Jews (and Gentiles, see Acts 17:30-31) who reject Christianity. But to describe this belief as anti-Semitic hatred is inaccurate and unfair. To be sure, Luke believes that those Jews who reject the Christian message are wrong and face God's wrath. But this kind of sentiment was typical in religious debate and controversy in the first century. Luke's critical view of "unbelievers" is mild compared to the related expressions of various Jewish groups toward one another, not to mention Jewish views toward Gentiles. Pharisees, and later the rabbis, believed that Sadducees, Samaritans, and Gentiles were destined for hell (*m. Sanh.* 10:1; *y. Kil.* 9:4; *Sipre Deut.* §311 [on 32:8]). The people of Qumran believed that most of non-Qumranian Israel, including Pharisees, were destined for judgment (1QS 2:4–9; 9:21–22; 1QpHab 5:3–5). Even Paul calls fellow Jews "enemies of God" (Rom 11:28), who are hardened (2 Cor 3:12—4:6; Rom 11:7, 25) and oppose God's purposes (1 Thess 2:14-16).[157]

The only opponents of Luke (and all other early Christians, for that matter) in the interpretation of the Scriptures were Jews. Who else would contradict the apostles? Some Athenians made light of the resurrection (Acts 17:32), but in almost all other controversies, the interpretation of the Scriptures is at issue, and the opponents of Christian claims are "the Jews." One of Luke's major concerns is to show that Jesus is truly the fulfillment of the Scriptures, as seen in his numerous summary statements (Luke 24:25-26, 45-47; Acts 3:18, 24; 10:43; 17:2-3; 18:28; 24:14-15; 26:22-23; 28:23). These statements testify to the centrality of the scriptural debate between Christians (both Jews and Gentiles) and non-Christian Jews. Those who interpret the Scriptures in a non-Christian manner are Jews, and Luke-Acts is a Christian response to this debate. What appears as anti-Semitic polemic is an exegetical polemic that attempts to demonstrate that Jesus, the Gentile mission, and Jewish unbelief fulfill the prophetic Scriptures. Luke interprets the Scriptures in order to present Christianity, Gentile question and all, as the fulfillment and completion of the biblical story.[158]

---

157. For further discussion see my essay "Is Luke's View of the Jewish Rejection of Jesus Anti-Semitic?" in D. Sylva, ed., *Reimaging the Death of the Lukan Jesus* (BBB 73; Frankfurt am Main: Anton Hain, 1990) 29–56, 174–83.

158. See C. A. Evans and D. A. Hagner, *Studies in Anti-Semitism and Early Christianity: Issues of Polemic and Faith* (Minneapolis: Fortress, 1993).

─13─

THE PROPHETIC SETTING OF
THE PENTECOST SERMON

CRAIG A. EVANS

In the chapters above we have observed how Scripture contributes to the Lukan evangelist's historiography (e.g., Luke 7:11-17; 9:51-62; 19:28-40) and presentation of dominical tradition (e.g., Luke 4:16-30; 10:29-37; 22:24-30). It seems that Scripture makes a similar contribution in Acts as well; behind the narrative leading up to the Pentecost sermon (Acts 2:1-16), as well as the sermon itself (2:17-40), are words and themes drawn from the prophet Joel, including Joel 2:28-32, the passage that the Lukan Peter quotes at the outset of the Pentecost sermon (Acts 2:17-21). But the Joel quotation looks back since it parallels in an important way Luke's extended quotation of Isaiah 40 in Luke 3, and it looks forward in that it anticipates the quotation and interpretation of Amos 9:11-12 in Acts 15. This chapter will investigate the literary context of the Pentecost sermon to determine the extent and significance of Joel's contribution to this portion of the Acts narrative and to the broader context of Luke-Acts.

THE FUNCTION OF JOEL IN ACTS 2

The Lukan Peter explains the perplexing charismatic phenomena by an appeal to Joel 2:28-32 (MT/LXX 3:1-5). The use of Joel is not, however, ad hoc but plays a major role in Luke's theology of universal salvation. We begin with a comparison of the quotation with the LXX and the MT and an assessment of Joel's contribution to the setting of the Pentecost sermon.

This chapter is a revision of my study, "The Prophetic Setting of the Pentecost Sermon," *ZNW* 74 (1983) 148–50.

Acts	LXX	MT
And in the last days it shall be, God declares,	And it shall be after these things	And it shall happen afterward
that I will pour out my Spirit upon all flesh,	that I pour out my Spirit upon all flesh,	that I will pour out my Spirit upon all flesh,
and your sons and your daughters shall prophesy,	and your sons and your daughters shall prophesy,	and your sons and your daughters shall prophesy,
and your young men shall see visions,	and your old men shall dream dreams,	your old men shall dream dreams,
and your old men shall dream dreams.	and your young men shall see visions.	your young men shall see visions.
Yea, even on my menservants and my maidservants in those days	Even on the menservants and the maidservants in those days	Even on the menservants and the maidservants in those days
I will pour out my Spirit; and they shall prophesy.	I will pour out my Spirit.	I will pour out my Spirit.
And I will show wonders in the heaven above	And I will show wonders in heaven	And I will give portents in the heavens
and signs on the earth beneath,	and on the earth,	and on the earth,
blood, and fire, and vapor of smoke.	blood and fire and vapor of smoke.	blood and fire and columns of smoke.
The sun shall be turned into darkness	The sun shall be turned into darkness	The sun shall be turned into darkness
and the moon into blood,	and the moon into blood,	and the moon into blood,
before the day of the Lord comes,	before the day of the Lord comes,	before the day of the Lord comes,
the great and manifest day.	the great and manifest day.	the great and terrible day.
And it shall be that whoever calls on the name of the Lord shall be saved.	And it shall be that whoever calls on the name of the Lord shall be saved;	And it shall be that all who call on the name of the Lord shall be delivered;
	for in Mount Zion and in Jerusalem	for in Mount Zion and in Jerusalem
	he shall be rescued,	there shall be those who
	as the Lord has said,	escape, as the Lord has said,
	and will be evangelized,	and among the survivors
	whom the Lord has summoned.	shall be those whom the Lord calls.

Luke's quotation varies from the LXX at several points. The evangelist adds a few phrases ("last days," "God says," "they shall prophesy"), reverses the dream and vision clauses, and omits the last part of Joel 2:32 (3:5). Martin Rese thinks that by stopping the quotation where he does Luke maintains the passage's universalistic tone.[1] But the centrality of Jerusalem in Luke-Acts, where, after all, the message of salvation begins (Acts 1:8), militates against this interpretation. This text does contribute to Lukan universalism but not by truncating Joel's prophecy. It will also be shown that language and ideas of Joel not quoted are nevertheless alluded to in

---

1. M. Rese, *Alttestamentliche Motive in der Christologie des Lukas* (SNT 1; Gütersloh: Gerd Mohn, 1969) 50–54.

Acts 2 and elsewhere in Acts. Luke's usage of Joel, in fact, is very much in keeping with early Jewish eschatological themes.[2]

Ernst Haenchen argues that Luke designed the setting for the sermon to explain and describe the arrival of the Spirit.[3] He believes that the association of rushing wind with the Spirit is natural enough (*pnoē*/ *pneuma*),[4] while the tongues of fire hovering over the apostles' heads is external evidence that the Spirit had indeed indwelt them. Haenchen also notes that fire is an appropriate symbol, because of Pentecost's association with the fire of Sinai.[5] The ecstatic speech is further proof that the Spirit is

---

2. See D. L. Bock, *Proclamation from Prophecy and Pattern: Lucan Old Testament Christology* (JSNTSup 12; Sheffield: JSOT, 1987) 168–69. See also Chap. 12 above.

3. E. Haenchen, *The Acts of the Apostles* (Philadelphia: Westminster, 1971) 172–75.

4. Haenchen, *Acts*, 167–68, 174; cf. H. Conzelmann, *Acts of the Apostles* (Hermeneia; Philadelphia: Fortress, 1987) 13.

5. Haenchen, *Acts*, 174; cf. Exod 19:18. Conzelmann (*Acts*, 16) thinks however that the association of Pentecost with the giving of the covenant at Sinai is not intended by Luke. I. H. Marshall (*The Acts of the Apostles* [Grand Rapids: Eerdmans, 1980] 68) is also skeptical. E. Lohse ("*Pentekoste*," *TDNT* 6.49) concludes that "the story of Pentecost in Ac[ts] 2 bears no relation to the Sinai tradition." Other scholars have come to the opposite conclusion: G. Kretschmar, "Himmelfahrt und Pfingsten," *ZKG* 66 (1954–55) 209–53, esp. 243–53; O. Betz, "The Eschatological Interpretation of the Sinai-Tradition in Qumran and in the New Testament," *RevQ* 6 (1967) 89–107, esp. 93; P. H. Menoud, "The Lukan Version of Pentecost and History," in Menoud, *Jesus Christ and the Faith: A Collection of Studies* (PTMS 18; Pittsburgh: Pickwick, 1978) 180–91, esp. 184, 190, n. 8, "The place of [Pentecost] in the calendar made it inevitable that it should recall the events at Sinai."

Evidence before 70 c.e. for associating Pentecost with Sinai is admittedly slight. Such an association occurs in *Jubilees* (see 6:17, taken with 1:1). Luke's description, Conzelmann (*Acts*, 16) says, reflects only the language of theophany in general (he notes LXX Isa 66:15, 18). Perhaps, but Philo's description of the event at Sinai (which Conzelmann notes) parallels Luke's description of the Pentecost miracle: "I should suppose that God wrought on this occasion a miracle of a truly holy kind by bidding an invisible sound to be created in the air . . . which giving shape and tension to the air and changing it to flaming fire, sounded forth like the breath through a trumpet an articulate voice. . . . Then from the midst of the fire that streamed from heaven there sounded forth to their utter amazement a voice, for the flame became articulate speech in the language familiar to the audience, and so clearly and distinctly were the words formed by it that they seemed to see rather than hear them" (*On the Decalogue* 9 §33; 11 §46); translation by F. H. Colson, *Philo* (LCL 7; Cambridge: Harvard University Press) 23, 29. Note the common vocabulary: "a sound from heaven" (*ek tou ouranou ēchos*, Acts 2:2; *phonē* in v. 6)/"a voice from heaven" (*phonē . . . ap' ouranou, Decal.* 11 §46; *ēchos* in 9 §33); the heaven-given speech is in a familiar "dialect" (*dialektos*, Acts 2:6, 8; *Decal.* 11 §46); the miracle could be "seen" (*ōphthē*, Acts 2:3; *horan, Decal.* 11 §46); what was visible was "fire" (*pyr*, Acts 2:3; *Decal.* 9 §33); the manifestation was "marvellous" (*thaumazein*, Acts 2:7; *thaumatourgesai, thaumasioteron, Decal.* 9 §33). On the basis of Exod 19:1, some tannaic rabbis concluded that God gave the covenant fifty days after the people arrived at Sinai (*Seder 'Olam Rabba* §5). Therefore, Pentecost "is the day on which the Torah was given" (*b. Pesah.* 68b). Another rabbinic tradition could also be relevant: "It says: 'And all the people perceived the thunderings' (Exod 20:18). Note that it does not say 'the thunder' [*ha-qol*, lit. "the sound" or "voice"], but 'the thunderings' [*ha-qoloth*]. Therefore Rabbi Yohanan said that God's voice, as it was uttered, split up into seventy voices, in seventy languages, so that all the nations should understand" (*Exod. Rab.* 5.9 [on 4:21]; see also *b. Shab.* 88b; *Midr.* Ps 92.3 [on 92:1]; *Midr. Tanh.* on Exod 20:18; *Frag. Tg.* Deut 27:8); translation based on S. M. Lehrman, *Midrash Rabbah: Exodus* (London and New York: Soncino, 1983) 86. Although this midrash has nothing to do with Pentecost, Luke's account of the Pentecost miracle is probably not unrelated

present and is recognized as such by the astonished crowd. Haenchen believes that Luke's "others" (v. 13) was inserted to provide a transition from ecstatic speech to Peter's sermon. These "others" therefore wrongly interpret the ecstatic speech by suggesting that the apostles are intoxicated.[6] This incorrect assessment thus becomes the occasion for Peter's correction, explanation, and sermon.[7] I basically agree with Haenchen's analysis, but I think that the setting is fundamentally indebted to the prophetic tradition as found in Joel and not simply to Luke's literary imagination.[8]

The introductory formula, "This is that which was spoken through the prophet Joel" (v. 16), introduces the quotation of LXX Joel 2:28-32, which in turn serves the double function of explaining the ecstatic phenomenon (vv. 2-15) and of introducing the sermon (vv. 22-36).[9] The fact that Luke's

---

to the Sinai tradition. In another midrash, Joel 2:28 is actually cited as the eventual fulfillment of Moses' wish (Num 11:29), made shortly after leaving Sinai, that all Israelites had the Spirit (*Midr.* Ps 14.6 [on 14:7]; Deut 5:29 [Hebr. 5:26], Moses' wish at Sinai that Israel would obey the commandments is also cited in this midrash; see discussion in this chap.). For more rabbinic citations touching on themes in Acts 2 see Str-B 2.597–606.

6. On the religious significance of intoxication see Conzelmann, *Acts*, 15. Haenchen (*Acts*, 172, n. 1) is wrong when he says that there would have been no "new wine by Pentecost in Palestine."

7. Haenchen, *Acts*, 175; M. Dibelius, *Studies in the Acts of the Apostles*, ed. H. Greeven (London: SCM, 1956) 138–85; E. Schweizer, "Concerning the Speeches in Acts," in L. E. Keck and J. L. Martyn, eds., *Studies in Luke-Acts* (Philadelphia: Fortress, 1966) 208–16. The latter two scholars note that most of the speeches in Acts begin in this manner.

8. It has also been suggested that Isa 28:7-13 might underlie the Pentecost story; see O. Betz, "Zungenreden und süsser Wein. Zur eschatologischen Exegese von Jesaja 28 in Qumran und im Neuen Testament," in S. Wagner, ed., *Bibel und Qumran* (H. Bardtke Festschrift; Berlin: Evangelische Haupt-Bibelgesellschaft, 1968) 20–36, esp. 29–32. The parallels are impressive. The inhabitants of "Jerusalem" are addressed (Acts 2:5; Isa 28:14; "priest and prophet are mad [*existēmi*] through strong drink" (Isa 28:7), and those who heard the apostles "were amazed [*existēmi*] (Acts 2:12); the prophets are drunk with "wine [*oinos*]" (Isa 28:7), and the apostles are accused of being drunk with "sweet wine [*gluekos*]" (Acts 2:13); foreigners "through a different tongue [*dia glōssēs heteras*] . . . will speak [*lalesousi*] . . . to this people" (Isa 28:11), and the apostles "began to speak in different tongues [*lalein heterais glōssais*]" (Acts 2:4). Compare also Acts 2:17 ("in the last days") and Isa 28:5 ("in that day"). That glossolalia and Isaiah 28 were asssociated in early Christian tradition is seen in Paul's quotation and interpretation of Isa 28:11 in 1 Cor 14:21 (see Betz, "Zungenreden und süsser Wein," 23–29). Isaiah 28 quite possibly made a contribution to the Pentecost story. As shown in this chap. and n. 12 below, the setting of the Pentecost sermon has even closer verbal and thematic affinities with Joel. Of course, the citation of Joel 2:28-32 is concrete evidence that Joel was before the evangelist as he composed his account.

In *Tg.* Isa 28:11 the people mock the prophets in a strange tongue. In 1QH 4:16–18 the Isaianic passage is alluded to but is understood as the stammering utterances of false prophets.

9. Some scholars consider Luke's introductory formula to be cognate to the pesher exegesis of Qumran (e.g., 1QpHab 3:2; 5:6; 4QpIsa[b] 2:7); see R. N. Longenecker (*Biblical Exegesis in the Apostolic Period* [Grand Rapids: Eerdmans, 1975] 201) who cites Acts 2:16 and 4:11 ("this is the stone"); E. E. Ellis, *Prophecy and Hermeneutic in Early Christianity* (WUNT 18; Tübingen: Mohr [Siebeck], 1978) 195, n. 35, 205–6; Conzelmann, *Acts*, 19.

The Lukan evangelist is not alone in applying this passage to the Christian proclamation. Joel 2:32a is cited in Rom 10:13 with essentially the same meaning as in Acts 2; see C. H.

setting for Peter's sermon is laced throughout with language taken from
the Greek version of Joel has, however, gone unobserved.[10] In the verses
immediately leading up to the sermon (i.e., vv. 2-15) are numerous words
and images also found in Joel. Approximately twenty words in Luke's
narrative and Peter's opening remarks (not counting the Joel citation
itself) may be traced to Joel,[11] and many of these words contribute essential details to the narrative itself. The motif of the residents "from all
nations" (Acts 2:5, 8-11) recalls Joel's concern with the nations (cf. Joel
1:6; 2:17, 19; 4:2, 8, 9, 11, 12). The reference to the Jews of the Diaspora,
from "every nation" (*pan ethnos*) of the world (Acts 2:5), seems to echo the
prophet's angry imprecation against those who have scattered the Jewish
people among "all the nations" (*panta ta ethnē*) (Joel 3:2-3). The expression "all those who inhabit" (*hoi katoikountes*) (Joel 1:2) is verbally identical
to Acts 2:14. Just as the prophet Joel spoke to those who lived "in Jerusalem" (Joel 2:32), so Peter addresses the people of Jerusalem (Acts 2:14).
The word "hearken" (*enōtisasthe*) in the same verse of Acts is also found in
Joel 1:2.[12] The theme of intoxication (Joel 1:5; Acts 2:15), including identical vocabulary (*methuein*), should be noted. Finally, Peter's sermon is
interrupted by an audience "pierced to the heart" (Acts 2:37; compare
Joel 1:5, 13; 2:13) who cry out asking what to do. As had the prophet Joel
(2:13), Peter urges the people to "repent" (Acts 2:38-40).[13] It is the time of

---

Dodd, *According to the Scriptures* (London: Nisbet, 1952) 46–48, and B. Lindars, *New Testament
Apologetic* (Philadelphia: Westminster, 1961) 36–38. In some rabbinic tradition Joel 2:28-32 is
interpreted eschatologically. It is believed that in the time to come God would pour out the
Spirit on Israel, thus fulfilling Moses' wish in Num 11:29 that all Israelites would be prophets
(see *Midr. Ps* 14.6 [on 14:7]; *Num. Rab.* 15.25 [on 11:17]; *Deut. Rab.* 6.14 [on 24:9]). See
further discussion in this chap. below.

10. Conzelmann, Haenchen, Dibelius, and Marshall, among others, make no mention of
this fact. Familiar with my work, D. L. Tiede (*Prophecy and History in Luke-Acts* [Philadelphia:
Fortress, 1980] 90) speaks of "phrases and words" from Joel "elsewhere in Acts 2," but he
does not specify which ones.

11. They are as follows: *ouranos* (Acts 2:2; Joel 2:10, 30; 4:16), *pyr* (Acts 2:3; Joel 1:19, 20;
2:3, 5, 30), *pimplēmi* (Acts 2:4; Joel 2:24), *andres* (Acts 2:5; Joel 1:8; 2:7; 4:9), *ethnos* (Acts 2:5;
Joel 1:6; 2:17, 19; 4:2, 8, 9, 11, 12), *katoikountes* (Acts 2:5; Joel 1:2, 19; 2:1; 4:20), *Ierousalēm*
(Acts 2:5; Joel 3:5; 4:1, 6, 16, 17, 20), *Ioudaios/Ioudaia* (Acts 2:5, 9; Joel 4:20), *phonē* (Acts 2:6;
Joel 1:20; 2:5, 11; 4:16), *sygchein* (Acts 2:6; Joel 2:1, 10), *akouein* (Acts 2:6, 22; Joel 1:2),
gleukos/oinos (Acts 2:13; Joel 1:5), *enōtizesthai* (Acts 2:14; Joel 1:2), *methuein* (Acts 2:15; Joel
1:5), *tauta* (Acts 2:22; Joel 1:2), *metanoein* (Acts 2:38; Joel 2:13, 14), *tekna hymōn* (Acts 2:39;
Joel 1:3; 2:23), *eis makran* (Acts 2:39; Joel 3:8), and *genea* (Acts 2:40; Joel 1:3). Of special
importance are the following verbs: *methuein* ("to be drunk"), which occurs only six times
elsewhere in the New Testament; *sygchein* ("to bewilder"), which occurs in only three other
places in the New Testament (all in Acts, cf. 9:22; 21:27, 31); and *enōtizesthai* ("to pay attention"), which is a New Testament *hapax legomenon*. This last word makes it clear that Luke has
used Joel's vocabulary.

12. LXX Job 32:11 offers a very close parallel to the last part of Acts 2:14, "Pay attention
to my words [*enōtizesthe mou ta rhēmata*]." From this we might infer that Peter's admonition
would have been interpreted from a wisdom perspective.

13. Repentance was understood to be a condition for national restoration (*T. Judah* 23:15;
24:1, 3, 6; *T. Moses* 18:1; *b. Sanh.* 97b). See also this chap. below.

decision (Joel 4:14); the "promise" is for everyone whom the Lord calls (Acts 2:39, citing the last part of Joel 2:32).

Luke has evidently utilized Joel's language and setting and molded them into his own material. The theme of drunkenness, or insensitivity in the case of Joel, becomes the occasion for Joel's message quoted by Peter, and for the Pentecost sermon as well. Likewise is Jerusalem faced with the day of "God's verdict" (compare Joel 4:14, *eggus hēmera kuriou en tē koiladi tēs dikēs/qrwb ywm yhwh b'mq hhrws*). Since the people have shed the blood of an innocent man (compare Acts 2:22-23, 36; Joel 4:19), they are grieved and cry out to Peter in desperation. The people of Jerusalem can call upon the Lord and be saved or ignore God and face judgment.

In the following selection of verses taken from Joel 1 and Acts 2 we may observe the striking similarity of their respective literary and historical contexts:

JOEL 1

The prophet speaks:

Hear these things, O Elders
And pay attention, all who inhabit the land.
Has anything like this happened in your days
Or in your father's days? (v. 2)

Tell your children about it,
And let your children tell their children,
And their children the next generation. (v. 3)

Awake, those who are drunk, and weep
And wail, all you wine drinkers,
On account of the sweet wine,
That is cut off from your mouth. (v. 5)

ACTS 2

Peter speaks:

Fellow Judeans and all who inhabit Jerusalem,
let this be known to you
and pay attention to my words. (v. 14b)
For these men are not drunk, as you suppose. . . . (v. 15a)

Fellow Israelites, hear these words . . . (v. 22a)
[Having heard this, they were pierced to the heart. . . .] (v. 37a)
For this is the promise for you and your children . . . (v. 39a)
Be saved from this perverse generation. (v. 40)

Seen against its scriptural backdrop the Pentecost sermon becomes an acting out of the prophetic message of the prophet Joel. Joel warns of the coming day of the Lord, a day of judgment (2:1-11). He calls to the people to repent. "Rend your hearts and not your garments" (2:13; cf. Acts 2:37). If the people repent, God's blessings and Spirit will be poured out on Israel (2:18-29). It is an opportunity for salvation, "And in Jerusalem he shall escape [*anasōzein*], as the Lord said, and be evangelized [*euaggelizesthai*], whom the Lord has summoned" (LXX Joel 3:5 [ET 2:32b]). It will be a time of restoration of Judah and Jerusalem (3:1). Israel's enemies will be punished for having scattered God's people (3:2-12, 19, 21). Jerusalem will once again be holy (3:17), fruitful (3:18), and inhabited (3:20).

Peter promises his hearers that if they repent, they will receive the gift of the Holy Spirit (Acts 2:38). This promise is to those in Palestine and to those who are "far off" (Acts 2:39); those scattered in the Diaspora now have the opportunity to receive the promise. Similarly, in the sermon following the healing on the temple steps, Peter promises Israel "times of refreshing" if they repent (Acts 3:19).

Scripture has a systemic function in the Lukan narrative—its presence is neither superficial nor secondary. The explicit citation, the verbal allusions, and the thematic similarities invite the reader to compare the Christian narrative with the words of Israel's ancient prophets.

THE FUNCTION OF JOEL IN LUKE-ACTS

The passage quoted from Joel also makes an important contribution to Luke's pneumatology. The Holy Spirit plays a prominent role from beginning to end, from Luke 1 to Acts 28. It fills John the Baptist before his birth (Luke 1:15), generates Jesus (Luke 1:35), enables him to defeat Satan (Luke 4:1-13) and to claim the fulfillment of Isa 61:1-2 (Luke 4:14-30), and it is promised to his disciples (Luke 11:13; 24:49). In Acts the Holy Spirit fills Jesus' disciples (Acts 2:1-4; 4:31), fills Samaritans (Acts 8:17), and fills Gentiles (Acts 10:44-48). The Holy Spirit also speaks to believers (Acts 8:29; 13:2), through believers (Acts 21:11), and through Scripture (Acts 4:25; 28:25).

Joel's prophecy provides the scriptural basis for Luke's pneumatology. The prophecy predicts not only that the Holy Spirit will be poured out (and therefore is a necessary ingredient in the age of Jesus and the church) but that it will be poured on a universal scale. By using Joel as the foundation text for his pneumatology, Luke found important supporting evidence for his universalistic theology.[14] But the prophecy also serves a pivotal function in Luke-Acts, for it looks back to the Isaiah prophecy

---

14. The implications of Luke's pneumatology for his universalist theology are explored above in Chap. 3.

found in Luke 3 and forward to the Amos prophecy found in Acts 15, making it possible for Luke to link the earliest beginnings of the Gospel story with the gospel message preached in Gentile lands. What are the indications that this is the case?

First, the coming of the Holy Spirit, the quotation of Joel, and the Pentecost sermon cohere with the preaching and ministry of John the Baptist. John's "baptism of repentance for the forgiveness of sins" (Luke 3:3) and promise of one who "will baptize with the Holy Spirit and with fire" (Luke 3:16) were realized on Pentecost. On that day the Holy Spirit appeared as "fire" (Acts 2:3) and filled the disciples (Acts 2:4). That Luke has John's preaching in mind is clear from the reminder at the beginning of Acts, "Wait for the promise of the Father [cf. Luke 11:13; 24:49], which, he said, 'you heard from me, for John baptized with water, but before many days you shall be baptized with the Holy Spirit'" (cf. Acts 1:4-5). As John had said from the very beginning, those who followed the one mightier than he would be baptized by the Holy Spirit and fire.

Not only has John's preaching been fulfilled on Pentecost, but the prophecy of Isaiah 40, cited in connection with John's wilderness ministry, has been fulfilled as well. Whereas Mark quotes only Isa 40:3 (Mark 1:3), Luke extends the Isaianic prophecy to include vv. 4-5 (Luke 3:5-6). In Luke the passage concludes with "all flesh [*pasa sarx*] shall see the salvation of God," which coheres with Joel's outpouring of the Spirit on "all flesh [*pasa sarx*]" (Joel 2:28; Acts 2:17). Perhaps the evangelist viewed the experience of Zechariah, the father of John, who was "filled with the Holy Spirit and prophesied" (Luke 1:67) as proleptic of the outpouring of Acts 2.

Second, the Joel quotation also anticipates the quotation and interpretation of the prophecy of Amos 9:11-12 in Acts 15. Joel's "whoever shall call on the name of the Lord" (Joel 2:32; Acts 2:21) is echoed in Amos, "The Gentiles who are called by my name" (Amos 9:12; Acts 15:17). According to Peter and James, God has "visited the Gentiles, to take out of them a people for his name" (15:14). Joel says that those who call on the name of the Lord "shall be saved" (Joel 2:32; Acts 2:21). This issue arises in Acts 15, when some asserted, "Unless you are circumcised according to the custom of Moses, you cannot be saved" (Acts 15:1). The council agrees that both Jews and Gentiles "shall be saved through the grace of the Lord Jesus" (Acts 15:11). Joel's prophecy also predicted "wonders and signs" (Joel 2:30; Acts 2:19), and the Jerusalem council is told that God has worked "signs and wonders" among the Gentiles (15:12). Thus at several points there is coherence between the quotations and contexts of Joel and Amos. Other particulars about Amos 9:11-12 will be discussed below.

Third, not only does the Joel quotation look back to John's preaching in Luke 3 and forward to the Jerusalem council of Acts 15, its essential elements are expressed throughout Luke-Acts. Joel says that in the last days God will pour out the Spirit on "all flesh." If "all flesh" is interpreted as including Gentiles, as the "all flesh" of Isa 40:5 (Luke 3:6) seems to imply, then we should expect to find that in Acts it has been poured out on Gentiles. Luke does not disappoint us. Following the conversion of Cornelius and his household the Holy Spirit is "poured out even on the Gentiles" (Acts 10:45). Joel also speaks of people prophesying (Joel 2:28; Acts 2:17). This they do in Acts. Some disciples of John are baptized in the name of Jesus and then "they spoke with tongues and prophesied" (Acts 19:6). We are also told that Philip the evangelist "had four unmarried daughters, who prophesied" (Acts 21:9). Joel says that "young men shall see visions [*horasis*]" (Joel 2:28; Acts 2:17). Luke tells us in Acts that many saw visions (*horama*); Ananias sees a vision relating to Paul's recent conversion (Acts 9:10). Both Cornelius and Peter see a vision (10:3, 17; 11:5); Paul sees two visions (16:9, 10; 18:9). Joel speaks of "wonders [*tera*] and signs [*sēmeia*—not in Joel, but added by Luke; see parallel columns above]" (Joel 2:30; Acts 2:19). Peter avers that during his ministry Jesus performed "mighty works and wonders and signs" (Acts 2:22). Now the apostles themselves could perform "wonders and signs" (Acts 2:43; 4:30; 5:12; 6:8; 14:3). Joel's "day of the Lord, great and manifest" (Joel 2:31; Acts 2:20) may be echoed when Paul tells the Athenians that "God has appointed a day on which he will judge the world" (Acts 17:31). Joel's prophecy urges people to "call on the name of the Lord" (Joel 2:32; Acts 2:21). Paul testifies before the Sanhedrin that Ananias came to him and told him to be baptized, "calling on the name" (Acts 22:16). Indeed, the frequency of the expression "the name of the Lord" (Acts 2:38; 9:21; 10:43; 22:16—many of these passages speak of "calling on the name of the Lord Jesus"; cf. Luke 24:47, "That repentance and forgiveness of sins should be preached in his [Jesus'] name to all nations, beginning from Jerusalem") may have been influenced by Joel's prophecy. Joel's promise to be "saved" is paralleled or echoed in many places in Luke-Acts (Acts 2:47; 4:12; 11:14; 15:1, 11; 16:30, 31; 27:20, 31; cf. Luke 7:50; 8:12).

In view of these considerations, I think that it is correct to say that Joel's prophecy is not only foundational to Luke's pneumatology but serves as a major contributing element to the evangelist's understanding of the Gospel itself.

PARALLEL EXAMPLES

The function of Joel in Acts 2 is not an isolated example. The Lukan evangelist does something similar in Acts 4:25-26 where Ps 2:1-2 is cited. After the disciples have been threatened by the Sanhedrin and released, they rejoice and quote Scripture: "Why did the Gentiles [*ethne*] rage, and the peoples [*laoi*] imagine vain things? The kings of the earth set themselves in array, and the rulers [*archontes*] were gathered together [*synachthēnai*], against the Lord and against his Anointed."[15] In anticipation of the scene leading up to this quotation, Luke tells his readers that the "rulers [*archontes*] and elders and scribes were gathered together [*synachthēnai*] in Jerusalem" (Acts 4:5). A few verses later the Lukan Peter addresses them, "Rulers [*archontes*] of the people [*laos*] and elders" (Acts 4:8). The verse following the quotation (Acts 4:27) identifies who "were gathered together" [*synachthēnai*] against Jesus. Apparently Herod represents the "kings of the earth," Pontius Pilate (and the Jewish leaders addressed earlier) the "rulers," the Gentiles [*ethnē*] the "Gentiles," and the peoples [*laoi*] of Israel the "peoples." The latter is plural because the corresponding word of the quotation is plural.[16]

Once again the prophetic Scripture is lived out in the experience of the believing community. The violence of those who oppose the Lord's Anointed had been foretold in Scripture and now has been played out in history. At yet another point the experience of Jesus, the Lord's Anointed, and the community is in continuity with Israel's sacred history.

In the sermon in the synagogue of Antioch of Pisidia the Lukan Paul quotes Hab 1:5, "Behold, you scoffers, and marvel, and perish; because I work a deed in your days, a deed that you will not believe if some one should narrate [*ekdiēgētai*] it to you" (Acts 13:41). The warning is fulfilled when many of the Jews contradict Paul and Barnabas and drive them from the city (vv. 44-52). This and the acceptance of the apostolic preaching by the Gentiles lead to the citation of Isa 49:6, "I have set you to be a light for the Gentiles, that you may bring salvation to the ends of the earth" (Acts 13:47). Both of these prophetic Scriptures were hinted at in the very beginning of the Lukan Gospel. According to Luke 1:1 the evangelist regards his work as a "narrative" (*diēgēsis*) of the things accomplished by the apostles and early believers. This narrative, unfortunately, is some-

---

15. We know little about pre-Christian interpretation of Ps 2:1-2. Although 4QFlor 1:18–19 quotes Ps 2:1-2, little of the exegesis is extant. The interpretation that follows the citation is clearly eschatological ("At the end of days"), but whether or not it is messianic is difficult to tell. Aside from Acts, the only other NT writing that makes use of Ps 2:1-2 is Revelation. Parts of these two verses are echoed in Rev 6:15; 17:18; 19:19 ("The kings of the earth"); 11:15 ("Our Lord and his Anointed"); and 11:18 ("The nations raged"). As in 4QFlorilegium, Ps 2:1-2 contributes to the seer's vision of the establishment of the messianic kingdom, which from the seer's perspective is still to come. In Acts, however, the psalm is understood as already fulfilled in the experience of Jesus and his apostles. Some of the rabbis also understand Ps 2:1-2 in an eschatological and messianic sense (*Midr.* Ps 2.2 [on 2:1-2]; 2.3 [on 2:2]; cf. *b. Ber.* 7b; *b. 'Abod. Zar.* 3b). For further discussion see Chap. 12 above.

16. The original Old Testament reference, of course, was to the Gentile "peoples," not to the people of Israel.

times met with unbelief, precisely as the prophetic Scriptures forewarned. According to Luke 2:31-32 the righteous Simeon, upon seeing the infant Jesus, said, "My eyes have seen your salvation . . . a light for revelation to the Gentiles. . . ." Simeon's words allude to the prophecy of Isa 49:6 (and 42:6), which will eventually be fulfilled in the preaching of the Gospel to the Gentiles in Acts.

The language and ideas of Habakkuk are not restricted to the formal quotation in Acts 13:41. In vv. 38-39 the Lukan Paul says that "through this one the forgiveness of sins is proclaimed, and in this one everyone who believes [*pisteuein*] is justified [*dikaioun*]. . . ." Here we have a succinct summary of Hab 2:4, "The just one [*dikaios*] will live by faith [*pistis*]." The importance of this verse for Paul's theology is well known (Rom 11:7; Gal 3:11; cf. Heb 10:38). Of course, the reference to believe (*pisteuein*) in v. 39 anticipates the citation of Hab 1:5 where this verb occurs. But Hab 1:5 says nothing of being justified—Hab 2:4 supplies this element. The phrase "in your days" from Hab 1:5 may moreover explain the similar phrase at the beginning of the citation of Joel in Acts 2:17 ("in the last days"), a phrase that does not derive from Joel itself.

Let us consider a final example. When the second Jerusalem council debates the question of whether or not circumcision is necessary for salvation, James quotes Amos 9:11-12. He more or less follows the Septuagint, which in places is at variance with the MT. Let us consider the quotation and the two versions side by side.

Acts	*LXX*	*MT*
After these things I will return	In that day	In that day
and I will rebuild the tent of David, which has fallen;	I shall raise up the tent of David, which has fallen; and I will rebuild its fallen parts,	I shall raise up the booth of David, which has fallen; and I will repair its breaches,
I will rebuild its ruins, and I will set it up,	and I shall raise up its ruins, and I will rebuild it, just as days of eternity.	and I will raise up its ruins, and I will rebuild it, as the days of eternity;
that the rest of men may seek the Lord,	in order that the rest of men	so that they may possess the remnant of Edom,
and all the Gentiles who are called by my name,	and all the Gentiles may seek, who have been called by my name	and all the Gentiles who are called by my name,
says the Lord, who has made these things known from eternity.	says the Lord the God who does these things.	says the Lord who does this thing.

Minor changes in the vocalization of the Hebrew text account for the different reading in the LXX, though it is not certain that the MT represents the original form. Since "Edom" was often understood as Rome (as is well attested in the Targums), it is entirely possible that *adam* ("man" or "men") was repointed by the Masoretes as *edom* ("Edom"), to reflect Jewish hope during the Roman period. To accommodate this change, *yidresu* ("They may seek") could have been easily altered to *yiresu* ("They may possess"). In any case, the LXX's rendering lends itself more readily to the Lukan context.[17]

How does this prophetic text fit in Luke? Calling upon (*epikalein*) the name of the Lord appeared in Acts 2:21; 9:14, 21; and will appear in 22:16. The word shows that not only Jews but also Gentiles must call on the name of the Lord to be saved (Acts 2:21). In the immediate context, "from days of old" (Acts 15:7) anticipates the quotation's "things known from eternity," a phrase borrowed from Isa 45:21. The implication is that going to the Gentiles was part of God's plan all along; it was not ad hoc or unexpected. Moreover, James's recognition that "God had visited the Gentiles, to take out of them a people for his name" (Acts 15:14) anticipates the quotation's "the rest of men" and the "Gentiles" who "have been called by [the Lord's] name." The verb "to visit" (*episkeptomai*) recalls Zechariah's song. "Blessed be the Lord God of Israel, for he has visited (*episkeptomai*) and redeemed his people, and has raised up a horn of salvation for us in the house of his servant David, as he spoke by the mouth of his holy prophets from of old" (Luke 1:68-70). There are several echoes here. James's comment also recalls the exclamation of the amazed crowd in Luke 7:16, "God has visited (*episkeptomai*) his people!" Indeed God has. God has visited Jews and Gentiles and from them has called out a people. This quotation from Amos and its re-contextualization by Luke tie together themes linking Jews and Gentiles. Both belong in the tent of David; both are working together to restore it.

CONCLUSION

In these various passages from Acts, Scripture is used to give shape to the narrative. This is not unique to the Lukan evangelist, of course. The Matthean and Johannine evangelists also correlate tradition with Scripture, especially in some of their "fulfillment" citations. Luke has absorbed language and themes from the prophetic Scriptures, so that we might describe the phenomenon as "prophetic narrative." Thomas L. Brodie has already suggested, with regard to other portions of Luke-Acts, that this type of literary activity be called *imitatio*.[18] To be sure, "imitation" does

---

17. For further discussion of this passage, the components that make up the Lukan quotation, and early interpretation of it, see Chap. 11 above.

18. T. L. Brodie, "Greco-Roman Imitation of Texts as a Partial Guide to Luke's Use of Sources," in C. H. Talbert, ed., *Luke-Acts: New Perspectives from the Society of Biblical Literature*

describe a certain aspect of the phenomenon, which he has also called "rewriting and updating." These words too describe certain aspects of the evangelist's technique—as long as we remember what Luke is actually rewriting and updating.[19] But in all of this a fundamental feature may be overlooked—Luke's conviction that what happened long ago in the experience of the people of God is once again happening. Joel the prophet had said that a special day was coming when God would pour out the Spirit, and the peoples of the world would hear the gospel. Long ago the fire was seen on Sinai and the voice of God was heard (in many languages according to some); now once again God has spoken. The Lukan narrative illustrates and testifies how these prophetic traditions had come to be experienced in the Christian community. Acts 2 certainly tells us something about how Joel is interpreted (or "updated") from a Christian point of view, but the real issue is how Christian history and experience are understood from a scriptural point of view. It is Joel that informs Luke's community, and it is Joel that "rewrites" the history and experience of this community.

Seminar (New York: Crossroad, 1984) 17–46; idem, *Luke the Literary Interpreter: Luke-Acts as a Systematic Rewriting and Updating of the Elijah-Elisha Narrative in 1 and 2 Kings* (Rome: Pontifical University of St. Thomas Press, 1987).

19. As the title of his work clearly states (second item in preceding note), Brodie views Luke as a rewriting and updating of 1 and 2 Kings. This is incorrect. Luke rewrites and updates the stories of Jesus and the early church in the light of 1 and 2 Kings (and other parts of the LXX); the distinction is crucial. See C. A. Evans, "Luke and the Rewritten Bible: Aspects of Lucan Hagiography," in J. H. Charlesworth and C. A. Evans, eds., *The Pseudepigrapha and Biblical Interpretation* (JSPSup; Sheffield: JSOT, forthcoming).

RELATED STUDIES

BY JAMES A. SANDERS

"Habakkuk in Qumran, Paul, and the OT," *JR* 39 (1959) 232–44; repr. in C. A. Evans and J. A. Sanders, eds., *Paul and the Scriptures of Israel* (JSNTSup 83; SSEJC 1; Sheffield: JSOT 1993) 98–117.

"*Nazoraios* in Matt 2:23," *JBL* 84 (1965) 169–72.

"Torah and Christ," *Int* 29 (1975) 372–90; repr. in J. A. Sanders, *From Sacred Story to Sacred Text: Canon as Paradigm* (Philadelphia: Fortress, 1987) 43–60.

"Hermeneutics," *IDBSup* (1976) 402–7; repr. in J. A. Sanders, *From Sacred Story to Sacred Text: Canon as Paradigm* (Philadelphia: Fortress, 1987) 63–73.

"Hermeneutics in True and False Prophecy," in G. W. Coats and B. O. Long, eds., *Canon and Authority: Essays in OT Religion and Theology* (Philadelphia: Fortress, 1977) 21–41; repr. in J. A. Sanders, *From Sacred Story to Sacred Text: Canon as Paradigm* (Philadelphia: Fortress, 1987) 89–105.

"Torah and Paul," in J. Jervell and W. A. Meeks, eds., *God's Christ and His People: Studies in Honor of Nils Alstrup Dahl* (Oslo: Universitets-forlaget, 1977) 132–40; repr. in J. A. Sanders, *From Sacred Story to Sacred Text: Canon as Paradigm* (Philadelphia: Fortress, 1987) 111–23.

"The Gospels and the Canonical Process: A Response to Lou H. Silberman," in W. O. Walker, Jr., ed., *The Relationships among the Gospels: An Interdisciplinary Dialogue* (San Antonio: Trinity University Press, 1978) 219–36.

"Text and Canon: Old Testament and New," in P. Casetti, O. Keelaud, and A. Schenker, eds., *Mélanges Dominique Barthélemy: Études bibliques* (Orbis Biblicus et Orientalis 38; Fribourg: Editions universitaires, 1981) 373–94.

"Extravagant Love," *New Blackfriars* 68 (1987) 278–84; repr. in *Scripture in Church* 20 (1990) 97–103.

"Annunciations," *Scripture in Church* 18 (1988) 115–20.

BY CRAIG A. EVANS

"The Voice from Heaven: A Note on John 12:28," *CBQ* 43 (1981) 405–8.

"On the Quotation Formulas in the Fourth Gospel," *BZ* 26 (1982) 79–83.

"The Function of Isaiah 6:9-10 in Mark and John," *NovT* 24 (1982) 124–38.

"On the Vineyard Parables of Isaiah 5 and Mark 12," *BZ* 28 (1984) 82–86.

"Paul and the Hermeneutics of 'True Prophecy': A Study of Romans 9–11," *Bib* 65 (1984) 560–70.

"The Isaianic Background of Mark 4:1-20," *CBQ* 47 (1985) 464–68.

"Obduracy and the Lord's Servant: Some Observations on the Use of the Old Testament in the Fourth Gospel," in C. A. Evans and W. F. Stinespring, eds., *Early Jewish and Christian Exegesis: Studies in Memory of William Hugh Brownlee* (Homage 10; Atlanta: Scholars, 1987) 221–36.

"The Genesis Apocryphon and the Rewritten Bible," in É. Puech and F. G. Martínez, eds., *Mémorial Jean Carmignac* (*RevQ* 13; Paris: Gabalda, 1988) 153–65.

To See and Not Perceive: Isaiah 6.9-10 in Early Jewish and Christian Interpretation (JSOTSup 64; Sheffield: JSOT, 1989).

"The Function of the Old Testament in the New Testament," in S. McKnight, ed., *Introducing New Testament Interpretation* (Guides to New Testament Exegesis 1; Grand Rapids: Baker, 1989) 163–93.

Luke (New International Biblical Commentary 3; Peabody: Hendrickson, 1990).

"The Old Testament in the Gospels," in J. B. Green, S. McKnight, and I. H. Marshall, eds., *Dictionary of Jesus and the Gospels* (Downers Grove, IL: Inter Varsity, 1992) 579–90.

"Typology," in J. B. Green, S. McKnight, and I. H. Marshall, eds., *Dictionary of Jesus and the Gospels* (Downers Grove, IL: Inter Varsity, 1992) 862–66.

" 'It Is Not as though the Word of God Had Failed': An Introduction to Paul and the Scriptures of Israel," in C. A. Evans and J. A. Sanders, eds., *Paul and the Scriptures of Israel* (JSNTSup 83; SSEJC 1; Sheffield: JSOT, 1993) 13–17.

"Ascending and Descending with a Shout: Psalm 47:6 and 1 Thessalonians 4:16," in C. A. Evans and J. A. Sanders, eds., *Paul and the Scriptures of Israel* (JSNTSup 83; SSEJC 1; Sheffield: JSOT, 1993).

"Luke and the Rewritten Bible: Aspects of Lucan Hagiography," in J. H. Charlesworth and C. A. Evans, eds., *The Pseudepigrapha and Biblical Interpretation* (JSPSup; Sheffield: JSOT, forthcoming).

INDEX OF
ANCIENT WRITINGS

INDEX OF
MODERN AUTHORS